A History of
the Virgin Islands
of the United States

by
Isaac Dookhan

WITH AN INTRODUCTION
by

Richard B. Sheridan
Professor Emeritus
Department of Economics
The University of Kansas

Canoe Press

JAMAICA • BARBADOS • TRINIDAD and TOBAGO

Canoe Press

1A Aqueduct Flats Mona Campus
University of the West Indies
Kingston 7   Jamaica   W I

First published in 1974 for the College of the Virgin Islands, St. Thomas,
U.S. Virgin Islands, by the Caribbean Universities Press in association with the
Bowker Publishing Company, Epping, Essex, England.

Second impression, 1994
Third impression, 1995
Fourth impression, 2002
Fifth impression, 2005

CATALOGUING IN PUBLICATION DATA

Dookhan, Isaac
   A history of the Virgin Islands of the United
States / Isaac Dookhan.

      p. cm.
      Includes bibliographical references.
      ISBN 976-8125-05-5
      1. Virgin Islands of the United States—
History. I. Title.
F2136.5.D66 1994   972.9722   dc–20

Cover illustration (taken from first edition, 1974): Artist's impression of
''Black Beard'' the pirate Captain Edward Teach (cf. pgs. 118-19 of this volume).
Front cover design reproduced by F. W. and Associates Ltd., Kingston, Jamaica
Printed in Jamaica by Stephensons Litho Press

Contents

List of Illustrations

Introduction

The Virgin Islands in the course of centuries have witnessed the coming and going of Ciboney, Arawak and Carib peoples, European discovery by Christopher Columbus, temporary occupation by pirates and adventurers, colonization, commercial and plantation development by Danes and other North European settlers, African slavery and its abolition, American purchase, colonial government, social and political change, and in recent years remarkable tourist and industrial developments.

These and other topics have been narrated and interpreted by Dr. Isaac Dookhan in this first comprehensive history of the U.S. Virgin Islands. Dr. Dookhan is eminently well qualified for this undertaking. He was born in the British colony of British Guiana, now independent Guyana, where he was educated in the public schools and served as teacher and headmaster. He did his baccalaureate and doctors degrees at the University of the West Indies in Jamaica. Under the direction of Professor Douglas Hall, he researched and wrote a Ph.D. dissertation history of the British Virgin Islands. These islands are in geographical proximity to and have had close historical ties with the U.S. Virgins. More recently he has published *A Pre-Emancipation History of the West Indies.* [1] The author has drawn upon primary and secondary sources in recounting the experience of the Virgin Islands and their peoples. He is concerned with successive waves of immigrants, how they affected the physical environment and cultural life of the islands, the impact of international wars and politics, commodity price movements, and technological changes.

The Virgin Islands of the United States comprise St. Thomas, St. John, and St. Croix, along with some fifty-odd islets and cays. They were purchased from Denmark in 1916 and the transfer effected the following year. Permanent settlement of St. Thomas dates from 1672, St. John from 1718, and St. Croix, which was acquired by purchase from France, from 1734. St. Thomas, with its excellent harbor, was uniquely placed to become a great trading center, while St. Croix and to a lesser extent St. John became centers of cotton and especially sugar production. These islands, which occupy the keystone of the West Indies arch, are located about 18° north of the equator and 64° west of Greenwich, 40 miles east of Puerto Rico, and about 1400 miles southeast of New York City.

Standing on the periphery of both the Greater and Lesser Antilles, the Virgin Islands have seen a succession of Indian cultures. After destroying the labor supply of Espanola in their lust for gold, the Spaniards turned to the inhabitants of other islands and are thought to have depopulated the Virgin Islands. For a century or more before the coming of the Danes, the islands attracted pirates and poor settlers who came from the eastern Caribbean islands which had been settled by Englishmen, Frenchmen and Dutchmen. Dr. Dookhan shows how piracy, in turn, gave way to buccaneering and privateering, to regulated and exclusive trade by the Danish West India Company, and eventually to modified free trade.

Today it is difficult to understand why tiny Caribbean islands were once valued highly by the leading maritime nations of Europe. In part, they afforded the Protestant nations of northern Europe the opportunity to establish bases from which to launch attacks on Spanish strongholds and especially the galleons which carried precious metals to Seville and Cadiz.

The seventeenth century witnessed the decline of silver mining and trade of New Spain and Peru and the pirates and buccaneers who preyed on this trade. During the same century more and more Europeans came to the West Indies to grow tobacco, cotton, indigo, ginger, and especially sugar-cane. So popular were these commodities in Europe that voluntary white laborers could not meet the demand. Resort was had to forced laborers, first to white indentured servants, and then in growing numbers to African slaves.

Some islands, such as English Barbados and Danish St. Croix, were well endowed by nature to become sugar islands. St. Croix, as Dr. Dookhan explains, had fertile plains and valleys, sufficient rainfall of seasonal variability, adequate harbors and anchorages, and the northeast trade winds which filled the sails of incoming vessels, energized the windmills which crushed the sugar-canes between iron rollers, and moderated the climate so that it was tolerable for European and African inhabitants. Small islands generally had certain advantages over large islands and continental coastal plains. They had a high ratio of coastline to land area which had the effect of economizing on difficult and costly land transport, were relatively less costly to defend against outside aggressors, and, once populated and cleared of forests, afforded few places of refuge for runaway and rebellious slaves. Together with such man-made advantages as the influx of experienced planters and merchants from the English and Dutch islands to windward, St. Croix became the sixth ranking island — well ahead of Cuba and Puerto Rico — in the production of cane-sugar by the eve of the American Revolution.

Dr. Dookhan says that the Danes regarded St. Thomas as a combination of plantation colony and trading entrepot. Not only was it a distributing point for its sister islands, but it carried on an extensive trade with neighboring foreign islands and the Spanish Main. European manufactures, North American foodstuffs and building materials, and African slaves crowded the wharves and warehouses of the port city of Charlotte Amalie. The kingdom of Denmark-Norway remained neutral during the numerous wars of the later part of the seventeenth and eighteenth centuries. This meant that St. Thomas was able to conduct a lucrative neutral trade with the colonies of belligerent nations. Here was found a money market for the sale of captured ships and cargoes and courts to dispose of prizes brought in by the privateers of different nations. In time, St. Thomas became a free port which attracted foreign traders in times of peace.

Dr. Dookhan devotes three full chapters and parts of other chapters to the African slave trade and the institution of slavery. That this is by no means a disproportionate emphasis is revealed by the facts that slavery existed in the Virgin Islands from 1672 to 1848, a longer time span than that following emancipation, and the black people made up ninety per cent or more of the population during the greater part of the slave era. Slave trade topics include trading forts in West Africa, tribal origins, trading methods, mutinies on slave ships, death toll on the Middle Passage, numbers transported, 'seasoning' the slaves for the routine of plantation life, and the abolition of the slave trade. Slavery as an institution involved such matters as occupations and work loads, feeding, housing, clothing and medical care, and regulations which governed the behavior and social status of slaves. Slaves found ingenious ways to resist their white oppressors, ranging from malingering to armed revolt. Indeed, emancipation came in 1848 after a mass uprising in St. Croix which was ably led by 'General' Buddhoe.

St. Thomas has been described by Professor Gordon Lewis as a Protestant city-state in which Calvinist and Lutheran were permitted freedom to worship and Catholic and Jew the right to hold private services.[2] As in north Europe and the colonies of North America, there were close relationships between religion and capitalism in the development of the Virgin Islands. Lacking people to settle their colonies, Denmark welcomed immigrants from Europe, North America and especially the English and Dutch islands to windward. Ethnic and religious diversity thus became marked features of Danish colonial society. Included in the polygot society of planters and merchants were Lutherans, Anglicans, Moravians, Sephardic Jews, French Huguenots, and members of the Dutch Reformed Church. Probably the outstanding religious development in the islands' history was the coming of the Moravian missionaries in 1732. These were men of humble birth who practiced their trades while they educated and won black converts. Planter opposition to the missionaries subsided when religion was given credit for encouraging the slaves to work harder and obey their masters.

The economy of the Virgin Islands, which rested upon sugar capitalism in St. Croix and the entrepot trade of St. Thomas, declined gradually in the nineteenth century. For a time, however, St. Thomas benefited from the steamships which called there to refuel and reprovision and to participate in the lucrative transit trade. The sugar industry fell on evil days as it faced growing competition from other cane growing countries and especially the beet sugar growers of Europe. Planters sought to reduce costs of production by means of mechanization and exploitation of their workers. Under the leadership of Queen Mary, who was an ordinary cane field worker, laborers in St. Croix staged a massive uprising which led to much loss of life and property. Dr. Dookhan asserts that 'many laborers came to believe that there was no difference between slavery and freedom.' Following the laborers' revolt of 1878, conditions improved somewhat as plantations were subdivided into farms which were leased to rural families. Yet the decline of both agriculture and trade continued down to the outbreak of the first World War despite an ambitious program by the Danish government to improve basic conditions.

After nearly a century of discussion and negotiation, the Virgin Islands were transferred from Denmark to the United States on March

31, 1917, for the sum of $25,000,000. Motivating the United States to action was the need for naval bases to defend the approaches to the Panama Canal, together with fear of German acquisition and use of the islands against her enemies in World War I. From 1917 to 1931, United States naval officers governed the Virgin Islands, retaining many of the Danish colonial laws that had been enacted in 1906. Race relations were frequently strained when officers and sailors from the southern states of America attempted to force their Jim Crow rules on to the black inhabitants. Though the social services – especially public health and education – were improved by the naval officers, little progress was made in reviving the economy after the postwar boom collapsed in 1920. Rum production was hurt by the extension of the Prohibition Act to the Virgin Islands, although some relief was provided when the distilleries turned to the production of bay rum. Virgin Islanders sought opportunities abroad during the lean years of the 1920's, many emigrating to New York and other cities along the Atlantic seaboard.

The year 1931 saw the arrival of two personalities. Herbert Hoover, the first President of the United States to visit the islands, is remembered for his derogatory observation that the Virgin Islands were the 'effective poorhouse' of the United States. Dr. Paul D. Pearson became the first civilian governor. His governorship (1931-1935) was marked by economic rehabilitation which went far to improve the well-being and morale of the people. Dr. Dookhan relates the numerous programs which the public corporation, known as the Virgin Islands Company, carried out. These included the encouragement of homestead farms, the revival of the sugar industry in St. Croix, port improvement in St. Thomas, and the promotion of tourism by constructing the Bluebeard Castle Hotel in St. Thomas. Despite these ambitious programs, the level of unemployment remained high and rioting took place in St. Thomas in 1934. Two years later the constitution of the islands was altered to permit universal manhood suffrage, and shortly after the first political party was organized. From this time onwards the political life of the islands was to be lively and at times acrimonious.

Contrasted with the isolation and backwardness of the depression years was the bustling activity during World War II. Anti-submarine warfare and the routing of U.S. convoys through Caribbean waters gave St. Thomas and St. Croix strategic military importance. Shore personnel manned the naval bases and air bases, while liberty parties from the warships anchored in the harbors increased the tempo of business and pleasure. Construction of military structures and roads drew workers away from agriculture. Other workers came from the British and French islands to windward. Though unforeseen at the time, the postwar tourist industry was the chief beneficiary of the military airbases which were converted to commercial aviation and the informal advertising of the islands by ex-servicemen.

'Tourism and tourist expenditures have been responsible for the dynamic growth of the Virgin Islands since the 1950's,' writes Dr. Dookhan. A complex of factors explain the remarkable transformation which has enabled these islands to develop in the course of a few years from little known Caribbean backwaters into rivals of Florida and Southern California. The continued decline of agriculture, which culminated in the phasing out of sugar production in 1966, turned the attention of islanders to programs of economic diversification. Beginning in 1952, a Tourist Development Board was established. In 1954, slightly more than 60,000 tourists came by cruise ship and air to the Virgin Islands where they spent an estimated $4 million. Among other things, American tourists were attracted by the scenic beauty and tropical climate, the political security which the islands enjoyed as American territories, low prices and duty exemptions on 'free port' luxury goods, easy access by air and water, and promotional activity by the tourist board. The big boom in tourism followed the closing of Castro's Cuba to Americans in 1959. The following year saw the arrival of over 200,000 tourists who spent almost $25 million in the shops and hotels and marinas. In 1970, after a decade of phenomenal growth, over one million tourists came to the Virgin Islands where they spent approximately $100 million.[3]

Diversification has also taken the form of measures to promote industrial activity. Tax exemptions and industrial subsidies, together with duty-free entry into the United States of certain articles assembled in Virgin Islands factories, have stimulated the growth of industry. These industries include watch assembly operations, textile manufacturing, oil refining, and the processing of bauxite into alumina. Industry has been handicapped, however, by the limited supply of native skilled and unskilled labor, high living costs, inadequate power and water supplies, lack of raw materials, and small market size.

Tourism and industry soon exhausted local labor supplies and turned to sources outside the islands. Thousands of immigrant West Indians have come from Puerto Rico and the British, French and Dutch islands. Other newcomers were U.S. citizens, or 'Continentals' who were attracted by business opportunities or came to retire in the Virgin

Islands. Official census returns show that the population of the three islands increased from 26,665 in 1950, to 32,099 in 1960, and to 63,200 in 1970. Recently the Virgin Islands Bureau of Statistics and Economic Studies has estimated the total population at 85,600, or over thirty per cent higher than the U.S. Census count of 63,200. St. Thomas has an estimated 45,710, St. Croix, 37,578, and St. John, 2,312. Though the wealth and income is maldistributed, per capita income in 1970 was estimated at $3,880 per year, which compares favorably with the mainland figure of $3,942, and was far above the per capita income of any Caribbean territory. At the low end of the income and welfare scale are the 'down islanders' or 'aliens' who are estimated to number 15,000 out of an employable labor force of 35,810.[4]

Economic and social change has been so rapid in recent years that Virgin Islanders have found it increasingly difficult to preserve their rich heritage. But a close reading of Dr. Dookhan's *History* reveals historical themes which help one to comprehend the truth that the islands' history shows the coexistence of continuity and change. The variegated racial and national groups in the society today should remind one that the Virgin Islands have seen wave after wave of immigrants — Danes, Dutchmen, Englishmen, Frenchmen, Jews, and especially people of African descent. Reminiscent of the 'down islanders' today were the immigrants from Madeira, Barbados, St. Bartholomew, and India who were employed in agriculture following the emancipation of the slaves in 1848. When it is considered that the population is largely 'down island' only a few generations removed, there is little justification for the attitude of superiority and snobbishness which citizens display towards 'aliens'. The lush growth of the religious denominations has gone hand in hand with the influx of nationality and ethnic groups. Much as it was in past centuries, St. Thomas continues to be a Protestant city state where the people turn out on Sunday in their best clothes, carrying Bibles and prayer books as they enter their chapels and churches. St. Croix, and to a lesser extent St. Thomas, has seen the growth of Catholicism in recent decades owing largely to the influx of Puerto Ricans.

Connecting links can be noted between the entrepot trade of St. Thomas in the seventeenth and eighteenth centuries and the free port trade today, between the tourists who came on nineteenth century steamship packet lines and those who come by cruise ship and air today. Charlotte Amalie and its waterfront is a happy mixture of the old and the new. There are centuries-old warehouses with thick brick walls, wide doors, and wrought iron grills which once contained hogsheads of sugar, puncheons of rum, prize cargoes brought in by privateers, and assortments of European trade goods. These structures have been converted into retail shops which display luxury wares from all corners of the globe and draw thousands of shoppers daily during the tourist season from the numerous cruise ships which make St. Thomas and St. Croix regular ports of call. Besides the American tourist's duty-free allowance of $200, one gallon of liquor can be entered free of duty. The liquor trade is so vast that one wag has said that there is enough booze to float the island should the Caribbean sea dry up. Lest it be thought that tourism is a post-World War II phenomenon, Dr. Dookhan points out that most European visitors to the West Indies in the middle decades of the nineteenth century passed through St. Thomas on their way to or from other parts of the Caribbean.

Numerous windmill towers and factory ruins remind one that St. Croix, and to a lesser extent St. John, once had important sugar industries. Near the port of Frederiksted, St. Croix, is Estate Whim where the great house and outbuildings have been restored and a fine museum added by the St. Croix Landmarks Society. On the north coast of St. John are the ruins of Annaberg sugar factory which has been cleared of brush and the masonry stabilized by the National Park Service. To a considerable extent the sugar capitalism of St. Croix has been replaced by the incentive-based alumina and petroleum industries of today. Whereas the incentives today are largely tax exemptions and duty remissions, sugar capitalism more than two centuries ago was encouraged by a seven-year tax free incentive to intending settlers, many of whom were experienced planters from 'down island'.

Dr. Dookhan emphasizes the fact that Virgin Islanders, like other peoples in dependent territories, have been influenced more and more by the 'revolution of rising expectations.' No longer are they tolerant of low living standards, poor public services, political and economic dependency, cultural deprivation, and invidious comparison with white 'Continentals'. New leadership has emerged in government, business, and the professions. Black Virgin Islanders are encouraged to take pride in themselves, their race and heritage, and to work towards personal development and self confidence. The people who were uprooted from Africa and transported to the Virgin Islands to cultivate plantations, build forts and harbor towns, unload and load ships, and today fill responsible positions in a complex insular society are conscious of their centuries-old achievements. Local leaders have chronicled their people's rise to recognition.[5] No longer is Virgin Islands' history written from the standpoint of Denmark and the United States. Instead, attention is focused on slave resistance and rebellion, laborers' revolts, the rise of trade unions and political parties, and the progress that has been made towards self-government, material betterment, and cultural excellence. Carnival is by far the most colorful spectacle of the year in the Virgin Islands. As Herman Wouk, a writer in residence for some years, describes it: 'Africa was marching down the main street of this little harbor town today; Africa in undimmed black vitality, surging up out of centuries of island displacement, island slavery, island isolation, island ignorance; Africa, unquenchable in its burning love of life.'[6]

That achievements have fallen short of objectives in the 'American Paradise' is clearly evident to all but the superficial observer. Along with the phenomenal growth of tourism have come certain social and economic ills. These include such problems as traffic congestion, high living costs, housing pressure, alien labor, concentrated ownership and soaring land values, absentee ownership and control of the economy, ecological abuse, and social disorganization. Efforts to cope with these problems and achieve a viable way of life have and continue to tax the moral and material resources of the people. One newly-created institution to cope with these and other problems is the College of the Virgin Islands. Founded in 1962 as a junior college and later expanded into a four-year, baccalaureate degree-awarding college, it is a focal center for ideas and programs that further the cultural and social life of the people. 'By 1970,' as Dr. Dookhan writes, 'the Virgin Islands had not yet attained complete economic self-sufficiency, political fulfilment in statehood, or a fully satisfactory system of social services, but the stage was set for a further thrust forward.'

[1] Isaac Dookhan, *A Pre-Emancipation History of the West Indies* (Collins, 1971).
[2] Gordon K. Lewis, 'An Introductory Note to the Study of the Virgin Islands,' *Caribbean Studies*, Vol. 8, No. 2 (July 1968), p. 8.
[3] Al Bill, 'V.I. Tourism — Is the Life Blood Waning or Waxing?' *Carib: The Weekly Magazine*, St. Thomas, November 11, 1971, pp. 2-3, 12-13.
[4] 'Local Bureau Sets V.I. Head Count at 85,600,' *The Daily News*, St. Thomas, November 18, 1971, pp. 1, 18.
[5] Valdemar A. Hill, Sr., *Rise to Recognition (An Account of Virgin Islanders from Slavery to Self-Government)*, Printed in the U.S.A., 1971.
[6] Herman Wouk, *Don't Stop The Carnival*, Garden City, New York: Doubleday and Company, Inc., 1965, p. 343.

This book is dedicated to
G. James Fleming and Jane E. Tuitt,
two prominent Virgin Islands educators

Dr Isaac Dookhan was born in Guyana on June 7, 1935, of James and Mangree Dookhan, both of Indian descent. He was educated in Guyana and in Jamaica. He obtained a class 1, grade 1, training teacher's certificate from the Government Training College in Guyana in 1956 and a bachelor's degree with honors in history and doctorate in history from the University of the West Indies in Jamaica. He taught at the elementary- and secondary-school levels and was an education officer in Guyana before coming to the College of the Virgin Islands in 1970. He held the position of professor of history and historian-writer in residence. Dr Dookhan researched and wrote extensively on the history of the Virgin Islands, Guyana, and the Caribbean in general.

Among his many publications are the first comprehensive histories of the Virgin Islands of the United States and the British Virgin Islands. Other studies on the Virgin Islands relate to popular attitudes toward acquisition by the United States, the naval administration, national prohibition, labor relations, expansion of higher education, the role of the American Civil Liberties Union, the Virgin Islands Company and Corporation, and military and civilian defense during World War II. He also co-authored with Governor Ralph M. Paiewonsky the autobiography *Memoirs of a Governor.*

Isaac Dookhan died in 1990, leaving behind a valuable and abundant academic treasury.

Chapter 1

Historical Geography

The geography of the Virgin Islands has exerted a profound influence on the islands' history, probably more so than most other West Indian islands. The Virgin Islands are situated at the head of the arc of the chain of islands stretching northward from Trinidad known as the Lesser Antilles, and they stand on the threshold of the group of larger islands continuing westward known as the Greater Antilles. As such the islands can be said to occupy the keystone of the West Indian arch.

For a long time, the Virgin Islands formed the hub of sea-routes extending north, south, east and west to Europe, North America, and to the other islands and mainland territories in the Caribbean. In this sense, St. Thomas has been rather aptly described as 'the place which is on the way to every other place'.[1] The strategic position of the Virgin Islands was enhanced by their proximity to the traditional points of entry into and departure from the West Indies of ships from North America and Europe. Combined with the purely commercial aspect of their position is that of the military. Situated almost in the center of the Caribbean, the Virgin Islands survey not only the island-territories but also the lands of Central and South America bordering the Atlantic from Mexico to the Guianas. Their position, relative to Panama, for example, should be noted.

The central position which the Virgin Islands occupy made them particularly desirable as trading entrepots for the early colonizing European nations and consequently became the object of much international dispute as these nations debated with each other the question of right of possessing them. Like other West Indian islands, but for slightly different reasons, the Virgin Islands became the pawn on the chessboard of international politics. More recently, the purchase of the hitherto Danish West Indies, by the United States of America, has been influenced by the strategic position which the islands occupy for military purposes. The fear was that the acquisition of the islands by a nation hostile towards the United States could be inimical to American interests in the Caribbean and prejudicial to its influence in the Western Hemisphere.

The Geology and Size

Extending eastward from the end of Puerto Rico like a crescent curving to the northward, is a submerged oceanic bank about one hundred miles long and from thirty to thirty-eight miles wide. This bank is hardly more than 165 feet under water, and from it rise the numerous islands of the Virgin archipelago.[2]

These have been divided, since their discovery by Columbus in 1493 and after the diplomatic wrangle over them had been settled, into two separate groups — the British Virgin Islands and the Danish West Indies or, after they had been sold in 1917, the Virgin Islands of the United States. The irregular line of demarcation extends from the north between Little Hans Lollik and Little Tobago, passes through the narrows between St. John and Great Thatch Island, and curves around the eastern end of St. John, between Flanagan Island and Pelican and Norman Islands.[3] The Virgin Islands are more properly a part of the Greater Antilles chain of islands, since the Virgin Bank is the eastward continuation of the same platform which makes the Greater Antilles. However, because of its separation by the Virgin Sound, geographically St. Croix can probably be better classed with the Lesser Antilles.[4]

The separateness of the Virgin Islands is one of their most outstanding features. This has been the product of their geological history. So too have been their varying sizes and topography. Of the group with which we are concerned, the most important are St. Thomas, St. John and St. Croix, which are small. At its greatest extremity St. Thomas is about thirteen miles long and from two to three miles wide; St. John is about nine miles long and five miles wide; and St. Croix is about twenty-two miles long and six miles wide. Their respective areas are 28.25, 19.77 and 84.25 square miles, giving a total of 132.27 square miles. The cays adjacent to these islands are usually considered their dependencies. They include Hassel Island, Water Island, Hans Lollik

Island and Thatch Cay near St. Thomas, Lovango Cay and Flanagan Island near St. John, and Buck Island near St. Croix. If the outlying cays are considered in the overall computation, the area of the entire group may be as much as 150 square miles or more.

The smallness of the islands together with their lack of precious metals such as gold and silver, help to explain their neglect by the Spaniards as worthwhile areas of colonization and exploitation. Spanish neglect consequently created an opening for other Europeans to enter and establish plantation colonies and trading entrepots.

The position of the main islands relative to each other indicate their separateness. Thus St. John is situated three or four miles at the nearest point east from St. Thomas, while St. Croix is situated to the south forty miles away from both. When Columbus discovered the islands in 1493, he was impressed by their geographical separateness and consequently named them for St. Ursula and her eleven thousand sea-going virgins of Christian mythology. After the settlement of the islands, their diffusion created problems of communication and administration.

Physical Features

To a greater or less extent all the islands are hilly. St. Thomas rises abruptly from sea level into a high ridge attaining an elevation of 1,550 feet in Crown Mountain and 1,504 feet in St. Peter Mountain or Signal Hill. These are in the western part of the island. To the east the island widens and the ridge fans out into a broad dissected upland less than 1,000 feet high and becomes progressively lower towards the eastern end of the island. St. John also rises abruptly to an upland ridge to an average height of about 1,000 feet. The highest elevation, Bordeaux Mountains, stands 1,277 feet high. St. John terminates in the east in a narrow curving neck.

St. Croix shows greater diversity of structure than either St. Thomas or St. John. From the western end of the island to Salt River Point, the island has an almost uniform width; further eastward, it narrows. The northern side is an upland rising to a maximum elevation of 1,165 feet in Mount Eagle.[5] The northern portion of the western half of the island is rugged and rises sharply from the water's edge. The southern portion is a broad, rolling, coastal plain, and the eastern end beyond

Christiansted is a rough, hilly tract which becomes progressively more arid towards East Point.

Except for St. Croix, as here suggested, the Virgin Islands are practically devoid of flat land. There are certainly gentle slopes in St. Thomas and St. John, but dips of 50° and over are more common. Even in St. Croix, inclinations of 80° and more can be observed.[6] Of the smaller islands, Water and Hans Lollik Islands and Thatch Cay are more than a mile long; they also are elevated, Hans Lollik reaching an elevation of 713 feet. The other cays are smaller and are less than 300 feet high.

A noteworthy feature of the islands is the innumerable bays which indent their coasts. St. Thomas and St. John are relatively more embayed than St. Croix. Some of these bays are very deep, and though large, have comparatively small entrances. As such they make not only good harbors for ships, but also offer protection against rough seas and high winds. Three outstanding examples of these are St. Thomas Harbor and Krum Bay in St. Thomas and Coral Bay in St. John. Christiansted Harbor in St. Croix though large, is more open, making vessels in it more susceptible to the ravages of inclement weather. These bays have been useful in promoting shipping and trade of the islands.

The white sandy beaches which fringe the bays have added to the natural beauty and attractiveness of the islands, and more recently have assisted in the promotion of tourism. In another respect they proved disadvantageous. The numerous indentations, all of which could not be supervised, offered facility to smugglers to land their cargoes without the knowledge of responsible officers. Smuggling might have had the effect of swelling colonial exports or of enabling the inhabitants to indulge in more conspicuous consumption than they could otherwise have done, but it tended to deprive the local treasury of much needed revenue.

The smallness of the islands and the steepness of the land account for the absence of rivers in the Virgin Islands. The exception, again, is St. Croix where there are a few streams bearing the names of rivers. In keeping with the topography of the land, most of these are found in the southwestern part of the island. One of the rivers in St. Croix is permanent; this is the Salt River. The others become dry in the absence of rains. When they otherwise contain water it is because of the action of ocean tides. In St. Thomas and St. John, because of the steep coastline, gullies or "ghuts" are the order and these serve more to drain away rainwater rather than to conserve it.

Soils

Associated with the subject of geology is that of soils of which the Virgin Islands have a wide variety.[7] Indeed, any sizeable piece of land in any one of the islands would have a number of different types of soil. The boundaries between different soils are not sharp and clearcut and one kind of soil tends to grade into another. Another feature of the soils is that there are different ranges in the properties they possess. Also, soil behavior tends to differ from one soil to another, and the same type of soil in different localities may respond differently to agricultural and other efforts.

In all three of the major islands many kinds of interpretative soil groupings for agricultural purposes can be established.[8] St. Croix contains a greater proportion of the most productive soils than the other Virgin Islands. These soils exist chiefly in the southwestern and central parts, and very little in the eastern section of the island. St. Thomas and St. John contain very little and these are more or less confined to the slopes adjoining the bays. Less productive soil types dominate the greater part of St. Thomas and St. John, and the northern highland and eastern section of St. Croix. These are not suitable for agriculture, but can be used for pasture, woodland or wild-life purposes.

The soils of the Virgin Islands suffer from a number of limitations which interfere with plant cultivation and growth. Chief among these are erosion, water in the soil and certain other inherent characteristics. Erosion by wind and water is due largely to the steepness of the slopes, requiring special techniques such as terracing to overcome it, and discouraging the use of agricultural implements. Water in the soil can partly be corrected by artificial drainage, but the real drawback is not too much but too little moisture in Virgin Islands soils. This is due to a relatively low incidence of rainfall. The problems raised by lack of adequate rainfall are aggravated by the low moisture holding capacity of the soils, which is an inherent soil characteristic. Similar features include the small depth of soil or shallowness to rock, which implies a shallow rooting zone and tendency to rapid exhaustion of soils, and high clay or slowly permeable subsoil which leads to soil acidity and high alkali content. Numerous gravels and rocks mixed throughout the soil and land surface are common features. In some instances, the physical conditions of the soil make it impracticable to make improvements, such as, for example, liming and fertilizing.

The type of soils which particular areas of the Virgin Islands contain, would naturally determine what can grow and what was actually grown. Like other West Indian islands, the agricultural potentials of the Virgin Islands were exploited by Europeans. The production of commercial crops, especially the staples, sugar and cotton, has served to determine the value of the islands as colonial possessions. St. Croix especially was one of the foremost producers of West Indian staples during the second half of the eighteenth and early nineteenth centuries. When the Virgin Islands were high producers they were attractive possessions to Denmark. The decrease of their productive capacity to the extent that it was no longer able to meet ordinary administrative expenses, but made substantial grants from the mother-country necessary, led to the desire, initiated and sustained, to get rid of the islands. The failure of agriculture also led to its progressive abandonment and to the promotion of alternative revenue-producing enterprises, primarily tourism.

Temperature and Rainfall

Situated between the latitudes 17°.40' and 18°.30' north of the equator, the Virgin Islands are well within the Torrid Zone, but sufficiently north to benefit from the moderating influence of the north temperate climate. Their position, too, places them within the belt of the northeast trade winds which afford them a mild uniform climate and a moderately well distributed rainfall. These conditions combine to give the Virgin Islands a sub-tropical rather than a tropical climate. The temperature is equable and ranges from a minimum of around 67° Fahrenheit during the winter months, November to February, to a maximum of around 95° Fahrenheit during the summer months, July to September. For most of the year the temperature is in the mild seventies.[9] The moderate temperature produced, in part, by trade winds, has certainly made the climate of the Virgin Islands less enervating and so conduced to European settlement in the days of colonization. More recently, the climate has promoted the Virgin Islands into a popular resort for people escaping the bitterness of North American cold and so boosted a tourist industry.

The average annual rainfall for the entire group of islands is only about 41 inches, but the variation from year to year is considerable, ranging from around 30 inches in dry years to more than 60 inches in wet years.[10] These features pertain in the larger islands; the smaller islands are poorly watered and are commonly characterized by extreme aridity. The larger islands which rise to higher altitudes receive a more regular supply of rain which varies locally in amount with topography and position in relation to the trade winds. Generally, the north side of the islands which face the winds can be expected to have a slightly higher rainfall than the southern sides, and the higher lands more than the lower. St. Croix exhibits the anomaly of being arid in its attenuated eastern point.

During the year the rainfall shows a somewhat erratic monthly distribution, varying from a fraction of an inch in a dry month to as much as eighteen inches. Unlike other regions in the tropics, the Virgin Islands do not show marked climatic seasons, beyond possibly a slightly higher precipitation during the so-called rainy seasons. In May and June, and again during September and October, rainfall is slightly heavier, and the heaviest single showers of the year can be expected in these months. The seasonal rainfall can be related to the seasonal pattern of cane-planting and harvesting. The practice was to plant slightly in advance of the rainy season and to reap during the dry season.

Droughts are regular occurrences in the Virgin Islands and have posed problems of water conservation for both domestic and industrial purposes. Under-ground water resources are limited and often unsuitable because of mineral properties which they contain.[11] A number of shallow wells serve to meet the water needs of the people but these tend to fail in times of drought. Since the American occupation, catchment areas with base reservoirs have been constructed to take advantage of rainfall. More recently, the conversion of sea-water into potable water has been attempted but the process is expensive and can be done only on a limited scale. In many instances, the reliance is still on basement cisterns. Water conservation has become a way of life in the Virgin Islands.

Winds and Ocean Currents

The prevailing winds of the Virgin Islands for most of the year are the North East Trades. In the days of the prosperous sugar plantations, winds turned the sails of windmills to set in motion the rollers which squeezed the juice out of canes for processing. This function led to windmills being located near the seashore — preferably on hills if possible — in order to take full advantage of the prevailing winds.

Distortions of the normal wind pattern sometimes result in hurricanes which owe their effect to velocity and direction. Winds rotate about a low-pressure center in a counterclockwise direction spiralling at the rate of over seventy-five miles an hour. Hurricanes tend to develop over water of about 82° Fahrenheit between latitudes 10° and 30°. In the West Indies, they occur principally during the hottest months, from July to October.

The Virgin Islands lie in the track of hurricanes moving across the Atlantic in the direction of Central America or curving upward towards North America. Though hurricanes are annual occurrences in the region, the Virgin Islands have been rather fortunate to have been visited only spasmodically. Among the most destructive were the hurricanes of 1772, 1785, 1819, 1837, 1867 and 1916. Destruction by hurricanes to plant and animal life and to buildings was considerable; human lives were also lost on occasions. In every instance, they had to be followed by considerable readjustment and reconstruction at high financial cost. By under-mining the credit-worthiness of planters and by diverting finance that would normally have been used for further extension projects and development to the job of repair and rehabilitation, they have set the pace of social and economic progress in the Virgin Islands.

The heavy precipitation accompanying hurricanes can result in disastrous floods, but the elevation of the Virgin Islands reduces these possibilities. However, considerable erosion of the soil inevitably occurs during such torrential downpours. The effects of hurricanes have been worsened by the fact that they are invariably followed by tidal waves with telling effects on vessels at sea or lying at anchor in the harbors, safe though these normally are against the ravages of ordinary storms. When a tidal wave, during the hurricane of 1867, threw the American warship 'Monongahela' on Strand Street in Frederiksted, it helped to seal the fate of the islands for the next fifty years. Occurring as it did in the middle of the Unites States' consideration of the question of purchase, it contributed to the alienation of American opinion to acquire the islands.

The Virgin Islands lie in the mainstream of the ocean currents flowing from east to west throughout the Caribbean. These are the North Equatorial Current and the South Equatorial Current which originate around the Canary Islands and the Gulf of Guinea respectively. In the Caribbean, the former becomes the Antilles Current and moves gradually upward towards Florida. The South Equatorial

Current flowing along the northern shore of South America as the Guiana Current, moves upward along the curve of the Central American coast. Around Florida it merges with the Antilles Current, and the combined current flows upward along the American coast as the Gulf Stream Current then across the Atlantic in the general direction of Britain.[12]

The currents have the effect of modifying the force and facilitating travel against the general direction of the prevailing north-east trade winds. Currents and winds created certain natural entrances into and exits from the West Indies, for sailing ships from Europe and America. Some of these were of significance to the history of the Virgin Islands. Among the entrances may be mentioned the Anegada Passage between the Lesser Antilles and the Virgin Islands. Among the exits were the Windward Passage between Cuba and Hispaniola, and the Mona Passage between Hispaniola and Puerto Rico. Vessels using these routes passed in the vicinity of the Virgin Islands.

Currents, in conjunction with winds, have influenced the course of the history of the Virgin Islands. Before the appearance of Europeans, they undoubtedly facilitated the movement of the native Indians through the Lesser Antilles from South America to the Virgin Islands. In the days of sailing ships during the period of European colonization, they undoubtedly enabled European vessels to reach the islands faster than if they had been contrary. Also, because of the north-easterly direction of the winds, it was more difficult for attacks organized from Puerto Rico to be executed than it was for attacks launched from the Leeward Islands. And, of most importance, they aided the progress of slaving vessels sailing for the Virgin Islands from the west coast of Africa. The proximity of trade routes to the Virgin Islands made of them a haven for pirates and privateers. Scope was given to their activities by the long and frequent wars among European nations in the eighteenth century, and by the political condition of neutrality adopted by Denmark during these wars.

Flora and Fauna

As with other islands in the West Indies, the position of the Virgin Islands in the tropics has given them a widely-varied flora.[13] Though the relative paucity of rainfall has retarded somewhat the growth of large evergreen forests as are common in South America, it is undoubted that at one time, the islands sustained considerable forests which have since been depleted by the extension of cultivation and the use of timber for construction purposes and for domestic use such as fuel. The early destruction of local timber meant that essential supplies had to be obtained through importations, thereby placing reliance on external suppliers.

The vegetation can be divided into two parts: indigenous, that is native to the islands, and naturalized, that is, introduced since the entry of Europeans. Among the former may be mentioned plants used as food, trees used for construction and those used for a variety of miscellaneous but useful purposes.

Food plants influenced the consumption habits not only of the native Indians but also of the Europeans who came after them. Among the native fruits were the coconuts, grapes, sour-sop, mamee, custard-apple, sugar-apple, cashew and papaua. Ground-provisions included cassava, arrowroot and the sweet-potato. In addition, corn, peppers, various species of squashes, beans and cacao were also grown. Corn was eaten either green or ground into meal to make bread. Cacao was used to make a nourishing drink called chocolate. Two other very important native plants were the tobacco used mainly for smoking and the cotton for making clothes. Both were later developed by Europeans as plantation staples for commercial purposes.

Indigenous construction woods included the ceiba or silk-cotton, lignum vitae, fustic, white cedar and probably the mahogany. Other useful woods were balata important for its gum, the mahoe whose bark could be used as rope, the genipa for its dye, and the bay-rum tree which produces bay oil, the essential ingredient in bay rum. Among these plants may be mentioned the annatto or roucou introduced by the native Indians for its dye, and the flamboyant whose resinous stem can be used to make torches. The manchineel produces a poisonous sap. A number of woods can be used for fuel and posts, or to make charcoal.

The plants introduced were valued for their export potentials and generally had been cultivated elsewhere in the West Indies before being brought to the Virgin Islands. Of primary importance was the sugarcane. Indigenous to south-east Asia, it was dispersed to the Middle-East and Mediterranean before reaching the New World. It reached the Caribbean from two directions: in 1480 the Spaniards introduced the plant into the Canary Islands and from there it was taken to Hispaniola by Columbus on his second voyage; in 1425 the Portuguese carried the sugar-cane from Sicily to Madeira, and from there it was introduced into Brazil about 1515. From Brazil and Hispaniola the plant was introduced into the Lesser Antilles. Other plants brought into the Virgin Islands included the breadfruit from the South Pacific Islands, the jackfruit from Asia, and several varieties of citrus from Spain. Other naturalized plants include the star-apple, okra, sorrel, tamarind, mango, and probably the plantain.[14]

The fauna of the Virgin Islands includes fishes, birds and animals. The last two include those both domesticated and wild. The seas around the Virgin Islands abound in a variety of fishes, and the Virgin Bank is a convenient fishing ground.[15] Fishes recognized or caught for food in the vicinity of the Virgin Islands include several varieties of tarpon, herring, sardine, shark, macherel, snook, and snapper. Many varieties of fish can be found only in the deeper waters, but others such as flounders, whiffs and soles, can be caught in the shallows. Lobsters, crabs, and shrimps can also be caught, as well as various species of shell-fishes such as the conch, oyster, and snail. Land and sea turtles were at one time very common.

As far as bird-life is concerned, it is generally conceded that there has been continuous extinction of the various species, especially of those used for food.[16] Among birds which inhabit the islands are the blue heron, pigeons, parakeets, yellow-legs, doves, boobies, noddies, shearwaters and other water-birds. The honey-creeper and Newton's owl are peculiar to the Virgin Islands. While all these are indigenous to the Virgin Islands, others such as the domestic rooster and. hen, were introduced. The troupial is supposed to have been introduced into the Virgin Islands, but the bird may be of bona fide status for St. Thomas specimens show peculiarities of color not found elsewhere. A form of quail was brought to St. Croix, and at one time was common, but it is now extinct.

Mention should also be made of migrant birds that visit the Virgin Islands from the mainland of North America during the winter months. As in Puerto Rico, some of these such as the green heron, bobolink and yellow-bellied sapsucker form an important part of the avifauna of the islands. Others are rare and are little known. Two birds, the Caribbean martin and the Jamaican vireo, nest in the Virgin Islands, but migrate in autumn to South America where they pass the winter.

Other land fauna of the Virgin Islands is, in general, rare.[17] Of peculiar interest is the fact that the only surviving indigenous mammals are the bats, the other native land mammals such as the Capromys,

Isolobodon, and the agouti (said to be introduced by the Indians) which are all rodents, are now extinct. Existing mammals such as the deer, mongoose, rats and mice were all introduced since the arrival of Europeans. Also native to the islands are the various species of lizards and snakes, the iguana and the land tortoise which are becoming rare. Frogs and toads are common, and so are spiders, ants and mosquitoes.

As in the case of plants which were grown, the fishes, birds and animals that could be obtained for food have naturally influenced the economic behavior of the people and their style of living. Compared with just the nuisance value of other pests, the fever-transmitting mosquito, with its toll on human lives, certainly did much to retard the development of the Virgin Islands. Early settlements were ravaged by diseases such as malaria and yellow-fever. For Europeans who came it meant quick death or much impaired efficiency and their fate dissuaded others from taking the risk. The consequent shortage of labor, especially for the plantations, led to the importation of laborers from Africa, who were better able to withstand the adverse health conditions in the Virgin Islands.

Among the animals in the Virgin Islands must be mentioned those that were imported by the Europeans. The most important were the horse, cattle, sheep, goats and pigs. Horses were used primarily for transport and draft purposes. The latter function was shared by the cattle especially in turning the mills of sugar plantations. Furthermore, in common with sheep, goats and pigs, cattle were used for food.

Conclusion

The diversity of the physical environment of the Virgin Islands was matched by an equally wide range in the activities of the people, all of which have been directed, more or less to the utilization or production of the means of existence. Though they had a tendency to become less effective with the development and application of new improved techniques, geographical conditions undoubtedly exerted a strong influence over the activities of the people.

The close relationship between economic alignments and political organization in the Virgin Islands should be noted, all the more so, since the islands were under a colonial status for so long. While the conditions of geography provided opportunities for the inhabitants of the Virgin Islands, the decisions regarding the manner and pace of their exploitation rested with the people themselves either through their own initiative, or with the help, sometimes compulsion, of others. Much of the history of the Virgin Islands revolved around the central theme of the plantation and slavery.

[1] Quoted in Theodoor de Booy and John T. Faris, *The Virgin Islands: Our New Possessions and the British Islands.* (Philadelphia & London, J. B. Lippincott Company, 1918) p. 54.
[2] Charles Schuchert, *Historical Geology of the Antillean-Caribbean Region, or, The Lands Bordering the Gulf of Mexico and the Caribbean Sea.* (Hatner Publishing Co., New York and London, 1968) p. 474.
[3] West Indies: *Virgin Islands, Virgin Gorda to St. Thomas and St. Croix.* A Map. No. 905. (Washington, 1969).
[4] T. Wayland Vaughan, 'Stratigraphy of the Virgin Islands of the United States and of Culebra and Vieques Islands, and Notes on Eastern Puerto Rico.' (*Journal of the Washington Academy of Sciences*, Vol. 13, No. 14, 1923) pp. 303-317; Howard Augustus Meyerhoff, 'Geology of the Virgin Islands, Culebra and Vieques.' (*The New York Academy of Sciences*, Vol. 4, Part 2, 1927); O. B. Boggild, On the Geology of the Danish West Indies. (*The Caribbean Journal of Science*, Vol. 1, No. 4, Nov., 1961) pp. 135-141.
[5] Meyerhoff, op. cit., pp. 80-81; O. B. Boggild, 'The Danish Islands in the Atlantic Ocean: Geologic Formations, Their Kinds and Uses.' (*The Caribbean Journal of Science*, Vol. 1, No. 2, May, 1961) pp. 61-65.
[6] Schuchert, op. cit., p. 479.
[7] Luis H. Rivera, William E. McKinzie, Henry H. Williamson, *Soils and their Interpretations for various Uses: St. Thomas, St. John, Virgin Islands.* (U.S. Department of Agriculture, 1966); William E. McKinzie, Bobb F. Scott, Luis H. Rivera: *Soils and their Interpretations for various Uses.* (U.S. Department of Agriculture, 1965.); Luis H. Rivera, Wayne D. Frederick, et al., *Soil Survey of the Virgin Islands of the United States.* (United States Department of Agriculture, Soil Conservation Service, 1970).
[8] Ibid.; Cf. James Thorp, *Soil Survey (Reconnaisance) of St. Croix, Virgin Islands.* (Technical Bulletin No. 315) pp. 10-18.
[9] Martin J. Bowden, et al., *Climate, Water-balance, and Climatic Change in the North-west Virgin Islands.* (Published under the auspices of the Caribbean Research Institute, College of the Virgin Islands, St. Thomas, 1969).
[10] Ibid., D. J. Cederstrom, *Geology and Ground-Water Resources of St. Croix, Virgin Islands.* (Washington, 1950) p. 10.
[11] Cederstrom, op. cit., pp. 69-91.
[12] Gerhard Neumann and Willard J. Pierson, Jr., *Principles of Physical Ocean-ography* (Prentice-Hall, Inc., 1966) pp. 424-425.
[13] Heinrich Franz Alexander Eggers, *The Flora of St. Croix and the Virgin Islands.* (Washington, n.d.); Elbert L. Little, Jr., and Frank H. Wadsworth, *Common Trees of Puerto Rico and the Virgin Islands.* (Agriculture Handbook, No. 249, U.S. Department of Agriculture, Washington, 1964).
[14] Carl O. Sauer, *Agricultural Origins and Dispersals.* (New York, 1952) pp.

20-22.

[15] J. T. Nichols, 'The Fishes of Porto Rico and the Virgin Islands.' (*Scientific Survey of Porto Rico and the Virgin Islands,* Vol. X, Parts 2 and 3. New York Academy of Sciences, New York, 1929) passim.

[16] Alexander Wetmore, 'The Birds of Porto Rico and the Virgin Islands.' (*Scientific Survey of Porto Rico and the Virgin Islands,* Vol. IX, Parts 3 and 4. New York Academy of Sciences, New York, 1927) passim.

[17] G. A. Seaman, *Mammals, Reptiles and Amphibians of the Virgin Islands.* (Brodhurst's Printery, 1961); Karl Patterson Schmidt, 'Amphibians and Land Reptiles of Porto Rico, with a List of Those Reported from the Virgin Islands.' (*Scientific Survey of Porto Rico and the Virgin Islands,* Vol. X, Part 1. New York Academy of Sciences, New York, 1928) pp. 150-155.

Chapter 2

Pre-Columbian Inhabitants

When Christopher Columbus discovered the West Indies, he did not reveal to Europeans an uninhabited New World. Rather, the region had been peopled for several thousands of years before his arrival. In common with other West Indian islands, the Virgin Islands were also inhabited, but no first hand study was made of the society which existed here on Columbus' arrival. However, studies carried out by archeologists in the twentieth century enable us to reconstruct the situation both before and after Columbus arrived.

Before the fifteenth century, three main groups of people, or Indians as they came to be called, had entered the West Indies: the Ciboneys, the Arawaks and the Caribs. In physical features, all three groups of Indians were of medium height; they had high cheek bones, high brows, fairly flat noses with wide nostrils, and straight black hair. Their bodies were well-proportioned; those of the Arawaks were lithe and supple, while those of the Caribs, because of their greater emphasis on muscle-development for fighting, were well-developed but flexible with broad buttocks and powerful shoulders.

Entry into the Virgin Islands and Site Locations

The Ciboneys reached the Greater Antilles travelling either southward from Florida, northward from South America, or eastward from Central America, while the Arawaks and Caribs moved northward from South America through Trinidad and the Lesser Antilles. The Virgin Islands which stand on the periphery of both the Greater and Lesser

Antilles, occupied the unique position where cultures clashed and turned. The Ciboneys had reached as far as St. Thomas in the Virgin Islands[1] before they were conquered and driven backwards or eliminated by the Arawaks who continued their passage from the Lesser into the Greater Antilles. The Arawaks established settlements throughout the Virgin Islands, and there they were met by the Caribs, not long before Columbus reached the islands. It has not been definitely established that Carib settlement in the Lesser Antilles had advanced beyond St. Croix though they apparently raided the east coast of Puerto Rico.[2] Both the Arawaks and the Caribs were destined to vanish before the European advance.

It has been suggested that the Ciboneys entered the Virgin Islands between 300 and 400 B.C. and that the Arawaks arrived at about 100 to 200 A.D. In addition, it has been estimated that the Caribs who were advancing behind the Arawaks reached here about 100 to 150 years before the arrival of Columbus.[3]

The Caribs were encountered by the Spaniards, in November, 1493, on Columbus' second voyage, at Salt River in St. Croix, where they had undoubtedly defeated the Arawaks and taken over their settlements there. It was at Salt River that the Spaniards had their first reported fight with the indigenous peoples of the New World.[4]

While Ciboney sites have been discovered only in Krum Bay in St. Thomas, Arawak sites have been located at several places such as at Magens Bay and at Botany Bay in St. Thomas, Salt River and Longford in St. Croix, Coral Bay and Cruz Bay in St. John, and on Water Island.[5] According to the archeologists Bullen and Sleight, the first Arawaks in the St. Thomas-St. John group settled near Coral Bay. Another settlement was made at Cruz Bay. As the population of these two settlements expanded, the Arawaks moved to other sites. These included Cinnamon Bay and Francis Bay in St. John and Magens Bay and Botany Bay in St. Thomas. Other smaller and less prosperous settlements were made elsewhere in the two islands.[6]

Manufactures

The most outstanding feature of the civilization of the Indians was their manufactures. The Ciboneys, Arawaks, and Caribs were more or less stone age peoples and the basic materials with which they worked were stone, shell, bone and wood. The principal, and for the Ciboneys probably the only, technological processes were battering with stone hammers, chipping with shell gouges and stone axes, and cutting with flint chips. There is an absence of pottery in Ciboney middens.[7] In addition to stone, shell, bone and wood, the Arawaks and Caribs worked with clay, hemp, fiber, grass, cotton and skins from which a variety of articles were made. Stones were used to make bowls, grinders, pestles, mortars, flints and celts. Shells and bones were used to make celts as well as picks and chisels, and wood was used to make canoes, bowls, the digging sticks used in agriculture, stools, and drums.[8]

The native Indians had developed the art of producing and using fire. An Arawak produced fire by using a fire drill, that is, a stick twirled between the hands and resting either upon a softer stick or upon two lighter sticks tied together. The Caribs produced fire by rubbing two sticks against each other.

Yellow and red clay was used to make pottery which was common among Arawaks and Caribs. The vessels were first shaped by hand and then fired. Most of them were undecorated except for white-on-red paintings done in geometric designs, and their sides were either straight or incurving.[9] Pottery vessels included cooking bowls, platter, bottles, and griddles on which cassava bread was baked. Leaves and fibers were plaited to make cordage and baskets, the latter being of outstanding production among Caribs. Mats were made only by Caribs. Cotton was used to make cloth and cordage, and skins were used to make drums. Sewing was done with bone needles or spines. In addition, gourds were converted into water containers by removing the pulp inside.

Carib and Arawak manufactures are difficult to distinguish. The reason for this is that when the Caribs conquered an Arawak settlement, they killed the men but kept the women as slaves. In an Indian community, women were responsible for making most of the artifacts, except those requiring much strength such as canoes and stone-works.

Food Collection and Preparation, and Dietary Habits

The Ciboneys were fish eaters. So too were the Caribs and Arawaks, though they ate proportionately less fish since their diet was supplemented from other sources. This is suggested by the remains in the sites where they lived. These include the bones of fishes, and great quantities

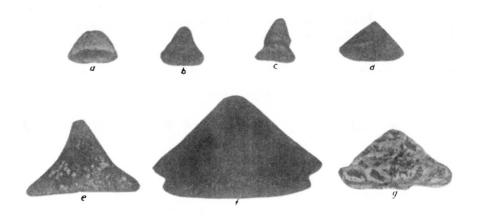

INDIAN DECORATIVE THREE-CORNERED ORNAMENTS

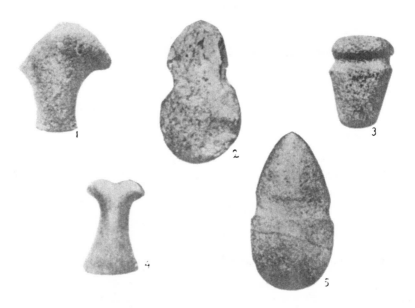

INDIAN STONE TOOLS

INDIAN POTTERY WARES

of shells, especially those of the clam, conch, mussel, oyster and snail. Land and sea crabs and turtles were also eaten.[10] Indeed, the staple food of the Caribs was crab. Ciboneys, Arawaks and Caribs also ate such animals, mammals, reptiles and birds as were to be found on the islands during their time. Though the Ciboneys had no cultivated crops, they probably nourished themselves with the various native fruits. Both the Arawaks and Caribs cultivated the soil, the Arawaks more so than the Caribs. Among the crops they planted were cassava (or manioc), both sweet and bitter, corn, potato, yams, beans and peppers.

The Indians used various devices to obtain their sea food. Fishing by Arawaks and Caribs was done by nets made of cotton or fiber, fitted with wooden floats and stone sinkers, and nets were probably used for dragging. The use of nets suggests shore fishing. So too does the use of the hook and line, the former being made of shell or bone. Fish spears were probably used also, the prongs being fish bones. Unlike the Ciboneys and Arawaks, the Caribs also used bows and arrows. Baskets were used both for fishing and for storing the catch.

On land, the hunting methods varied. The small round water-polished pebbles found in shell middens probably indicates that the Ciboneys used slingshots.[11] This however would raise questions concerning the means of propulsion. The Caribs used bows and arrows and domesticated dogs to secure animals and birds. The Arawaks resorted more to the use of dogs and imitating the cries of the hunted creatures. The game was dispatched with clubs, if necessary. Crabs were hunted at night by the light of a burning brand, and shell-fish was picked up along the shores.

The Arawaks and Caribs planted cassava, corn and other vegetables twice a year to coincide with the seasonal rainfall. All cultivation was done by women. Slash and burn agriculture was practiced in the sense that a plot was partly cleared, burned and planted. After some years, when a plot of ground had become exhausted, it was abandoned and another plot was cultivated.[12] The Indians fertilized the fields with urine and with ash from the burnt trees. Birds were kept from the fields by children stationed on platforms in the trees. Most fruits were gathered wild.

There were significant differences in the way food was prepared by Ciboneys, Arawaks and Caribs. Ciboneys are thought to have ground their vegetable foods in mortars and on milling stones, and to have mixed them in bowls made out of stone or wood. Animal food was either eaten raw, or roasted over fires.[13] The Arawaks and Caribs were more elaborate in preparing meals, both of them using cassava to make bread. The cassava was peeled, grated and squeezed in a basket-work or cotton tube, to extract its poison, if it were the bitter kind. The shreds were shaped into cakes, baked on a clay griddle set on stones over a fire, and then dried in the sun. The ordinary cakes were coarse, but those for chiefs were fine. The bread was then stored and used when needed. Corn was used to make soup or cakes by both Arawaks and Caribs. The corn was soaked overnight, ground between two bricks or in mortars hollowed out of tree trunks, mixed with water to form loaves, wrapped in leaves, and baked in the fire. Corn was also used to make beer. Corn kernels which had previously been chewed were put into large jars of water. This mixture was left to ferment, heated for three or four hours, allowed to cool, and then strained.[14]

The Arawaks had a unique way of preparing food in the pepperpot. This was a sauce made from the juice obtained from bitter cassava when making bread. In it vegetables and meat were kept at a continuous boil over a fire, portions being taken out as required, and fresh supplies added from time to time. The Caribs used a different method in preparing fish and meat and special pains were taken to cook these properly. They were either broiled, sometimes for a whole day over a slow fire, roasted on coals, or smoked in order to preserve them for future use. Caribs seasoned their fish and meat with a sauce made by boiling strained cassava juice with crushed peppers and cassava flour. A soup was made by boiling meat, fish, peppers, cassava juice and flour, and shellfish in which, when eating, they dipped their cassava bread or roasted yams and potatoes.

The eating habits of the Ciboneys are not known, and those of the Arawaks and Caribs varied. The Arawaks ate three times a day: morning, noon and evening. During festivals they took a fourth meal which was preceded by vomiting, as a form of ritual. In contrast, the Caribs, ate irregularly at odd intervals. The men sat on low stools in the carbet or men's house, and were served by the women on little tables which they covered with leaves. Afterwards, the women ate by themselves in the kitchen.

Dwellings

As suggested by their dwelling site in Krum Bay, the Ciboneys lived in sheltered positions, albeit in the open. Since they did not engage in agriculture, it did not matter that their sites were situated on stony ground with no good farm land nearby. Krum Bay, however, was well located for fishing. Ciboney dwellings were little more than the simplest of wind-breaks constructed of brush or palm thatch. Their villages were very small and semi-permanent, and more in the nature of camps than anything else.[15]

Because of their warlike inclinations which kept them on the move against other peoples, the Caribs also had impermanent settlements. The settlements of the Arawaks, however, were permanent, unless they were forced to flee from the attacks of the Caribs. Arawak and Carib settlements were located in areas where they could undertake agriculture, for example, at Magens Bay. Carib settlements, however, tended to be those belonging to conquered Arawaks such as at Salt River and were strategically located for defense.

The dwellings of Arawaks and Caribs consisted of single-roomed huts with thatched roofs, gabled sides and dirt floors. The house of the Arawak chief was large and rectangular, and this he shared with his wives. The dwellings of the commoners were small and round and were single family units or else occupied by several different families. Each had a single doorway and perhaps also windows. In a Carib village, the men occupied a single house called a carbet, while the women lived in smaller houses divided by partitions to separate the sleeping quarters from the kitchens. The only openings in Carib houses were doors in each end which were covered with mats.[16]

Caribs and Arawaks slept in hammocks made of cotton or reeds. In Carib houses small wooden tables or stools were common, while among the Arawaks carved stools of wood or stone were used only among the people of a high social class, and then principally during religious ceremonies.

Transportation and Clothing

Ciboneys, Arawaks and Caribs transported themselves on water by means of canoes which were dugouts from cedar and silk-cotton trees. The making of a canoe was a long process: first a tree had to be felled by alternately burning and chopping it, then the ends were squared, and finally the trunk was hollowed out by gouging it with fire and stone chisels. Canoes varied in size from those that could carry only one person, to those that could carry as many as seventy or eighty people.

The largest canoes belonged to the chiefs, and the smallest were used on fishing trips.

Generally, the canoes of the Caribs had a better finish than those of the Arawaks: their sides were smoothed, polished and often painted. Only the canoes of Arawak chiefs were painted. Again, the Carib canoes were propelled by two or three sails made from cotton or from palm-leaf matting and as in the case of the Arawaks by paddles which were spade-shaped with crossbar handles and very long blades. Bailing was done by gourds. Canoes were used not only in coasting, but also in travelling from island to island. Travelling inland was undertaken on foot since Indians lacked domesticated beasts of burden such as the horse, and burdens were transported in baskets on the back.

Very little clothing was worn by Indians, whether they were Ciboneys, Arawaks or Caribs. Both men and women, generally, wore girdles or breechcloths made from either cotton or vegetable fibers. The length of the apron worn by married Arawak women depended on their rank: the aprons of upper-class women, for example, extended to their ankles. For all Indians, the upper parts of the body were bare. Before the arrival of Europeans, Arawak and Carib men went completely naked.

As part of their dress, Indians wore pendants of shell or stone, and other ornaments. Arawaks sometimes wore ear and nose ornaments made of gold obtained in trade and these ornaments bore the shape of zemis or idols. Arawaks also wore armlets and leg bandages made of beads or from cotton, while Caribs wore bracelets on the arms, made of the same materials.[17] Carib men sometimes inserted the teeth and bones of slain enemy into their necklaces and bracelets.

Both Caribs and Arawaks flattened the heads of their children — the Carib doing so back and front, and the Arawak only the front — as this was thought to make them more beautiful. The Ciboneys did not indulge in this practice.[18] All three peoples colored their bodies principally during ceremonies or rituals. The paint was expected to make warriors appear fiercer, and in order to enhance this effect, Caribs scarred as well as painted their bodies, while Arawaks wore grotesque masks of wood or stone. All Indians wore their hair long: generally beards were scanty but such as they had, the Arawaks allowed to grow, while the Caribs plucked them out considering them a deformity.

Social Organization

Of all three peoples, the Ciboneys had the least organized social system. Each local group, consisting of several families living together, probably constituted an independent band. They probably held property in common and rarely engaged in trade.

Compared with the loose social organization of the Ciboneys, the settlements of the Arawaks were organized under and governed by hereditary chiefs. Beneath each chief was an hierarchy of other classes which can be referred to as nobles, commoners and slaves.[19] The nobles acted as assistants to the chief and performed judicial functions. Also, they attended meetings with the chief to decide village policies. The commoners did the actual work of the village with the assistance of the slaves. Crimes were judged by the chief who imposed the sentence, the death penalty on theft and adultery. The extent of private property is not clear. Personal property and other ornaments were inherited matrilineally. Agricultural land and storehouses were probably held in common and joint hunting enterprises were undertaken. Trading was common among the Arawaks. The existence of many Arawak communities in Puerto Rico must have been particularly favorable to the Arawaks in the Virgin Islands. In addition to these contacts, the Arawaks must have conducted an inter-community trading within the Virgin Islands themselves. Cassava, pepper, stools, wooden bowls, pottery, and carved stone objects were the principal articles bartered.

Compared with the hierarchical structure of an Arawak community, the Carib settlement was more or less an independent organization. It comprised an extended family which had broken away from a larger settlement and was headed by its founder who supervised fishing and cultivation and organized entertainment. He was respected but had little authority because Carib men were individualists, and respected fighting ability more than age or statesmanship. Each settlement had one or two war-chiefs who were elected to office. Rank was not as well-defined among the Caribs as among the Arawaks. Ancestry was unimportant: men were prominent because of their military prowess, or because of their knowledge and experience. Each settlement had its slave class consisting of captive women; their children, however, were free. In economic affairs, the Caribs were unique in that they used rolls of tobacco as a standard of exchange. Land and food were held in common, but canoes and ornaments were private property.[20]

Religious Practices

Little is known about Ciboney religion. Ceremonial stones discovered might have had a religious function while the presence of stone balls in burials, might be an indication of belief in life after death.[21]

In contrast with the Ciboneys, both Arawaks and Caribs believed in the plurality of souls: Caribs associated them with the heart and arteries, the former being good and destined for heaven, the latter being bad and destined to remain in the bones or to roam in forests or on seashores. The souls of the Arawaks were believed to have lived in their bodies and also in trees, rocks and natural phenomena. The Caribs believed the good spirits were invisible except at night when they took the forms of bats. So each Carib had a bat for his personal deity. An offering consisting of cassava bread and fruits was occasionally given to this deity in order to ensure good crops and to safeguard health. There were no ceremonies of worship and no idols or priests. Caribs believed that all disagreeable and frightening occurrences such as nightmares, sickness, hurricanes and earthquakes were due to evil spirits.[22]

Like the Caribs, the Arawaks believed that spirits had supernatural powers, and they sought to gain control over them. This they did by constructing idols of wood, stone, bone, shell, or clay where the spirits could reside.[23] These idols were called 'zemis' and each person had one or more. These were kept in homes except those of the priest which were lodged in a special building. Zemis were also carved on walls as petroglyphs such as those found at Reef Bay in St. John and on Congo Cay.[24] Arawaks also shaped their utensils and furnitures like their zemis. Most zemis were in the shape of grotesque human beings, birds, leaves, cassava and potatoes. Many zemis discovered, such as at Salt River, Longford and Sprat Hall in St. Croix, can be distinguished as three-pointed stones.[25] To the zemis were attributed the powers of spirits. Some were believed to influence the weather, some to regulate crops, some to improve hunting and fishing, some to produce wealth, and others to help in childbirth. Three-pointed zemis were believed to have the most power over crops.

Arawak chiefs depended for their power partly on the superiority of their zemis. Usually a chief constructed a speaking tube between his zemi and a hidden corner where a confederate spoke into the tube making it appear that the zemi was speaking.[26] Zemis were kept on tables with snuff in front of them and food was offered to them or they were rubbed with cassava in order to prevent illness.

A peculiarity among Arawaks was that they vomited for religious purposes in order to purify themselves. Caribs fasted on a number of occasions as a sort of penance. Arawaks and Caribs were served by witch doctors who attended to sick people.

Some Important Social Customs

Differences occurred in the marriage patterns of Arawaks and Caribs. An Arawak tended to marry into his own class, though marriage to a sister or niece was prohibited. Among the Caribs, marriage with mothers, sisters and stepsisters was tabooed, though a man could marry his cousin. Polygamy was practiced by those Arawaks who could afford it. Generally it was limited to chiefs, and all wives of a chief lived in the same house. Carib men, also, were allowed more than one wife, those with more wives being considered more prominent. Warriors could marry the women taken captive during a raid. The prospective Arawak bridegroom had to pay his intended father-in-law a price to have his daughter; if he was poor he paid in service. The Carib bridegroom had to obtain the consent of the girl's parents: if he was a warrior fathers were anxious to secure him for their daughters. Except in the case of chiefs, there did not seem to be much ceremony in Carib and Arawak marriages. An Arawak married couple usually lived with the bridegroom's family, while a Carib couple lived with the bride's family.[27]

Greater similarity was evidenced in the death and burial of Arawaks and Caribs. When it was clear that an Arawak person was to die, he was strangled, or he might be driven out of the house by his relatives, or he might be abandoned with food and water. The Caribs, also, sometimes killed the old and infirm. Disposal of dead bodies took two forms, burning or burial. If burnt, the body was sometimes consumed with the house in which the death took place. If buried, the body was flexed, wrapped and placed in a prepared grave. The Caribs usually painted and oiled the body. Carib dead was buried in the carbet, near the wall if the person was ordinary, and in the center if he was prominent. The deceased person's personal possessions were usually placed in the grave, and to these the Arawaks added a bowl of water and some bread.[28]

Of all three peoples, the Caribs were the most warlike. Carib men were trained from youth to be warriors and their armory contained more potent weapons. Carib youths were taught to value courage and endurance, and were trained in the use of weapons to be fighters. Even their rituals, such as being anointed with the fat of slaughtered Arawaks to make them brave, had military ends in view. The principal weapon used by the Caribs was the bow and arrow, the latter being tipped with poison to increase their killing quality. In the Virgin Islands there were a number of poisonous plants including the manchineel and milkweed whose sap could be used as poison.[29] The chief weapon used by the Arawaks, however, was the spear, bows and arrows being used only intermittently and more by nobles than by commoners. Both Caribs and Arawaks used javelins and clubs also.

In military tactics both Arawaks and Caribs depended on the element of surprise to achieve victory. The former attacked from ambuscades, while the latter attempted to catch the enemy asleep by attacking at dawn and at night from various directions. The Caribs allegedly ate the bodies of the people they vanquished; those killed in war were eaten immediately after victory was established, while prisoners were reserved for village celebrations. Female prisoners were kept alive and treated as slaves, but male prisoners were tortured and killed.

Both Arawaks and Caribs did sculpturing, carving and painting. Sculpturing and carving were done in stone and wood, those of the Arawaks being considered superior to those of the Caribs. It would appear, however, that the painting of the Caribs was more elaborate. Modelling in clay by Arawaks was generally poor and the overwhelming art motif was the zemi.

The Caribs were fond of wrestling and boat races. Wrestling was also done by Arawaks who, in addition, ran races, and engaged in a ball game played with a rubber ball. The game was played by both men and women though separately.

At feasts, the natives drank beer, sometimes getting quite drunk. They also smoked tobacco in the form of cigars, the dry tobacco leaves being wrapped in corn husk. The Caribs also chewed tobacco, while the Arawaks used snuff on religious occasions.

Dancing was a usual pastime for both Arawaks and Caribs. Singing accompanied the dancing, the songs of the Caribs telling of war. The musical instruments of both peoples included the drum which was a hollowed log covered at one end with animal skin, and the rattle which was a gourd with stones in it. In addition, the Arawaks used a castinet which comprised little plates of stone attached to the fingers and clicked to produce music. The Caribs used a stringed instrument made of a gourd with a single string, and a flute made of bamboo or hollow bone.

Disappearance from and Impact on the Virgin Islands

The entry of Europeans into the West Indies was very fateful to the Indians of the Virgin Islands as it was to those elsewhere. The overriding lust of the Spaniards was for gold and when they settled in the Greater Antilles they mined for the precious metal. The native Arawaks who were forced to work in the mines were unequal to the task. The harsh treatment meted out to them, combined with the inadequate food, and the diseases introduced by the Europeans, caused them to die out in large numbers.

The depletion of the local labor supply in the Great Antilles led the Spaniards to turn elsewhere, and it is probable that the Indians in the Virgin Islands were drafted into the labor force. As in the case of the Indians on St. Croix, who encountered Columbus in November, 1493, resistance to the Spaniards meant death. Indians who learned of the fate of their fellows in the Spanish colonies could have escaped eastward to the Lesser Antilles where they would feel more secure among people of their own kind. With their skill in navigation, this would not have been a serious problem.

It has been suggested, also, that about 1555 the Indians were driven away from the Virgin Islands as directed by Charles V of Spain who ordered that they should be treated as enemies and exterminated.[30] Why the Emperor should act thus against the Indians here since one of the purposes of Spanish colonization was the Christianization of heathens, was not stated. One of the reasons why Spaniards did not settle in the Lesser Antilles was that they feared the attacks of the warlike Caribs who could easily evade capture by resorting to mountain fastnesses. A similar fear could have motivated them in their relation with the Indians of the Virgin Islands. Whatever the causes may have been, it is a fact that the Danes found only a few Indians still living on the islands, at the colonization in 1672.

The Indians are supposed to have introduced some plants and animals into the Virgin Islands; but they influenced the history of the islands more significantly. The military encounter between the Spaniards and the Indians at Salt River in November, 1493, undoubtedly contributed to Spanish neglect in colonizing the Virgin Islands since people who came to seek wealth would not knowingly run the risk of death at the hands of warlike natives. Spain's failure to settle here, paved the way for the settlement and eventual colonization of the islands by other European nations, of whom the foremost were the

French and the Danes. Not too much should be made of the Indian scare, however, since Spanish neglect was influenced by other, probably more important, considerations such as the small size of the islands, their lack of precious metals, and especially in the case of St. Thomas and St. John, their comparatively hilly nature.

The Indians affected the history of the islands in another rather negative way. Their absence from the Virgin Islands at the time they were colonized for plantation agriculture and when they could have been used as laborers, meant that alternative sources had to be tapped. European indentured laborers generally proved unsuitable, and employers resorted to African labor. The requirements of a continuous and reliable supply of labor led to the institution of Negro slavery in the Virgin Islands. This took place at an earlier date than it would have had there been Indians here to work.

[1] Ripley P. Bullen, The Preceramic Krum Bay Site, Virgin Islands, in Relationship to the Peopling of the Caribbean. (In *Akten des 34. Internationalen Amerikanis tenkongresses,* Wien, 1960, Vienna, Ferdinand Berger, 1962) p. 398.

[2] J. Walter Fewkes, *The Aborigines of Porto Rico and Neighboring Islands.* 25th Annual Report of the Bureau of American Ethnology. (Washington, 1907) p. 219; Sven Loven, *Origins of the Tainan Culture, West Indies.* (Goteborg, Elanders Bokfryckeri Akfiebolag, 1935) pp. 53-58. Loven believes that the Caribs had reached as far as Vieques, though this island could have been used as a base to launch attacks.

[3] Irving Rouse, 'Prehistory of the West Indies.' (*Science,* Vol. 144, 1964) pp. 499-513; José M. Cruxent and Irving Rouse, 'Early Man in the West Indies.' (*Scientific American,* Vol. 221, No. 5, 1969) pp. 42-52.

[4] Samuel Eliot Morison, *Admiral of the Ocean Sea. A Life of Christopher Columbus.* (Little, Brown and Company, Boston, 1942) pp. 415-417.

[5] L. H. Dudley Buxton, J. C. Trevor and Alvarez H. Julien, 'Skeletal Remains from the Virgin Islands.' (*Man,* Vol. 47, 1938); Folmer Andersen, *Notes on St. Croix.* (St. Croix Museum Commission, 1954) pp. 27-28.

[6] Ripley P. Bullen, 'Ceramic Periods of St. Thomas and St. John Islands, Virgin Islands.' (In *William L. Bryant Foundation American Studies.* Report No. 4, 1962); Frederick W. Sleight, Archaeological Reconnaissance of the Island of St. John, United States Virgin Islands. (In *William L. Bryant Foundation American Studies.* Report No. 3, 1962).

[7] Ripley P. Bullen, *The Preceramic Krum Bay Site,* pp. 398-399.

[8] Gudmund Hatt, 'On Pottery from the Virgin Islands.' (*Man,* No. 48, 1938); Loven, op. cit., pp. 149-150 and 195-196.

[9] Rouse, op. cit., pp. 508-509; Hatt, op. cit.; Loven, op. cit., pp. 271-278.

[10] Theodoor de Booy, *Archaeology of the Virgin Islands.* (Museum of the American Indian, Heye Foundation, New York, Indian Notes and Monographs, Vol. 1, No. 1, 1919).

[11] Ripley P. Bullen, *The Preceramic Krum Bay Site,* p. 399.
[12] Frederick W. Sleight, *Archaeological Reconnaissance of St. John;* Ripley P. Bullen, *Ceramic Periods of St. Thomas and St. John Islands.*
[13] Ripley P. Bullen, *The Preceramic Krum Bay Site,* p. 399.
[14] Julian Steward, *Handbook of South American Indians.* (New York, 1963) Vol. 4, pp. 523, 550-551.
[15] Gordon R. Willey (Ed.), *Prehistoric Settlement Patterns in the New World.* (New York, 1956) p. 167.
[16] Loven, op. cit., pp. 336-349; Steward, op. cit., pp 525 and 551-552.
[17] Steward, op. cit., pp. 525-526 and 552-553.
[18] Buxton, Trevor and Julien, op. cit., p. 5.
[19] Steward, op. cit., pp. 528-530; Loven, op. cit., pp. 498-506.
[20] Seward, op. cit., pp. 555-556.
[21] Ripley P. Bullen, *The Preceramic Krum Bay Site,* p. 399.
[22] Steward, op. cit., pp. 561-563.
[23] Alanson Skinner, 'Archaeological Specimens from St. Croix, Virgin Islands.' (*Indian Notes,* Vol. 2, April, 1925) pp. 109-115; Loven, op. cit., pp. 578-597.
24. Theodoor de Booy, 'Archaeological Notes on the Danish West Indies: the Petroglyphs of the island of St. John and of Congo Cay.' (*Scientific American Supplement,* Vol. 84, December, 1917) pp. 376-377.
[25] Gudmund Hatt, 'Archaeology of the Virgin Islands.' (In *Proceedings of the Twenty-First International Congress of Americanists.* The Hague, 1924).
[26] Ibid., pp. 36-37.
[27] Steward, op. cit., pp. 531 and 557.
[28] Ibid., pp. 532 and 558-559; Loven, op. cit., pp. 541-543; Theodoor de Booy and John F. Faris, *The Virgin Islands: Our New Possessions and the British Islands.* (Philadelphia, Lippincott, 1918) pp. 105-106.
[29] A. J. Oakes and James O. Butler, *Poisonous and Injurious Plants of the U.S. Virgin Islands.* (United States Department of Agriculture. Miscellaneous Publication. No. 882, Washington, 1962).
[30] De Booy and Faris, op. cit., pp. 41-42.

Chapter 3

Danish Colonial Expansion

The Virgin Islands were discovered by Christopher Columbus in November, 1493, on his second voyage of discovery to the New World. On the fourteenth of that month the expedition anchored off Salt River Bay in St. Croix and some men were sent ashore to collect water. From St. Croix unfavorable winds drove the expedition somewhere to the east or southeast of Virgin Gorda. When the winds changed, the fleet reformed and sailed in two divisions through the cluster of islands to the west of Virgin Gorda. Outside St. Thomas the two divisions rejoined on the evening of November 17 or next morning, and from there sailed for Hispaniola.[1]

The discovery of the Virgin Islands like the rest of the West Indies, was followed by Spain's assertion of exclusive right to them on the basis of prior discovery. However, these claims were rejected by other European nations who wanted a share of the territory and its trade.

While Spain was yet a powerful nation in Europe, other nations refrained from challenging directly its claim to monopoly of the West Indies. Hence, they were content to give 'unofficial' backing to private enterprise in the form of smuggling and piracy. Privateers were also commissioned to attack Spanish West Indian posessions. The result was that in the sixteenth century Spain was forced to grant certain important concessions to other Europeans to trade in the West Indies, though they were to do so at their own risk, their vessels and crews being subject to seizure and punishment.[2]

The concession granted by Spain to other European nations to trade in the West Indies was but the first step towards their establishment of colonies. The decline of Spanish power in the seventeenth century made it increasingly difficult for Spain to protect its monopoly. Accordingly, other nations were able to breach it. The direction of settlement was indicated by Spanish neglect to colonize the smaller islands of the Lesser Antilles in favor of the Greater Antilles.

Beginning with the English, followed by the French and the Dutch, the seventeenth century witnessed an increasing invasion of Spanish territorial claims to the West Indies. It was in keeping with this general European trend that Denmark was to establish its first colony in St. Thomas in the second half of the seventeenth century.

Early Danish West Indian Ventures

The attention of the Danes was drawn to the West Indies at an early date by the possibilities of trade here. Nevertheless, they were forced to follow the lead of other Europeans largely because Denmark was in a state of economic decline. In the sixteenth century energies were wasted in settling internal disorders, in feuds between king and nobles, in powerful peasant revolts and in religious controversy. Besides, Sweden was a constant thorn in the Danish side.[3] The result of all these troubles was that even the Danish trade came to be dominated by foreigners, notably the Dutch. It was the Dutch who introduced the Danes to West Indian trade and Danish sailors on Dutch trading vessels were able to observe the opportunities for trade which the West Indies possessed.

In contrast to the previous century, the seventeenth century was a period of increasing prosperity for Denmark. Danish agricultural and industrial production, especially of corn and cloth, called for wider overseas markets, and under Christian IV (1588-1648) attempts were made to find such markets.[4] The initiative for promoting trade between Denmark and the West Indies was taken by the Dutch residing in Copenhagen who petitioned the king in 1622 for authority to establish a company to trade with the West Indies. Permission was subsequently granted by the king in an open letter dated January 25, 1625 when the proposed company was given the privilege of trade for eight years with the West Indies, Brazil, Virginia, and Guinea.[5]

Nothing came of the proposed enterprise primarily because it was impossible to attract the necessary capital. People were wary of trading ventures which were likely to collapse, as did the Danish East India Company and the Iceland Company organized in 1616 and 1619 respectively. Equally important in thwarting the formation of the Company was the fact that Denmark became involved in the Thirty Years' War from 1625. Military involvement and defeat brought an unfavorable reaction towards commercial enterprise since it became impossible for Danes to devote attention to or assist in the launching of the new experiment in trade.

The failure of the 1625 attempt did not mean the end of the idea to promote Danish West Indian trade. Under the direction of Prince Frederik, later Frederik III (1648-1670), Gabriel Gomez organized a trading expedition in 1647 under two brothers surnamed de Casseres. With letters of introduction from the Danish king to the governor of Barbados, they visited that island to trade with its inhabitants. However, the expedition failed probably because of the Civil War in England between royalist and parliamentary forces, which led to social conflict among Englishmen in Barbados. It was not until 1651 that a second expedition was attempted. In that year, two ships were sent out to the West Indies with instructions to pick up some 'special items' and to collect certain claims outstanding from the first voyage.[6] It is not known how this expedition fared.

Apart from important and influential Danes, less prominent people became interested in the West Indies. While some Danes served on English and Dutch vessels trading with the region, others were engaged in trading on their own behalf. According to the customs records, the first ship to sail for the West Indies from Copenhagen passed Kronborg, a castle which guards the harbor of Elsinore and the entrance to the Sound, on March 20, 1652. The captain was Erik Nielsen Smit who was later to establish the first colony in St. Thomas. The ship returned to Denmark the same year and was granted exemption by the king from the payment of customs duties.[7]

The success of this voyage fired the imagination of its organizers who not only thought of a second voyage, but also of establishing a colony on one of the unoccupied islands in the West Indies. Subsequently, they applied to the king for certain special concessions including exemption from the payment of customs duties on ships' provisions. Royal interest in colonization was shown when the privileges requested were granted, even though these were of short duration.[8] In March, 1653 Erik Nielsen Smit set out again on a second voyage and returned in November of the same year with a substantial cargo of 4,000 bales of tobacco, 40,000 pounds of ginger, two hogsheads of sugar, and seven barrels each of sugar and indigo.[9]

Meanwhile, the success of Smit's first voyage had aroused the interest of other Danish merchants who began organizing themselves for similar undertakings. Eventually, five vessels — four from Copenhagen and one from Elsinore — sailed for the West Indies in 1654. One apparently perished while four returned safely with large cargoes totalling 225,437 pounds and 1,490 bales of tobacco, 241,170 pounds of ginger, 40,901 pounds and 29 barrels of sugar, and 628 pounds and one barrel of indigo.[10] The venture was highly successful, but the West Indies were becoming a dangerous place in which to trade due to enmity between Spain and England. When in 1655 Erik Smit undertook his third voyage to the West Indies his vessel along with another was captured, the combined loss amounting to 32,000 rixdalers. Though Smit was allowed to return to Denmark, the expedition was a complete failure.

To the difficulties imposed by the international conflict was added another due to unfavorable weather conditions. Yet a third vessel and its crew of 22 men were destroyed by a hurricane in August, 1657. In the same year war broke out between Denmark and Sweden and continued until 1660 making it necessary to postpone trading activities in the West Indies as well as plans for Danish acquisition of territory in the region.

The First Colonization Attempt, 1665-1668

In the history of Danish colonial expansion, the 1660's were important because of the establishment of absolute monarchy in Denmark. In a final struggle between the king and the nobility, the king was able to emerge supreme. In order to establish his supremacy the king fell on the support of the emergent industrial class, the new class of merchant traders and generally on the common people. With this concentration of government, the state began to take a leading and consistent part in encouraging industry and commerce. The establishment of colonies followed naturally the desire to develop trade since the king's support of overseas ventures was not without self-interest. The chartering of joint-stock companies in which the king himself held shares was not only a means of increasing his own financial position but made the success of overseas ventures dependent on mutual support between king and shareholders. Events in the West Indies after 1660 developed from such conditions within Denmark.

It was not until February, 1662 that conditions permitted the dispatch of a fourth expedition to the West Indies under Erik Smit's experienced leadership. Smit returned in February, 1663 with a cargo consisting of tobacco, ginger and other tropical West Indian products. But the voyage was equally important for another reason: from it stemmed directly the idea of establishing a colony in the West Indies. Smit had probably made the necessary reconnaissance as to the most suitable island to colonize.

A plan for the colonization of St. Thomas was laid before the Danish king in April, 1665. It projected the main advantage which the island possessed for trade, namely, a safe harbor against storms and hurricanes for both large and small vessels. It also expressed the intent to colonize St. Thomas with both Danes and foreigners undoubtedly to prevent attacks from other Europeans who were not likely to wage war against their own nationals. Lastly, the king was urged to follow the example of English and Dutch colonization efforts, as shown elsewhere in the West Indies.[11]

The royal response was favorable: only a little more than three weeks after the proposal had been submitted, on May 6, 1665 a royal commission was issued naming Erik Nielsen Smit as Governor of St. Thomas, and authorizing him to take possession of and to govern the island.

Preparation for the expedition was of short duration for by July 1, 1665 Erik Smit and his company were able to set sail on board the vessel 'Eendragt' bound for St. Thomas. The journey was very perilous for on one occasion off St. Bartholomew and again while actually in St. Thomas harbor, the vessel was almost destroyed by storms. Between these two events, a fire broke out on board and threatened to reach the powder-room and destroy the entire vessel.[12]

The incidents experienced on the voyage to St. Thomas seemed a precursor of things to come. At the time, the Second Dutch War (1665-1667) was being waged between England and the Netherlands and the West Indian area was the scene of much fighting and destruction. Although all settlements were in danger of being attacked the war at first appeared to favor the Danes. Because of the somewhat isolated position of St. Thomas from the rest of the Lesser Antilles, it was comparatively safe from attack. Consequently, English, French and Dutch settlers elsewhere in the Caribbean were willing to join the Danes in St. Thomas in order to escape from the ravages of war. Their coming increased the number of settlers in the infant colony.

St. Thomas did not escape the consequences of war. Smit had

reached the island either in late 1665 or in early 1666, and some time later English privateers attacked the settlement and plundered it of essential supplies. However discouraging this attack might have been, it did not lead to the abandonment of the settlement. The Danes had already become aware of the potentials of St. Thomas as a center of trade, and as a plantation colony. Even prior to the English privateering attack, a vessel had been dispatched to Denmark on February 15, 1666 with a small cargo of three hundred 'rolls' of tobacco and one-and-a-half hogsheads of sugar which had been obtained through trade with neighboring colonies.[13] In addition, the settlers had begun to clear the forests preparatory to cultivating the land.

From the beginning sickness had attacked the settlement and on June 12, 1666 the infant colony received its greatest blow when the Governor, Erik Nielsen Smit himself, died. His death created a void which no Danish settler in St. Thomas could fill adequately. The most qualified Dane was Kjeld Jensen Slagelse, a Lutheran theological candidate recruited for the voyage, who assumed the leadership of the settlement. The methods Slagelse adopted to govern the settlers showed good qualities of leadership. His first action was to summon a meeting and to get all the settlers to re-affirm their allegiance to the king of Denmark. He then got them to agree to repel attacks from outside by concerted action. These two measures were undoubtedly necessary since the foreigners combined out-numbered the Danes. In addition, a Council was created to help Slagelse to govern, which in its composition was designed to avoid sectional differences and conflict. Elected by the settlers, it consisted of book-keeper Jesper Beyr and constable Christen Hansen both Danes, Jan Brouer a Dutchman and captain Ralph Palmer an Englishman.[14]

Misfortune, however, dogged the settlement. It was again terrorized by English privateers who robbed it of supplies and powder and who seized the vessel which was used in the trade with the neighboring islands. Even after they left, the settlers lived in constant fear of their return. In addition, the settlement was devastated by a hurricane. As a result of these calamities, the settlers suffered from a shortage of food-stuffs. Trading was impossible since they had no goods to barter and they could not obtain credit. To add to their plight, sickness continued among the settlers. Under such conditions the settlement disintegrated. The English settlers left with the English privateers for St. Croix, then a French colony, in anticipation of better conditions there. Besides, the Dutch were also becoming troublesome as a result of their intolerance of Danish holidays, and the Dutch in Tortola were becoming hostile to the Danish settlement.[15]

After remaining for nineteen months on the island without receiving any assistance from Denmark, the Danes decided to abandon the settlement. After first visiting St. Christopher, where several Danes were living, they obtained passage for Denmark. Following their departure, the Dutch in Tortola visited St. Thomas and robbed it of everything of value that the Danes had left, including some guns and other ammunition. The English were also attracted to the island and some of them established residence here.

The Colonization of St. Thomas, 1672

It was not until 1672 that a second attempt was made by Denmark to colonize St. Thomas on a more ambitious scale than the previous effort in 1665. In order to give new impetus to trading enterprises, a Board of Trade had been established in Denmark in 1668, and its activities were boosted by the accession to the Danish throne in 1670 of Christian V. Among the first and most significant actions taken by that sovereign was the conclusion of a treaty of alliance and commerce between Denmark and Britain in July, 1670, which permitted the Danes to colonize St. Thomas without arousing British opposition. Further interest in colonization was shown when the king proceeded to charter the Danish West India Company on March 11, 1670. Under the charter and the 'reglement' which accompanied it, preparations for the settlement of St. Thomas were begun in the summer of the same year.

As governor of the new colony, the directors of the Company selected Jorgen Iversen who, though only 33 years of age, apparently had the experience necessary for the post of governor. He had lived and worked, first as a clerk and then as a manager, in St. Christopher. He thus had first-hand information about conditions in the West Indies. Also important were his West India trading ventures between 1660 and 1665, in partnership with three Dutch businessmen from Zeeland. This was what probably made him a man of some means. He was introduced to the harsh realities of West Indian trade when on one occasion his ship and cargo were seized by an English privateer. Besides his knowledge, experience, and wealth, Iversen was well married, occupied a fairly high social position, and was known in royal circles.[16]

About 20,000 rixdalers were expended in fitting out the two vessels which had been provided by King Christian V for use by the Company. A wide range of articles was loaded in one of them. These included foodstuff, kitchen utensils, wares and furniture. In addition, tools and materials for constructing a fort as well as houses for the Company's employees were shipped. So too, were a various assortment of arms, textiles and liquors.[17]

As a precautionary measure, it was decided to reconnoiter St. Thomas in order to ensure that the island was still unoccupied by another European nation. Because of English ambitions in the region as shown by their conquest of Jamaica from Spain in 1655, it was not certain that St. Thomas was not already occupied by them. Accordingly on August 31, 1671 the Dutch Captain Arent Henriksen, in the yacht 'The Golden Crown' was dispatched in advance to make the necessary survey. The 'Faero', with the governor on board, was to follow later, and an arrangement was made for the two parties to meet in St. Eustatius. However, when the 'Faero' failed to arrive within the expected time, Captain Henriksen returned to Denmark. Governor Iversen had left Copenhagen in October, 1671, but while he was still in the North Sea, his ship sprang a leak and he stopped at Bergen for repairs. It was not until February 29, 1672 that the expedition was able to continue.[18]

The quality of people secured by the Danish West India Company for its proposed colony was in keeping with the general difficulty experienced at the time by all European nations to recruit settlers for their West Indian colonies. In term of agriculture, St. Thomas was practically virgin territory and offered possibilities of individual enterprise as a new venture in colonial development. Two main factors deterred the Danish lower class from participating. In the first place, the enterprise for St. Thomas was regarded as a Company undertaking to engage in plantation agriculture. As such, the prospects of independent and private enterprise were seen to be extremely limited. In the second place, by the seventeenth century, yellow-fever and malaria were prevalent diseases in the West Indies, and Europeans did not have immunity to them. In 1671, Danes knew of the suffering and death of the settlers who had come to St. Thomas in 1665, and so were afraid to follow.

There was no enthusiastic rush of Danes to colonize St. Thomas in 1671. Of the 190 persons on board the 'Faero', 12 were officials and 116 were the Company's employees. The remaining 62 had been recruited from the prisons and places of ill-repute in Denmark. The Company's employees were indentured immigrants contracted to serve

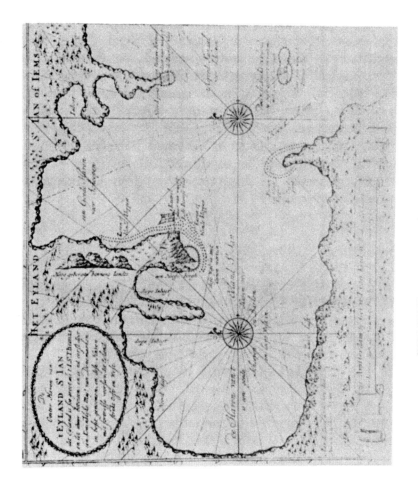

THE SETTLEMENT AT CORAL BAY

the Company for a period of from three to five years in return for food, clothing and housing. Lacking means of their own, they had their passage paid by the Company.[19]

The 'Faero', with its company, arrived at St. Thomas on May 25, 1672. Of the 190 persons, only 104 remained: nine had escaped and 77 had died. The deaths were due to a combination of over-crowding, poor and inadequate food, and insanitary conditions on board which made the passengers vulnerable to diseases. Those who survived would be depleted even further after colonization had begun. During the first seven months in St. Thomas, another 75 persons died, leaving a bare 29.

The Danes found no one living on St. Thomas when they landed. The English settlers who had occupied the island after the end of the first Danish settlement, had left six or seven weeks before, though the reason for their departure is not known.[20] The Danish flag was raised and formal possession was taken of the island. Denmark's long association with the Virgin Islands began with this occupation of St. Thomas in 1672. In later decades the Danes were to extend their colonization to other islands in the group.

The Settlement of St. John, 1718

According to the Charter issued to the Danish West India Company in 1671, the Company was empowered to establish settlements on St. Thomas and on any other uninhabited island in the West Indies. This general authorization was incorporated in the Commission given to Iversen as Governor of St. Thomas, and to his successors.

Until 1718, a few but unsuccessful attempts were made to colonize St. John. In 1675, Iversen took possession of the island and placed two men on it, but the occupation was not followed by any permanent settlement. In 1684, another attempt was made by Governor Adolph Esmit to settle the island through two merchants from Barbados. He was deceived in supposing that by involving the English he would thereby prevent English intervention to disrupt the settlement. Sir William Stapleton, then Governor of the English Leeward Islands, sent two sloops to the island and drove away the 40 men sent there by the Barbadian merchants.[21]

The opposition of the English governors explains in part why St. John was not colonized until forty-six years after St. Thomas. Also important was the opinion of some Danes that the colonization of St.

Thomas should be consolidated before a new colony was attempted on St. John. The Danish West India Company, however, had not abandoned the idea of colonizing other Virgin Islands. In 1688 when Esmit took up his second appointment as Governor, he was instructed to settle St. John by sending between four and six men there and encouraging them to begin cultivation.[22] Nevertheless, nothing seems to have been done towards implementing these instructions.

It was during the governorship of Erik Bredal (1716-1724), that active consideration was given to the colonization of St. John. The initiative was taken by the colonists themselves who were looking for better planting opportunities elsewhere. They first sought and obtained the approval of the directors of the Danish West India Company to settle St. John. Bredal's intention to establish a settlement on St. John published on March 23, 1718 was followed by fast action to prevent the English from intervening. The enterprise was headed by the governor himself in order to indicate beyond doubt its official nature and to give force to the Danish possession. On March 24, 1718, Bredal equipped a vessel with provisions, and guns and ammunition, and together with twenty planters, five soldiers and sixteen slaves landed on St. John. The next day he took possession of the island in the name of the king of Denmark and of the Danish West India Company.[23]

The first settlement was commenced in Coral Bay at the east end of St. John selected because of its strategic position and its supposed suitability for agriculture. From Coral Bay, the Danes could keep a watch on the English and from the fort constructed on a hill, now called Fortsberg, they had command over the harbor and the surrounding countryside. Any control of that part of St. John would first have to begin with the seizure of the fort. Agriculturally, the valley between the surrounding hills and the bay was large enough for plantation agriculture. Preliminary surveys, also, probably showed that it was fertile enough, and that it was more adequately supplied with water than other parts of the island. Moreover, the harbor had the capacity to accommodate more vessels than any other harbor in St. John and it promised safety against stormy weather.

The occupation complete, Eight Articles of Agreement were issued including the provision that English and Spanish settlers had to swear fealty to the commander of the settlement. This requirement was an obvious attempt to preserve the safety of the new settlement by reducing the possibilities of subversion in case of enemy attack. Provisions were also made for the proper distribution and settlement of the land, the granting of assistance by the Company in the form of slaves and essential plantation supplies, exemption of taxation for eight years, and the disposal of the island's produce to the Company.[24] These provisions were evidently intended to establish the settlement on firm foundations by seeking to attract new settlers and to encourage cultivation. The increase in population and production in turn would help to consolidate Denmark's claim to St. John against that of other rival claimants.

The Acquisition and Settlement of St. Croix, 1733-1734

One of the main reasons for the colonization of St. John was the limited agricultural potential of St. Thomas. The same reason dominated Danish acquisition of St. Croix in 1733. By that time trade had declined to the point where only one or two ships were required to carry off the annual products of the islands. Besides, since 1721 shareholders had gone without dividends and for several years prior to 1733 the Danish West India Company had been unable to meet its interest payments on outstanding debts. It became clear to the directors of the Company that, in order to prevent stagnation and revive the fortunes of the planters and Company, a fresh start had to be made elsewhere. Attention was directed to the nearby French island of St. Croix which had been unoccupied since 1696.

St. Croix had an eventful history of rival European claims and abortive settlements in the seventeenth century.[25] It is generally believed that as early as 1625, it had been occupied by the English and Dutch who, sometime later, were joined by the French. Foreign settlements in the Virgin Islands, however, were liable to be destroyed by the Spaniards in Puerto Rico when they raided other settlements in the Lesser Antilles. The position of the Virgin Islands en route between Puerto Rico and the eastern islands made settlements especially liable to attack.[26] As Thomas G. Mathews has pointed out, 'the frequent passing of Spanish ships offered a constant threat which only the most desperate English, French, or Dutch settlers would be willing to risk.'[27] What seemed to have saved St. Croix, however, was the Spaniards' apparent preference for the channel among the northern Virgin Islands when engaged in their raids on the Lesser Antilles.

The early English, Dutch and French settlers who inhabited St. Croix apparently lived separately. Though they seemed to have maintained the peace among themselves, they were seldom friendly. In 1645, a crisis was precipitated when the leader of the Dutch allegedly killed the leader of the English. A fight ensued between the English and Dutch in which the Dutch leader was mortally wounded. Peace was subsequently established and the English, under the pretence of friendship, invited the new Dutch leader to their quarter. He was seized and shot in retaliation for the loss of the English leader. Fearing further retaliation the Dutch evacuated the island and settled on the islands of St. Eustatius and St. Martin with their fellow-countrymen. The French, who sympathized with the Dutch, feared English reprisals and withdrew to the French island of Guadeloupe.

The English remained masters of St. Croix, but not for long. In August, 1650, the Spanish government of Puerto Rico launched a surprise attack against the settlement and the English survivors in their turn were forced to flee. The Dutch thought that it was safe to do so and returned to St. Croix. However, the Spaniards had not yet left for Puerto Rico and the Dutch were ambushed; those who were not killed were taken prisoners.

Meanwhile, Phillippe de Lonvilliers de Poincy, the French Governor-General in St. Christopher, learning of the expulsion of the English from St. Croix, organized an expedition to take the island. The Spaniards were defeated and expelled and French settlement and cultivation of St. Croix were begun towards the end of 1650 when de Poincy dispatched about 300 settlers to the island. From the beginning, however, the infant colony became a prey to disease with two-thirds of the colonists dying during the first year. In addition, dissatisfaction spread among the colonists because of heavy taxation and because they were forced to trade with the French West India Company instead of being allowed to deal on more favorable terms with Dutch traders.

When the decadent state of French colonies in the West Indies led to their sale by the Company to their respective governors, St. Croix was purchased by de Poincy. The colony remained unprofitable and in 1653 de Poincy transferred possession of it to the religious Order of the Knights of Malta. Even then St. Croix did not prosper despite the introduction of fresh settlers in 1659 and 1661, and the appointment of an energetic young governor named du Bois. A drought in 1661, followed by heavy rains, caused widespread sickness and death. In 1665, the administration of the island was taken over by the 'Compagnie des Indes Occidentales', which had been organized by Colbert, the French Minister of Finance, the year before. In 1674, however, the

'Compagnie' failed and St. Croix passed under direct royal control. None of these administrative changes benefited St. Croix so that in 1696 the remaining colonists were taken to Saint-Domingue, following the decision to abandon the island.

After 1696, the only people who lived on St. Croix were those who went there to collect timber. They were primarily English. Temporary dwellings were constructed but no permanent settlements were made.[28] It was evident that an unsettled island so near to St. Thomas would attract the attention of the Danes here. When economic depression due to drought and other causes struck St. Thomas and St. John from the late 1720's, thought was directed towards the acquisition of the island. Fear that the English intended to occupy the island was a spur to action. The French were willing to consider sale since they had no obvious or immediate interest to re-colonize St. Croix. Moreover, they were anxious to secure Danish neutrality in and money for the conflict with Russia and Saxony over the question of succession to the Polish throne.

Negotiations for the Danish purchase of St. Croix were conducted under the energetic leadership of Count Adolph von Plessen, a Danish Privy Councilor, and Frederik Holmsted, bookkeeper of the Danish West India Company. Von Plessen was specifically drafted into the Company to head its drive to revive the failing fortunes of its West Indian colony. He regarded the acquisition of St. Croix as the only way to improve the economic condition of the Virgin Islands and of the Company. Holmsted was interested in acquiring St. Croix since, as a cloth manufacturer, he was anxious for the expansion of the Danish linen industry. The acquisition of St. Croix meant the use of more slaves who would have to be clothed.

St. Croix became a Danish possession in 1733 when the treaty between France and Denmark, relating to St. Croix, was concluded at Copenhagen on June 15, and ratified shortly afterwards. It provided for the purchase of St. Croix from the French by the Danish West India Company for the sum of 750,000 livres, half to be paid in cash on the exchange of ratifications and the remainder within eighteen months.[29] An essential condition of the treaty was the provision that Denmark would not sell St. Croix to any foreign nation without the consent of the French. This provision became operative over 132 years later when Denmark sought to sell the Virgin Islands to the United States of America.

Under Instruments of Government drawn up by the West India

Company, Frederik Moth, formerly an acting-governor of St. Thomas, was appointed governor of St. Croix. The occupation and settlement of the island were delayed, however, since the Company's ship, 'Unity,' which bore the instructions and other orders to St. Thomas, did not arrive until June 11, 1734. But preparations for taking over St. Croix were begun by Moth immediately after he received his commission.

In June, 1734 Mothe visited St. Croix and decided to estabish the new settlement on the northside where Christiansted now stands.[30] Prayers were said for the success of the new enterprise on August 31, 1734 and on the following day, four vessels bearing Moth and his party, including planters and slaves, set off for St. Croix. By September 5 a site had been cleared for a fort and on the following day some cannon were placed there. The minister in attendance then preached a sermon and the royal flag was raised. Afterwards, the king's commission to the new governor was read and the cannon fired a salute.[31]

There were, at that time, about 150 British inhabitants on St. Croix, together with about 400 to 500 slaves, both men and women. These were permitted to stay, if they so desired, provided they took the necessary oath of allegiance to the king of Denmark.

The formal transfer of the island from France to Denmark took place in January, 1735. It had been postponed by the French authorities in Martinique because of the likelihood of hurricanes during the summer months. The French Captain Bonnoust and his party arrived on January 8, and accorded a nine-gun salute to the Danish flag planted near the fort, which the Danes answered shot for shot.Two days later, the official handing-over ceremony took place and Frederik Moth was acknowledged by the French as the legal governor, in full possession of the island according to the Treaty of Copenhagen.[32]

European Challenge to Danish Occupation of the Virgin Islands

By 1735, Denmark was in full possession of St. Thomas, St. John and St. Croix. However, its possession had not gone unchallenged for protests came from Spain and from England. After the Danes had established their settlement on St. Thomas in 1672, Spanish objections were raised by the Governor of Puerto Rico. In reply, the directors of the Danish West India Company, as the basis of their claim, asserted the principle of effective occupation, or the establishment of settlements, as their criterion for possession. In the face of this argument and, primarily because it was unwilling to support its claim by force of arms, the protests of the Spaniards dwindled down to no more than an occasional harmless reference.[33] Spain no doubt preferred to have the Virgin Islands colonized by the Danes rather than by the English and the French since the Danes obviously lacked the others' aggressiveness towards Spain.

England raised the question of Danish right to continue on St. Thomas in 1717 when it claimed that the Danes had forfeited all concessions given to them under the Treaty of 1670. The English charged the Danes with harboring runaway English slaves, maltreating Englishmen on the island and encouraging privateering activities against English ships. The English also protested against the Danish occupation of St. John and St. Croix and rested their argument mainly on a patent granted to the Earl of Carlisle in 1627 giving him control in the Lesser Antilles.[34]

The English were aware of the threat that these islands posed to English trade within the area, and were concerned about the defense of their colonies since the fighting force of the islands was being depleted as a result of emigration to the Danish colonies. Despite the grievances of the English, their position could not be maintained. Their claim to the islands occupied by Denmark, like that of the Spanish, broke down since they had failed to establish settlements on the islands. Of equal importance was the fact that no evidence could be produced to show that Englishmen had ever exercised sole right of possession even though they had lived and were living in the islands. Like the Spaniards, the English were averse to using arms in support of a claim that could not be firmly established in the first place by other means.[35]

Like other West Indian islands, the future of the Virgin Islands as Danish West Indian possessions, was bound up with the international wars of the later seventeenth century and those of the eighteenth century. Because of the plantation staples they produced, West Indian islands were regarded as valuable colonial possessions. As such, they became the prize in international warfare as each European nation sought to conquer those colonies belonging to its rivals. During most of these wars, however, the safety of the Virgin Islands was assured since Denmark assumed a neutral position.

Only once was the Danish position threatened in the seventeenth century. The Danes in St. Thomas carried on trade with the French settlers on St. Croix even though French laws of trade forbade this practice. An opportunity to put an end to this irregular traffic was obtained by the outbreak of war between France and the Netherlands in 1672. News of the outbreak of war reached St. Croix only in September, 1675 and a vessel belonging to the Danish West India Company then at the island was seized. Then on February 2, 1678 St. Thomas itself was attacked by the French. It is not quite clear why this attack took place except for the accommodation which St. Thomas gave to the Dutch. Governor Iversen put up a stout defense of the island and the French were eventually repulsed; they left after seizing a few slaves and free-Negroes.[36] The attack stimulated work on the fort, the tower of which had recently been completed and, in 1680, the governor reported that it was finished.

During the French Revolutionary and Napoleonic Wars (1793-1815), the Danish West Indies were twice seized by Britain — in 1801 and again in 1807. On the first occasion, the islands were held for a short while before being restored under the Treaty of Amiens in 1802. On the second, they were retained by England until 1815, when they were returned to Denmark under the Treaty of Paris in exchange for Heligoland, which Denmark ceded to Britain.[37]

The reasons for the British occupation in 1801 stemmed partly from the facility which the islands offered to privateers operating against British trade in the region. It resulted also from Denmark's seeming opposition to Britain when it formed an alliance of armed neutrality with Russia and Sweden to prevent Britain from searching Danish ships trading with France and confiscating their cargoes. The occupation of 1807 followed a Danish alliance with France after Britain had bombarded Copenhagen and had confiscated the entire Danish fleet in an unsuccessful attempt to force Denmark to form an alliance with it. The Franco-Danish alliance created a situation in which the Virgin Islands could be used as a base for French ships to operate against the British in the West Indies.[38]

The weakness of Danish colonial defense was shown by the ease with which the British captured the Danish islands. In the Virgin Islands there was no organized system of naval defense as was retained by Britain to protect its own colonies. By and large the Danes depended for the safety of the Virgin Islands on their neutral position during war. Their biggest fear was of privateers and pirates and to deal with these the three forts, Fort Christian in St. Thomas and Christiansvaern and Frederiksvaern in St. Croix, were considered adequate. Little attention was devoted to the problem of giving adequate naval protection to the islands. By the later eighteenth century, there were only two small

Danish vessels here to provide the defense against the naval might of Britain during the French wars.

In January, 1801, Britain began its operations against Denmark by seizing Danish ships in British ports, and other merchant vessels on the high seas. It was not until March, 1801, that the governor-general of the Virgin Islands was informed of the British actions. Even before then, the military activities of British against Danish shipping had been observed, and the governor-general W. A. Lindemann then living in St. Croix, had dispatched the brig 'Lougen' and the schooner 'Den Aarvaagne' to St. Thomas to strengthen the defenses here. These vessels were intercepted on the way and the 'Den Aarvaagne' was soon forced to return to Christiansted while the 'Lougen' put up a spirited but useless fight. It was later allowed to proceed to St. Thomas since it was so badly damaged that no further resistance was expected from it.[39]

The land forces in the Virgin Islands at the time consisted of a mixed assortment of Danish regulars stationed in the colony, volunteers, and free-negro corps. These could hardly be expected to put up an effective resistance against well-trained British troops. On March 27, 1801, the British under General Trigg and Admiral Duckworth attacked St. Thomas with 25 ships and 3,000 to 4,000 men and the Commandant capitulated on March 28, without firing a shot. Governor-general Lindemann on St. Croix likewise surrendered that island to the British on March 31, 1801.

The same attitude of non-resistance and capitulation was again exhibited in 1807 when the British, under General Bowyer and Admiral Cochrane, attacked with 17 ships of war and about 7,000 men. On December 22, the capitulation of St. Croix was demanded and on Christmas day the capitulation agreement was signed. On that same day, Casimir von Scholten, father of the later famous governor-general, capitulated in St. Thomas. He was later taken to England as a prisoner of war.

Conclusion

In keeping with a general European trend, the Danes had been at first attracted to the West Indies by the trading opportunities in the islands. Their settlement on St. Thomas was largely determined by the strategic position of the island for trade with the surrounding Spanish, English and French colonies. But when Danish settlement was first undertaken in the Virgin Islands, the enterprise was conceived, not only as a trading, but also as a planting venture. Indeed, the extension of Danish sovereignty, later to include St. John and St. Croix, was determined largely by the need to extend cultivation. The production of staple tropical commodities, like the promotion of trading enterprise, was to play an important part in the future of the islands and to influence their history to a considerable extent.

[1] Samuel Eliot Morison, *Admiral of the Ocean Sea. A Life of Christopher Columbus.* (Little, Brown and Company, Boston, 1942) pp. 412-420.
[2] Frances G. Davenport, *European Treaties bearing on the History of the United States and its Dependencies.* (Washington D.C., Published by the Carnegie Institution of Washington, 1929) Vol. 1, pp. 219-221, 246-249 and 258-263.
[3] W. Glyn Jones, *Denmark.* (Praeger, New York, Washington, 1970) pp. 25-31.
[4] Ibid., pp. 33-34.
[5] Waldemar Westergaard, *The Danish West Indies Under Company Rule (1671-1754). With a Supplementary Chapter, 1755-1917.* (New York, The Macmillan Company, 1917) pp. 18-19.
[6] J. O. Bro-Jorgensen, *Dansk Vestindien Indtil 1755: Kolonisation og Kompagnistyre.* (Fremad, Denmark, 1966) p. 12.
[7] Ibid., p. 13.
[8] Westergaard, op. cit., p. 20.
[9] Bro-Jorgensen, op. cit., p. 14.
[10] Ibid., p. 16
[11] Ibid., pp. 17-18.
[12] Ibid., p. 19.
[13] Westergaard, op. cit., p. 30.
[14] Kay Larsen, *Dansk Vestindien, 1666-1917.* (Copenhagen, 1927) p. 18.
[15] Cf. John Knox, *An Historical Account of St. Thomas, W.I.* (New York, Charles Scribner, 1852) pp. 44-46.
[16] Janus Fredrik Krarup, 'Jorgen Iversen (Dyppel) Vestindisk Compagnies forste Gouverneur paa St. Thomas.' (*Personalhistorisk Tidsskrift,* 11R. 6B, 1891) pp. 23-45.
[17] Bro-Jorgensen, op. cit., pp. 48-49.
[18] Ibid., p. 53.
[19] Ibid., p. 49.
[20] Westergaard, op. cit., p. 37.
[21] Ibid., p. 127.
[22] Ibid., pp. 127-128.
[23] Isaac Dookhan, A History of the British Virgin Islands. (Unpublished Ph.D. Thesis, University of the West Indies, 1968) p. 23.
[24] Ibid., p. 23.
[25] Knox, op. cit., pp. 33-41; Florence Lewisohn, *St. Croix under Seven Flags.* (The Dukane Press, 1970) pp. 20-74.
[26] Arturo Morales-Carrion, *Puerto Rico and the Non-Hispanic Caribbean: A*

Study in the Decline of Spanish Exclusivism. (University of Puerto Rico Press, Rio Piedras, P.R., 1952) p. 38.

[27] Thomas G. Mathews, 'The Spanish Domination of Saint Martin (1633-1648), (*Caribbean Studies,* Vol. 9, No. 1, April, 1969) p. 21.

[28] Dookhan, op. cit., pp. 29-30.

[29] Westergaard, op. cit., p. 206.

[30] Ibid., pp. 209-210.

[31] Lewisohn, op. cit., p. 84.

[32] Westergaard, op. cit., pp. 210-211.

[33] Manuel Gutierrez de Arce, *La Colonizacion de las Islas Virgenes.* (Sevilla, 1945).

[34] Dookhan, op. cit., pp. 21-24 and 30-32.

[35] Ibid., pp. 24-26 and 33.

[36] Westergaard, op. cit., p. 42.

[37] J. W. Fortescue, *A History of the British Army.* (London, 1912) Vol. VII, pp. 8-9; William James, *The Naval History of Great Britain from the Declaration of War by France in 1793 to the Accession of George V.* (London, 1837) Vol. III, p. 159 and Vol. IV, p. 354; Edward Pelham Brenton, *The Naval History of Great Britain from the year MDCCLXXIII to MDCCCXXII.* (London, 1823) Vol. II, pp. 449-450, and Vol. IV, pp. 178-179.

[38] Glyn Jones, op. cit., pp. 41-43.

[39] Jens Vibaek, *Dansk Vestindien 1755-1848: Vestindiens Storhedstid.* (Fremad, Denmark, 1966) pp. 219-220.

Chapter 4

Colonial Government under Company Rule

Although Denmark was interested in colonization in the West Indies, the Danish king was not prepared to take the initiative in establishing colonies or to assume direct control when colonies were founded. In this regard he acted like his European counterparts in the seventeenth century. In England, the responsibilities of West Indian colonization were often delegated to chosen favorites of the Crown, who became proprietors of the islands they settled.[1] On the other hand, in France and the Netherlands, the responsibility of establishing colonies and directing colonial affairs was delegated to national joint-stock companies.*[2] When Denmark established colonies in the West Indies, it resorted to the French and Dutch example. Both the 1665 and the 1671 colonial ventures were organized and executed by chartered companies. The more important of these, because of the success it achieved, was the Danish West India Company which received its Charter in March, 1671.

Colonial Administrative Machinery in Denmark

Even though the Danish king transferred the responsibility of establishing and controlling colonies to a Company, he nevertheless gave it personal and financial support and exercised supervision and direction of its activities. Control was exercised through Crown representatives on the directorate of the Company. Of the six directors of the Company, the king appointed three who were members of the Board of Trade established in 1668. Initially these were Jens Juel, Peter

Lerke and Hans Nansen through whom the Crown was able to exercise influence over colonial policy. In addition, through reserve powers contained in the Charter, the Crown had the power of confirming the appointment of the most important of the Company's colonial employees. Moreover, the king held the power of final decision concerning the powers which should be conferred upon the Company. These powers were outlined in the Charter granted by the king and the Charter itself was subject to modification and amendment by him as changing circumstances made this necessary. Indeed, it was tacitly acknowledged that the very existence of the Company was dependent upon the king's will. Lastly, because the king and other members of the royal family were among the largest shareholders of the Company, they could exercise control through the institutional machinery established to assist the directorate in the management of colonial affairs.

The Danish West India Company had been formed by selling shares, the minimum size of each share being 100 rigsdalers. In the discussions of the Company's affairs, each shareholder, or participant as he was called, had one vote. Besides the three directors of the Company appointed by the king, the shareholders elected by majority vote three other directors from among themselves. For any shareholder to be eligible for election to the directorate he had to have 2,000 slettedalers invested in the Company. It was this directorate of six members that had executive control over colonial affairs.

Participating in the government were the 'chief-participants' who had invested 1,000 or more rigsdalers in the Company. They were all eligible to serve as an advisory body to the directors. Four of them — two nobles and two burghers — formed a committee which had the power to inspect the Company's books at any time, and to audit the bookkeeper's accounts once yearly. In addition, occasional meetings of the general assembly of all shareholders were called to decide on matters of general interest and touching upon major changes. in policy.[3]

The powers and privileges given to the Danish West India Company through the Charter were wide-ranging. However, the Company did not have exclusive control or enjoy complete independence. It was authorized to occupy and take possession of St. Thomas 'and also such other islands thereabouts or near the mainland of America as might be uninhabited and suitable for plantations.' It was permitted to build offices, forts and other fortifications in the colonies established, and to take the measures considered necessary for their defense. War with another European nation could not be initiated by the Company though its colonies could defend themselves if attacked. Direct relations with foreign nations was reserved for the Danish Crown. The Company could administer justice to everyone in its employment or within its immediate jurisdiction, but direct appeal to the Supreme Court in Copenhagen was allowed.

The Company was given a monopoly of the trade with the West Indies and no other person except captains associated with it could participate in that trade. In addition to this, the Company could keep the proceeds of all undertakings except the usual tenth which was the king's share. It was exempted from the payment of export duties on goods which it shipped from Denmark to the West Indies. However, imports from the West Indies were subject to a 2.5 percent duty if they remained in Denmark, and to a one percent duty if they were re-exported. By having a lower re-export duty than an import duty, the aim was undoubtedly to increase foreign trade.

The Company could appoint governors for its colonies but these appointments were subject to approval by the Crown. It could appoint ministers of religion for the settlements, and recruit settlers from among both Danes and foreigners in order to develop its colonies. Lastly, it was permitted to have its own weights and measures though these had to conform to Danish standards.

The well-being of the colony owed much to the number and characteristics of its settlers. The Company was empowered to recruit its skilled workers, such as artisans and carpenters, from among the men enlisted in the Danish military forces. These were to be 'strong industrious men who are married and know some trade'. On the other hand, the Company was to recruit its plantation laborers from among Danes who were condemned to prison or to labor in irons, and from among those women whose disorderly lives had led them to prison or houses of correction. Sustained effort and constructive performance could hardly be expected from the latter category of recruits, and the progress of the infant colony in St. Thomas was to be severely hampered by their presence.[4]

The active control of the business of the Danish West India Company rested almost solely on the directors of the Company. The directors appointed the governors and chief colonial officials and gave them their instructions. They obtained captains for their sailing vessels, and secured ministers of religion to cater to the spiritual welfare of the colonists. In addition, they were expected to find markets either in

Denmark or elsewhere in Europe for the West Indian produce, and to send supplies for use by the colonists in return. This responsibility was delegated to factors.† The directors were to keep in touch with the Dutch money market and to buy insurance for both ships and cargoes from Dutch insurance firms. When disputes arose between the Company's employees and the planters in the Virgin Islands, the directors were expected to act as arbiters. Even when colonial appeals were made directly to the king, the directors were consulted before any judgment was passed. Lastly, the directors were supposed to maintain the royal authority and dignity both in relation to the colonists and to foreign nations.

The authority of the directors in the regulation of colonial affairs was enormous, but they did not have exclusive power of control. For instance, the general assembly of all shareholders was convened to consider subjects like the need to secure additional funds to enlarge the Company's activities, and on such occasions each member had one vote regardless of the number of shares which he had purchased. In addition to this limitation, serious problems affecting the Company were sometimes referred by the king to a special commission appointed from among the members of the Board of Trade, or to special bodies called 'Commissions in the Council Chamber of the Royal Castle.'

Colonial Administration: The Governor and Privy Council

The directors' control over colonial affairs was limited by other very important considerations. These were, firstly, the distance which separated Denmark and the Virgin Islands, and, secondly, the irregularity and slowness of communication between the two places. Because of these conditions, the directors had to delegate to the Company's officials in the Virgin Islands many of their powers given by the Charter. The chief colonial official was the governor through whom the Company exercised executive and administrative control in the Virgin Islands. The governor was assisted by a Privy Council which was primarily an advisory and executive body. It consisted initially of a merchant (or factor), a bookkeeper and a secretary. From 1703, a treasurer was added to the list of the Company's officials, and he also became a member of the Privy Council. All these officials were appointed by the directors from among Danes.

The governor was responsible for carrying out the instructions given to him by the directors of the Company, and for directing the day-to-day activities of the colony. His main duties included the maintenance of law and order, and the establishment of effective means of defense and protection. In keeping with these duties, he had to attend to the construction of forts and other fortifications and to the organization of a local militia. He was responsible for the construction of such public facilities as jails and roads, and for the levying and collection of taxes. He presided over meetings of the Privy Council and listened to delegations of colonists.

In judicial matters, the governor had the power to pardon or punish offenders. Together with other members of the Privy Council he was originally responsible for settling differences among the colonists but after 1703, selected planters were allowed to assist in this also. Appeals from their decisions could be made to the directors of the Danish West India Company or to the Supreme Court in Copenhagen. Unlike similar people in the British colonies, the Danish governor and the members of the Privy Council did not legislate; however, they were allowed to make regulations for the proper administration of the colony.[5] The governor was required to report his actions to the directors and to keep them informed on colonial affairs.

The duty of the governor often extended beyond the formal authority of his commission. In the matter of trade, for instance, he distinguished between what was legitimate and what was not, and sought to encourage those enterprises which benefited the colony. He tried to keep on good terms with the planter-colonists, avert slave rebellions, and maintain good relations with the neighboring foreign colonies. At the same time, he was concerned that the Company's plantations yielded favorable returns and that the Company's ships had worthwhile cargoes on their return to Denmark. The success of a governor was judged by his ability to satisfy these and other requirements. Even though he could refer some of these matters to his assistants, the final responsibility for their successful outcome was his.

With the expansion of Danish possessions in the Virgin Islands, it was necessary to widen the base of administration. Because St. John was so near to St. Thomas and because it had a very small population, it was not considered necessary to have a separate administration there. From the outset, it was different in St. Croix. The distance of forty miles separating this island from St. Thomas made it necessary to have a separate governor here from the beginning. However, the governor of St. Croix was subordinate to the governor of St. Thomas whose title was changed from governor to governor-general in 1736. Thereafter, while St. Thomas and St. John continued under a single administration, St. Croix was permitted after 1747 to have its own Privy Council in addition to its own governor.

Much of the success of the colonization attempt depended on the quality of the men selected as governors. The first governor, Jorgen Iversen, was competent and honest enough; his retirement in 1680 on account of illness, and his death at the hands of mutineers in 1682 when he was returning to St. Thomas on a reappointment, was a serious blow to the Company. During his governorship, he had, indeed, been charged with brutality, but his high-handed behavior is understandable considering the low quality of the first colonists, and the mammoth task of laying solid foundations for a new colony.[6]

Iversen's three immediate successors appear to have been men of inferior caliber and unsuited for the role of governor. Nicolaj Esmit, who assumed office in July, 1680, tended to favor lawless elements, and lacked the firmness and vision necessary to direct a pioneer venture. In the autumn of 1682 he was deposed by his brother Adolph at the head of a faction of unruly planters, but Adolph himself became notorious for his encouragement of privateering and piracy. During his governorship from 1682 to 1684, St. Thomas became a haven for privateers and pirates and attention was diverted from the development of trade and agriculture. That his irregular assumption of office in 1682 should have been approved by the directors, in commissioning him as governor, was due largely to the intrigues in Copenhagen of Adolph's wife, Charity, and to Iversen's unexpected death. But that they should have re-appointed him governor in 1687, in the light of his past misconduct, illustrates the difficulty experienced by the Company in securing competent employees. In June 1688, three months after his resumption of office as governor, Adolph Esmit was returned to Denmark as a prisoner, a victim of his incapacity to govern.[7]

As successor to Adolph Esmit in May, 1684, the Company appointed Gabriel Milan, a Jew. Milan was a talented, strong-willed man, given to independent action. He executed a heavy-handed justice by meting out extravagant fines and punishments, and in his relation with the Council he was arbitrary and willful. Because of his conduct he alienated the support of both planters and officials. Dissatisfaction against him led to a plot for his assassination, but he crushed the conspiracy with great cruelty. In the end, Milan was recalled and imprisoned. Later, he was tried for his misdeeds and sentenced to death. In March, 1689, he was beheaded in Copenhagen.[8]

In contrast with the inefficiency and mismanagement of the colony by the Esmits and Milan, were the energy and enthusiasm with which governors like Christoffer Heins and Johan Lorentz approached the Company's affairs. Heins acted as governor from June, 1686 to March, 1688, and again from June, 1688, to his death in October, 1689. During both periods, he brought St. Thomas a much required calm in administration, and prepared the way for the governorship of Johan Lorentz.

Lorentz had some experience in the Company's service and, in 1689, was employed as bookkeeper. He was governor of St. Thomas, in succession to Heins, from 1689 to 1692 and again from 1694 to 1702 when he died in office. He was a dedicated servant of the Company and worked in its best interests. He was largely responsible for muzzling the ambition of the Brandenburgers who had been allowed to establish a trading station in St. Thomas in 1685, to expand in St. Thomas and to the neighboring islands. Equally important for the future interest of the Company was his suppression of piracy. Under his guidance, stability was brought to St. Thomas, and the Company was rescued from bankruptcy and placed on the road to economic solvency and prosperity.

Elaborate sets of instructions intended to cover every emergency were issued to the colonial officials by the directors of the Danish West India Company. However, the officials were prone to interpret these instructions very flexibly or even to ignore them. Sometimes they used their position for embezzlement and graft. For instance, as a result of his operations during the later years of the War of the Spanish Succession (1702-1713), Governor Crone was accused of gross fraud in the conduct of the Company's affairs. He died before the suit that was brought against him came to an end. Nevertheless, Christian Soeberg, the treasurer at St. Thomas, who apparently collaborated with Crone, was finally convicted of fraud and forced to pay a large fine. While some officials were dishonest, there were governors, such as Bredal (1716-1724) and Gardelin (1733-1736), who owed their advancement to their reputation for integrity and to their ability to expose corruption in the management of the Company's affairs.

The dishonesty and disloyalty which occurred among the colonial officials were partly the fault of the Company. Salaries were low while the cost of living in the islands was high. Employees were forced to seek outside employment, and were open to bribery and corruption. Officials, if they so desired, could engage in cultivation, though they were forbidden to trade on their own account. They were compelled to sell their produce to the Company, but it often happened that they used their positions of authority to indulge in illegal trading. In this respect, the Company's produce also was considered fair prize. In order to raise their standard of living more in keeping with their status and closer to that of the planters and merchants, the officials resorted to the expedient of making purchases for their personal use in the name of the Company or of buying from the Company on credit. By the end of 1725, it was estimated that of a total of 181,897 rigsdalers owed to the Company, 71,309 rigsdalers were owed by its employees.[9]

After the initial experiment of appointing its West Indian governors from among men in Denmark, the Danish West India Company secured considerable success from its policy of recruiting its administrators from among officials who had seen service in St. Thomas. This policy was established with the appointment of Johan Lorentz as governor and after his death in 1702, the policy was continued. Of the eight governors who held office in St. Thomas between 1702 and 1733 when Gardelin became governor, only two men did not have preliminary training in St. Thomas.[10] Neither of these two men, Otto J. Thambsen (1724-1727), and Henrik Suhm (1727-1733), was able to get along well with the inhabitants of St. Thomas or found their work congenial to them.

Colonial Administration: The Burgher Council

The success of the Danish West India Company as a commercial venture depended very largely on the ability and integrity of its West Indian representatives. The success of these representatives, in turn, depended very largely upon their relationship with the local inhabitants. Thus, if the Company's officials wanted full cargoes to send to Denmark, they had to keep on good terms with the planters. This was especially necessary since planters were often attracted by better offers from Dutch and other foreign traders. This dependence on the local planters forced the Company to recognize the desires of the colonists. At the same time, awareness of their strong position led the planters to demand a greater role in the administration of the colony. This pressure became greater as the numbers and the prosperity of the planters increased. The tendency of the Company's officials, including the governors, to marry into the families of wealthy planters, ensured that the planters obtained the sympathetic support of the officials in their struggle with the Company for greater control over local affairs.

From an early date the planters had a part in the selection of governors. The deposition of Nicolaj Esmit and the institution of his brother Adolph was achieved with their assistance. More often, the death of a governor in office made it necessary that a new executive be appointed so that the business of government could go on. To wait until the directors in Denmark acted was seen as unnecessary delay likely to throw the political situation into confusion. Consequently, acting governors were selected from among the Company's officials. In the appointment of governors, the directors did not abdicate or delegate their right to anyone, but they paid close attention to the wishes of the local inhabitants, especially since appointments were made in consultation with the Privy Council. So long as the person recommended had never acted against the interests of the Company, he could be assured of confirmation as governor by the directors.

The local inhabitants obtained an officially recognized medium of expression in 1703 when they were permitted to organize a common or burgher council. This council consisted of six reputable planters who were selected by the planters themselves from among their number and approved by the governor. The council was presided over by the secretary of the colony and as outlined in the instructions given by the directors on March 27, 1703, its functions were purely judicial. Whenever the governor was unable to settle disputes among the inhabitants, he was directed to refer them to the burgher council. From this council acting as a court, the cases might be appealed to the Privy Council of the colony sitting as a superior court.[11]

The colonists of St. Thomas were not satisfied with this token recognition of their importance. As their economic power increased, they became more critical of their lack of political power. Until they were allowed more effective means of expressing themselves, the colonists were forced to petition and, when this failed, to send delegates to Denmark to air their grievances and make their demands. The use of delegates was resorted to in 1706-1707 and again in 1715-1716 and their success made it only a question of time before they received greater recognition. Finally, on November 16, 1734, Christian VI issued a list of new privileges for the colonists in which the selection of members and the rights of the burgher council were stated in detail. The first members of the burgher council were to be appointed by the governor. Thereafter, one of them was to retire every three years and this vacancy, as well as any other that might arise, was to be filled by the governor from a list of three planters submitted to him by those members of the burgher council who remained.[12]

The powers of the burgher council were increased even though its judicial functions were apparently not retained. The council was given the right to confer with the governor and Privy Council whenever it had any matter to propose touching on the public welfare. Proposals had to be submitted in writing, and copies might be forwarded to the directors of the Company whether the governor-in-council offered a reply or not. The burgher council provided a means by which the colonists could make their desires known to the authorities in St. Thomas and Copenhagen. Its powers were advisory rather than executive, and though it lacked the power to initiate action, the right to advise was not far removed from the right to implement that advice.

Members of the burgher council often met separately to consider ways and means by which money could be raised and spent. Decisions were usually expressed to the governor-in-council at joint meetings, records of which were kept. The burgher council generally consisted of between four and seven members: thus it was usually larger than the Privy Council. Hence, when joint meetings were held to consider general issues such as the market price of plantation produce, a sufficient number of its members usually withdrew in order to make the numbers of each council even.

In the burgher council, the planters had a legally sanctioned instrument which became more effective with use. Through it they were able to bring to the Company's attention all manner of alleged abuses and grievances. However, they still resorted to the use of delegations to Copenhagen when they saw fit. Delegates had proven effective before, and they were used again in 1747 in response to a royal edict issued at the Company's request forbidding trade by private shipowners with St. Thomas.[13] The planters saw this restriction as a threat to their prosperity since they would be denied the advantages of that trade. The vehemence of their opposition was effective in securing some very important concessions with reasonable promptness.

The Company's Abdication of its Colonial Responsibilities

Under the Charter of March, 1671, the Danish West India Company was given control over the islands which it settled in the West Indies. At first control was confined to St. Thomas, and later it was extended to include St. John and St. Croix when these islands were settled. Company rule in the Virgin Islands, however, was neither continuous nor permanent. For three years, from 1691 to 1694, the Company abdicated its authority and allowed St. Thomas to pass under private ownership; and in 1754, it transferred the entire group of islands to the Danish Crown. The reasons for these transfers varied being mainly, on the first occasion, the poor economic condition of St. Thomas during the first two decades of colonization, and on the second occasion, the political pressures exerted by the colonists themselves to be removed from the monopolistic control of the Company.

The years immediately following the establishment of the settlement in St. Thomas comprised a difficult period in the history of the island. The colonists who settled on St. Thomas after 1672 were a varied lot; in addition to the Danes, there were Dutch, French, German, English and Jewish settlers. To keep such a mixed collection of people under reasonable control was a difficult task. The situation was made worse by the low quality of the Danes who had been brought over as laborers. Besides, the island was ravaged by disease, mortality being especially high among the Danish laborers. Those who died were replaced by their fellow-countrymen equally unsuited to plantation labor. To make matters worse, it was well-nigh impossible for the Company to obtain honest or capable employees for St. Thomas.

In the early years, therefore, the growth of the colony was naturally very slow and dividends for the shareholders of the Company were scarce. The low economic state of the Company made some action necessary if it were to remain in existence. An attempt was made to boost the fortunes of the Company in 1674 when it was allowed to take over the slave-trading interests of the Guinea Company.‡ The increased privilege, however, was not based on solid foundation since the Company was not equipped, either psychologically or materially in ships and men, to take over the trade.

A major drawback of the Company was that not all of the shareholders had paid their full share. By a resolution of February 8, 1675, the capital of those shareholders who had not paid in full was ordered to be forfeited to the Company. This resolution was re-confirmed by a royal order of March 3, 1680 which further sought to improve the finances of the Company by 'inviting' all Danish Government employees who earned more than 300 rigsdalers a year to invest ten percent of their salary in shares. Compulsion in this invitation was evident in the condition laid down that, if they did not pay in the required amount within four to six weeks, the money would be deducted from their salaries. In addition, it was required that all owners of carriages whose shares did not amount to 500 slettedalers must make a once-for-all investment of 60 rigsdalers. § The administration of the slave-trade was re-organized by the appointment of a committee of four, headed by the Danish Councilor of War, Admiralty and Commerce, to take charge of supplying the Guinea forts with men and munitions and of equipping slave ships to operate between Guinea and the West Indies. [14]

These measures proved unsuccessful to stimulate the finances of the Company and thus further action was taken. In 1685 the Brandenburg African Company was allowed to establish a trading station in St. Thomas to dispose of its slave cargoes acquired through the Brandenburg slave factory at Cape Three Points in Africa. The Brandenburgers were authorized to operate the station for as long as thirty years since to the Danes the concession was a business undertaking. The Brandenburg African Company was to pay the Danish West India Company, in addition to weighing fees, five percent in kind of all produce exported, and one percent and two percent duty on all slaves imported and re-exported respectively. In lieu of these payments, in 1692 the Brandenburg African Company was required to pay an annual rental of 3,000 rigsdalers, increased to 4,000 rigsdalers in 1695. By the agreement of 1685, also, the Brandenburgers could cultivate a plantation large enough to employ 200 slaves. Because of the poll tax on slaves, this further concession promised to return a substantial revenue to the Company. [15]

Further transfer of the Company's control for business reasons took place in 1689 when the Danish West India Company leased its Guinea factories to Nikolaj Jansen Arf, one of the foremost ship-owners in Copenhagen. The lease was for eight years, and Arf was to pay the Company a 'recognition' of two percent of the value of all slaves transported to the West Indies. [16] Then in 1690, the Company leased St. Thomas itself to Jorgen Thormohlen, a private merchant of Bergen. The contract between the Company and Thormohlen was signed on February 13, 1690, but the transfer of authority did not take place until February 7, 1691.

Under the contract with Thormohlen, St. Thomas and the surrounding islands were leased for ten years, but the Company reserved the right to resume trade with the colony at the end of three years. At that time also Thormohlen might terminate the lease if he did not care to continue it. Thormohlen was to take charge of all the Company's properties including the fort, plantations, negroes and magazines and he was to return them in the same condition on the termination of his lease. He was permitted the same trading privileges to which the Company itself had been entitled and it was agreed that if he colonized any of the surrounding islands, the Company would have the right to purchase them from him. The annual rental to be paid by Thormohlen for St. Thomas was 4,630 slettedalers with which the Company hoped to satisfy the shareholders. Of great importance was the condition that failure to make punctual payment of the rental would invalidate the contract.[17]

The experiment in proprietorship was doomed to failure due partly to mismanagement, partly to the opposition of staunch supporters of the Company, and partly to conditions inherent in the 1690 contract. Francois de Lavigne who succeeded Johan Lorentz as governor was quite untrained for the business of administering a distant colony at a difficult time in its history. He made a poor start when he tried to implement schemes to raise revenues. One of his main duties was the collection of the Brandenburger rental which, by the time of Thormohlen's proprietorship, had fallen into arrears. Lacking success with his amiable approach, De Lavigne then sought to get the rent by seizing Brandenburger goods to the value of 9,320 rigsdalers. Both actions worked to his discredit. Johan Lorentz and the pro-Company faction in St. Thomas viewed his initial friendship with the Brandenburg director-general in the island with suspicion. They, therefore, witheld their cooperation from him. Later, his seizure of the Brandenburger possessions was regarded as contrary to the wishes of the Danish king who wanted mutual friendship and confidence to exist between Danes and Brandenburgers in St. Thomas.

Meanwhile Thormohlen was having problems of his own in Denmark stemming from his two proposals to obtain financial assistance to administer St. Thomas. The first one was to get the colonists to share in bearing the burden of defense, and the second was to raise the duties on exports from St. Thomas from five to six percent. Both schemes were rejected by the directors of the Company on the grounds that any increase in taxation was contrary to the terms of the lease, and that planters would be driven away from the island.

While Thormohlen was having difficulties in raising extra revenue, he found that he had inherited the financial problems of the Company.

One of these pertained to a seizure of 16,000 rigsdalers worth of sugar which Lorentz, as governor, had made from the Brandenburgers in payment of rents due. Thormohlen was requested in 1692 to make restitution and the financial impasse made him quite unable to pay his own rental. When in March, 1694, he filed a suit for damages against the Company, the directors promptly resumed control and named Johan Lorentz as their governor of St. Thomas. Their action was soon after approved by the Danish king. On Lorentz's arrival in St. Thomas, Thormohlen's proprietorship over the island came to an end.

Transfer of the Virgin Islands to the Danish Crown

The last years of the seventeenth century witnessed a rejuvenation of Company interest in West Indian affairs. St. Thomas was reacquired from Thormohlen in 1694; the treaty with the Brandenburgers was allowed to lapse after 1695, even though the Germans were allowed to remain; and, in 1697, the Company did not renew Arf's lease of its Guinea factory. Reports made by Lorentz describing the gains obtained from the slave trade by the Brandenburgers in St. Thomas aroused the enthusiasm of the directors. Consequently, they made preparations for the resumption of the slave trade in earnest.

A new charter, issued by the king to the Company in 1697, reflected the renewed interest. While retaining the essential provisions of the Charter of 1671, the new charter underscored the Company's intention to engage in the Guinea trade. Charter status was given to the Company's possession of Fort Christiansborg in Guinea and all other slave forts and lands the Company might acquire there in the future.

At the same time, the directorate of the Company was reformed in order to secure closer cooperation of the participants. The directorate continued to have six members, with the possibility of an increase should the need arise. All members were to be elected by the shareholders though one-third of the directorate were to be ministers or servants of the Crown; the remaining two-thirds were to be elected from among the shareholders who were reputable merchants. The qualification of those who sought to become directors was reduced from a 2,000 slettedaler to a 1,000 rigsdaler investment in the Company, which constituted a reduction of one-fourth. Of significance, also, was the new power given to the Company to enter into financial negotiations with people outside the Company to obtain capital for undertaking trading ventures.[18]

During the first half of the eighteenth century, the Company's possessions in the Virgin Islands expánded; St. John was occupied and St. Croix purchased, and settlement and cultivation were commenced in both. In St. Thomas, agriculture was not very productive for long, but there was increasing emphasis on trade. In St. John, agriculture was brought to a standstill by a serious slave rebellion in 1733, and though it took some years for the island to recover, production was restored to its previous state by 1739. In St. Croix, after a slow start, agricultural production boomed from the 1740's onward.

The bright economic standing of the Virgin Islands was accomplished by a growing population whose energy in productive enterprise was matched by its increasing ability to articulate its grievances. Agitation had resulted in an increase in the political power of the colonists that was more in keeping with their economic power. With increased prosperity, a major source of colonists' dissatisfaction was the regulations with which the Company restricted their freedom to trade. This resulted in the above-mentioned crisis of 1747 which ended in success for the colonists.

The crisis of 1747 high-lighted the tensions which existed between the directors on the one hand and the colonists on the other. The participation of the colonists in the control of colonial affairs brought much grief to the Company, and proved to be one of the chief causes for its dissolution. Further signs of increasing independence and dissatisfaction by the colonists with centralized control became evident again in 1747. In keeping with the rapid economic growth of St. Croix, the colonists demanded and the Company conceded, a governmental system for St. Croix separate from that of St. Thomas and St. John.[19]

The early 1750's was a period of increased prosperity for the Company as seen in the almost doubling of receipts from customs duties. Also, the number of ships sent out by the Company to Guinea and the West Indies increased from three or four in 1747 to thirteen in 1750-1751.[20] Despite this prosperity, the end of the Company's monopoly was fast approaching. As a planting venture, the Company had not achieved much success and its ownership and operation of plantations were not to its credit. For instance, its plantations in St. Thomas made increasingly disappointing returns: in 1746 one had to be sold and, while the other was kept, it showed an annual deficit between 1749 and 1754. As a trading venture the Company was experiencing a boom in the early 1750's though, at the same time, it suffered from a number of important maritime losses. Between 1751 and 1752, three of the Company's ships were lost at sea followed by the disastrous slave mutiny on board the 'Patientia' in 1753. In addition to these losses, the Company had a debt of some 1,000,000 rigsdalers. Its financial position was very insecure and doubts were raised as to whether it should continue to operate.

The idea had been expressed in a general assembly of the shareholders as early as 1746 that the king should take over the shares of his subjects and assume entire control over the Virgin Islands. This decision, however, was rejected by the members of the Board of Trade. The question was again raised in 1754 an immediate cause being the losses, estimated at about 20,000 rixdalers, experienced by the 'Patientia'. Pressures from the colonists themselves, however, were largely responsible. Even before the news of the 'Patientia' mutiny reached Copenhagen, the burgher council of St. Croix had presented an urgent petition to Frederik V for the colonists of St. Croix to be brought under the immediate sovereignty of the king. The colonists considered that such an act would be an 'inestimable act of grace and benefaction' from which they anticipated considerable benefits.

In a proposal to the king, dated July 24, 1754, the directors and chief shareholders set forth the various drawbacks to the prosperity of the Company, and recommended its dissolution. By this time, the membership of the Board of Trade had changed, and the members were now more willing to consider proposals for dissolution. In view of the decision of the directorate of the Company, the Board of Trade decided in favor of the plan of dissolution and showed how it might be effected. On the recommendation of the directors and chief shareholders, the general assembly of shareholders accepted the offer of the king to take over, at par value, the 1,250 shares of the Company, and to assume its obligations.[21]

Conclusion

The Danish West India Company had directed colonial affairs since 1672 when it colonized St. Thomas. It had not only succeeded in extending its territorial sovereignty to include St. John and St. Croix, but it had managed to hold the islands against rival claimants. The rule by the Company was not without flexibility in its responses to the wishes of the colonists. Thus it allowed the colonists at times to indicate their choice of governors and to secure representation through burgher councils. It also entertained colonial delegates to Copenhagen and often granted their wishes. Its failing was that of any joint-stock company dedicated to the production of dividends for its shreholders.

The colony of the Virgin Islands was seen as a profit-making enterprise whose resources must be tapped for the benefit of the shareholders. Trade was consequently channelled within narrow restrictions thereby running counter to the aspirations of colonists who saw prosperity in terms of free trade. Restrictions caused irritation and conflict of interest leading the colonists to agitate for a greater measure of local autonomy and Crown control. The surrender of the Company to the demands of the colonists was a tacit acknowledgement that it was incapable of sustaining a conflict with an economically more powerful adversary.

Other aspects of the transfer must be recognized. The Company had been entrusted by the king with control over the islands which it settled. Therefore, in transferring its control over the Virgin Islands to the king, the Company was taking the legally appropriate step. The transfer of colonial authority from the Company to the Crown was followed by significant changes in the system of trade. Henceforth, also, important changes were made in the system by which the islands were governed.

[1] J. A. Williamson, *The Caribbee Islands under the Proprietary Patents.* (London, Oxford University Press, 1926).
*A Joint Stock Company is an organization consisting of a number of shareholders organized to conduct a business for profit.
[2] S. L. Mims, *Colbert's West India Policy.* (New Haven, 1912). Even Britain resorted to such Companies outside the West Indies as discussed in W. R. Scott, *Joint Stock Companies to 1720.* (Cambridge, 1910-1912; 3 Volumes).
[3] Waldemar Westergaard, *The Danish West Indies Under Company Rule* (1671-1754). (New York, The Macmillan Company, 1917) pp. 34-35.
[4] For a Copy of the Charter of 1671 of the Danish West India Company, see Westergaard, op. cit., pp. 294-298.
†A factor is a person who acts as an agent for another in the transaction of business, usually for a commision.
[5] For examples of regulations passed see, Governors of St. Thomas. Orders issued for Observance by Inhabitants, 1672-1726. (The Bancroft Collection at Berkeley)
[6] Janus Fredrik Krarup, 'Jorgen Iversen (Dyppel) Vestindisk Compagnies forste Gouverneur paa St. Thomas.' (*Personalhistorisk Tidsskrift*, 11R. 6B, 1891) pp. 23-45.

[7]   Westergaard, op. cit., pp. 66-68.

[8]   Janus Fredrik Krarup, 'Gabriel Milan og Somme af Hans Samtid.' (*Personal-historisk Tidsskrift*, 3R. 2B, 1893) pp. 102-130, and 3R. 3B, 1894) pp. 1-51.

[9]   J. O. Bro-Jorgensen, *Dansk Vestindien Indtil 1755: Kolonisation og Kompag-nistyre.* (Fremad, Denmark, 1966) p. 213.

[10]   For a list of governors of the Virgin Islands, see Kay Larsen, *Guvernorer, Residenter, Kommandanter og Chefer. Samt enkelte Andre Fremtraedende Personer i de Tidligere danske tropekolonier.* (Kobenhavn, Arthur Jensens Forlag, 1940) pp. 33-34.

[11]   Westergaard, op. cit., p. 185.

[12]   Ibid., pp. 214-215.

[13]   Georg Host, *Efterretninger om den Sanct Thomas og dens Gouverneurer, optegnede der paa Landet fra 1769 indtil 1776.* (Kjobenhavn, 1791) p. 139.

‡After 1674 the Company became known as the Danish West India and Guinea Company.

§Note for this and later reference: a rigsdaler = $1.10 U.S. = 96 skilling; a slettedaler = 64 skilling.

[14]   Georg Norregard, *Danish Settlements in West Africa* 1658-1850. (Boston University Press, 1966) p. 51.

[15]   Westergaard, op. cit., pp. 71-94.

[16]   Norregard op. cit., pp. 95-104.

[17]   The history of St. Thomas under Thormohlen is fully discussed in Westergaard, op. cit., pp. 79-94.

[18]   For a Copy of the Charter of 1697 of the West India and Guinea Company, see Westergaard, op. cit., pp. 299-302.

[19]   Host, op. cit., p. 136.

[20]   During the same periods the *total* number of ships from the West Indies and Guinea to Copenhagen declined from 30 to 24, P. P. Sveistrup and R. Willerslev, *Den Danske Sukkerhandels og Sukkerproduktions Historie.* (Kobenhavn, 1945) Table 5.

[21]   Edvard Holm, *Danmarks-Norges Historie, 1720-1814.* (Kobenhavn, 1897) Vol.3, pp. 164-239.

Chapter 5

Plantation Agriculture During Slavery

The early Danes came to the West Indies to trade and after a colony was established the interest in trade continued. However, a primary reason for establishing permanent settlements in the West Indies was to develop plantation agriculture. The intention was that the proceeds from agriculture would supplement the supplies obtained from trade. This aim was both explicit and implicit in the provisions of the Charter of the Danish West India Company of 1671.

The Charter of 1671 not only gave the Company a monopoly of trade with the West Indies, but it also permitted the acquisition and settlement of St. Thomas and other neighboring islands which were suitable for plantation agriculture. By reason of its central position, St. Thomas was strategically located to engage in trade with other West Indian islands, but the quality of its soils for agricultural purposes undoubtedly appealed to the colonizers. The occupation of St. John in 1718, and the purchase of St. Croix in 1733, were influenced more by the potentials which they possessed for cultivation than by the need to use them as trading entrepots.

Increase in Plantation Population

The development of the Danish West Indies in plantation agriculture was due less to the settlers brought out from Denmark than to those Europeans who already had experience in West Indian agriculture. The recruits who accompanied Governor Iversen in 1671 were chiefly laborers who possessed neither the capital nor the managerial ability to establish plantations. That the Company continued to recruit and send out to St. Thomas people of limited education and low character was of great concern to Governor Iversen. It was clear that the difficult pioneering period through which the Danes passed in the 1670's was due partly to this type of people. It must have been evident to all concerned that, if St. Thomas was to be developed, people with technical knowledge and regular work habits were clearly required. There was little hope of securing skilled people from Denmark because of rumors of death and disease in St. Thomas. Besides, even though vacant land was available for cultivation, they had little hope of acquiring any.

The colonization of St. Thomas in 1672 coincided with the outbreak of the Third Dutch War between England and France on one side and the Netherlands on the other. However, rather than hampering the colonization of St. Thomas (as did a similar conflict in 1666), the Dutch war promoted it. The Virgin Islands were removed from the main theater of warfare and as such they were comparatively safe from attack. The fear of war and actual wartime destruction in the Lesser Antilles forced many of their settlers to flee to St. Thomas.

The Danes had hardly begun their settlement when colonists of several other nations joined them. They included English and French as well as some Germans and Jews but the largest number was Dutch who exerted considerable influence in St. Thomas. The foreign nationals entered St. Thomas uninvited but were allowed to remain, thereby boosting the number of the colonists which was being rapidly depleted by death. More importantly, they brought their knowledge of plantation agriculture which was of inestimable value to the young colony.

Population grew in peacetime even more than it did during the war years: in 1673 the population of St. Thomas numbered barely 100 white and 100 Negroes; by 1680, it had risen to 156 whites and 175 Negroes; and, by 1688, after a heavier increase, it had doubled to 317 whites and 422 Negroes.[1] There was no war from 1678 to 1689 the interim between the Third Dutch War and the War of the League of Augsburg. Rather than war, it was the policy of accommodation of the Esmits which probably accounts for the heavy influx of population.

The white population engaged in planting totalled 148 in 1688, of whom 66 were Dutch, 31 English, 17 French, and 17 Danes and Norwegians. Additionally, there were four Irish, four Fleming, three Germans, three Swedes, one Scot, one Brazilian and one Portuguese. The same year Adolph Esmit issued a mandate offering an eight-year exemption from taxation to settlers who would come in from other foreign islands. This mandate, together with the War of the League of Augsburg (1689-1697) resulted in an increase in population to 389 whites and 555 Negroes by 1691.[2] Among the new white immigrants were some French Huguenots and more Dutch settlers. War was at this time a dominant factor in population increase and during the War of the Spanish Succession (1702-1713) there was another heavy influx of colonists. By 1715 the white population of St. Thomas had increased to 547 while there were as many as 3,042 slaves. Five years later the numbers of whites and slaves had increased to 565 and 4,187 respectively representing a relatively small increase in peacetime.[3]

When St. John was occupied in 1718, the first inhabitants came entirely from St. Thomas and as a consequence the population was varied in national composition. Of the 20 planters who landed with Governor Bredal on the islands, nine were Danes, five were French Huguenots and nearly all the rest were Dutch. Some were led to emigrate because they had become hopelessly indebted in St. Thomas, while others did not have well-located plantations here. All of them expected to improve their fortunes in St. John to which end they brought 16 Negroes with them. Among the regulations made by Bredal in 1718 was one granting exemption from the payment of taxes for eight years as an incentive for settlers to come in.

The white population of St. John increased unevenly: by 1728 there were 123 whites − an increase of 412.5 percent during the first decade − and five years later they numbered 208, a further increase of just over 68 percent. This decline in the rate of growth is understandable, since St. John's small size limited its capacity to absorb a planting population. The slave group also increased: by 1728 it was 677, and by 1733 it was 1,087, providing another clear indication of the expansion of agriculture.[4]

Given the black to white ratio of 5.2 to 1, it is not surprising that the slaves of St. John staged one of the most destructive rebellions in the West Indies.* Planters who were not killed by the slaves were forced to evacuate the island. For these planters, the acquisition of St. Croix by the Danish West India Company, and the commencement of settlement there in September, 1734, provided a means whereby they could recoup their lost fortunes. Accordingly, many of them seized the opportunity to settle in this island.[5]

Besides the displaced St. John planters and some others from St. Thomas seeking better lands to cultivate, St. Croix was settled by a large number of British some of whom were already on the island when Governor Moth landed there in September, 1734. Others came over from St. Christopher, Nevis, Tortola and Virgin Gorda after war broke out between Britain and Spain in 1739. Two years later there were about 300 British on St. Croix comprising by far the largest population group among the Europeans in the island. As a result, the English language and customs dominated those of the other national groups which made up the population. In addition to the British, a number of Dutch people arrived from St. Eustatius to escape the effects of the war.

As in the case of St. Thomas and St. John, immigration into St. Croix was encouraged by the use of the tax-free incentive to prospective settlers though for St. Croix the period was seven instead of eight years. The value placed on St. Croix as an agricultural island was indicated by the rigid selection of those who should possess estates. Transfer of land to small planters who had less than six slaves was delayed by the directors of the Danish West India Company. Alternately, the proposal to encourage refugee debtors to immigrate to St. Croix was opposed by the local authorities. Experience had taught that sober, industrious settlers could not be expected from Europeans in deprived circumstances. The emphasis on securing settlers with capital and knowledge of plantation agriculture helps to explain why St. Croix made a slow start. With the out-break of the War of Jenkins' Ear (1739-1748) and continuing after it progress was more rapid. The planter population of 207 in 1747 increased to 354 in 1753 while the growth in slave population was proportionally greater, increasing from 1,906 in 1742, to 2,878 in 1745 and to 7,566 in 1754.[6]

Number and Size of Plantations

The progress of plantation agriculture in the Virgin Islands tended to keep pace with the increase in the population. Nevertheless, much depended on the quality of the settlers and the leadership which they had. The poor quality of the settlers on St. Thomas retarded progress during the first decade of colonization. Thereafter, despite the increased population, progress in planting was impeded by political disorder during the governments of Nicolaj and Adolph Esmit and Gabriel Milan. Beginning with the quiet administration of Christoffer Heins and continuing under Johan Lorentz, progress was more rapid.

A census taken in 1688 showed that there were 90 surveyed plantations in St. Thomas, and by 1691 the number had increased to 101. Only 28 of these had been under cultivation for eight years or more, while the average time each had been cultivated was just about five years. The first two decades of the eighteenth century were the most progressive for St. Thomas agriculture and by 1715 the number of plantations had risen to 160, a rapid development compared with the slow start at the beginning of colonization. After 1715, however, the number of plantations increased very slowly; in 1720 there were 164 while in 1725 when the peak was reached, there were 177.

Compared with St. Thomas, plantation agriculture in St. John developed rapidly after its settlement and by 1721 39 planters had received deeds to land. Early in 1726 Governor Moth informed the directors of the Company that 'St. John is now entirely settled, [so] that there is no more land left to give away except at the Fort, and the Company's plantation, which is still lying idle, as it is not yet surveyed . . . There are already about 20 sugar works built, and others in process of building.'[7] Moth undoubtedly misrepresented the situation since there was still land for further distribution; in 1728 there were 87 plantations and five years later there were 109. Noteworthy is the fact that many of the planters in St. Thomas who acquired plantations in St. John managed them through hired overseers while they continued to reside in St. Thomas.

Although it was on a much larger scale, St. Croix's agriculture developed much like that of St. Thomas. There was a comparatively slow start because land was granted to selected colonists but development was more rapid following the out-break of war in 1739. According to the first census, there were as many as 264 plantations in the island in 1742 by which time almost all of the land had been taken up. Thereafter, the number of plantations remained practically stationary. The boom in agriculture in St. Croix in the 1740's was shown by the planters' willingness and ability to incur debts for the purchase of slaves and equipment.

The size of plantations varied widely; on an average, those in St. Thomas were the smallest while those on St. Croix were the largest. By the time St. John and St. Croix were settled, the colonists were able to benefit from their experiences in St. Thomas and elsewhere. They had learned that maximum benefit could be derived from plantations of large size, especially in the production of sugar which required an

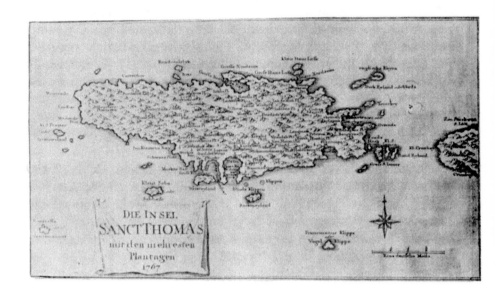

Above: ST. THOMAS
Below: ST. CROIX

expensive processing plant. Since the plantation and factory were generally single units of ownership and production, costs were minimized by spreading the fixed investment in the sugar works over a relatively large acreage. The average size of a sugar plantation in St. Thomas was between sixty and seventy acres while in St. John, the average sugar plantation was about a third as large again, or between eighty and ninety acres.[8] The numerous land disputes which arose between planters were indicative of the haphazard way in which lands in both St. Thomas and St. John had been distributed without proper prior surveys.

St. Croix benefited¹ from the experience of St. Thomas and St. John as shown in the systematic way the land was divided prior to distribution. The entire island was first divided into nine Quarters—East End Quarter A, East End Quarter B, The Company's Quarter, Queen's Quarter, King's Quarter, Prince's Quarter, West End Quarter, North Side Quarter A, and North Side Quarter B. Each Quarter was then sub-divided into a number of almost uniform plantations, rectangular in shape where possible. A normal plantation was 2,000 feet wide and 3,000 feet deep, with a area of 6,000,000 square feet, or approximately 150 acres. There were a number of smaller plantations which brought the average size of all plantations to about 120 acres.[9]

Many planters in St. Croix became the owners of more than one plantation and where these were adjacent to each other, they were referred to as a double-plantation, a triple-plantation, etc. 'La Grange' and 'La Grande Princesse,' for example, were equal in size to several normal plantations. Another unique feature of plantation ownership in St. Croix was that initially many owners did not cultivate their lands, but kept them for speculative purposes. Land values tended to rise with the prices of plantation produce so that speculators made substantial profits by selling their land. Even before such sale, the disposal of the timber found on the plantations often enabled them to recover their own purchasing costs. The problem of speculative buying became so acute that in 1756 an order was passed requiring that all plantations should be cultivated within a specified time. Defaulters could have their plantations confiscated by the colonial government.

Plantation agriculture was not confined to private individuals only for the Danish West India Company itself was a participant. In St. Thomas the Company operated four plantations: 'Sugar Plantation' on the southeast of Great Northside Bay, later renamed Magens Bay; 'New Quarter Plantation' on or near the present site of New Herrnhut;

'Mosquito Bay Plantation' on what is now Lindbergh Bay; and 'Krum Bay Plantation.' The last two plantations proved of so little value that they were sold in 1726.[10] In St. John the Company had only one plantation located at Coral Bay near the fort, while in St. Croix it possessed 'La Grange' and 'La Grande Princesse.' Several other plantations in St. Croix were held by the Company's directors and shareholders in a private capacity.

The greater emphasis by the Company on plantation agriculture in St. Croix stemmed from its efforts to recoup financial losses entailed by its abandonment of its slave trade monopoly in 1735. From plantation ownership also the Company's ships might be assured of full return cargoes and its refineries in Denmark of raw sugar. Besides, the plantations were intended to set an example to other planters in the methods and skills of production.

Land in St. Thomas was granted to the Brandenburgers in 1685 in the hope that the example set by the Brandenburgers in plantation enterprise would put new life into the colony. Moreover, receipts from poll taxes, weighing fees, and import and export duties levied on the Brandenburgers would substantially increase the Company's finances. The Brandenburgers, whose main interest was the slave trade, did not regard the operation of a plantation as obligatory. Failure to act in this direction helped to alienate Danish opinion from their continuation in trade in St. Thomas.

Crop Distribution: The Supremacy of Sugar

By the time St. Thomas was settled, the sugar industry was firmly established in the British and French colonies in the Lesser Antilles, and sugarcane cuttings were introduced into the island from Tortola by Governor Iversen in 1672. At first sugar was not the major industry though later decades were to see it dominate the economy of the Virgin Islands. Thus of the 101 plantations under cultivation in St. Thomas in 1691, only five were devoted to the cultivation of sugarcane.

Despite the high demand for sugar in Europe, sugar production in St. Thomas did not at first prosper due to shortage of capital, of technical knowledge, and of adequate labor among the early colonists. As a result, the early concentration focused on tobacco and cotton production since these crops could be grown on small plots by few people at little cost. Tobacco cultivation soon became insignificant, but of the 101 plantations in operation in 1691 as many as 87 were devoted primarily to cotton. Once cotton was planted on a particular plot there was little incentive to change to sugarcane unless circumstances warranted it or made it possible.

Unlike St. Thomas, sugarcane cultivation was the primary occupation of the colonists of St. John almost from the beginning. The first planters who went to St. John from St. Thomas were undoubtedly inclined to engage in sugarcane cultivation because of the greater profitability of this crop and the suitability of the soil there.

Land utilization was maximized in St. Croix by devoting the more fertile and well-watered lands to sugarcane, and the less fertile and more arid lands to cotton. In general, the western section of the island was placed under sugarcane cultivation and the eastern section under cotton. Of the 264 plantations recorded in 1742, 120 were listed as sugarcane plantations and 122 as cotton plantations.[11] The emphasis on cotton production in some areas was reflected in the names of places such as 'Cotton Grove,' 'Cotton Valley,' and 'Cotton Garden.'

Generally more than one crop was grown on a plantation, though greater emphasis might be placed on one than on others. Thus, a portion of a sugarcane plantation might be given to cotton, and a portion of a cotton plantation might be given to sugarcane. In addition, other crops of commercial importance, such as tobacco and indigo, might be grown. A section of each plantation, also, was generally set aside for the production of provisions such as cassava and corn for slaves. Another would be used as grassland to maintain the plantation livestock including cattle, donkeys and mules variously used as mill and cart animals and to supply manure to fertilize the fields. A portion of the plantation was reserved as woodlands, where the plantation supply of fuel and lumber could be obtained. This was particularly so in St. Croix, where there was a more abundant supply of timber. Plantations were laid out to achieve the best use of the topography, soils, roadways and sugar-mills.

The movement towards monoculture was pronounced, especially in St. Croix where lands devoted to subsidiary crops, to pasture, and to woodlands, tended to give way to the production of one or other of the staples, sugarcane or cotton. Even cotton lands were sometimes converted to cane lands as sugar became the more profitable commodity. Eventually, sugarcane production became the most important agricultural undertaking in the Virgin Islands.

Though not reflected in the number of plantations the expenses involved in sugar production far outpaced that of cotton. Compared with cotton sugar production required a large capital outlay to establish factories and to purchase the necessary machinery, tools, utensils, livestock and workers. Large quantities of sugarcane were necessary to make the capital equipment economical, and cane growing, in turn, called for large gangs of slaves. Sugar production thus differed markedly from cotton growing in the acreage, capital equipment, and labor force on the plantations. Moreover, the labor in the cane fields was more arduous, while in the sugar factory it called for special skills and techniques.

A sugar plantation was too large to be cultivated entirely as a single unit and so it was divided into a number of fields. Ranging from eight to ten acres, these fields were separated by paths and roads to facilitate transport and to serve as fire guards. Fruit trees were usually planted along these paths to produce additional food supplies, and cattle fodder was obtained here.

Planters faced hazards such as droughts which stunted plant growth, occasional heavy rains which weakened the sugar content of canes, and attacks from insect pests and rats. Because of these hazards new varieties of sugarcane — Otaheite and Bourbon — were introduced from the East in the later years of the eighteenth century, which were more resistant to adverse weather and pests and yielded more sugar. Other vicissitudes included storms and hurricanes which occasionally levelled whole fields and destroyed buildings, livestock and slaves. Moreover, constant watch had to be kept to ensure that fires, either deliberate or accidental, did not destroy the sugarcane fields.

Despite the adverse conditions, the production of agricultural staples in the Virgin Islands was promoted by a number of favorable factors including financial assistance and the availability of ready markets. In the initial stages, capital for investment and expansion was supplied by the Danish West India Company and by the Dutch from St. Eustatius who were willing to encourage cultivation in order to develop their own trade. The advantageous market which the Dutch provided for the Danish colonial products was one reason why the colonists objected strenuously to the monopolistic trading restrictions adopted by the Danish West India Company. But even while they objected, they were assured of a guaranteed market for their produce in Denmark.

Conditions became even more favorable for sugarcane planters when the Company was permitted to refine its Virgin Islands muscovado in Denmark beginning in September, 1729. At first it was unable to handle all of the sugar so that by an edict of July, 1733, the Danish king required all privately owned refineries to use only the raw sugar which came from the Virgin Islands as long as supplies permitted thereby assuring the Company of a ready market for its colonial sugar. In order to prevent evasion, private refineries had to pay an import duty of 10 skillings for every 100 pounds of foreign sugar they imported. Moreover, the private refineries were instructed to pay a negotiated price for the Company's sugar or pay the Amsterdam or world price; they could not arbitrarily reduce the buying price. Finally, royal permission was given in December, 1733 for the Company to buy either or both of the private refineries in Denmark owned by the Weyse and Pelt families. By 1737, the Company held a virtual monopoly of the refining business in Denmark and absorbed most of its own sugar.[12]

The Prosperity and Decline of Agriculture in the Virgin Islands

Plantation agriculture did not run a lengthy course in the Virgin Islands except in the case of St. Croix. St. Thomas seemed to have reached peak production in 1725, by which time St. John had come into prominence, after which there was continuous decline. Perhaps this can be illustrated by reference to the Company's plantations, two of which were sold in 1726 after their failure to yield profits. During the nine years, 1726 to 1734, the Company's 'Sugar Plantation' yielded only meager profits, and the 'New Quarter Plantation' made no profit for four years, and for three years suffered actual loss. During the period 1735 to 1745, the income from the 'Sugar Plantation' fell to less than half of what it had been during the previous ten years, and from 1749 to 1754, it showed an annual deficit. The 'New Quarter Plantation' produced such disappointing returns that it was sold in 1746.[13]

That the private plantations in St. Thomas probably did not fare any better than the Company's plantations is shown by their reduction in numbers from 177 in 1725 to 154 in 1754. The number of sugar plantations sank from 63 to 38 and cotton plantations from 87 to 70. St. John showed the same tendencies as St. Thomas, although the situation was slightly better. The plantations did not recover from the 1733 slave rebellion until 1739 but from that year to 1754, the sugar plantations declined from 24 to 21 and cotton plantations from 65 to 51. In both St. Thomas and St. John the reduction in the number of plantations can be explained not by consolidation but by abandonment.[14]

Plantation agriculture was not of much importance in St. Thomas and St. John after 1754. Thus, it was reported in 1796 that of the 119 wind-mills and 211 animal-mills in the Virgin Islands, only 4 of the former and 67 of the latter were in St. Thomas and St. John. In terms of yield, St. Thomas and St. John produced 1,300,000 pounds and 850,000 pounds of sugar respectively.[15]

Compared with St. Thomas and St. John, the second half of the eighteenth century was a period of increasing prosperity for St. Croix due partly to the possibilities which the planters had to obtain money. While the Danish West India Company yet had control over the islands, planters obtained loans from it and in 1754 outstanding claims due to the Company amounted to 1,290,000 rigsdalers compared with 136,000 rigsdalers in 1747. This debt was taken over by the Crown when it assumed control but because of its bad financial management planters were forced to look outside Denmark for further financial assistance.

Beginning from 1768-1769 loans were obtained from Holland, the principal Dutch creditors being the banking house of Abraham ter Borch & Zonen. However, on loans obtained from the Dutch, planters had to pay interest as high as six to seven percent, and they had to consign their sugar to the creditors and import supplies from Holland. As a result, the Danish government adopted the policy in 1770 to take over the debt and implemented it in 1786 when the debt was purchased at a reasonable price. At that time the indebtedness of planters amounted to 9.91 million rigsdalers and the purchase led to a reduction in the interest rate to 4.5 percent for their benefit. A debt commission was set up in the islands to handle the collection of repayments.[16]

Though plantations in St. Croix did not increase in number after the 1740's, enhanced prosperity was seen in the increased price of land, in the increasing number and price of slaves, and, to some extent, in the continued importance of exports. At the inception of its settlement, a standard plantation in St. Croix of approximately 150 acres was sold for 500 rigsdalers, or roughly 3.3 rigsdalers an acre. As early as 1754, the price of the same property had more than trebled, selling at 11.8 rigsdalers an acre while by 1786, the cost had gone up to between 160 and 196 rigsdalers an acre.[17]

The slave population in St. Croix numbering 1,906 in 1742, increased to 7,566 in 1754, and to 16,956 in 1766. Though the cost of slaves varied according to conditions such as sex, age, skills, tribal origin and their general conduct, nevertheless, a rise in price was noticeable. Thus while a 'capable' male field slave, that is, one fully mature and industrious, was sold for 200 rigsdalers in 1758 his price had increased to 255 rigsdalers by 1786.[18]

Because of the smuggling, inter-colonial trade and privateering which went on in St. Croix, the exports of the island did not accurately reflect the state of its agriculture. Smuggling, inter-island trade and privateering tended to increase during wartime as did plantation production in response to high wartime prices in Europe. Consequently they were favored by the condition of almost continuous warfare in the West Indies during the second half of the eighteenth century. When Denmark maintained a neutral position during these wars the Virgin Islands escaped attack, and planters were able to expand agricultural production.

Though irregular, the sugar exports of St. Croix increased markedly during the second half of the eighteenth century. Exports in 1755 amounted to only a couple thousand barrels,† but in the 1760's, following the Peace of Paris in 1763, they increased to an average of 21,233 barrels (or 17,411,060 lb.) a year. A smaller annual average of 18,455 barrels (or 15,133,100 lb.) were exported during the decade of the 1770's but in 1774 and 1775 exports totalling 23,749 and 24,672 barrels respectively were produced. During the period of the American War of Independence (1776-1783) an average of 20,472 barrels (or 16,787,040 lb.) of sugar were exported a year, decreasing to an annual average of about 15,157 barrels (or 12,428,740 lb.) between 1788 and 1794.[19]

A decline in peacetime was evident resulting partly from the diversion of American trading enterprise to St. Eustatius after the end of the War of Independence. Of great importance also was the continuous period of drought from which the islands suffered for three years from 1789 to 1791. In addition, peace led to the resumption of normal trading relations between European nations and their West Indian colonies and reduced the volume of foreign colonial produce coming into the Virgin Islands.

With the outbreak of the French Wars in 1793, coinciding with favorable weather conditions in the Virgin Islands, exports again increased. The high prices of sugar during the war tended to sustain production which was unimpaired by the British occupation of the Virgin Islands between 1801 and 1802 and again between 1807 and

1815. Instead, sugar production in St. Croix rose from an annual average of 32.46 million pounds during the first few years of the nineteenth century, to a maximum of 46 million pounds in 1812. At that time the island was clearly among the foremost sugar producers in the West Indies.[20]

After the end of the Napoleonic Wars in 1815, plantation agriculture in the Virgin Islands showed an overall decline. Between 1796 and 1847 the area devoted to sugarcane in St. Thomas, St. John and St. Croix dropped from 2,496 to 1,125, from 1,863 to 843, and from 27,655 to 23,971 acres respectively.[21] By 1850, only 20 plantations in St. Thomas were still producing sugar, the rest of the island being converted into pasture or allowed to run to brush. One estimate of sugar exports from St. Croix shows a steady decline: the average annual export for the ten years 1815 to 1824 was 25.4 million pounds; for the nine years 1825 to 1833, 24.1 million pounds; and for the eight years, 1834 to 1841, 21.4 million pounds.[22]

The French Wars witnessed a decline in the cotton industry of the Virgin Islands. Maximum exports from St. Croix were reached in 1792 when 157,000 pounds were shipped after which the decline was rapid, the average for the decade of the 1790's being only 60,000 pounds. In the nineteenth century Danish West Indian cotton, like that of the rest of the West Indies, suffered from competition with the United States. It was not until American production was disrupted at the outbreak of the Civil War in 1861, that an attempt was made to revive cotton cultivation in the Virgin Islands. Even so, results fell short of the commodity output in the late eighteenth century.

Causes of Agricultural Decline

A variety of factors contributed to the decline of plantation agriculture in the Virgin Islands. From the standpoint of world markets the dominant cause was the decline in prices for plantation produce. This left the high-cost Virgin Islands producers of sugar and cotton unable to compete with the low-cost producers elsewhere. Contributory causes were the heavy debt burden of planters and the general exhaustion of the soil whose fertility the planters did not take any appropriate measures to maintain.[23]

Agricultural methods practiced by planters were inefficient as shown, for instance, by the little use of manure beyond what was provided by the plantation animals. Small effort was made to maintain the natural fertility of soils which was particularly necessary in view of the hilly nature of the islands and the tendency for soils to erode during rainfall. From evidence still existing today it can be seen that very little terracing was done as a means of soil conservation. Besides, planters generally were reluctant to introduce such labor-saving devices as ploughs and harrows where these could be used, reliance being placed on slave labor which was both costly and inefficient.

Milling operations in the production of sugar were wasteful and consequently uneconomic. The most common mills were those driven by wind or animal power but their rollers were only powerful enough to squeeze about 56 percent of the juice out of the sugarcanes thereby making for considerable loss.[24] Steam-mills could extract as much as 70 percent of the juice but they were not introduced until late. The first one was built in 1816 on the Hogensborg plantation in St. Croix, but it performed so poorly that no additions were made until the 1830's. As late as 1845 there were only three steam-mills in St. Croix, though by 1852 as many as 40 were reported.

Another cause for decline was absentee-landlordism, that is, the practice of owners to live away from their plantations leaving the management of their lands to managers or even overseers. The problem was not as serious in St. Thomas and St. John as it was in St. Croix where planters, mainly British, having made their fortune, retired to live abroad. Some managers and attorneys who were neither capable nor honest, sought to maximize incomes by driving slaves hard and by pursuing soil-exhausting practices. In order to force absentee owners to return and reside in the Virgin Islands, a tax was levied from 1817 on all owners who lived more than six months in a foreign country. The tax ranged from four to ten percent of the value of crops, and from five to ten percent of the rental value of houses. However, the law did not produce the desired results since many owners preferred to pay the tax rather than return to live in the islands.

Hurricanes and droughts made their contribution to the decline of agriculture in the Virgin Islands. Four hurricanes in 1772, 1785, 1819 and 1837, were particularly severe causing considerable damage more or less similar on each occasion. In 1772 ships in the harbors were thrown ashore, and throughout the islands, sugarcane and cotton fields were devastated while many sugar works collapsed. Slave houses and many buildings belonging to the whites were destroyed. In 1785 damage estimated at 2.25 million rigsdalers was caused in St. Croix alone. The

D

destruction of the hurricane of 1819 had the long-term effect of convincing many islanders that the future of plantation agriculture was bleak. Finally, the hurricane in 1837, with the usual destruction to fields and buildings, came at a time when plantation agriculture was much depressed and it contributed to the lowering or abandonment of production.

The effects of droughts in the first half of the nineteenth century were particularly severe. According to Heilbuth, a planter of St. Croix, the period was one of 'regular and constantly occurring drought' which aggravated the 'ill-effects of the impoverished system of culture.'[25]

Ever since the Virgin Islands had been taken over by the Danish Crown in 1754, the inhabitants of St. Thomas had increasingly turned their attention towards trade and away from plantation agriculture. When St. Croix was colonized, a number of the most wealthy and productive planters of St. Thomas and St. John had seized the opportunity to transfer their already failing fortunes to St. Croix. The continued attraction of St. Croix as a very productive island, drew enterprising planters away from the two other islands, and served to reinforce the adherence of the colonists in St. Thomas to trade.

The West Indian sugar industry generally suffered from two developments in the early nineteenth century. During the Napoleonic Wars sugar production had expanded in Cuba, Brazil, India, Mauritius, and other parts of the East Indies. In addition, European governments began to experiment with the sugar-beet to meet some of their sugar requirements. The new sugarcane areas had the advantage of more fertile soils and, especially in Asia, of cheaper labor, while beet sugar production had the advantage of subsidies. The extra sugar thrown on the European market lowered the price of the commodity. Because of their high cost of production, the Virgin Islands, like the other older sugar-producing regions in the West Indies, were unable to compete. Sugar was sometimes produced at a loss and many plantations went out of operation.

The Virgin Islands were further adversely affected by policy changes in Denmark. Colonial sugar was dealt a severe blow in 1813 when the Danish government permitted unrestricted importation of both raw and refined sugar. To make matters worse, Denmark lost two of its important re-export markets after the war, namely, Norway and the Baltic States.[26] Under such conditions, the legal restrictions confining the produce of the Virgin Islands to the Danish market were particularly severe. It meant that until they were removed in 1833 the

Virgin Islands legally could not take advantage of more favorable markets.

Conclusion

Drawing on a reputable study of St. Croix in 1841, Augustin Cochin stated that '60 plantations had been abandoned to the state for lack of being able to repay its advances. Heavy mortgages burdened the greater portion of the other plantations.' The Journal 'Faederlandet' was also used to show the low state of the plantations in St. Croix. It affirmed that 'of 151 plantations, 76 belonged to non-residents of the colony, that 16 had reverted to the state, and that 60 had fallen into the hands of creditors.'[27]

Both before and after the beginning of the nineteenth century a large number of plantations in the Virgin Islands went out of agricultural production. Cotton cultivation practically ceased and sugar production dropped considerably. However, a relatively large amount of sugar was still being produced in St. Croix, which remained predominantly agricultural. St. Thomas contined to produce a small amount of sugar, but it had diversified its economy by developing as an important trade entrepot. The situation in the Virgin Islands by 1848 was such that while agriculture was declining trade was expanding.

[1] Waldemar Westergaard, *The Danish West Indies Under Company Rule (1671-1754).* New York, The Macmillan Company, 1917) pp. 41 and 121-122.
[2] Ibid., p. 122.
[3] Ibid., p. 126.
[4] Ibid., p. 130.
[5] Waldemar Westergaard, 'A St. Croix Map of 1766: with a Note on its Significance in West Indian Plantation Economy.' (*The Journal of Negro History*, Vol.XXIII, No.2, April, 1938) pp. 216-217.
*Chapter 10 below discusses the causes and consequences of the 1733-24 slave rebellion in St. John.
[6] Westergaard, *The Danish West Indies Under Company Rule*, pp. 222 and 225.
[7] Quoted in Ibid., p. 130.
[8] P. P. Sveistrup, *Bidrag til de Tidligere Dansk-Vestindiske oers Okonomiske Historie. Med Saerligh Henblik paa Sukkerproduktion og Sukkerhandel.* (Kobenhavn, Nielsen & Lydiches Bogrrykkeri, 1942) p. 23.
[9] Westergaard, *A St. Croix Map of 1766*, pp. 224-228.
[10] Westergaard, *The Danish West Indies Under Company Rule*, pp. 130-131.
[11] Ibid., p. 319.

[12] Sveistrup, op. cit., p. 11.

[13] Westergaard, *The Danish West Indies Under Company Rule*, p. 219.

[14] Ibid., pp. 318-319.

[15] Peter Lotharius Oxholm, *De danske vestindiske oers Tilstand i Henseende til Population, Cultur og Finance-Forfatning i Anledning af nogle Breve fra St. Croix* ... (Kjobenhavn, 1797) 'Statistisk Tabelle'; Westergaard,*The Danish West Indies Under Company Rule*, p. 255.

[16] Jens Vibaek, *Dansk Vestindien 1755-1848: Vestindiens Storhedstid.* (Fremad, Denmark, 1966) pp. 55-62.

[17] Ibid., pp. 98-100.

[18] Ibid., p. 107.

†A barrel was equal to 820 pounds.

[19] P. P. Sveistrup and R. Willerslev, *Den Danske Sukkerhandels og Sukkerproduktions Historie.* (Kobenhavn, 1945) pp. 52 and 54.

[20] Sveistrup, op. cit., p. 72; Eric Williams, *From Columbus to Castro: The History of the Caribbean 1492-1969.* (Andre Deutsch, 1970) p. 366.

[21] Holger Utke Ramsing, 'Naeringsveje; Landbrug og Havebrug.' In *Foreningen Danske Samvirke, de Dansk Atlanterhavoer.* (Copenhagen, 1908) Vol. 4, p. 795.

[22] Sveistrup, op. cit., p. 103.

[23] Lowell Joseph Ragatz, *The Fall of the Planter Class in the British Caribbean, 1763-1833: A Study in Social and Economic History.* (New York, The Century Co., 1928).

[24] For a first-hand account of the manufacture of sugar, see Peter Lotharius Oxholm, *De danske vestindiske oers Tilstand i Henseende til Population, Cultur og Finance-Forfatning i Anledning af nogle Breve fra St. Croix* ... (Kjobenhavn, 1797).

[25] E. Heilbuth, *Denmark und St. Croix in their Mutual Relations.* (Buffalo: Lee & Thorp's Press, 1845) p. 18.

[26] Steffen Lindvald, *Sukker & Rom.* (Kobenhavn, 1967) p. 71.

[27] Augustin Cochin, *The Results of Emancipation.* (Boston, Walker, Wise and Company, 1863) p. 390.

Chapter 6

The Trade Emporium until 1850

Seen in the particular context of European settlements in the West Indies, the basis of colonization was trade, and trade was the essence of colonization. Colonies were founded to supply essential and sometimes luxury goods which could not be produced in Europe, and to provide a market for the manufactures of the mother-country. On the other hand, the conditions of trade determined the well-being of colonies; unless colonists could be provided with the commodities they needed, and unless they could find somewhere to dispose of the goods they produced, they could not prosper. The value of trade both to Europeans and to the colonists explains, as far as the Virgin Islands were concerned, why Denmark adopted regulations confining colonial trade to Denmark, and why colonists, on the other hand, applied almost constant pressure to have trade freed from restrictions.

According to prevailing mercantilist theory, colonies were established for the benefit of the mother-country and when the Virgin Islands were settled, the principle was extended to them. In the application of mercantilism a double monopoly was established over colonial trade. By the terms of its Charter of 1671, the Danish West India Company was authorized to trade with the colonies which it established in the West Indies; all other traders were debarred, the king guaranteeing not to issue any passports or authorizations to private traders. In addition, colonial trade was confined to Denmark so that the manufactures of the mother-country could be exchanged for the tropical staples of the islands.

From the beginning, however, the concept of mercantilism was broadly interpreted: the Virgin Islands were regarded not only as a plantation colony, but also as an entrepot or trading center. Manufactures from Denmark could be exchanged for such products of the surrounding foreign colonies as sugar, cotton, tobacco, indigo, coffee and dyewoods. All colonial commodities, whether Danish or foreign, had to be carried directly to Denmark and European manufactures obtained from Denmark could be marketed in the Virgin Islands or re-exported from them to foreign colonies. In short, the Virgin Islands were seen as Danish trading outposts in the Atlantic.

Whenever colonial trade was confined or restricted to one market, it meant that the condition of that market would determine the welfare of the colonies concerned. Alternatively, where trade was free, advantage could be taken by the colonies of the best markets. The commercial history of the Virgin Islands was a struggle by colonists to free themselves from the restrictions on their trade. This constant pressure, and the willingness of the Company, or of the Crown when it took over in 1754, to give way to that pressure, or its inability to withstand that pressure, explain the irregular movement towards free trade.

The Danish West India Company's Trade Regulations

The low economic status of the Company during the first two decades led to the first changes in commercial policy. Between 1671 and 1680 only about six ships in all engaged in the West Indian trade. The first action taken was not a relaxation of the exclusive trade principle, but one designed to give financial rewards to the members of the Company. By a mandate issued on February 22, 1675, the Company permitted its own shareholders to trade with St. Thomas on their own account. The ten percent duty they were required to pay on all the goods they imported into the island was evidently an attempt also to secure government revenue for internal development and expansion. This reason underlay two further concessions: in 1674 the Company had been given control over the Guinea slave trade, and its members were now permitted to import slaves into St. Thomas on payment of a 'recognition' or duty of one slave for every fifty imported; and in addition, each captain, under a penalty of 20 rigsdalers, had to bring to St. Thomas two capable Danish workingmen for whom the Company would pay 10 rigsdalers each.

When these measures failed, permission was granted in 1685 to the

Brandenburg African Company to establish a trading factory in St. Thomas. Subsequently, the Guinea slave factories were leased to Nikolaj Jansen Arf, and St. Thomas itself was leased to Jorgen Thormohlen. In each case it was hoped that the fortune of the colony would revive under the stimuli given by these enterprises. These actions constituted not only a partial transfer of sovereignty but also a negation of the exclusive trade policy hitherto maintained by the Company.

Prosperity first came to St. Thomas because of favorable wartime conditions and the energy of devoted Company governors such as Johan Lorentz and Claus Hansen. Already in the mid-1690's, the Company had re-acquired its interests in Africa and St. Thomas from the lessees, and the Brandenburgers were made to suffer a lingering death until their agreement with the Company expired in 1715.

The outbreak of the War of the Spanish Succession and its aftermath resulted in unprecedented prosperity for St. Thomas. Planters were encouraged by the profits of clandestine trade to attack the Company's trade restrictions. Since it was useless to protest locally, the planters organized delegations which they sent to Copenhagen in 1706-1707 and again in 1715-1716. Success was achieved in 1707 when the Company's directors granted to the inhabitants of St. Thomas the right to export West Indian goods to any place in Europe outside of the Danish dominions. In return they had to assist the Company in securing full return cargoes for its vessels, and they were forbidden to export elsewhere while any of the Company's ships was in the harbor of St. Thomas.[1]

Further concessions were granted in 1716 when the import as well as the export trade with non-Danish dominions was thrown open to the inhabitants of St. Thomas. The only requirement was an ad valorem duty of six percent on exports and five percent on imports. Again the planters were expected to assist the Company in securing full return cargoes for its ships, though they could sell at the current market rates rather than suffer a discount of one-sixth of the value of the goods which the directors had previously insisted on.[2]

Planters were not satisfied by the concessions already won and conscious of their growing numbers and importance, they pressed for further concessions. Consequently, the Company gave up in 1724 its prior right to buy planters' produce and abandoned its monopoly to all trade at St. Thomas except the trade in slaves. Ships of all nations were permitted to buy and sell here on payment of the six percent export and five percent import duty fixed in 1716.[3]

The need for some action to boost trade was recognized in the decade prior to the emergence of St. Croix as an important agricultural island. Trade restrictions were further relaxed by the royal mandate of April 25, 1735 allowing all Danish subjects the right to trade freely with the Virgin Islands in merchandise and slaves and to take colonial produce to all foreign countries and to all Danish ports except Copenhagen. When this mandate did not have the desired effect of stimulating trade, private Danish traders were allowed by the mandate of June 18, 1743 to sell their cargoes in Copenhagen also.[4]

Any relaxation of monopoly was welcome to the planters of the Virgin Islands, since it promised more favorable prices through greater competition among buyers. But the Danish West India Company moved quickly to prevent needless competition with the private traders. An arrangement was made on December 3, 1745 by which certain European goods could be taken to the Virgin Islands by the Company and other goods by the private traders. In addition, Company's ships and those of private traders were given preference over foreign vessels in the carriage of Virgin Islands produce.[5] After much agitation, adoption of the 'Plan and Convention of Union' of February, 1747, resulted in the merging of the interests of the Company and of the private traders. On the basis of this Convention, an edict was issued in March, 1747, abrogating trade with the Virgin Islands by all other traders.

The edict of March, 1747, annulled the free trade concessions granted in 1724 and 1735 and reimposed the monopoly which the Company had previously held. Planters feared that their prosperity would be undermined by the new restrictions now that agriculture was expanding rapidly in St. Croix.[6] Threats were made of emigration, boycott, and hoarding of sugar to prevent the Company's ships from securing adequate cargoes. Governor Christian Suhm and his Privy Council believed that the islands would be ruined if planters left the islands and if others who were desirous of coming in were frightened off.

The regulations of 1747 were no doubt influenced by the Company's desire to secure some of the benefits accruing from the improved agricultural situation. However, the vehemence of planter opposition made some concession necessary without breach of the monopoly principle. Consequently, the colonists were allowed to import cocoa, coffee, tobacco, dyes and dye-woods, hides and timber, free of duty, and to export them at half the 'outgoing recognition'. But these goods had to be exported in vessels belonging to the colonists themselves, and they had to be taken to Copenhagen from where they could then be reexported to foreign ports. These provisions tended to nullify the concessions granted and to restore the Company's monopoly.

Trade Regulations under the Crown

After the Company was dissolved and its West Indian interests transferred to the Crown in 1754, the Danish West Indian trade was thrown open to all Danes whether they lived in Europe or in the West Indies. This privilege included the right to take slaves from Guinea to the Virgin Islands. Nevertheless, Danish monopoly over colonial trade was not greatly relaxed; goods produced in Denmark could not be imported into the Virgin Islands from elsewhere, and colonial goods loaded in Danish vessels could be taken only to Denmark. This was a re-assertion of prevailing mercantilist theory.

The retention of the restrictions on the trade of the Virgin Islands lasted for just about one decade when a partial but nevertheless important break was effected by the famous Ordinance of April 6 1764.[7] The Ordinance threw open the trade of St. Thomas and St. John with other foreign colonies in America to the ships of all nations. To some extent this was not a breach but an extension of mercantilist principles. Trade with Europe was still reserved for Danish subjects and the products of the Virgin Islands if sent to Europe at all (and these included all the products of St. Croix) could be disposed of only in Danish territory. Additionally, foreign ships were permitted to bring in only plantation supplies (foodstuffs, livestock and lumber) and manu-factured goods which could not be obtained from Denmark at all or only in limited quantities. Mercantilism was breached, however, when foreign traders in America, primarily from the British North American colonies, were allowed not only to sell such supplies and goods to the Virgin Islands as could be obtained from Denmark but also, in return to buy sugar and cotton to the value of half the imports the remainder to be made up of rum and molasses.

A further departure from the tenets of mercantilism was made in 1767 when the European trade of the islands was opened to the ships of other nations though they had to pay higher rates of duties. Free trade, thus established, lasted for ten years, when shortly after the outbreak of the American War of Independence, it was abrogated. In 1777 the Danish king ordered that all products from the Virgin Islands should be sent to Copenhagen to prevent the sugar trade from being diverted from Denmark. In addition, foreign trade between Europe and St. Thomas and St. John was forbidden. These restrictions, in turn, proved too difficult to maintain and in 1782 they were relaxed.[8]

Partly to handle the European trade created by the regulations of 1777, the Royal Danish West India Trading Company was chartered on May 11, 1778. Earlier in 1778, France had joined the revolting British North American colonies in war against Britain. Therefore, with its West Indian headquarters in St. Thomas, the Company could take advantage of the trade with the French colonies, especially in coffee from Saint-Domingue. However, the Company could function only behind the facade of trade regulations and war; when the 1777 trade restrictions were removed in 1782 and the war ended in 1783, the Company suffered. By 1786 its Charter preferences had lost their significance though the Company continued to operate in competition with other traders until 1824 when it was liquidated. A second Company, the Aarhus West India Trading Company, organized in 1782 and similarly designed, sent two trading vessels to St. Thomas. They did not achieve any success and the Company was liquidated in 1786.[9]

Britain's capture of the Virgin Islands during the French Revolutionary and Napoleonic Wars brought a temporary halt to the free port privileges and practices of St. Thomas. Under British navigation laws the trade of the Virgin Islands was confined to Britain, and unauthorized foreign vessels were prohibited from calling here with imports or to carry away exports. A free port was established in the British island of Tortola which, however, failed to measure up to expectations, and when the Virgin Islands were restored to Denmark in 1815, St. Thomas regained its previous entrepot privileges.[10] At the same time, the trade of St. Thomas and St. John were freed from all restrictions which meant that Danish as well as non-Danish vessels could trade with these islands on equal terms.[11]

The changes made after 1764 did not affect St. Croix whose trade was still governed by strict mercantilist principles. To avoid a breach of these principles St. Croix sugar and cotton were forbidden to be taken to St. Thomas for exportation; had this happened, the produce could then have been shipped elsewhere. Not until 1823 was a royal ordinance issued allowing the importation of provisions and plantation supplies from any foreign port to St. Croix and the exportation of sugar of equal value to such port. Unrestricted trade between St. Croix and foreign ports was instituted in June, 1833, one hundred years after the purchase of the island from France and St. Croix was thus placed on an equal footing commercially with St. Thomas and St. John.[12]

The late relaxation of the restrictions governing the trade of St. Croix stemmed from the continuing importance of the island as a producer and exporter of sugar which made it worthwhile to continue to channel the product to Denmark. Production had to sink beyond any hope of immediate revival before the trade restrictions were removed. As in the case of St. Thomas and St. John, free trade was intended to bolster an economy whose former prosperity could no longer be maintained purely through agriculture.

Inter-Colonial Trade

Besides the trade with Denmark, the islands developed strong trading relations with the surrounding West Indian colonies and with the mainland British colonies which later became the United States of America. A certain amount of smuggling was also undertaken although it is difficult to calculate its extent because of its secret nature.

Trade with neighboring islands was permitted to the colonists by the Danish West India Company in order to secure full cargoes, and to some extent it was forced upon them by the conditions of the Danish trade. Before Danes had even thought of establishing a colony in the West Indies, their excursions into the region had been purely trading ventures. After the colonization of St. Thomas and before cultivation became established, the Company continued to permit trade with other European colonies. The colonists exchanged European merchandise for cargoes of tropical produce and such trade was welcome to the Company. Once trade relations had been established, such Virgin Islands products as sugar, molasses, rum, cotton and woods, were exchanged for other colonial merchandise.

Besides the exchange of complementary products of Caribbean origin, inter-island trade stemmed from deficiencies in Danish trade. One was the infrequency with which the Company's vessels visited the Virgin Islands to bring European supplies and to collect colonial produce. Denmark, moreover, supplied only a limited range of colonial needs so that it was necessary to procure additional requirements from other convenient places.

The Company's sugar, cotton and other products of Virgin Islands origin were usually warehoused until ships arrived from Denmark or

Guinea to collect them. Commercial intelligence was supplied to the directors by the Company's factors who resided in the islands. When poor communication stopped the flow of information, the directors leaned on the side of caution. If cargoes were uncertain, they relied on the Guinea vessels to convey to Denmark whatever colonial cargoes were on hand. This practice led to the development of a triangular traffic from Denmark to Guinea, Guinea to the Virgin Islands, and the Virgin Islands to Denmark.

Prior to the 1740's, the Company never had more than two vessels in the triangular trade and planters complained of the irregularity of service since they depended on the sale of their produce to keep their plantations in operation. As an alternative they became staunch supporters of the petty trade which developed with the neighboring islands of Tortola, Antigua and St. Christopher which were British; Saba, St. Eustatius and Curacao which were Dutch; and St. Croix which was French, prior to its abandonment in 1696. The English seemed to have been attracted by the better prices offered for their produce in St. Thomas, and the cheaper rates at which they could obtain necessary supplies. The Dutch seemed to have outbid the Danes for Virgin Islands products and sold European merchandise more cheaply. Moreover, Dutch traders were more liberal in selling goods on credit and in granting loans for agricultural development and were thus popular among the colonists.

The fact that the Company, through its factors, offered only fixed prices for planters' produce, was good enough reason for them to seek other markets which offered better terms. Through the burgher council, the planters exercised some influence in fixing the market price of their produce, but their decision could be over-ruled by the Company. In any case, the Dutch seemed to have had the ability to offer better prices and so were favored trading partners with the colonists.

The system of 'indirect' taxation imposed by the Company was another source of grievance to the planters. So long as the planters were compelled to ship their produce to Denmark in the Company's vessels, an excessive freight rate became in itself a species of tax. When to this was added the underpaying of planters for their produce, which was also regarded as an indirect tax, the planters seemed to have had strong reasons to protest. Partly for these reasons they sought greater freedom of trade and a place in the local law-making process. For these reasons, also, they were encouraged to seek wider trading opportunities nearer at hand.

Virgin Islands Trade with North America

Apart from the conditions described above, colonists dealt with foreigners because they could be assured of regular supplies of essential commodities in adequate quantities. The most notable example of this was the trade with the British American colonies. It is not known exactly when this trade started, but by 1707 it was sufficiently strong for the Company to impose a four percent duty on provisions coming from New England. It must have been given considerable impetus by the relaxation of restrictions in 1724 and 1735.

The American trade figured prominently in the colonists' opposition to the Company's Plan of Convention and Union of 1747. It was feared that the new regulations would exclude ships from New York and New England coming to the Virgin Islands. Not only did these American vessels bring provisions such as flour and dried codfish, but also essential plantation supplies as hoops, barrel staves, planks, shingles and horses. The efficient operation of the plantations depended on these supplies, though this was only one side of the trade. In return for the foodstuff, lumber and livestock, the Americans took sugar and molasses for which they paid good prices. The prospect of having this trade curtailed was irritating to the West Indians.[13]

The American trade helped to compensate for low commodity prices in Europe where sugar prices in particular tended to fall for a time following the peace of Aix-la-Chapelle in 1748. The demand in New York and New England remained quite steady, so that with a fairly free market, the colonists stood to gain by continued trading there. However, it was not until 1758 that the trade with the American colonies was again permitted and planters were allowed to export thither one-sixth of the volume of sugar which they sent to Denmark. A most liberal interpretation was given to this regulation while the navigation law of 1764 gave unrestricted scope to the Virgin Islands—American trade.

Eighteenth century wars generally tended to benefit trade between the Virgin Islands and North America, even when European branches of Caribbean trade were impeded. This advantage was due to the entrepot facilities in the Virgin Islands which were available to all nations and colonies. The War of American Independence from 1776 to 1783, however, had a depressing effect since American trading-vessels were liable to seizure by British naval vessels and privateers. The Americans sought to prevent this by establishing trading depots in the Virgin

Islands and by operating privateers themselves in an effort to give protection to their trading vessels operating in the West Indies.[14] Despite these attempts, direct American trade with the Virgin Islands decreased with the swing in favor of Denmark. Conditions improved after 1780 when Spain and the Netherlands joined the Americans and the French in war against Britain. When the British Admiral Rodney sacked St. Eustatius in February, 1781, St. Thomas benefited greatly from the transfer here of American trading interests from that island.[15]

With the establishment of American independence in 1783, the ex-colonies were free from the restraints of the British laws of trade and navigation. Thereafter, their trade with the Virgin Islands showed a general increase despite some adverse circumstances. Between 1783 and 1793 the trade fluctuated widely: from 1784 it rose gradually to reach a peak in 1788; for the next three years it declined; and then it rose substantially the following two years. The cause for this uneven progress was primarily the severe drought which lasted for three years from 1789 to 1791.[16]

Improved weather conditions from 1792 and the outbreak of the French Wars in 1793 led to improved trade, and until 1802 there was a general increase with the best years being 1796 and 1797. After those two years, there was a slight setback in exports from the Virgin Islands to the United States. It resulted from French spoliation of American trading vessels and the quasi-war between France and the United States from 1799. By 1801, however, normal trade relations were once more restored.

American trade with the Virgin Islands grew at a considerable rate from 1802 to 1807 after which it dropped sharply. The capture of the Virgin Islands by British forces in March, 1807, was not in itself damaging to the American trade since by the terms of the treaties of capitulation, Americans were permitted to take the products of the islands and to provide them with essential supplies. The trade suffered, rather, from the American embargo of December, 1807, which forbade United States vessels to clear for foreign ports. Until about 1815 the bulk of the trade between the United States and the Virgin Islands was conducted directly through smuggling or indirectly through Canada. With the end of the war and continuing thereafter, trade was once more restored to its normal channels.[17]

Interloping, Neutral Trade and Privateering

Besides Denmark and North America, the Danish colonies traded with the British, Dutch, French and Spanish colonies in the West Indies. This inter-colonial trade was encouraged by the relaxation of restrictions in 1716, 1724 and 1735. Despite the attempts of the imperial nations to restrict their colonial trade to their own nationals, and despite the seizures that were often made of Danish vessels, the St. Thomas traders were willing to assume risks which the Company could not afford. American shipyards supplied cheap and seaworthy vessels in which Virgin Islanders faced the dangers of privateers and men-of-war and successfully evaded the vigilance of the West Indian authorities who sought to uphold their respective navigation laws. When the Danish interlopers were fortunate enough to encounter permissive officials their fears of capture and punishment were allayed.

Virgin Islanders were not the only people to engage in the interloping trade; other West Indian traders were quite willing to come to the Virgin Islands to dispose of or secure fresh cargoes. This practice is best seen in relation to the trade in African slaves in which commodity St. Thomas from an early date seemed to have transacted a brisk business. Slaves were brought in by the Company's vessels, by private traders and by the Brandenburgers while they held their factory in St. Thomas. In addition, a considerable number of slaves sold in St. Thomas were brought in by interlopers most of whom were Dutch. Total numbers were more than could be absorbed locally so many slaves were re-exported. Advance notice was given of the arrival of ships from Guinea, at which time traders from other islands came to the Virgin Islands to have first choice of the slave cargoes.[18]

It has been emphasized that wars, generally, favored the trade of the Virgin Islands. The declared neutrality of Denmark during the wars of the eighteenth century enabled Danish trade with the Virgin Islands to go on more or less unmolested, and even at times to increase. There were some seizures of Danish vessels but commerce did not suffer any major disruption. The neutrality of Denmark also promoted a wide neutral trade between the Virgin Islands and the colonies of the belligerent nations. St. Thomas especially, and St. Croix to a less extent, became a clearing house where foreign colonial products could be disposed of and where foreign colonies could obtain essential supplies of foodstuff. The Americans seemed to have transacted a brisk entrepot trade during all the wars, including their war of independence when St. Thomas carried on a substantial transit trade in foreign coffee with the revolting colonies. The transit trade in sugar was also important, especially after the capture of St. Eustatius, but this trade came to an end when peace was restored in 1783.[19]

Despite Denmark's profession of neutrality, Danish and Danish colonial vessels were liable to seizure. The Rule of 1756, proclaimed by Britain during the Seven Years' War worked some hardship for the Virgin Islands. Under it, any vessel which traded with enemy territory in contraband of war was liable to seizure. Under the pretext that the Danish vessels trading with the French colonies took war supplies, even 'innocent' cargoes were seized by the British. To make matters worse, seizure was often extended to vessels which did not even trade with enemy colonies.

Twelve Danish-Norwegian vessels, nine of them from Copenhagen alone, trading with the Virgin Islands were seized in 1758. The protests made by the Danish minister of foreign affairs, J. H. E. Bernstorff, eventually led in 1759, to an agreement with Britain by which a Danish captain who was challenged would be allowed to proceed on giving surety for that part of his cargo which was charged with being French. As an added precaution against seizures, the Danish government adopted the convoy system by which trading vessels could sail between Denmark and the Virgin Islands under armed escort.[20]

During the American War of Independence, the facilities given to the Americans to establish trading depots in St. Croix aroused the anger of the Governor of the Britsh Leeward Islands who encouraged the seizure of Danish vessels by British privateers operating from Tortola. Captures were taken into Road Town, tried by the Vice-Admiralty Court there and confiscated. Following the storm over the seizure of two Danish vessels, 'La Dorothea' and 'L'Elizabeth Christine', the British Government was forced to order the removal of the Vice-Admiralty Court from Tortola lest its operation lead to war with neutral nations.[21]

Privateering had an important bearing on the wartime trade of the Virgin Islands. Privateers were armed vessels whose captains were commissioned through letters of marque issued by their respective governments to sail against enemy commerce and shipping. Because of the nearby presence of Tortola, it was never necessary for the British to use St. Thomas or St. Croix as privateering bases. It was otherwise with the French and the Americans who, lacking bases in the vicinity, made full use of the Virgin Islands to organize privateering attacks against British shipping in the area. Privateers were able to repair and refit, and to obtain supplies here. Moreover, from a commercial point of view, they were able to dispose of the cargoes which they had seized including both European merchandise and colonial produce.

The use made of the Danish islands as bases for privateers so antagonized the British that they questioned the right of the Danes to St. Thomas in 1717 to 1718, sought to prevent the occupation of St. John at about the same time, and questioned the legality of the French sale of St. Croix to Denmark in 1733. Again, the potentials of the islands as privateering bases during the French Revolutionary and Napoleonic Wars was the main reason why Britain seized and held them between 1801 and 1802 and again between 1807 and 1815. That the Virgin Islands gained from the purchase and export of goods seized by privateers while they were under Danish control is undoubted.

Privateering in the Virgin Islands did not end with the close of the French wars in 1815 but continued to be favored by the revolt of the Spanish American colonies against Spain. Those captains issued with letters of marque by the infant republics of Venezuela and Columbia preyed on Spanish vessels, several of which were captured and brought into St. Thomas for disposal. Privateering in the Caribbean and the Virgin Islands finally ended with Spain's recognition of the new republics in 1825.[22]

Smuggling in the Virgin Islands

Smuggling seemed to have been an activity of some importance in the Virgin Islands. Facility for it was given by the large numbers of bays and coves where cargoes might be loaded or landed without detection. It was aided also by the inadequacy of supervising personnel, though some customs officers were unable or unwilling to prevent illicit trade.

The bribing of Danish officials was not altogether impossible since many of them were badly paid and living costs in the Virgin Islands were high. The Danish West India Company's policy of buying cheap and selling dear, coupled with onerous import and export duties and other charges were all incentives for the colonists to deal with smugglers. To those who owed money to the Company smuggling was one way by which they sought to escape payment of debts. Others sought merely to export their produce in the name of another planter who was not so encumbered, and who had opportunities to smuggle.

Smuggling became a fine art in the Virgin Islands where many smugglers were bold enough to enter or clear their cargoes at the colonial ports. The means of enforcing observance of the regulations were often lacking; a customs house, whether in St. Thomas or St. Croix, was no deterrent to smugglers unless it was properly staffed and equipped. In the face of inadequate law-enforcing machinery, ships were accustomed to slip away during the night without securing clearance or paying their dues.

That smugglers did not always have their own way was evidenced during the time Peter Clausen was assistant factor and treasurer after 1748. Up to 1747 receipts from customs duties averaged less than $26 for each planter; thereafter they increased rapidly and until 1754 averaged about $46 as a result of the unprecedented enforcement of customs regulations by Clausen. When Clausen later became governor-general, his vigorous administration soon revealed a regular system of smuggling especially on the south side of St. Croix opposite Christiansted, where it was unlikely that any customs officials kept watch.[23]

Smuggling was less rewarding and tended to decline as trade restrictions were gradually removed. However, the evasion of duty payments continued to be a problem of some importance. Obliging officials reportedly reduced the burden by means of false entries in the customs books. Under-registering the size and volume of cargoes might thus mean that the duties paid would amount only to a fraction of the legal rate charged on goods that came from or went to non-Danish European and American ports.

St. Thomas: The Mail Packet Rendezvous

St. Thomas continued as a trade emporium after the plantation base of its commerce began to shrink. This was due largely to the rendezvous here of vessels belonging to the Royal Mail Steam Packet Company, a British shipping concern. St. Thomas was first made a station for British packet vessels in 1819 when a severe hurricane destroyed the harbor facilities in Road Town, Tortola, hitherto the packet station.[24]

St. Thomas was a logical choice for the packet station since it had a suitable harbor and the island was already well established as a communication center. Besides, heavy British capital investment had already been made in the Danish islands. The selection of St. Thomas was not so much a preference of a foreign over a British colony, as a choice of a prosperous over a poor colony. Subsequent attempts to return the packet station to Road Town were unsuccessful.

When the Royal Mail Steam Packet Company received its charter in 1839, St. Thomas was retained as the rendezvous for its vessels touching at several points in the Caribbean.[25] Special privileges were granted to the Company with regard to the transfer of passengers, mail and cash. Most European visitors to the West Indies from the 1840's passed through St. Thomas on their way to or from other parts of the Caribbean. These people continued to give the island the cosmopolitan character it has retained to the modern age of cruise ships and jet planes.

The focal point of St. Thomas as a rendezvous for the Company's ships was the coaling station established in 1841 with coal ships exempted from the payment of customs duties. The station gave employment to large numbers of local people, but the special attraction was that wages offered here in unloading ships or fuelling them were better than elsewhere in agriculture. Until 1885 when the packet station was removed to Barbados, St. Thomas benefited greatly as a transit center, as a coaling station, and as a maritime dockyard where vessels were repaired. From four to six ships were always waiting in the harbor to take passengers, mail, and other commodities to other West Indian Islands or to Latin America. As an aid to navigation, a light was installed at the entrance of the St. Thomas Harbor in 1843 to facilitate the safe entry of vessels.[26]

Importance of St. Thomas as a Trading Center

Representative figures show the trend of trade which, in general, was away from Denmark and towards the United States of America, non-Danish European nations and other West Indian islands. Existing statistics bear upon legitimate or official trade and do not include the vessels engaged in smuggling and privateering. While smuggling continued, privateering was progressively phased out after the end of the Napoleonic Wars in 1815. Another change was the prohibition of the Danish slave trade in 1803.

St. Thomas benefited from the conjunction of full free-port privileges and the establishment of the packet station after 1819. In 1800 there were entered at St. Thomas a total of 1,300 vessels, between 1816 and 1819 the numbers had decreased to 1,169 on an average each year, while between 1820 and 1829, an average of 2,829 vessels of 177,444 tons entered each year. Between 1831 and 1840 there was a small reduction to 2,557, and between 1841 and 1850 a further reduction to 2,146 vessels a year. Comparing the last two periods, however, an actual increase in tonnage from 161,408 to 207,623 tons is noticeable. Besides, statistics for the period 1841 to 1850 do not include steamships and mail-ships which entered St. Thomas. Between 1840 and 1850, the steamships entering increased from 36 to 91, which included the vessels engaged in the Royal Mail Steam Packet service.[27]

The United States moved ahead of Denmark in the St. Thomas trade in which Britain and France also featured prominently. Table 1 gives the percentage of vessels calling at St. Thomas from the several countries during specified periods.[28].

TABLE 1
Country of Origin of Ships entering St. Thomas

Country	1821-1830	1831-1840
U.S.A.	35	35
Denmark	22	14
Britain	21	18
France	11	11
Others	11	22

Commercially, St. Thomas was a flourishing port with life concentrated around the harbor in the town of Charlotte Amalie. In the 1840's over eighty percent of the island's population of about 14,000 were engaged in occupations other than agriculture and bearing largely on trade and commerce. In St. Croix where the emphasis was on agriculture most of the people lived in the rural districts. In 1839 there were 41 large importing houses in St. Thomas; 13 English, 11 French, 6 German, 4 American, 4 Italian and Spanish, and only 3 Danish.[29]

As a shipping center and distribution point for the West Indies, St. Thomas held an enviable position after 1819. West Indian and Central American vessels called for mail and passengers while smaller boats came to collect cargoes. Thirty to forty boats were engaged in the trade with Puerto Rico alone and trade to that colony averaged about 4 million rigsdalers yearly. Next in importance was the transit trade with Haiti, while trade of less value was conducted with other West Indian colonies and Central America. In addition, by 1850 St. Thomas had a very large transit trade in European goods with several large South American republics, including Brazil, Argentina and Venezuela. From Europe ships of various nations called here while United States vessels visited regularly.[30]

As a result of the boom in trade which occurred in St. Thomas and in order to facilitate business transactions a marine insurance company and two banks were established in Charlotte Amalie.[31] The first bank was the St. Thomas Bank, a private enterprise, which began operations in January, 1837 with a capital outlay of half million dollars. It was such a success that during the first six months it realized a dividend of 12 percent. Shortly after, also in 1837, the second bank, the British West Indian Colonial Bank was established. Both banks depended on the conditions of trade for their success: while trade flourished they prospered; alternatively, when trade decreased they suffered. The St. Thomas Bank lasted until 1898 and the Colonial Bank until 1916 when depressed trade and bad economic conditions eventually forced them to close.

Conclusion

By the nineteenth century, the Virgin Islands were declining in plantation agriculture; on the other hand, they were becoming increasingly important as a center of trade with the swing being away from Denmark. This double alienation from the mother-country both as a source of colonial produce and as a market for Danish manufactured goods was to have serious consequences for the islands in the future. That Denmark was already aware of the loss of benefits was indicated in 1846 by the talk of disposing of its islands. That the islands were later offered for sale to and were eventually bought by the United States was an acknowledgement of the hold which that nation already had on their economy. That the proposed sale was to meet with popular consent locally was an indication that Virgin Islanders were already aware of the benefits to be derived from association with the United States.

[1] J. O. Bro-Jorgensen, *Dansk Vestindien Indtil 1755: Kolonisation og Kompagnistyre* (Fremad, Denmark, 1966) pp. 187-188; Waldemar Westergaard, *The Danish West Indies Under Company Rule* (1671-1754). (New York, The Macmillan Company, 1917) pp. 185-188.

[2]   Bro-Jorgensen, op. cit., pp. 194-196; Westergaard, op. cit., pp. 188-191.

[3]   Westergaard, op. cit., pp. 194-195.

[4]   Ibid., pp. 219-220.

[5]   Ibid., pp. 220-221.

[6]   Ibid., pp. 221-222 and 233-234; Bro-Jorgensen, op. cit., p. 264.

[7]   Jean Louise Willis, The Trade between North America and the Danish West Indies, 1756 to 1807, With Special Reference to St. Croix. (Unpublished Ph.D. Thesis, Columbia University, New York, 1963) pp. 73-78; Annual Register, 1764, pp. 89-90.

[8]   Jens Vibaek, *Dansk Vestindien 1755-1848: Vestindiens Storhedstid.* (Fremad, Denmark, 1966) p. 64; Westergaard, op. cit., p. 250.

[9]   Willis, op. cit., pp. 116-119; Emanuel Sejr, 'Aarhus Vestindiske Handels Selskab. Oprettelse og sammenbrud.' (*Erhvervshistorisk Aarbog, Meddelelser fra Erhvervsarkivet*, Vol. 13. Aarhus, 1962).

[10]   Isaac Dookhan, A History of the British Virgin Islands. (Unpublished Ph.D. Thesis, University of the West Indies, 1968) pp. 106-111.

[11]   Vibaek, op. cit., p. 301.

[12]   E. Heilbuth, *Denmark and St. Croix in their Mutual Relations.* (Buffalo: Lee & Thorp's Press, 1845) p. 22.

[13]   Herbert C. Bell, 'The West India Trade before the American Revolution.' (*The American Historical Review*, Vol. XXII, No. 2, Jan., 1917) pp. 272-287.

[14]   Dookhan, op. cit., p. 101.

[15]   J. Franklin Jameson, 'St. Eustatius in the American Revolution.' (*The American Historical Review*, Vol. VIII, No. 4, July, 1903) pp. 683-708.

[16]   Willis, op. cit., pp. 164-207.

[17]   Ibid., pp. 208-253.

[18]   Westergaard, op. cit., pp. 148-149.

[19]   Willis, op. cit., pp. 126-151.

[20]   Vibaek, op. cit., p. 81.

[21]   Dookhan, op. cit., p. 102.

[22]   John P. Knox, *A Historical Account of St. Thomas, W.I.* (New York, Charles Scribner, 1852) pp. 104-105.

[23]   The American Journal, 1770-1771, July 29, 1770 and January 3, 1771.

[24]   Dookhan, op. cit., p. 132.

[25]   Royal Mail Steam Packet Company. (*Encyclopaedia Britannica*, Vol. 25) p. 854 (d).

[26]   Vibaek, op. cit., p. 306.

[27]   Adolph Frederik Bergsoe, *Den danske Stats Statistik.* (Kjobenhavn, 1853) Vol. 4, p. 666.

[28]   Ibid., p. 667.

[29]   Westergaard, op. cit., p. 252.

[30]   [John van Voorst], *Letters from the Virgin Islands.* (London, 1843) pp. 92-93, conveys a sense of the importance of St. Thomas as a recipient of the world's trade in the observation that 'India goods, tea, spices, Canton crape, Madras coifs, nankeens, &c.; wines, spirits, and preserved fruits from France; dried meats, medicinal waters, linen, &c.; from Germany; lumber, shingles, maize, salt fish, &c. from the States; the coffee, cotton and rum of the Antilles; — these with articles of

European manufacture, whether for use or luxury, from a toy to a steam boat, may find purchasers at St. Thomas.'
[31] Thurlow Weed, *Letters from the West Indies, 1843-1862.* (Albany, Weed, Parsons and Company, 1866) p. 365.

Chapter 7

Piracy in the Virgin Islands

As already mentioned, the early history of the West Indies was characterized by Spain's assertion of monopolist rights over the entire region and by the opposition of other European nations desirous of obtaining a share of its territory and trade. Almost from the beginning of Spanish colonization, the attitude of defiance was shown in the high-handed actions of foreign intruders who were bold enough to venture into the Caribbean in violation of the Spanish prohibitions. By the middle of the sixteenth century, religious and patriotic enthusiasm was made to justify a policy of deliberate robbery of Spanish subjects by Protestants from Europe.

Pirates were attracted to the West Indies by the wealth which was offered by the newly-discovered lands and, accordingly, they attacked settlements and shipping. They received the blessings of their respective national governments who were either jealous or afraid of the power of Spain, but lacked the means of open defiance. Even when the Spanish monopoly was broken, by the establishment of foreign colonies, non-Hispanic nations turned upon each other in order to seize each other's possessions in the West Indies. In this situation filled with almost continuous international rivalry and conflict, pirates continued to operate in peace and war to devastate and seize the property of those who lived and traded in the region.

A Pirate Haven

It is not known to what extent the Virgin Islands were used by pirates before they were formally colonized, but it is possible that pirates resorted here to careen and water their vessels as they did in the more easterly of the Lesser Antilles. The islands were probably used also as a rendezvous for corsairs assembled to launch their more ambitious operations. In addition, spontaneous, irregular and non-permanent settlement of the islands might have been made by pirates before effective occupation was accomplished.

Piracy was in the decline by 1672 after having been in existence for almost 150 years in the Caribbean. In the second half of the seven-teenth century, it was being superseded by buccaneering whose star was then in the ascendant. Another rival was privateering, though at the time privateering was partly abated, only to run its tempestuous course with renewed vigor in the eighteenth century. In this twilight zone of both buccaneering and privateering, when piracy could be conducted under the legitimate cover of the buccaneer's letter of reprisal and the privateer's letter of marque, the day of the private operator was nearly over.

Nevertheless, for some time after the colonization of the Virgin Islands, piracy flourished here openly, sometimes almost respectably. Colonists of all classes, even colonial governments, tolerated them, and were prepared to do business with them. Conditions were almost ideal for the operation of piracy: the large number of small islands afforded safe anchorage and refuge, and the forests provided suitable woods for repairing. Situated as the Virgin Islands were in proximity to the regular trade routes used by sailing ships entering or leaving the West Indies, they were well located for use by pirates. Moreover, the poverty-stricken inhabitants who comprised the bulk of the early settlers felt no qualms of conscience to traffic with pirates in buying their loot and providing them in return with foodstuff and other needed supplies.

The Virgin Islands had all the qualifications necessary for an extended and energetic practice of piracy, and for two or three decades pirates used St. Thomas before being forced to abandon their traffic here.

The Esmits and Piracy

The governorship of Jorgen Iversen from 1672 to 1680 was marked by a conspicuous absence of piracy in St. Thomas, even though the colony was struggling to maintain its existence. It was during the period when the Esmit brothers, Nicolaj and Adolph, were responsible for the government of St. Thomas, that the island gained its reputation as a pirate resort.

The Esmits had a propensity to tolerate and even to indulge in illegalities; runaway white indentured servants and black slaves from the English colonies in the Lesser Antilles were sheltered here and their return refused. The governors, also, did not hesitate to seize and retain on somewhat questionable pretexts English vessels which came into the St. Thomas harbor. For instance in August, 1682 the sloop 'Prosperous' under the captaincy of Thomas, Watson, on its way from Barbados to Jamaica, came into Charlotte Amalie in order to re-victual. Watson had received Nicolaj Esmit's permission to land, but the vessel and its cargo were seized and declared good prize, on the charge that Watson had overstayed his time and had sold spirits and an assortment of textiles and apparel to the inhabitants. Watson and his mate, John Campion, were condemned to be hanged and the sloop's cargo was confiscated.

When Adolph Esmit seized the government of St. Thomas from his brother in the autumn of 1682, he at first refused to return the sloop; later he agreed to do so but only after the vessel had already been sold at an auction. In addition to seized vessels, the English suffered from the Danish governor's refusal to return seamen and debtors who had run away from the English colonies to St. Thomas, on the rather untenable ground that St. Thomas was a free port, and that all those who sought refuge here were entitled to protection.

In contrast to the treatment meted out to legitimate traders, another incident during 1682 illustrates the welcome that was being accorded to sea rovers. The event was reported by Nicolaj Esmit himself and his account implicates the settlers of St. Thomas also in harboring lawless elements.

There arrived here February 8, [1682] a ship of unknown origin, some two hundred tons in size, without guns, passport or letters, and with seven men, French, English and German. On being questioned they replied that they had gone out of *Espaniola* [Hispaniola] from the harbor of Petit Guava (sic) with two hundred men and a French commission to cruise on the Spaniards . . . [They were sailing] for Petit Goava, but on the way the boat leaked, so they asked to come in to St. Thomas and there careen the boat, which was done at *Strand Slucken* [Gregerie Beach?] by the aid of thirty men sent out by me. I bought what little cacao they had, the rest of their plunder they brought ashore and divided among our people. The ship was no longer usable. I have decided not to confiscate it, in order to avoid any unfriendliness with sea-robbers. The inhabitants of St. Thomas have decided that the said seven men shall remain among them.[1]

The behavior of the Esmits so exasperated the Governor of the English Leeward Islands, Sir William Stapleton, that on November 11, 1682, he wrote a vigorous letter of protest to the Lords of Trade and Plantations in London recalling several instances in which the English colonies were suffering from their seizure of English vessels and their sheltering of runaways. This complaint was forwarded to the Danish envoy in London, Christian Lente with the result that within a fortnight the Danish king had written a letter reprimanding Adolph Esmit, and ordering him to restore all English property on pain of death. Adolph was further informed that repeated charges of the same kind would certainly lead to his execution.

The 'La Trompeuse' Affair

It is hardly to be expected that an order given in distant Denmark would have much effect on a man of Adolph Esmit's temperament and ability to pull political strings to get his way. Early evidence that he was not to be bound by instructions was shown around the middle of 1683 in the case of the French pirate ship, 'La Trompeuse', the treatment of which, as one writer has rightly pointed out, 'rocked not alone the harbour of St. Thomas, but the chancellories of England, Denmark, and France.'[2]

Captain Peter Paine (or Le Paine), commander of 'La Trompeuse' arrived at Jamaica from Cayenne in March, 1682. He asked for and obtained permission to sell the ship's cargo of sugar, and afterwards to settle in the island. Unknown to the Jamaican authorities then was the fact that 'La Trompeuse' had been stolen by Le Paine and that orders for its seizure and return to France had been given.

Meanwhile, two Jamaican merchants, Banks and Ward, had hired the ship and sent it to the Bay of Honduras to load logwood. It was then to be sailed for Hamburgh, and arrangements were made for the ship to be delivered to the French agent there. However, these plans were foiled by a French pirate named Jean Hamlin who, on hearing of the ship's trip to Central America, followed it in a sloop, and seized it after first inviting its master and mate on board his vessel. 'La Trompeuse' was then fitted out as a pirate ship.

The first captures made by 'La Trompeuse' were seven or eight vessels from the island of Jamaica, and by February, 1683 an estimated sixteen to eighteen more English ships had been captured by it off Hispaniola. Earlier, in December, 1682 a man-of-war had been dispatched by the Governor of Jamaica to capture it, but it failed to encounter the pirate ship. For some time 'La Trompeuse' obtained shelter and supplies of food and men at the Ile à Vache from where it operated against passing ships. It was made for speed and was able to evade capture, but the hope was expressed in February, 1683 that as 'the pirate is a weak and unsheathed ship and is growing foul',[3] it would not be long before it was captured. Nevertheless, a Jamaican frigate, the 'Guernsey' after trying for three months, failed to find it.

Part of the time in which it was being hunted, 'La Trompeuse' found shelter in the Virgin Islands where it received friendly reception from Adolph Esmit. However, when in early July, 1683, the English frigate 'H.M.S. Ruby' under Captain Richard May, visited St. Thomas, he failed to find the pirate ship. The reply of Adolph Esmit to an inquiry about the pirates was indicative of his evasiveness, his lack of cooperation and his sympathy for the pirates. Instead of giving the required assistance to locate the vessel, he accused May of conducting himself improperly because his ship had come 'into his Danish Majesty's harbour without paying his fort the proper respect.'[4] At the time 'La Trompeuse' was off the African coast where it was doing extensive plundering with no less than seventeen ships being taken. Nevertheless, on July 27, 1683, it was back at St. Thomas where finally the English Captain Charles Carlile of 'H.M.S. Francis' caught up with it.

When Carlile appeared off the harbor of St. Thomas 'La Trompeuse' was lying within it along with some five or six other pirate vessels in which the English had no immediate interest. Carlile had with him a letter from Sir William Stapleton, desiring Governor Esmit's assistance to capture 'La Trompeuse', but when within cannon shot, he was fired upon by both the pirate and the Fort. The next day Carlile protested against the shooting and when no explanation was given, he made preparations to burn the pirate ship that very night.

Three days later Esmit explained that prior to Carlile's arrival he had taken 'La Trompeuse' into his custody and had put his men on board it. Even had this explanation been given on the first day it might not have been believed; neither would it have stopped the preparations to burn the ship. Proof of this was seen in the fact that even gifts of fresh meat and an invitation from Esmit for Carlile to land to do business and then to have dinner with him next day were considered mere pretexts to postpone or prevent violence. But Carlile was in no mood for delay since this might enable the pirates to secure assistance, and he went through with and executed his plans to burn 'La Trompeuse.' To ensure proper completion of the job, a boat load of men waited nearby to see that no one went to put out the blaze. When the ship exploded, fire caught another pirate ship lying nearby and destroyed it also.

Carlile sailed away after burning 'La Trompeuse,' but returned shortly afterwards and demanded of Esmit the delivery of four English pirates who were on shore, threatening to summon three more frigates to his assistance if Esmit refused. The governor did not accede to this request, but as if to prove his non-complicity with pirates, he sent over in irons the man who had shot against the 'Francis' with the explanation that the others had fled.

The others had indeed fled, but with Esmit's assistance apparently given in return for much financial gain. According to Andreas Petersen Brock, the official reporter and Government Secretary for St. Thomas, Hamlin had been housed by Esmit in the Fort.

He has eaten and banqueted with Esmit and has slept with Esmit in a room. He has brought much gold. Esmit would not deliver the said Hamlyn to the English. Furthermore, Esmit sent Hamlyn together with his comrades and pirates out of the harbour with a barque and a fishing net belonging to the company. They sailed around the island and went into Mosquito Bay . . .

Besides the gold, money and silver and other goods he has received from the pirates, Esmit bought 3 to 24 negroes from La Trompeuse . . . The privateers, officers as well as crew, Esmit helped and let go free. Five or six of them that have stayed here, he had married to landladies and girls and then sold them negroes and plantations very cheap to get hold of their money and gold.[5]

From other sources, Governor Stapleton learned of the protection and shelter given by Esmit to the pirates; accordingly, he demanded that Esmit should deliver up Jean Hamlin. To show how serious he was, he added the threat, 'I warn you, have a care. I shall come from the Leeward Islands with an armed force, blow you up as quickly as the Trompeuse, and pound any pirate that you may have fitted out'.[6]

English governors were not empowered to use force against the nationals of friendly countries in the West Indies. Whether Esmit knew this or not, or whether he was willing to call Stapleton's bluff, he was not daunted by the English governor's threat. He seized English vessels whenever he could, and his promotion of piracy continued unabated. Indeed, he sold Jean Hamlin a new sloop which was probably one of those he had seized from the English, and Hamlin was soon back at his old trade. Before long he was reported as captain of 'La Nouvelle Trompeuse,' which Stapleton claimed had been fitted out and protected by New Englanders.

Another person turned pirate through the agency of Esmit was Captain George Bond who was until then master of the ship 'Summer Island' of London. At St. Thomas, Bond was able to buy a Dutch vessel and to fit it out as a pirate. Soon he was capturing vessels one of which, the 'Gideon,' was sent into St. Thomas where it was unloaded and the pirates given protection by Esmit.

Change in the Old Order: Johan Lorentz and Bartholomew Sharp

Under Adolph Esmit, St. Thomas became, in the words of Stapleton, a 'receptacle of thieves and sea-robbers.'[7] As later events showed, however, piracy in the Virgin Islands was a plant of tender growth, which received its nurture only if the governors supported it. Adolph Esmit was removed from the governorship in 1684 and was replaced by Gabriel Milan under whom St. Thomas continued chaotic, and as backward and as poor as ever. Under such conditions piracy could and probably did continue, though from the absence of written reports, the activities of pirates were not noteworthy.

Acting Governor Heins and Governor Johan Lorentz were men of greater integrity than either Esmit or Milan and were not likely to suffer pirates gladly. They saw piracy for what it was, a drag on the progress of a young colony; lawlessness could appeal only to the lawless or to those of lawless tendencies. The establishment of a colony on a firm basis required people of greater moral rectitude, who were prepared to settle and to plant and trade legitimately. Besides, once a colony had acquired the reputation for harboring pirates, prospective colonists would be discouraged from coming in. Others would be disinclined to sink their capital and labor in plantations which could produce more lasting progress.

.neir effort to promote the development of St. Thomas, the Da. .sh governors regarded the friendly attitude of foreign governors to be important especially since they had been ordered to suppress buccaneering and piracy. The treatment of 'La Trompeuse' showed that the English would not tolerate the seizure of their trading vessels by pirates; if St. Thomas sheltered these sea-robbers, it could only expect to earn the English wrath. Such unfavorable international repercussions could not but be detrimental to the welfare of the colony.

During the period when St. Thomas was leased to Thormohlen, Lorentz had no authority; but no sooner had he resumed the governorship than he made strenuous efforts to dissociate St. Thomas from piracy. The success which he achieved was partly responsible for the increasing numbers of new settlers who came into St. Thomas. Lorentz was saved some embarrassment in his attitude towards piracy by the War of the League of Augsburg (1689-1697) when pirates operated more or less under cover as privateers duly commissioned to wage war against enemy ships. As such, therefore, St. Thomas as a neutral port could not properly be accused of sheltering or dealing with lawless elements.

The cessation of hostilities in 1697 no longer made the issuing of privateers' letters of marque necessary to European governments, with the result that those who had operated hitherto as privateers were reduced to the rank of pirates. After 1697 the attitude of Johan Lorentz towards pirates was definitely unfriendly, and this was illustrated quite convincingly in his relationship with the notorious English pirates Bartholomew Sharp and Captain William Kidd.

Bartholomew Sharp was an English buccaneer who for fifteen or sixteen years had been engaged in ravaging ships and settlements in the Caribbean in quest of loot. When at the end of his buccaneering days he was not allowed to settle in any of the English colonies, in 1696 he sought and obtained permission to settle in St. Thomas. The authorities, however, kept watch on his activities to ensure that he remained a law-abiding member of the community and that he did nothing to interfere with the progress of the colony.

By 1697 Sharp had a small plantation which he worked with the labor of seven slaves. As a planter, however, Sharp was a failure; he was soon in debt, and in order to escape paying his creditors, he decided in 1698 to leave St. Thomas. Secret arrangements were made with the captain of an English vessel to send a boat ashore to collect him, his slaves, and other belongings, but knowledge of what he was planning became known. His slaves ran away, and while he himself was about to leave, he and the boat's crew were seized by soldiers from Fort Christian. During the trial that followed it was shown that Sharp had threatened to harm St. Thomas as much as possible to prevent which, he was sentenced to life imprisonment and his property confiscated.[8]

The Captain Kidd Affair

At the close of the War of the League of Augsburg in 1697, Captain Kidd had been commissioned by the English Government to suppress piracy in the Indian Ocean, but finding the opportunities for gain favorable he himself turned pirate. So successful was he that his name has passed into legend, and he is memorialized in the words of the sea-chanty entitled *Captain Kid's Farewel to the Seas; or, the Famous Pirate's Lament.*[9] As the words suggest the song was probably written by Kidd himself; part of the first stanza reads as follows:

> ". . . My name is Captain Kid, who has sail'd;
> My name is Captain Kid.
> What the laws did still forbid
> Unluckily I did while I sail'd . . ."

Kidd's piratical exploits caused the English Government to outlaw him and in the beginning of 1699, he sailed for the West Indies on the ship 'Quedah Merchant'. He was refused permission to land at Anguilla, and fearing capture he did not go to Antigua. Instead he decided to make for St. Thomas, whose reputation as a neutral port gave him hope of a friendly reception. However, he was refused permission to land reasons for which were stated in a letter from Johan Lorentz to the directors of the Danish West India Company; fear of English reprisal was paramount in the Danish governor's mind. He wrote:

6th April this year at the harbour arrived a ship, showing an English flag, anchoring outside the harbour and giving no salute. The captain thereupon, namely Cidd (sic), sent his chaloupe ashore and with it a person, carrying a letter, in which he requested to be allowed with his ship to enter. I thereupon sent my written parole indicating that, if he is an honest man and can prove nothing unlawful to have done, he can come in freely, with which answer he was not satisfied, but required me to protect him against the arrival of English Royal ships, which might want to challenge him without royal orders, from which I concluded that his circumstances were not quite straight, and therefore the following day called together the council, consulting it whether he should be given another parole. Considering that great jealousy between this island and the British might arise, if he came in here and upon their challenging him this island did not extradite him, it was decided not to allow him another parole, of which decision he was notified. There was no doubt that the English general would challenge him immediately, as he sailed from England on a royal English passport, and had he not been handed over, the royal ships would close this harbour that neither ships nor boats would be able to get out or in to the great damage for our country. By another message he tried to get in and stay under protection, until he would be able to send a bark to New England there to introduce his case and prove that he was no pirate, the governor there, my Lord Bellomont, being the main owner of the ship, upon which he three years ago sailed out of England, to the East Indies and the Red Sea cruising for pirates. I still did not find him reliable enough to give such allowances but answered: that if he wanted to accept the parole already given, he could come in, if not, I prohibited him from sending his chaloupe ashore any more. Upon which he the 8th inst. has sailed away again, at the point of the harbour setting ashore 5 persons, of which 4 were passengers and the fifth a person who for two long years had been lying ill on board the ship.[10]

On leaving St. Thomas, Captain Kidd sailed for Hispaniola where he bought a smaller vessel and left for New York. There he was arrested and sent to England where he was tried for piracy and eventually hanged. At Hispaniola Kidd had sold the cargo of the 'Quedah Merchant' to a number of traders from Curacao, Antigua and St. Thomas who were there.[11] One of these men, William Burke, an Irishman, bought between 120 and 130 bales of muslin. Soon after, Burke came to Lorentz and offered him a part of Kidd's cargo, if the latter would help him to get rid of the rest. Lorentz refused and developments shortly after led to the exposure of a channel of illegal trade hitherto unknown.

After leaving Lorentz, Burke went to Van Belle, the Brandenburger factor in St. Thomas, who did not share Lorentz's scruples in receiving stolen goods, and that very night, pirate booty was landed and stored in

E

the Brandenburger warehouse. The unusual nocturnal movements aroused the suspicion of the guard and he reported them to Lorentz who began an investigation next day. Some of the goods were eventually found in the home of a merchant and taken to the Fort by soldiers, while Burke was arrested and a suit brought against him.

The trial implicated other merchants from Curacao and from Barbados whose share of Kidd's cargo had been sold, and showed that Burke was the middleman between the foreign traders and Van Belle. The Brandenburger factor was subsequently fined 5,000 rigsdalers while Burke was fined 300 rigsdalers and required to make a further deposit of 5,000 rigsdalers as security that Kidd had acquired the goods by legal means. Those goods already within the Brandenburger warehouse were allowed to remain there until the Germans sent them away in one of their ships, the 'Seven Provinces.'

Meanwhile, the English had heard of Burke's doings, and in October, 1699 an English squadron arrived here under the command of Rear-Admiral Benbow who demanded both Burke and the 5,000 rigsdalers deposit. Having dealt with Burke in the courts already and considering that he was sufficiently punished, and learning that Benbow was exceeding his orders, Lorentz refused the English Admiral's request and later allowed Burke to escape to the French part of St. Christopher. It was undoubtedly this uncooperative reception by the Danes which led Benbow to term St. Thomas 'a receptacle for thieves' a rather old charge by this time, and less justified.[12]

Lorentz's instructions as governor had expressly prohibited him from dealing with pirates and his adherence to these instructions was well illustrated by the Bartholomew Sharp and Captain Kidd affairs, though not exclusively so. The incident involving 'Tempest' Rogers, another English pirate, is a case in point.

Rogers had operated in the Indian Ocean where he had known Captain Kidd before coming to St. Thomas in July, 1699. He had a cargo of African slaves and East Indian goods which, he claimed, Kidd had forced upon him in payment for other goods. He sought permission to repair his ship in the harbor, and this request was granted; but when he started to sell some of the goods here, Lorentz intervened, and Rogers was forced to leave the islands. Later on, when he had sold his ship and cargo elsewhere, he returned to the island, and expressing his desire to settle permanently was allowed to remain. He was permitted to engage in inter-island trade and was even employed by the Danish West India Company as Surveyor of Customs.[13]

BLACKBEARD

St. Thomas had need of men who were willing to contribute to its development: those who were not so disposed were not welcome. The unfavorable reception of freebooters was demonstrated in April, 1700 when Lorentz meted out exemplary punishment to four pirates who had come into St. Thomas, by confiscating their goods to the value of 2,600 rigsdalers. He left five others to be dealt with by the directors of the Danish West India Company as they thought fit. Under such conditions, it is to be expected that pirates would stay clear of St. Thomas.

Pirates either did not come to St. Thomas after 1700, or else they preferred to enter as smugglers. The outbreak of the War of the Spanish Succession in 1702 enabled pirates to operate under the guise of privateers, and by its end in 1713, piracy was virtually at an end. In the Virgin Islands, the war-period clinched the establishment of plantation agriculture and the emergence of a class of capitalist planters who apparently were not prepared to traffic with pirates and thus prejudice their reputation as 'law-abiding' colonists.

Conclusion

Stories of pirates in the Virgin Islands after 1713 fall into the category of fables associated with the names 'Blue Beard' and 'Black Beard' and connected with two so-called 'castles' in St. Thomas. These 'castles' were actual buildings which still exist on Smitberg and Government House Hill, though they were in reality two fortified watchtowers designed to give warning of the approach of enemy craft, and to give support to Fort Christian in defending St. Thomas. It would appear that the pirate 'Blue Beard' was pure fancy and never existed, but 'Black Beard' was the pirate Captain Edward Teach, 'a swaggering merciless brute' supposedly a native of Bristol in England.

Teach came to prominence as a pirate during the War of the Spanish Succession but it was not until 1716 that he secured an independent command. Thereafter until his death in 1718, he was a scourge of unwary ships in the Caribbean. That he visited St. Thomas at all is based on conjecture rather than on documentary evidence. The stories told of him are lurid but attractive, even though they had no bearing on the history of the Virgin Islands. [14]

Inasmuch as the exploits of the pirates make interesting reading, their contribution to the development of the Virgin Islands cannot be said to have been either substantial or real. The period of their greatest ascendancy under the Esmits also coincided with the critical period in the history of St. Thomas. For the relatively short period that it lasted, piracy had the effect of keeping out prospective settlers and of distracting the attention of those already settled here, from the job of production. Under Heins, and more decidedly under Lorentz, piracy was frowned upon as a hindrance to the prosperity of St. Thomas. Once the island was relieved of the stigma as a pirate haven which had drawn upon it the ire of English colonial governors, it could forge ahead, with less restraint, to become a worthwhile colonial possession.

[1] Waldemar Westergaard, *The Danish West Indies Under Company Rule* (1671-1754). (New York, The Macmillan Company, 1917) pp. 48-49.

[2] Isidore Paiewonsky, Account of the burning of a pirate ship La Trompeuse in the Harbour of St. Thomas, July 21, 1683. (1961). Foreword.

[3] Ibid., Letter from Lynch to Blathwayt, February 22, 1683.

[4] Ibid., Letter from Esmit to May, July 2, 1683.

[5] Ibid., Extract of letters and documents from Andreas Brock to Albert Gyldensparre and other Directors, West India-Guinea Co., Copenhagen, 1683-1684.

[6] Ibid., Letter from Stapleton to Esmit, August 15, 1683.

[7] Ibid., Stapleton to the Lords of Trade and Plantations, January 13, 1684.

[8] J. O. Bro-Jorgensen, *Dansk Vestindien Indtil 1755: Kolonisation og Kompagnistyre.* (Fremad, Denmark, 1966) pp. 156-157.

[9] J. Franklin Jameson, *Privateering and Piracy in the Colonial Period. Illustrative Documents.* (New York, August M. Kelly, 1970) pp. 253-257.

[10] Quoted in Dunbar Maury Hinricks, *The Fateful Voyage of Captain Kidd.* (Bookman Associates, Inc., 1955) pp. 114-115.

[11] Dunbar Maury Hinricks, 'Captain Kid and the St. Thomas Incident.' (*New York History,* July, 1956).

[12] Calendar of State Papers, Colonial Series, America and the West Indies 1699. No. 907. Benbow to Vernon, October 28, 1699.

[13] Bro-Jorgensen, op. cit., p. 160; Jameson, op. cit., p. 257.

[14] W. G. Palgrave, 'St. Thomas.' (*Littell's Living Age,* Vol. CXXII, July, August, September, 1874) pp. 609-619; Hugh F. Rankin, *The Golden Age of Piracy.* (Published by Colonial Williamsburg, Williamsburg, Va., New York, Holt, Rinehart and Winston Inc., 1969) pp. 105-129; Captain Charles Johnson, *A General History of the Robberies and Murders of the Most Notorious Pyrates . . . etc. 1717 to the Present Year 1724.* (London, 1724) pp. 45-66.

Chapter 8

The Danish West Indian Slave Trade

The practice of using Africans as slaves in the West Indies began when the native Indians were unable to perform the labor Spaniards required of them in the mines and on plantations and ranches. The first slaves were brought from Spain, but as the demand for them increased, they were brought directly from Africa. In time, a regular traffic in slaves developed in which all the maritime European nations participated either legitimately or illegitimately. Slave cargoes were traded for such tropical produce as tobacco, sugar, cotton, spices, dyes and dyewoods, or for coin, bullion, and bills of exchange.

When non-Hispanic Europeans began to colonize the West Indies, they soon followed the Spanish example of using African slaves when they could not get enough Europeans to perform plantation labor. The introduction of the sugarcane in the 1640's gave impetus to the trade in human chattels from Africa, since its cultivation for sugar production made a large, relatively cheap and stable labor force essential. By the time the Virgin Islands were settled in 1672, sugarcane cultivation by slaves was fairly well established in the British and French colonies and that example was followed by the Danish colonists.

African slaves replaced European indentured workers quite early in the plantation history of the Danish colonies because of the poor quality of the indentured laborers brought out by Governor Iversen from Denmark. The ravages of disease, and the lack of suitable replacements made it expedient to secure Africans who were physically capable of plantation labor under West Indian climatic conditions. Participation in the slave trade offered a possible solution to the labor problem faced by the Danish West India Company; without slaves, plantation agriculture could not have been developed in the Virgin Islands. Indeed, the rise of a class of small and medium sized capitalist planters in the Virgin Islands as elsewhere in the West Indies was made possible only through the labor of slaves.

The Origin of the Danish Slave Trade

Danish involvement in trade with Africa antedated the formation of the Danish West India Company and the colonization of St. Thomas.[1] It is almost certain that Danish sailors were engaged on Dutch ships trading along the West Coast of Africa from around the end of the sixteenth century. The first plan for a Danish government-sponsored trading venture was made in 1624 by William Usselinx who had organized the Dutch West India Company three years earlier. His attempt was frustrated by opposition from Danish merchants in Copenhagen who, under the leadership of Johan de Willum, were successful in securing royal letters patent granting them permission to form a Company. This project proved abortive as did the king's authorization to Johan and Godert Braem and others in May, 1636 to found a Guinea and Africa Company. The overriding cause for this second failure was financial depression in Denmark.

Meanwhile, trade had commenced between Sweden and Africa under the leadership of Louis de Geer, and in December, 1649, the Swedish Asiatic and American Trading Company received its Charter. The Danes could not ignore the challenge from their traditional enemy and in 1649 they sent a ship to Guinea. It returned safely and unofficial trade was continued from 1650, while the city of Gluckstadt was granted privileges to engage in the African trade in 1651. Copenhagen merchants also became active, and in 1654 an expedition to Africa was organized by Jens Lassen, Secretary to the Danish Exchequer. It proved highly successful, the ship dispatched returning with a rich cargo of sugar, ivory, palm-oil, and a quantity of gold.

Permanent Danish contact with the African continent stemmed indirectly from these ventures which created a desire for a more fixed base. The war between Denmark and Sweden from 1657 to 1660 put an end to the trading enterprises to Africa; but under a privateer's commission, Hendrik Carlof succeeded in capturing the Swedish African fort of Carlsborg and the stations at Takoradi, Anamabo, Gemoree, and Accra. These captures marked the beginning of the Danish dominions in Guinea.

Above: FORT CHRISTIANSBORG
Below: FORT FREDENSBORG

Above: THE SLAVE TRADE AREA
Below: A SLAVE RAID

With the assistance of the Dutch and native Africans, the Danes were able for a while to prevent the Swedes from reconquering the fort and stations. Nevertheless, with the help of the King of Fetu, the Swedes were able to recover Carlsborg in 1659. Despite this assistance, the Fetu were anxious to stimulate competition among European nations engaged in the slave trade. Consequently, they 'sold and transferred' Frederiksberg to the Danes and on this hill, the Danes constructed their first fort in Africa.[2] Then in August, 1661 Jost Cramer, a Danish merchant bought a piece of land from King Kankoy of Great Accra, and there a second fort called Fort Christiansborg was built. It was within cannon shot of the Dutch fort of Crevecoeur and the English Fort James, both to the west.[3]

The Danish West India Company takes over the Slave Trade

The Guinea trade was at first controlled by the Gluckstadt Company which seemed to have traded directly only between Guinea and Portuguese Sao Thomé, an island off the West African coast, and presumably never carried out any large-scale slave-shipments. However, the Gluckstadt Company was on the verge of ruin by 1669; though its charter was renewed in 1671 on the accession of Christian V, the Company was incapable of continuing the Guinea trade. The king's forts, therefore, were in danger of falling into foreign hands, and to prevent this a royal patent was issued on December 10, 1672, for the foundation of a Guinea Company in Copenhagen. When there were no applicants, the king advised the Danish West India Company to take over the Guinea trade, especially since there was now need to provide slave labor for the newly-founded colony of St. Thomas. From a business point of view, it seemed most advantageous to adopt the triangular trade route by which ships with Danish merchandise would be sent to Guinea where they would purchase slaves for the plantations, and at St. Thomas, West Indian produce would be collected and taken back to Denmark. After some hesitation, the Danish West India Company assumed control of the Guinea trade in November, 1674, when a royal charter was issued.[4]

In granting the Company a monopoly over the slave trade, the king accorded to it a position which was beyond its capability to maintain. The Company lacked the finances necessary to provide the vessels and to maintain the forts in Africa, and several years sometimes passed without a single Company vessel sailing for Guinea. The Company's property deteriorated, Fort Frederiksberg beyond the point of reclamation. Consequently, it was allowed to pass into English hands in 1685, and the Danish slave trade was confined to Fort Christiansborg. It was not until more than fifty years later that the Danes acquired another fort and established lodges or trading stations on the Guinea coast.

From the very beginning the Company relaxed its monopoly over the slave trade and, as in the case of the West Indian trade, concessions to private slave traders were given almost to the end of the Company's existence. Shareholders were allowed in May, 1675 to trade with St. Thomas if they paid a 'recognition' or duty of 10 percent of the value of the outgoing cargo. During the war between Denmark and Sweden, from 1675 to 1697, no Company's vessel went to Guinea, and the Guinea trade was left to private enterprise. The king promised in March, 1680 to send a ship to Guinea at his own expense, to carry soldiers to the fort and slaves to the West Indies. However, this promise was fruitless, and in January, 1682, the Company made an agreement with some citizens of Gluckstadt allowing them to trade with Guinea in return for the transportation of a little capital, merchandise, and garrisons for the forts.

Shortly afterwards, the king granted the Company the right to allow outside participation in the Guinea trade in return for the payment of a 'recognition.' He also promised to contribute 1,500 rigsdalers annually for the upkeep of the forts in Guinea, again with no good result. Accordingly, in 1684, the Company was forced to make an agreement with Oliger Pauli, its book-keeper, permitting him to trade without paying a 'recognition', and in March of the following year, a group of Portuguese Jews in Holland were allowed to trade with Guinea.

Upkeep of the forts was left to private enterprise with the result that the Danes lost Fort Frederiksberg in 1685, since private traders were not interested in spending money to maintain such establishments. During the same year, the Brandenburgers were allowed to establish a trading station or factory in St. Thomas where they could dispose of their African slaves obtained through their Fort Gross Friedrichsburg near Cape Three Points. Then in July, 1689 the privileges of the African trade were transferred to Nikolaj Jansen Arf, one of the most important shipowners of Copenhagen.[5]

After a promising beginning, Arf's business failed; the Guinea trade was dominated by English and Dutch interlopers and after 1693 Arf did not send out any ships. As a factor in the slave trade to the Virgin

Islands, the Arf episode seems to have been negligible. This state of affairs was unsatisfactory to the Danish West India Company and to the Danish Government: the Danish interests in Africa were worth preserving and the demands of the St. Thomas planters for slaves needed to be satisfied. From his observations of the Brandenburger slave trade and the profits they made, Governor Lorentz reported in 1696 that 'all other trade is as nothing compared with this slave trade.'[6] To the directors of the Danish West India Company searching for a profit-yielding enterprise, this seemed to be the answer. Next year, the Guinea slave trade was resumed and thereafter pursued with a greater degree of earnestness.

The Slave Trade in the Eighteenth Century

Misfortune plagued the Company at a time when it was implementing a policy of trade expansion. Three of its largest ships were lost in the course of a few years: the 'Cron Printzen' in 1705, followed by the 'Christianus Quintus' and the 'Fridericus Quartus' in 1710. The Company lost no fewer than eight ships between 1697 and 1733 and its slave trade naturally suffered. The number of sailings from Africa were far too few and irregular to meet the demand for slaves in the expanding Danish West Indies. The need for large supplies of slaves became particularly urgent after the settlement of St. Croix in 1734, and to meet this contingency, the Company was forced to relax its monopoly. Permission was given on April 25, 1735 for all Danish subjects to engage in the slave trade between Guinea and the Virgin Islands in return for a fee of one rigsdaler for every ton burden of the participating vessels.

Although the Company lost its slaving monopoly, its sphere of influence in Africa was extended: a lodge or station was established on the island of Ada in 1731; and, through the efforts of Commanders Waeroe and Schiellerup, land was procured in Ningo territory and Fort Fredensborg was constructed in 1736. The fort was located about 75 kilometers east of Fort Christiansborg, that is, near enough for the two forts to give each other mutual support in time of need, and yet far enough from the Dutch and English forts not to suffer from competition. Unlike Fort Christiansborg, its locality offered fine landing facilities and good trade.

In response to an application from the colonists in St. Thomas for annual sailings of 'slave-haulers,' the Company became more active after 1744. Nevertheless, it was forced to grant certain concessions to private traders with regard to trade with the Virgin Islands in order that they might transport slaves here.

When the Danish Crown took over the assets of the Danish West India Company in 1754, it acquired control over the slave trade also. However, it showed even less activity than the Company, and several of the Company's ships were sold or given away. By a mandate of August 30, 1754, confirmed by a decree of April 22, 1755, the privileges previously held by the Company were abolished and trade was thrown open to all Danish subjects. Later, in March, 1765 the control of the Danish African forts, with wide trading privileges, was given to the Royal Chartered Danish Guinea Trading Company better known as the Bargum's Trading Society. This Company became bankrupt in 1775 and it was succeeded by the Royal Danish Baltic-Guinea Trading Company in 1782.[7]

Irrespective of which Company was in control, Danish slave-ships were very irregular in their arrival at the African forts to collect slaves. Consequently stocks were sold to foreign purchasers when there were numerous slaves on hand.[8] The first decades brought many Portuguese interlopers to Fort Christiansborg; later the Dutch came, and then the French, while English interlopers flourished during the second half of the eighteenth century. Of the total number of slaves brought to the West Indies and America, only a tiny fraction was brought in by Danish vessels. Even when there were as many as three or four Danish vessels engaged in the Danish slave trade, the English and Dutch would have several hundred.

The Danish slave trade was concentrated around Fort Christiansborg prior to 1736, after which it was expanded to include smaller Fort Fredensborg also. In addition, some slave-trading was conducted at outlying lodges or stations, under the charge of factors: Ada was acquired in 1731, Keta in 1744, Way in 1757, Popo in 1772, and Aflahu in 1784. The foundation stones of two new forts, Fort Kongensten and Fort Prinsenten, were laid in October, 1783 and June, 1784 respectively; when completed these forts replaced the former lodges at Ada and Keta.

Generally speaking, the forts rarely provided full cargoes for the Danish vessels calling there, either because their visits were inopportune, or because factors preferred to deal with foreigners to their own financial advantage. As such, cargoes had to be supplemented at other places along the African coast and the Company issued orders to this effect in November, 1731. This procedure was considered preferable to waiting at the forts, since to do so meant loss of time, money and the lives of sailors. Considering the speed of collection and transhipment, the Company's policy seemed to have been justified. At the same time that slave-cargoes were procured, supplies of water and food, especially millet for the slaves, were collected.

The Recruitment of Slaves

Slave cargoes were obtained in a variety of ways by the Danish factors operating on the West African coast. Continual wars among African tribes, which were either provoked deliberately or were the genuine outcome of tribal differences, provided a steady flow of prisoners of war. Besides, some tribes carried out large-scale robberies of human beings from conquered or simply weaker neighboring tribes. Moreover, some Africans became slaves because they were unable to pay their debts. On several occasions, Africans were brought in singly or in very small groups to pay for purchases of European merchandise bought at the fort or lodge. In return for tribute paid in European goods, some chiefs bound themselves to provide the fort or lodge with Africans. When they could not meet their contract by war or theft, they would sell some of their numerous wives and male slaves to the European traders in the knowledge that replacements would be forthcoming.[9]

Slave supplies were always difficult to predict since normally it was not possible to place orders with native chiefs or slave traders for specified numbers of slaves. One important consideration which governed the recruitment of slaves was their tribal origin. The Accra slaves were regarded as the best workers because of their endurance, but they were regarded as the most difficult to subdue, while the El Mina slaves were noted for their spirit of resistance when enslaved. However, when slaves were difficult to obtain, dealers were prepared to accept those from any tribe who came their way. Africans who were young, industrious and peaceable were preferred to those who were old, lazy and given to violence. Slaves were drawn for all stations of life in Africa including rich and poor, skilled and unskilled, literate and illiterate, free and unfree.

Because of uncertain supplies, it was often necessary to accept

Africans how and when they were brought in, even if it were singly and at dead of night. These were stocked until they could be sold; usually Africans were kept in special rooms in the forts which, however, were too small to hold as large a number as a whole ship-load. The excess were therefore housed in the foreworks outside the forts or in the native villages attached to them.

Each fort was under the control of a Commandant but the military support was weak. Fort Fredensborg, for instance, was manned by only three or four soldiers. Consequently, male slaves were frequently retained in irons from fear of revolt or to prevent them from running away. Usually rings of iron were placed around their necks and ankles with an inter-connecting chain, and often they were fettered to heavy blocks of wood or iron which hindered free movement. Such precautionary measures were taken since the Africans desired freedom to escape their uncertain future. Thus, in August, 1727, some captives fell upon their overseer, himself an African, killed him and escaped; half of them were subsequently caught and the ringleader was broken on the wheel and then beheaded. Another mutiny broke out in August, 1738 costing the life of one soldier, but it was quickly suppressed.[10]

Runaways rarely achieved freedom unless they lived in the neighborhood because the Europeans had the active support of natives who stood to gain from the success of the slave trade. Chiefs usually received monthly tributes from the fort, or were compensated on a per capita basis, to return runaways. Because of the lack of adequate storage space, the risks of escape and mutiny, and the high feeding costs especially during times of food shortage, the Africans were disposed of as quickly as possible, even if it meant dealing with interlopers.

Danish factors at the forts and lodges became shrewd appraisers of the Africans brought in by native traders themselves adept at concealing the flaws of their victims resulting from age, sickness, or injury. If there was a doctor at the fort the medical condition of the Africans would be examined thoroughly. Factors were most interested in vigorous and ablebodied men and women who could later be sold at the highest prices. Women fetched lower prices than men since their capacity for strenuous physical labor was assumed to be lower than that of the men; boys and girls were bought at even lower prices than the women. Ablebodied men in the prime age range were used as the basic standard in computing prices; women, boys and girls were valued at such fractions of the standard price as three-fourths, two-thirds, and one-half.[11] Payment was made in European goods and not cash.

Slave prices in Africa rose and fell depending on such conditions as the number of European ships and cargoes destined for West Africa, the supply of slaves on the coast, the availability and price of provisions and, indirectly, the price of slave-grown produce in the West Indian plantations. African chiefs conspired to have several European nations establish forts in their territory in order to have a competitive advantage.

Some indication can be given of slave prices on the West African coast, though the quotations can be nothing but rough estimates. Around 1700 male slaves cost about 32 rigsdalers each, and women about 28-32 rigsdalers each; by 1705 prices for men had risen to an average of 40-48 rigsdalers. Thereafter, slave value rose even higher, and by 1714 men fetched 64 rigsdalers each and women 40 rigsdalers each. Some slave captains were sometimes prepared to pay more in order to be able to get away quickly to the West Indies to take advantage of favorable markets, and in 1720 English interlopers paid as much as 100-120 rigsdalers each for men and 80 rigsdalers each for women.[12] Even after 1720, however, men more regularly cost 88-96 rigsdalers each and women 64-72 rigsdalers each; but between 1744 and 1754 the usual prices were 112 rigsdalers each for men and 80 rigsdalers each for women. Largely because of the expansion of sugar cultivation in the West Indies, prices of Africans increased after 1754, and in the 1770's first class male slaves were bought at Fort Christiansborg for 128-144 rigsdalers each and females for 96-112 rigsdalers each.[13]

The Journey across the Atlantic

After sale, slaves were taken on board ship by the captain. Whenever ships were unable to berth along-side the shore, loading was effected by means of smaller boats or canoes. On such occasions, much care was taken to prevent them from capsizing, otherwise the slaves might be lost.

Slave-ships were frequently overcrowded for in addition to the regular cargo, captains and crews often took private slaves to be sold in the West Indies for their own gain. To prevent overcrowding, in 1747 captains and officers were forbidden, under severe penalty, to take slaves on board on their own account. This regulation did not have the desired effect since it was modified by another measure providing a progressive bounty ranging from seven to twenty rigsdalers for each slave above 300, to encourage large slave cargoes. Slaves were kept in the holds for most of the time with the men usually in chains, and they were packed as closely as possible, lying side by side. If the weather was fine, groups of them were brought daily on deck to ease them from their cramping position, but in foul weather, they had to remain below.[14]

Another dominant characteristic of slave ships was their poor sanitary condition. Since ventilation in the holds was bad, the stench was unbearable, and slaves died of suffocation. Both contagious and infectious diseases such as itch, ringworm, smallpox and dysentery were common in the insanitary environment while the possibilities of epidemic outbreaks were great. Each ship had one or two doctors but sometimes there was little they could do to prevent or cure diseases.

The treatment of slaves naturally differed from ship to ship depending on the temperament of the ships' captains and crews. All things considered, it can hardly be expected that slaves were always sufficiently or adequately fed. The main item of diet was millet, to which pork, beans and barley gruel were added. Since the trans-Atlantic crossing at best took several weeks, fresh fruits were a rarity if given to the slaves at all, and water was more often stale than not. In order to keep up the spirits of the slaves, tobacco and alcohol were sometimes given to them. Evidence indicates that some captains even arranged for music and gave their slaves the opportunity to dance in small groups on the main deck, but it is not known to what extent they indulged in this practice.[15]

Slaves who embarked on the long journey or 'Middle Passage' across the Atlantic to the West Indies, seldom knew where they were going or what was in store for them. Most, if not all, had never been to sea before; fear of the unknown led to depression and despondency which aroused their worst apprehensions. They imagined all kinds of horrors, and it was natural that they should seek to escape an uncertain fate. Suicide was one way out: some threw themselves overboard, while others wounded themselves mortally with such weapons as they could put their hands on. Occasionally they mutinied, encouraged by their large numbers, usually in the hundreds, compared with the relatively small crews on the slave ships of from 25 to 50 men.

Since slaves were not trained sailors their mutinies often took place near the shore which contributed to their failure. If a mutiny was discovered in time, it could be put down easily by the crew who had arms at their disposal. In such cases it was only a question of not killing too many slaves and thereby making the voyage unprofitable. If slaves were able to arm themselves, the situation became more critical since crew members were then forced to act ruthlessly to save their own lives.

Existing records show few mutinies on board Danish slave ships; the most consequential of these was that on board the 'Patientia' on August 5, 1753 when three slaves broke loose, killed three of the sailors and wounded the captain, Ole Eriksen, and forced the rest of the crew to evacuate the vessel. With the assistance of English sailors aboard the 'Triton' the Danes recovered the 'Patientia,' but nevertheless suffered losses estimated at 20,000 rigsdalers.[16]

While it can hardly be said that slaves were humanely treated, it is probable that excessive ill-treatment was not deliberately practiced or allowed to become habitual if slaves were to retain their value as merchandise. It was to everyone's advantage that as many slaves as possible should reach the West Indies safely. If slaves died or were severely injured, it meant a loss of investment or profit. Nevertheless, it was impossible to prevent deaths whether these were caused by disease, ill-treatment, suicide or mutiny. Death tolls were sometimes very large, the average estimated loss from a normal slave cargo being between 20 and 25 percent.

Estimated loss does not take into consideration instances in which whole slave cargoes perished when ships foundered, such as happened to the 'Cron-Printzen' in 1706 with its huge cargo of 820 slaves. Again, of a cargo of 506 slaves which left Fort Christiansborg on a Danish West India Company's vessel in 1697, only 259 reached St. Thomas. On a third occasion, 242 slaves out of an original cargo of 443 on board the 'Laarburg Galley' were lost in 1734, which was partly responsible for the Company abandoning its monopoly of the slave trade in April, 1735. Lastly, out of a cargo of 334 slaves on board the 'Jaegersborg' sailing in 1748, 174 died constituting a loss of over 52 percent. During the period, 1698 to 1754, over 10,000 slaves were taken from West Africa in the Company's vessels, but no more than 7,500 or about 75 percent were landed in the Virgin Islands — the rest had perished in the crossing.[17]

Slave mortality on the Middle Passage after 1754 showed no improvement if annual variations alone are considered. As evidenced by the case of the 'Ada' in 1774, 121 out of a cargo of 221 slaves reached the Virgin Islands; besides, substantial numbers of those landed alive were so debilitated that they died within a few days time. Another ship, the 'Acra' which sailed in 1782, suffered a loss of 257 out of a cargo of

592 slaves, or 43.4 percent. However, the range, or average over a period of several years, was apparently lower, even though statistics are not very encouraging. For example, a recorded total of 6,513 slaves on seventeen ships were taken to the Virgin Islands between 1778 and 1787 of which 441 belonged to two vessels 'Count Schimmelmann' and 'Count Bernstorff' whose statistics are incomplete since they do not show deaths. In all, 1,056 deaths are recorded, giving an average loss of 17.31 percent for the ships with complete statistics.[18]

On arrival in the Virgin Islands, the slaves were sold on board ship if the demand for slaves was pressing, or else they were sold on shore. Whenever possible, slaves were rested and fed for a few days before being sold in order to improve their physical appearance. In the meantime, their arrival was announced either orally, by handbills or posters, or by advertisements in the *Royal Danish American Gazette* after that newspaper began publication in 1770.

The method of sale varied depending on the place of sale. If slaves were sold on deck, the snatch system was adopted, that is, prospective buyers were allowed to pounce upon a cargo of slaves and separate those they intended to buy from the main group by way of establishing a right of prior purchase. If slaves were disposed of on shore, sale was achieved by auction, and slaves were sold in small lots until they had all been purchased.[19] Payment for slaves was received in the form of cash, sugar, or cotton.

Conditions governing the price offered for individual slaves in the Virgin Islands were very much the same as at the West African slave fort, namely, the sex, age, health, and tribal origin of the slaves, though the demand of the estates for labor was always an over-riding factor. The price at which slaves were sold was naturally higher than the price at which they had been bought, and as a result dealers were able to obtain substantial profits. Generally, the selling price ranged between 25 percent and 100 percent above the buying price. Indeed, the cargo of 259 slaves landed from the Danish West India Company's 1697 expedition, was sold at 85 rigsdalers each, or three times their price on the African coast, so that the venture proved highly profitable despite the loss of 247 others. Similar high profits were obtained in 1752 when slaves bought for 100 rigsdalers were sold for as much as 353 and 354 rigsdalers. The profits on one voyage in 1724, which landed 351 slaves amounted to 28 percent, two others the following year realized 29 percent profit, while another cargo of 140 slaves in 1754 resulted in a profit of 50 percent.[20]

The selling price of slaves continued to be high after 1754. Three voyages of the 'Cron-Printzens Onske' in 1756, 1761 and 1764 landed a total of 768 slaves in the Virgin Islands, who were sold for 152,082 rigsdalers or an average of 198 rigsdalers each. Again, between 1778 and 1787, a total number of 5,116 slaves were landed and sold in St. Croix for 1,090,135 rigsdalers, or an average of 211 rigsdalers each.[21] Considering the price at which slaves were being bought in West Africa at the time, the profits were undoubtedly large.

Planters seldom purchased several slaves of the same tribe, preferring instead to have slaves of different tribes and languages so as to avoid concerted resistance on the plantations. Once bought the slaves were branded with the initials of the owner, or otherwise marked, to ensure identification. They were given clothing and taken to the plantation where they were placed under the supervision of experienced slaves who introduced them to the working arrangements of the plantation. This process of being broken into the routine of plantation life was known as 'seasoning' or apprenticeship.

The Abolition of the Slave Trade

The stimulus for the abolition of the Danish slave trade came from England rather than from within Denmark itself. From the seventeenth century there was a growing aversion to slavery in that country where it was denounced by religious groups such as the Quakers and Methodists, political and economic theorists such as John Locke and Adam Smith, and writers such as Daniel Defoe and Dr. Samuel Johnson. As a result of the efforts of Granville Sharp, slavery was outlawed in England in 1772, and British humanitarians organized themselves in the *Society for Effecting the Abolition of the Slave Trade* in 1787. Two years later a Royal Commission was appointed to study and report on the conditions of the slave trade and slavery.[22]

British agitation was one of the factors which moved the Danes to action though there were humanitarians in Denmark who were stirred by the brutality and evils of the slave trade.[23] It was not only the suffering and death of slaves which caught their attention; the death of Danish sailors engaged in the trade was for them also very important. Investigation showed, for instance, that out of 2,004 sailors engaged on Danish slave ships between 1777 and 1789 as many as 691, or 34 percent had lost their lives.[24] Besides, the slave trade was a costly undertaking, and it was even suggested that it might be cheaper for the planters to purchase slaves from British and Dutch traders.

The Danish Government had never shown much interest in pursuing and conducting the trade itself. Rather, it had preferred to hand over this business to some other organization, such as the Bargum's Trading Society and the Baltic-Guinea Trading Company. Even so, the Government was financially involved, and after 1787 subsidies amounting to 30,000 rigsdalers annually were given to the Baltic-Guinea Trading Company to enable it to build and maintain the African forts. The unwillingness of the Danish Government to continue spending money to maintain the trade was an important reason for its abolition.

The emancipation of serfs in Denmark in the 1780's and other progressive reforms motivated by Enlightenment principles, provided an impetus for the abolition of the slave trade. By the end of that decade also Danes were considering the possibility of establishing plantations in Africa itself.[25] It became necessary, therefore, to retain there whatever labor was available rather than to transfer it to the West Indies. In any case, apart from St. Croix which was still actually and potentially a highly productive island, the Virgin Islands did not show much need for slaves. Moreover, urgent reform was considered necessary to avoid a repetition of the Saint-Domingue slave rebellion of 1791 which took a heavy toll of European lives.

The abolition of the Danish slave trade was to a large extent due to the efforts of Ernst Schimmelmann who was one of the directors of the Baltic-Guinea Trading Company. He set up a committee in 1786 to look into the Guinea trade, and its report of June 4, 1787 showed that the Danish slave trade was not supporting itself. In another proposal of 1791, Schimmelmann suggested a Commission to investigate the slave trade, though he believed that before the trade was abolished, planters should be allowed ample time to secure the number of slaves they would require. After abolition, with good treatment of slaves, their numbers could be maintained by natural increase.

At Schimmelmann's suggestion, and because there was wide-spread feeling that something should be done, a Commission was appointed later in 1791 to make a complete study of the slave trade from a wide range of Danish and British evidence. In its report, the Commission considered the slave trade morally wrong, and from a national point of view not very profitable since the cost of the trade on the African coast had usually been borne by the government.[26]

The report of the Commission and the recommendation of the West

Indian and Guinea General Finance and Customs Office which had control over colonial affairs, led to the abolition of the slave trade. By a Royal Resolution of March 16, 1792, the Danish slave trade was to come to an end ten years later on December 31, 1802, in order to give planters adequate time to procure the number of slaves they needed.[27]

Under the terms of the Resolution, all nations were to be allowed to import slaves into the Virgin Islands during the ten-year period of grace. In order to assist importers to take advantage of this concession, for every mature slave imported, they were allowed to take 2,000 pounds of sugar to whatever port they desired. Since female slaves were in great demand, and would be of great importance for slave reproduction, they were allowed to be imported duty free. Also to encourage the importation of females, the poll-tax on female field slaves was to be replaced after 1795 by a double poll-tax on all males slaves. The re-exportation of slaves was strictly prohibited, except when they were ordered by a court of law to be sold off the islands. This regulation was intended to prevent foreign sales and thus help to build up the desired slave population.

Denmark was the first European nation with West Indian colonies to abolish the slave trade, and it carried the scheme of abolition a step further. It offered loans at five percent interest to planters who needed to purchase slaves to maintain staple production, and 1,042,116 rigsdalers were appropriated for this purpose. Loan recipients were required to maintain their slaves properly; should a slave die or be sold, the unpaid debt on that slave had to be cleared before any further loan was given. By mid-October 1793 requests for loans numbered 790, and by 1799 loans for 5,302 slaves had been granted. About half as many slaves again were imported without government backing.[28]

Applications for financial assistance apparently stopped after 1799, and on July 1, 1802, a group of slave owners on St. Croix petitioned the king for a three year extension of the dead-line from January 1, 1803. Their argument that an epidemic in 1799 and a bad year in 1800 had made it impossible for them to make the necessary purchases of slaves was not convincing, and their request was denied.

Though officially it came to an end, the slave trade did not cease from January 1, 1803, since a small number of vessels was given permission to exceed the time limit. Some captains even sailed without having such authorization, and one of them was fined for illegally importing slaves into St. Croix. Illegal traders were encouraged by the commandants of the Guinea forts, who reputedly claimed that the natives were willing to tolerate them there only because of the slave trade. They feared that compliance with the Resolution would lead to loss of native respect and possible expulsion from the coast. Slave trading at the forts continued and as late as 1821, Africans maintained that its abolition had never been announced to them. It was only in the 1820's that a real effort was made to put an end to the slave trade in Guinea.[29]

Conclusion

The Danish West India slave trade was begun in response to the need for labor in the West Indies; but the colonists were interested in it not only to supply laborers for the local plantations but also in order to strengthen their inter-colonial trade through re-exportation. Neither were they content to depend upon the legal channels of trade to obtain the number of slaves required. Because of this consideration it is safe to assume that recorded statistics indicate only a part of the number of slaves imported into the Virgin Islands.

From his examination of statistics of slaves imported into the Virgin Islands, Professor Curtin considered one estimate of 75,000 slaves imported in the course of the trade, given by Noel Deerr in his book, *The History of Sugar* to be too high. Alternatively, he gave more credence to statistics provided by Waldemar Westergaard showing retained imports of 16,899 during the period 1687-1754, or an annual average of 248 slaves. He qualified the statement, however, by admitting that 'the Danish slave trade was much larger than this but most of it went to foreign colonies'. Commenting on the extent of the slave trade after 1754 he stated, 'It may not be unreasonable simply to extend Westergaard's annual average to the remaining years of the century, giving a further sum of 11,160 for 1755-1799, and a total estimate for the whole period of the slave trade in the neighborhood of 28,000'.[30] On the basis of computations made by Curtin, this number represented 0.3 percent of all slaves brought to the New World in the history of the slave trade.

The end of the slave trade, decreed in 1792 and effected in 1803, was due largely to economic factors, the principal one being the cost to the Danish government of maintaining the establishments on the Guinea coast. Despite the profits being made by dealers, the trade did not repay the expenses incurred by the Danish Exchequer in the form of substantial subsidies. Danish disillusionment with their colonial enterprise began with their disenchantment with the slave trade. As yet, however, the growing prosperity of the entrepot trade in St. Thomas, and the flourishing state of agriculture in St. Croix, made the islands worth keeping. When, at first, agriculture and then trade, began to fail, the Danes sought to get rid of the islands, as they had got rid of the slave trade.

[1] Georg Norregard, *Danish Settlements in West Africa 1658-1850.* (Boston University Press, 1966) pp. 7-20 and 29-46.
[2] John Barbot, Description of the Coast of North and South Guinea. In A. & J. Churchill, *A Collection of Voyages and Travels.* (London, 1732) Vol. V, p. 172.
[3] Ibid., pp. 182-183; William W. Claridge, *A History of the Gold Coast and Ashanti.* (London, 1935) Vol. 1, pp. 119-120.
[4] Norregard, op. cit., pp. 21-28 and 47-54.
[5] Waldemar Westergaard, *The Danish West Indies Under Company Rule* (1671-1754). (New York, The Macmillan Company, 1917) pp. 95-97; Norregard, op. cit., pp. 55-62.
[6] Lorentz to the Directors of the Danish West India Company, November 30, 1696. Quoted in Westergaard, op. cit., p. 145.
[7] Norregard, op. cit., pp. 113-130.
[8] Jean B. Labat, *Voyage du Chevalier des Marchais en Guinee isles voisines et à Cayenne fait en 1725, 1726 & 1727.* (Paris, 1730) Vol. 1, p. 312.
[9] [C. G. A. Oldendorp], *Fuldstaendigt Udtog af C. G. A. Oldendorps Missions-Historie om den evangeliske Brodres Mission paa de carabaiske Oer St. Thomas, St. Crux og St. Jan.* (Kjobenhavn, 1784), p. 179.
[10] Norregard, op. cit., p. 86.
[11] Westergaard, op. cit., pp. 149-150.
[12] Cf. Elizabeth Donnan, *Documents Illustrative of the History of the Slave Trade to America.* (Octagon Books, Inc., New York, 1965) Vol. 11, p. xvi.
[13] Norregard, op. cit., pp. 87 and 123 and 124.
[14] P. E. Isert, *Reise nach Guinea und den Carabaishen Inseln.* (Kjobenhavn, 1788) pp. 305ff.
[15] Norregard, op. cit., pp. 87-88.
[16] Georg Norregard, 'Slaveproret pa Patientia 1753.' (*Arbog for Handels og Sofartmuseet pa Kronborg,* 1950) pp. 23-44.
[17] Westergaard, op. cit., pp. 320-326.
[18] Jens Vibaek, *Dansk Vestindien 1755-1848: Vestindien Storhedstid.* (Fremad. Denmark, 1966) pp. 172-173.
[19] Westergaard, op. cit., p. 144; Cf. Orlando Patterson, *The Sociology of Slavery. An Analysis of the Origins, Development and Structure of Negro Slave Society in Jamaica.* (Fairleigh Dickinson University Press, 1969) p. 150.
[20] Donnan, op. cit., pp. xvi-xvii.
[21] Georg Norregard, *Danish Settlements in West Africa 1658-1850,* pp. 143-157;

Vibaek, op. cit., pp. 172-173.

[22] Reginald Coupland, *The British Anti-Slavery Movement.* (London, 1933).

[23] The classical accounts of the abolition of the Danish slave trade are C. C. Alberti, 'Den danske Slavehandels Historie.' (*Nyt historisk Tidsskrift,* 3B., Kjobenhavn, 1850) pp. 201-244; C. A. Trier, 'Det danske-vestindiske Negerindeforselsforbud af 1792.' (*Historisk Tidsskrift,* Series 7, Vol. 5, Kjobenhavn, 1904-1905) pp. 405-508.

[24] Norregard, op. cit., p. 152.

[25] Isert, op. cit., pp. 338-340.

[26] Dckumenter vedk. kommissioner for negerhandelens bedre indretning og ophaevelse samt efterrentninger om negerhandelen og slaveriet i Vestindien 1783-1806.

[27] Donnan, op. cit., pp. 616-617.

[28] Vibaek, op. cit., p. 184.

[29] Norregard, op. cit., pp. 183-184.

[30] Philip D. Curtin, *The Atlantic Slave Trade. A Census.* (The University of Wisconsin Press, Madison, Milwaukee and London, 1969) p. 85.

Chapter 9

The Slave Society

Like other West Indian communities which shared similar experiences of plantation agriculture, the Virgin Islands were a slave society. Slavery became a fixed and indispensable institution almost from the time of the colonization of St. Thomas when English, French and Dutch immigrants from other West Indian colonies brought slaves with them. As has already been discussed, the slave trade fed a constant stream of Africans into the Virgin Islands in response to the demands of the plantations for a continuous and dependable labor force.

Slavery dominated every aspect of life in the Virgin Islands: socially, it led to the development of classes based on degrees of color, wealth and education; politically, it led to the adoption of measures for the suppression of the inferior classes and the support of the ruling class; and economically, it led to the exploitation of slave labor in the production of colonial staples. Slaves were employed in a wide variety of occupations, but the vast majority performed manual labor under the direction of white colonials who appropriated the slave-produced wealth.

The White Community

The European population dominated every aspect of the economic, social and political life of the Virgin Islands. All of the Company and Crown officials were white men as were the planters, their managers, overseers and book-keepers. Similarly, the merchants engaged in the import and export trades, and lawyers, doctors and other professionals were of European descent. The officials, planters, merchants and professional people were the most prominent economic groups and occupied a higher social status than other white people in the Virgin Islands. Even for the lower classes of whites, however, the society offered opportunities for them to improve their economic condition, and hence, their social position.

The white population was varied in its social composition and economic condition: highest on the social ladder was the governor or governor-general, as the case might be, while below him were the senior government officials who were less wealthy and socially less prominent than the leading planters. In order to compete with the planters, officials sought to become planters themselves or, failing this, used their positions for financial reward and gain. The merchants comprised another group of colonial whites who combined plantation agriculture with their trading activities to augment their economic standing. Included among the 'lesser whites' were lower officials, petty traders, plantation overseers and book-keepers, soldiers and sailors. If ambitious or talented enough, these people could gradually work their way up in the social hierarchy of the white group, by seeking to acquire their own land and engage in planting.

Not all members of the white segment of the population were involved in the political process. The members of the Privy Council whether under the Company or the Crown, were drawn from among the colonial officials mostly recruited in Denmark with a few appointed from among qualified white colonials. Members of the common or burgher council were drawn from among the most powerful and influential planters in the islands. Laws were not passed locally but took the form of royal mandates or resolutions; nevertheless, important regulations for the better ordering of society were passed by the governor-in-council. These protected the position and privileges of the whites, at the same time that other classes were kept in various degrees of subordination. Since only whites served as judges, the legal system could be made to serve the interests of the white community as against those of the other classes. Legal privileges for the lower orders of society, when they came, stemmed largely from the benevolence of the Danish monarchy.

The social prominence of the whites in the Virgin Islands was marked not only by their control of the administrative, political and legal machinery but also in the ostentatious way they lived. Even though differences existed among them depending on their wealth, their social life differed greatly from that of the free-blacks, free-coloreds and slaves. The most prosperous among them lived in large and elegant stone mansions with chiefly European furnishings and convenient out-buildings. These 'great houses', as they were called, were conspicuously located, but while in St. Thomas and St. Croix they were not far removed from other plantation buildings, in St. John they occupied a commanding position on nearby hills.

Again depending on their wealth and importance, whites fared sumptuously on both locally produced and imported foods and drinks. In towns like Christiansted and Frederiksted, there were theaters where whites could attend plays like Shakespear's 'King Lear', 'Hamlet' and 'William III'. In Charlotte Amalie, there was an Athenaeum (or library) and Reading Room in which there was a wide selection of foreign reviews, magazines and newspapers.[1] As early as 1770 a local newspaper named the 'Royal Danish American Gazette' was started in St. Croix, and from 1844 continued as the 'St. Croix Avis'. In St. Thomas, the newspapers were the 'St. Thomas Gazette' (1812-1814) and the 'St. Thomae Tidende' which began publication in 1815. Local newspapers carried notices, advertisements, and local and foreign news; they catered to the intellectual life of the community and facilitated the expression of the local white viewpoint. Among the most popular sports was cock-fighting.[2] Internal travel was by means of horse-drawn coaches (attended by servants in livery), cabriolets and gigs.

Despite its importance, the white community was a comparatively small one, and as time passed its numbers tended to decrease both absolutely and comparatively. In 1758 the white population of St. Croix which even at that early date was the most densely peopled of the Virgin Islands, comprised 12.5 per cent of the inhabitants. It decreased even further and was eight percent in 1775 and only 6.5 percent in 1803.[3] In terms of nationality, though the islands were possessions of Denmark, the Danish population was very small, being hardly ten percent ever. Danes were chiefly officials and soldiers though the Danish origin of many of them was doubtful.[4] In St. Croix most of the foreigners were British and many were Irish, while in St. Thomas, at least for the first 75 years, the dominant group was the Dutch whose numbers, however, tended to decrease towards the end of the eighteenth century.

Almost from the beginning, the Virgin Islands had a cosmopolitan white population consisting mainly of Danes, Dutch, English and French. The various national groups lived in peace with each other with only an occasional outbreak of strife which, however, was of an individual nature. Duels were prohibited but were sometimes secretly fought in Tortola or on Vieques in order to settle personal grievances.[5]

As time passed, the differences in occupation between the white population in St. Thomas and St. Croix was reflected in differences in their residential locations. From around the second half of the eighteenth century about 75 percent of the population of agricultural St. Croix lived in the rural areas while half of the population of commercial St. Thomas was concentrated in the town of Charlotte Amalie. In both islands, however, the tendency was towards greater urbanization as more and more free people flocked to the towns in search of better employment opportunities.[6]

Free-blacks and Free-coloreds: Their Composition and Social Position

Among the white population there was a great numerical disparity between males and females due, firstly, to the fact that not many European women came out to the islands as settlers, and secondly, to the fact that many European men who came to the Virgin Islands, preferred to leave their wives and children in Europe. Not many men were willing to expose their families to the hazards of West Indian conditions, especially the harsh tropical climate and the deadly diseases. Children in particular were left behind in Europe so that their education could be provided for.

The disproportion between European men and women in the Virgin Islands led the men initially to seek conjugal comforts from the class of numerous female slaves in the society. From this relationship there emerged a group of colored people who were born slaves since the children of slaves assumed the status of their mothers. In many instances, however, they obtained their freedom from their white fathers; those who were not freed tended to receive more privileged positions than their black counterparts and so were better circumstanced to purchase their freedom. In time, the off-springs of the union between white men and colored women, and between colored men and women, added to the numbers of the colored group. It should be noted that the sexual permissiveness was not confined to the lower ranks of whites but extended even to governor-generals and other high officials and planters.

In addition to the free-colored or racially-mixed population, there was a class of free-blacks, which developed from among those slaves who had been given their freedom by their masters because of faithful or meritorious service, or because these masters had been affected by their moral conscience or scruples. In addition, an indefinite number of slaves obtained their freedom through purchase effected by themselves or by others interested in their welfare. Thus a freedman desirous of marrying a slave would think it fit first to remove her from her servile status.

The number of slaves who bought their freedom could not have been large, since slave-owners generally were loath to part with property which could contribute substantially to their material welfare and prosperity. Owners more readily manumitted those slaves who could no longer, because of infirmity of old age and sickness, give effective service but rather constituted a drain upon their financial resources for maintenance and welfare. In cases where freed blacks were still capable of bearing children, such off-springs contributed to the increase of their numbers.

The free-coloreds and free-blacks occupied a similar medial status in society, and during slavery their combined numbers increased. St. Thomas had 1,157 free-coloreds and free-blacks by 1767, while in St. Croix, their numbers increased from 368 in 1775, to 1,656 in 1803, to 2,179 in 1812, and to 2,892 in 1826.[7] While they were few, they suffered from a number of restrictions which were removed or relaxed when they became more numerous and powerful.

Free-Coloreds and Free-Blacks: Privileges and Disabilities

Free-coloreds and free-blacks could own land to the extent of small holdings as well as slaves with whom to work these lands. In the towns the men could engage in small trade in competition with the merchants, and the women could set themselves up in such occupations as dress-making and laundering. The security of the islands was strengthened by means of the Free Negro Corps of which a free-negro Mingo Tamarin was appointed captain in 1721. He was to play a very important role in the suppression of slave revolts and at his death in 1765, was succeeded by his son Peter.[8]

Despite these evidences of privilege, the opportunities of free-coloreds and free-blacks were severely limited, and their inferior social position was given expression in a number of declarations. In the mandate issued by Governor Gardelin in September, 1733, it was provided that free-negroes implicated in runaway plots or found to have encouraged stealing were to be deprived of liberty and property. Additionally, they were to be flogged and then banished. Like slaves, free-coloreds and free-blacks could not do violence to a white person without being punished, even though in their case the punishment was less severe.

In a proclamation of 1775, free-negroes were forbidden to bear the name of the master granting them their freedom, as was the custom among them hitherto. Furthermore, according to a regulation issued by Governor-General Peter Clausen on October 11, 1776, they were required to carry at all times a 'letter of freedom' issued by the governor-general; for those who were already free the 'letter of freedom' had to be obtained within a year, otherwise they had to leave the islands, or lose their freedom and be sold at public auction as slaves. In addition, the 'letter of freedom' had to be produced whenever the right to freedom of the person was challenged and even when mothers sought to baptize their children.[9]

Despite the restrictions from which they suffered, the free-coloreds and free-blacks were proud of their freedom. The mixture of repression and class pride was nowhere better reflected than in the behavior of the colored women. Dressed in clothes of the finest cotton, muslin, or chintz, with long trains, and wearing gold necklaces, rings and bracelets, they were very attractive; but lack of worth-while economic opportunities drove them to a life of prostitution and degradation.[10] The pride of the free-coloreds and free-blacks was also indicated by the address 'Sir' or 'Madam' used among themselves.[11] The restrictions, especially the 'letter of freedom' were annoying, but they had to wait until more propitious times to be relieved.

By the 1830's racial distinctions had been blurred by the economic decline of white planters and the relative rise in prosperity of the free-coloreds and free-blacks. Some coloreds had themselves become large proprietors through the bequeathal of property to them. Consequently, the oppressed people themselves assumed the initiative for the removal of the restrictions from which they were suffering.

Two representatives of the free-negro community went to Copenhagen in 1816 and presented the king with a petition signed by 331 of their number. In it they complained of severe and 'ignominious punishments' sometimes without trial for the slightest offenses committed, the denial of the privilege to sell liquor by retail, and the compulsion to which they were subject to hunt runaway slaves. They pointed out too that they could not open 'houses of accommodation or entertainment' and that they were denied bail even for the most trivial offenses. They showed the extent to which they contributed to the defense and public peace of the islands, the amount of property they held in lands, buildings and slaves, and their contributions in support of the civil establishment through the payment of taxes. In return they asked that they might be permitted to obtain burgher briefs (that is, trade licenses), that 'letters of freedom' might be abolished, and that they might be placed under the 'same regulations and establishment' as white people.[12]

The petition probably exaggerated both the contributions and sufferings of the free-negroes generally; nevertheless, they had real grievances. The response of the Danish authorities, however, was different from that of the Danish West India Company's officials towards similar delegations of colonists. In the eighteenth century, white delegates had been given a hearing and had their requests granted whereas in 1816 the colored delegates were reprimanded for having left the Virgin Islands without the permission of the governor-general, and were ordered to return immediately. Even when the Danish Crown relented and requested Governor-General Bentzon to enquire whether equality could be established, Bentzon took no action since he had only recently assumed the office of governor-general and preferred to ignore the subject.

What had been denied to the free-negroes in 1816 was achieved by Peter von Scholten, Governor-General of the Virgin Islands after 1827. Von Scholten began by reorganizing the existing Free Negro Corps by which colored men were appointed as officers from among whom he chose some of his adjutants to serve along with those who were white.

By a further action in 1830 King Frederik VI approved von Scholten's plan to divide the free-negro population into two classes.[13] Members of the first class would be the most progressive of the group and would include some specified officers of the Free Negro Corps and some civilians who deserved 'distinction more or less, on account of superior education, mental capacity, good conduct, situation in life, or from other considerations'. These were to receive certificates of citizenship and were entitled to the same treatment as white persons.

Members of the second class would comprise all other free-negro officers and those registered in the protocols of free-negro persons, who were to receive certificates of legitimation signed by the governor-general's secretary. However, these certificates merely recognized a state of freedom of the persons concerned and did not significantly alter their situation.

It was no longer necessary for free-negroes to carry 'letters of freedom'. Moreover, the governor-general was empowered to classify colored persons as whites 'where free persons of color, of both sexes, assimilate in color to the whites, and they otherwise, by a cultivated mind and good conduct render themselves deserving to stand, according to their rank and station in life, on an equal footing with the white inhabitants.'[14]

The king's decree opened the way for the most successful free-negroes to attain social and political equality with the whites and even, under certain circumstances, to identify themselves completely with the white group. The creation of class distinctions among the free-negro group, however, aroused sectional animosity and threatened to wreck the plan. Consequently, a further royal decree of April 18, 1834 granted citizenship to all free-negroes with all the rights and privileges of white colonists. The only exceptions were those slaves who should obtain their freedom in future: these had to wait for three years after their freedom to achieve full equality.[15]

Under the law, free-negroes had been granted equality with white people, but the problem of their acceptance into the white community remained. At first there was rejection by the whites while the free-negroes were cautious in assuming their new position. Von Scholten sought reconciliation by inviting members of both groups to common dinner parties and other social functions at Government House. When at first he invited whites and non-whites to a ball, the colored ladies did not appear, but by 1846 both sides had more or less adjusted to the new situation.[16]

The Slave Population: Its Composition and Functions

The free-black and free-colored population increased steadily during the period of slavery. In comparison the slave population reached a maximum towards the end of the eighteenth century, and thereafter decreased steadily. While the increase was a result of the slave trade solely, the reduction was due to a variety of causes including death by violence or disease, desertion, and manumission. Table 2 illustrates the number of slaves in the Virgin Islands between 1755 and 1846.[17]

TABLE 2
Total Number of Slaves in the Virgin Islands, 1755-1846

Year	St. Thomas	St. John	St. Croix	Total
1755	3,949	2,031	8,897	14,877
1761	3,632	2,020	13,489	19,141
1773	3,980	2,293	21,698	27,971
1791	4,214	1,845	21,549	27,608
1802	5,737	2,492	27,006	35,235
1815	4,848	2,445	24,339	31,632
1826	4,548	2,206	21,356	28,110
1835	5,032	1,971	19,876	26,879
1846	3,494	1,790	16,706	21,990

Slaves were the sinews of the colony, but they occupied the lowest social and economic position; politically they did not count at all. Their inferior position was in keeping with their servile status: slaves were chattels and could be bought and sold, even exchanged in payment of debts. Within the colony there were several categories of slaves though the largest number was engaged in agriculture; for instance, in 1797 it was estimated that about 82 percent of the slaves in St. Croix were field workers.[18] Even among the field slaves there was a division of labor based on the physical capabilities of the laborers.

The most robust men and women performed such heavy field operations as clearing the land, terracing, digging cane holes, planting, reaping, feeding the sugar-cane into the mills, and seeding and baling cotton. These slaves were also engaged in making and repairing roads and in building various structures of wood and stone. Pregnant women and young mothers, youths between twelve and eighteen years of age, and elderly slaves performed lighter field work such as weeding, manuring and picking cotton. Children under twelve years of age were also employed in such tasks as weeding and manuring gardens to keep them occupied and to give them training for plantation work later on.

In addition to the field workers, there were other slaves who were engaged in the boiling-house, curing-house and still-house associated with the production of sugar and rum. Slaves, chiefly of mixed blood,

Above: PLANTER-QUARTERS
Below: SLAVE-QUARTERS

served as skilled artisans such as masons, carpenters, coopers, wheel-wrights, and smiths. Others, again mainly colored, were employed as domestics in the capacity of cooks, butlers, cleaners and chambermaids. A few were even kept as mistresses by their masters. In the towns, when not otherwise engaged as domestics, slaves were employed as saddlers, coopers, barbers, sailors and fishermen. A number of slaves were employed by the Danish West India Company, and later by the Crown, to work in the warehouses, and to construct works of fortification and defense. These slaves were appropriately distinguished as the 'Company's Negroes' or 'His Majesty's Negroes'. Slave-owners engaged in trade, especially in St. Thomas, employed their slaves in warehouses and on the wharves as packers, porters and loaders.[19]

Working and Living Conditions of Slaves

By far the hardest lot was that of the field slaves whose working week extended from Monday to Saturday. They were awakened at around four o'clock each morning by the sound of the 'tutu' or conch-shell blown by a 'bomba', or slave driver. The stock animals were grassed, the slaves ate, and by five o'clock they were marched to the fields to begin work. They toiled until about eight o'clock, when they rested and breakfasted for about one hour. Then they worked until about noon when they were given about two hours off to have their meals and to rest from the hot noon-day sun.[20]

After their noontide break slaves were worked further until about six o'clock which, however, was not the end of the working day since they then had to collect grass for the stock animals next day. During crop time, slaves had to work longer hours; though the cutting of canes ceased at sundown, the cutters might be required to assist the regular mill-hands to complete the processing of the sugarcane already cut.[21] Quick milling of canes was necessary since their sugar-content decreased if milling was delayed.

The living quarters of slaves were thrown promiscuously together, and each family was assigned a separate hut usually from twelve to twenty feet in length, eight or nine feet high, and from ten to fourteen feet wide. The framework was of wood, the walls were made of wattles plastered over with mud to keep out the rain and wind, and the roof was thatched. By the nineteenth century, the houses of some field slaves were being made of stone and covered with shingles to make them more resistant to the climate. The floor was the bare earth on which mats or rugs were spread, and depending on the industry and neatness of the occupants, there might be a few pieces of furniture. The hut was divided into two rooms, a kitchen and a bedroom, and its small size invariably made it overcrowded; in fair weather, therefore, much time was spent out of doors.[22]

As was to be expected, the living quarters of the domestics and town slaves were of a better quality than those of the field workers. The dwellings of the artisans, for instance, would almost invariably be roofed with shingles, floored with boards, and have a few pieces of furniture including a bed raised from the floor. However, whatever the quality of slave houses, these would contrast sharply with those of their owners.

The feeding of slaves was the responsibility of the owner; some food was grown on the plantations, but a greater quantity was imported especially when agricultural staples expanded to take in as much of the cultivable land as possible. It became cheaper to import food than to grow it when the price of land rose substantially. In any case some foods which could not be produced locally such as flour, salt-fish and bacon had to be imported. Wars seldom threatened food imports because of the neutral status of the Virgin Islands; even when Britain captured the islands in the early nineteenth century, it does not appear that any food shortage occurred.

In addition to imported foods, slaves were given the opportunity to grow some provisions of their own. Small plots of land were attached to their living quarters, and they were given Sunday and a half-day on Saturday each week to cultivate them for their own benefit. On these plots slaves grew such food crops as yams, cassava and corn, and reared livestock such as poultry and pigs. They also supplemented their diet by fishing in the surrounding waters of the Atlantic wherever possible.[23] That slaves often had enough locally-produced food and to spare was evident from the fact that they operated Sunday markets where surpluses could be sold. Many white and colored people obtained much of their vegetable and meat supplies at the Sunday markets.[24] Advantages accruing to slave-owners were reduced outlays for food-stuffs and greater stability in the family life of slaves. However, reliance on slave-grown food had its disadvantages; when plots failed, slaves starved and became dissatisfied. Thus, food shortage contributed to the slave rebellion in St. John in 1733, and resulted in much suffering during the drought and crop failure of 1789 to 1791.

Slaves had different ways and means by which they could earn money. In addition to the sale of surplus vegetables and livestock which they reared, they sold some of the fish they caught. Besides, there were opportunities in town for selling firewood for fuel as well as grass to those who kept horses. Instead of, or in addition to, cultivating their plots, some slaves used the free time given on Saturday and Sunday, to hire themselves out as laborers.[25] The money so earned was used to buy necessaries and luxuries not otherwise provided, or else saved to purchase freedom.

Besides housing and food, slaves were provided with clothing and medical care by their masters. The amount of clothing supplied was the barest minimum necessary to keep the slaves within the bounds of tolerable decency. It was confined to a few suits a year and these were made of a coarse but strong linen. However, slaves were permitted and sometimes encouraged to buy the clothes they needed or desired out of the money they earned through sale of their provisions, livestock or services.[26]

With regard to medical attention, the Virgin Islands were not in the fortunate position of having many doctors. Unlike plantations in other West Indian colonies which were more favorably circumstanced, plantations in the Virgin Islands did not have their own doctors to cater to the medical requirements of slaves. Instead, financial provision was made to pay for the services of a visiting doctor whenever necessary.[27] Some estates, however, had 'hot houses' where sick slaves could be kept and treated until they recovered. In these cases the services of nurses who were themselves slaves, were provided. In addition, slaves used their knowledge of medicinal herbs, acquired in Africa or inherited, to cure ailments.[28]

Slaves' yearly routine was broken by the Christmas and New Year festivities. One eye-witness account of slave celebrations in 1845 in St. Croix gives some idea of what they were like in the later years of slavery:

... The Holidays of the slaves commence with Christmas, and although the law gives them that and the following day, they contrive ... to do very little work between Christmas and New Year ... For several weeks preceding Christmas they are busied with preparations for their festivities. Indeed their toil through the whole year is cheered by their anticipation of holiday happiness. For these festivities, all there is of turban, calico, ribbon, gewgaw and trinket, among them, is reserved to adorn their persons. DANCING is their only festive resource. The slaves on each estate elect their Queen and Princess, with their King and Prince, whose authority is supreme. They have their Maids of Honor, Pages &c., &c. A Queen retains her rank until by age or otherwise she voluntarily retires as Dowager. The instrument which, on these occasions, 'discourses most eloquent music,' is a large keg or half barrel, over the head of which a goat skin is drawn, and upon which a negro beats with his hands, as proudly and triumphantly as Ole Bull draws his cat gut. The Dance is opened by the King and Queen. The Prima Donna sings ballads, while the whole gang unite in the chorus, to which the Drums furnish a *very* base, but truly appropriate accompaniment. When the Royal pair are exhausted, they introduce the Prince and Princess, who in turn call up those of inferior rank. The Dance opens with much gravity, but in its progress Dancers and Singers warm into enthusiasm. The voice of the Prima Donna rises; the chorus swells; the drummer turns up the white of his eyes and displays his ivory; the Queen swoons; is supported by maids of honor, who sprinkle 'Bay Rum' and ply their fans until she recovers, and joins in the Dance with renewed energy. And thus the revelers consume the day and night. Not more than a dozen of a gang of sixty, seventy or eighty, participate in the Dance, the remainder seeming to find equal enjoyment by straining their lungs and cracking their voices in the Orchestra. Towards the close of the festivities, however, all join in the Dance, all, at the same time, singing most vociferously. Flags, held by the maids of honor, are waving over the heads of the Queens during the Dance.

The first privilege (or duty as they esteem it) of the slaves, on Christmas and New Year's days, is to pay their respects, in a body, to their master, before whom they Dance for an hour or more, paying tribute, in their songs, to his liberality, generosity, &c., after which they are regaled with cakes, cordial, &c., and generally receive presents from their mistress. They then return to their own domicils to pass the day and night in festivities. In the Town the Free Colored People and House Slaves form their parties, elect their Kings, Queens &c., and Dance in like manner. We went the rounds among them, and and were generally received by some complimentary line thrown, impromptu, into their songs'.[29]

The Genesis and Nature of Slave Laws

Conflict was inevitable in a slave society where social status was established on the basis of wealth and whiteness of skin color, and where social and political privileges rested in those at the top. The tendency was for the elite to preserve their exclusive and privileged position by seeking to maintain the status quo, while those lower down should seek to advance their status in as many ways as possible. Because of the most inferior position of the slaves, the greatest threat to the preservation of the existing social order came from them. To counter these threats the most repressive regulations were applied to them. Regulations rarely specified the rights of slaves which were left to the generosity and benevolence of the slave-owners to grant at their discretion. The concern of the insular administration was the maintenance of order and prevention of the breakdown of society.

Beginning in the very year that St. Thomas was colonized and continuing thereafter, numerous regulations were passed governing the behavior and social status of the slaves. Slave laws became more and more severe as the ratio of slaves to Europeans increased as can be seen from those issued in 1672, 1684 and 1733.[30] According to the slave law of 1672, 'no man must let his negro leave the estate after sunset, without good cause, that he may not go to his neighbor's estate, and do injury; and whoever at night observes a strange negro on his estate, shall catch him and carry him in the morning to the fort, where he shall be punished.'[31] Though implied, there was nothing in this regulation which was mandatory on the slaves; masters were responsible for their good behavior, though the punishment was to fall on the offending blacks.

The regulations of 1684 differed by placing definite restraints upon the freedom of slaves who were now held responsible for observing the laws. Slaves were forbidden to carry knives or clubs, they were to be at home by drum-beat on week-days and by sunset on Sundays, and they were prohibited from holding feasts and 'drum dances'. Breaches of these regulations were punishable by whipping for the first offence, by having the ears severed for the second offence, and by hanging for the third offence. In the last instance, the head of the slave was to be placed on a stake and exhibited as an object lesson to would-be offenders.[32]

The ratio of whites to slaves was roughly even in 1684, and seven years later there were three adult white persons to every five adult slaves. In such situations, the white colonists had little to fear from concerted slave resistance. However, when adult slaves outnumbered adult whites by a ratio of eight to one, as was the case between 1720 and 1725, the situation became vastly more dangerous.

It was in order to protect the white colonists and to prevent slaves from taking advantage of their numbers that Governor Gardelin issued the mandate of September 5, 1733, to be proclaimed three times a year as a constant reminder to slaves.[33] The severity of these regulations reflected the tensions which existed in the society and their repressive nature was shown firstly in those clauses relating to runaway slaves. Leaders of runaways were to be pinched three times with red-hot irons and then hanged. Slaves found guilty of conspiracy were to lose a leg each unless their owners requested leniency when the sentence could be reduced to 150 lashes and the loss of the slaves' ears. Slaves who failed to report a plot of which they were aware were to be branded on the forehead and, in addition, were to receive one hundred lashes. Alternatively, those who reported plots could secure financial rewards and have their names kept secret. Runaways who were caught within a week were to receive 150 lashes in punishment; those who remained hidden for three months were to lose a leg each; and those who stayed away for six months were to lose their lives. In the last instance, if the owner interceded, the punishment could be reduced to the loss of a leg. Slaves who stole, or received stolen goods, and those who assisted others to run away were to be branded and given 150 lashes each.

Regulations governing relations between whites and slaves were also very harsh: a slave raising his hand in violence against a white person was to be pinched three times with a hot iron; whether he should in addition be hanged or only lose a hand was left to the discretion of the person assaulted. The testimony of a reputable white person was sufficient evidence against a slave; in case of doubt, the latter might be tortured. A slave meeting a white person on the road had to step aside until the latter had passed; if he did not do so, he could be whipped. Slaves were prohibited from carrying sticks and knives and from practicing witch-craft, subject to a flogging, while slaves who attempted to poison their masters were to be pinched with a hot-iron and then broken on the wheel.

Dancing and feasting to music were forbidden unless the slave-owner or his representative had first granted permission. The authorization of masters was likewise necessary before slaves could sell provisions of any kind. Lastly, slaves could not be found loitering after drumbeat without being subject to imprisonment and a flogging.

Maintenance of order was the sole purpose of the slave laws passed in the Virgin Islands during the period of Company rule. The welfare of slaves, whether it was physical or spiritual, was left to the discretion of the slave-owners. An attempt to correct this anomaly was made with the passing of the slave law of February 3, 1755 by the Danish Crown. Though apparently not brought into operation in the Virgin Islands, this law formed the basis of a number of slave regulations passed locally.[34]

The slave law of February 3, 1755, clearly expressed owners' responsibilities to their slaves while reaffirming their rights over them. The law confirmed the owners' right to sell their slaves who were considered property without the right of possession. Slaves could not marry without their owners' consent though, on the other hand, masters could not force them to marry. Polygamy and homosexuality among slaves were prohibited, but otherwise their sexual behavior was left unregulated. Slave-owners had to provide their slaves with rations and were forbidden to give 'kill-devil' or alcohol instead of food. Furthermore, masters had to see that their slaves were decently dressed, and that old and sick slaves were treated properly. If it could be proved that masters failed in these essentials, ownership of the slaves would go to the Crown.

Slaves could not hold official positions and could not be used as witnesses in court, though they were otherwise allowed to give testimony. They could be punished for misdemeanors, and if found guilty of violence against a white person, could be put to death. If a condemned slave was executed, compensation had to be paid to the owner by the colonial government, according to appraisal. Owners could punish their slaves by flogging or putting them in irons; but torture or maiming was not permitted on penalty of loss of the slaves while the killing of slaves was prohibited. Married slaves belonging to the same owner were not to be separated, and minor children could not be taken away from their mothers or parents. The religious education of slaves was to be encouraged, and missionaries were to be allowed to preach on the plantations.[35]

Punishment of Slaves and Amelioration

In general slave laws had two objectives applicable to both slave-owners and slaves, namely, to correct existing abuses and to anticipate others in an attempt to prevent them. By recognizing the slave-owners' property rights over slaves and by regulating the behavior of slaves, the law tended to work in the interest of the slave-owners. At the same time, by outlining the areas of responsibility of the owners to slaves, the law worked in the interest of the slaves. The slave-owners' treatment of their slaves also showed a double purpose. Slaves as property constituted an investment in capital; their labor was a source of profit. Both investment and profit would be lost if they were punished harshly, imprisoned, or killed. At the same time, resort was had to extreme measures to maintain the system of forced labor and inequitable distribution of wealth and income.

The more regular punishment meted out to slaves was flogging since it allowed them to resume work almost immediately after the punishment was administered. In addition, the number of lashes could be varied in number and intensity according to the circumstances of the case. Moreover, if the whipping were witnessed by other slaves, it could be used as an object lesson to teach the folly of disobedience and recalcitrance. A flogging of from 50 to 100 lashes was generally considered normal, though on occasion as many as 500 are said to have been given, in lieu of the death penalty. After the beating, the welts were rubbed with salt and pepper: this increased the punishment and suffering of slaves but was believed to avoid complications.[36] Other types of punishment such as castration, dismemberment and execution were resorted to after flogging had failed to produce the necessary results. Imprisonment was more a colonial government type of punishment though plantations usually had a small jail for the temporary confinement of refractory slaves.

A condition which contributed to the harsh punishment of slaves was absentee-landlordism which resulted in the plantation being left in the hands of a manager or overseer.[37] Slaves tended to suffer more at the hands of men like these because they had no vested interest in the welfare of slaves except to please their employer and enhance their own income. In the 'busal' or slave driver, who was himself a promoted slave,· they had a good ally, since the busal himself was anxious to please. However, the busal did not always take the side of the plantation authority, but associated himself with his fellow bondmen in resistance to the slave system.

In contrast to the restrictive laws hitherto in force, a Royal decree of November 22, 1834, due largely to the efforts of Peter von Scholten, granted some valuable concessions. Slaves were permitted to buy their freedom, although this was merely legalizing custom; and they could change owners if maltreated, thereby forcing their superiors to administer more limited punishments. Slaves could dispose at will of their earnings, of the gifts they received, and of those things they bought or inherited. Working hours were shortened: hitherto slaves had to work for their masters on Sundays when requested; now they were given the option between working and not working. If they decided to work they had to be paid for their labor. Moreover, pregnant women were exempt from hard labor.[38]

Self-interest in terms of profits and the preservation of the peace of society dictated that the punishment of slaves should be modified. This was especially so after the abolition of the slave trade when slaves could no longer be imported, and when those who died or ran away could not be replaced by fresh purchases. Food, clothing, housing, and medical care had to be given to the extent necessary for the maximum efficiency of slaves.[39]

Beyond the provision of essentials, however, slave-owners were not prepared to accept any responsibility, as was most evident in the field of formal education. Religious education was offered by the Christian denominations, and though it was desirable and given encouragement, nevertheless its availability to slaves was left to the discretion of slave-owners. It was not until the 1830's, during the governor-generalship of Peter von Scholten that an attempt was made to introduce a system of free, compulsory, and universal education in the Virgin Islands, by which even the children of slaves should benefit.[40] However, in order to make the plan acceptable to planters it was necessary to grant them certain tax concessions.

Conclusion

In a slave society such as existed in the Virgin Islands, the maximum power of control was in the hands of slave-owners. Indeed, on the plantations, the authority of the planters over their slaves was paramount. In a situation where slave-owners looked to each other for mutual support, it rarely if ever happened that they went against each other as far as the treatment of slaves was concerned. It would be a rash slave who would seek to invoke the law against his master. Even if he did, the arm of justice was on the side of his master in so far as the colonial magistrates were themselves slave-owners.

Colonial officials gave slave-owners largely a free hand in the management of their slaves; many officials were themselves slave-owners and they sympathized with and supported other slave-owners. Governor-Generals and governors were not willing to excite planter opposition by undue interference in their domestic affairs. The major exception to the general attitude was von Scholten, and his actions on behalf of the free-negroes and slaves, cost him the governor-generalship.

In a situation where the freedom of slaves was so much circumscribed and the opportunities of advancement, or even of securing justice, were so much limited, it is natural that the protest of slaves should be continuous and even vehement. One of the outstanding features of slavery was slave protest.

[1] Thurlow Weed, *Letters from Europe and the West Indies.* (Albany, Weed, Parsons and Company, 1866) p. 365.
[2] Philip C. Yorke , *The Diary of John Baker, Barrister of the Middle Temple, Solicitor-General of the Leeward Islands, Being Extracts therefrom, Transcribed and Edited with an Introduction and Notes.* (Hutchinson & Co., London, n.d.) p. 92.
[3] Jens Vibaek, *Dansk Vestindien 1755-1848: Vestindiens Storhedstid.* (Fremad, Denmark, 1966) pp. 102-103.
[4] J. P. Nissen, *Reminiscences of a 46 Years' Residence in the Island of St. Thomas in the West Indies.* (Nazareth, Pa., Senseman and Company, 1838) passim.
[5] Vibaek, op. cit., p. 191.
[6] [Ole Sevenson, (Ed.)] , *Three Towns: Conservation and Renewal of Charlotte Amalia, Christiansted and Frederiksted of the U.S. Virgin Islands.* (Tutein & Koch, Copenhagen, 1964?).
[7] Vibaek, op. cit., p. 193; *Census of Free-Coloured in 1826.* (Private Collection in Christiansted Public Free Library).
[8] Kay Larsen, *Dansk Vestindien,* 1666-1917. (Copenhagen, 1927) p. 87.
[9] Vibaek, op. cit., p. 193.
[10] N. Parker Willis, *Health Trips to the Tropics.* (New York, Charles Scribner, 1853) pp. 41-45 and 63-64; Cf. Weed, op. cit., pp. 339-340, which shows that as late as 1845 colored ladies shopped their clothing after the white ladies had already taken their pick of newly-arrived cargoes.
[11] Hans West, 'Beretning om det danske Eiland St. Croix i Vestindien, fra Juniimaaned 1789 til Juniimaaneds Udgang 1790.' (*Maanedskriftet Iris,* Kjobenhavn, Julii, 1791) pp. 49 ff.
[12] Petition from the Free-Colored Population of the Virgin Islands to the King of Denmark, 1816. (Private Collection in Christiansted Public Free Library.)
[13] Albert A. Campbell, 'St. Thomas Negroes — A Study of Personality and Culture.' (*Psychological Monographs,* Vol. 55, No. 5, 1943) pp. 15-16.

[14] Ibid., p. 16.

[15] Ibid., pp. 16-17.

[16] Carlo Christensen, *Peter von Scholten. A Chapter of the History of the Virgin Islands.* (Denmark, Gadgaard Nielsens Bogtrykkeri, 1955) p. 14.

[17] Vibaek, op. cit., pp. 102-103 and 327; P. P. Sveistrup, *Bidrag til de Tidligere Dansk-Vestindiske oers Økononfiske Historie.* (Kobenhavn, 1942) p. 15.

[18] Peter Lotharius Oxholm, *De danske vestindiske oers Tilstand i Henseende til Population, Culture og Finance-Forfatning i Anledning af nogle Breve fra St. Croix.* (Kjobenhavn, 1797).

[19] Ibid.; Emil Valdemar Lose, *Kort Udsigt over den Danske Lutherske Missions Historie paa St. Croix, St. Thomas og St. Jan.* (Nordisk Missions Tidsskrift, Vol. 1, Copenhagen, 1890) passim.

[20] Waldemar Westergaard, *The Danish West Indies Under Company Rule* (1671-1754). (New York, The Macmillan Company, 1917) pp. 158-159.

[21] Sylvester Hovey, *Letters from the West Indies: Relating especially to the Danish Island of St. Croix, and to the British Islands of Antigua, Barbadoes and Jamaica.* (New York, 1838) p. 28.

[22] Ibid., p. 26.

[23] Ibid., pp. 26-27.

[24] Weed. op. cit., pp. 352-354.

[25] West, op. cit., pp. 1-88.

[26] Hovey, op. cit., p. 27; Weed, op. cit., p. 331.

[27] Weed, op. cit., p. 384.

[28] For a discussion of herbs used for medicinal purposes in the Virgin Islands, see A. J. Oakes and M. P. Morris, 'The West Indian Weed-woman of the United States Virgin Islands.' (*Bulletin of the History of Medicine*, Vol. XXXII, No. 2, March-April, 1958) pp. 164-170.

[29] Weed, op. cit., pp. 345-347.

[30] For other regulations, see Governors of St. Thomas. Orders issued for Observance by Inhabitants, 1672-1726. (The Bancroft Collection at Berkeley).

[31] John P. Knox, *A Historical Account of St. Thomas, W.I.* (New York, Charles Scribner, 1852) p. 51.

[32] Ibid., pp. 55-56.

[33] Westergaard, op. cit., pp. 166-168.

[34] U. N. Fugl, 'Om Negerslaveriet i Westindien og sammes Ophomed specielt Herisyn til de Danske Besiddelser.' (*Juridisk Tidsskrift*, Vol. 24, 1834).

[35] H. Lawaetz, *Peter v. Scholten. Vestindiske Tidsbilleder fra den sidste Generalguvernors dage.* (Kobenhavn, 1940) p. 126.

[36] Campbell, op. cit., p. 7; Vibaek, op. cit., p. 150.

[37] Lawrence P. Spingarn, 'Slavery in the Danish West Indies.' (The *American Scandinavian Review*, Spring, 1957) p. 38.

[38] Ibid., pp. 42-43; Carlo Christensen, op. cit., pp. 15-16.

[39] Fugl. op. cit., passim.

[40] See Chapter 11, p. 195, below.

Chapter 10

Slave Protest and Emancipation

Plantation labor was the most onerous and unrewarding of all the work which slaves were called upon to perform. Compared with it, the work of domestics, artisans, fishermen and other categories of slaves, was comparatively light and easy, with greater privileges attached to them. Compared with other slaves too, the treatment of field slaves was marked by greater severity and cruelty, and over them, as over all other slaves, the domination of the master or his representative was complete. The exploitation of their labor power was more strenuously pursued, the authority of the whites being backed by their control of the means of exercising that authority. It was among these slaves that protest was particularly evident in the Virgin Islands.

Despite the strict control to which they were subject, slaves did not lack that sensitivity which made them desire, and on occasion demand, their freedom. Though their subordination seemed complete, slaves were not subdued: the will to resist persisted in them, and expressed itself in a variety of ways. The spirit of protest was not stilled by suppression; on the contrary, it was nurtured by the experiences and conditions of enslavement and continued as long as slavery existed.

Slaves originating from certain African tribes imbued with a warlike spirit and a propensity for resistance would be expected to spearhead slave protests and to resist their enslavement. Likewise, slaves recently brought from Africa usually had lingering notions of the freedom they had once enjoyed and would strive to be free. This is not to say that only certain Africans cherished the idea of freedom while others were tolerant to the point of indolence. Neither should it be implied that slaves who had lived in the Virgin Islands for some years were reconciled to their depraved condition, or that their children who were born in the islands were content with their servile status and had no desire for personal advancement.

Individual Acts of Slave Protest

The desire for freedom was shared by slaves of all classes and conditions, though not all of them were willing to take any action to achieve freedom. Neither were all forms of resistance designed to effect escape from slavery or to achieve freedom; instead, certain forms of protest stemmed from the bondage in which the Africans found themselves.[1] Theft and lying, for instance, were definitely devices adopted by slaves to ease the burdens of servitude: goods stolen from the master, or more likely from another slave-owner, could be consumed or sold in order to add to the supplies provided by the master; lying was sometimes resorted to in order to evade work or to escape punishment.

The slaves' desire to settle personal injuries or to take revenge for wrongs done by white superiors found such outlets as doing violence to the person concerned, destroying crops and property, wilful neglect, and injuring the estate animals. The burning of fields of unripe cane was particularly feared by planters in the Virgin Islands, and many of them resorted to the expedient of setting trusted slaves to keep watch in order to prevent this singularly destructive practice.

The British political economist, Adam Smith, writing in 1776, stated that 'a person who can acquire no property, can have no other interest but to eat as much, and to labour as little as possible.'[2] Because slaves had no share in the result of their labor they had little incentive to work hard. Rather, whenever possible, they sought to evade work despite the knowledge that if caught, heavy punishment awaited them.

Slaves were versed in the art of going-slow, thereby making it necessary for planters to force their labor through the application of the whip wielded by a black slave-driver. The feigning of illness, or the prolonging of genuine illness, or self-inflicted illness or injury, were all effective ways of evading work, especially when there was no doctor present to determine the extent or verify the nature of the complaint. Women tended to capitalize on the complaints peculiar to them; thus, the weaning period was deliberately prolonged to lengthen the time they would be away from work. In addition, the deliberate refusal to work, either singly or collectively, was another method by which slaves resisted their lot.

Generally, however, malingering constituted a more effective protest against slavery, than outright refusal to work, for unless the slave-owner's suspicion of a deliberate act was aroused, the chances of escaping punishment were better. Malingering was not very destructive to the slave-owner, since it meant only a temporary loss of services which could be regained by additional work. What was more serious was self-mutilation by slaves, of a permanent nature, such as the severing of an arm or of both arms, to make them incapable of performing manual labor.

Some slaves, especially newly-arrived Africans or 'busals', to whom slavery was particularly odious and unbearable, preferred death by suicide to enslavement. Protest in this form was not confined to individual acts, and mothers especially killed their children also when they committed suicide. Death by poisoning and by hanging was the usual way out, but some slaves prolonged the agony by starving themselves. The German Moravian missionary leader, Oldendorp, writing in 1784, even told of a woman who slowly committed suicide by eating sand and gravel, even though her master tried to prevent her by giving her a muzzle made of leather.[3]

Running Away

Comparatively few slaves were courageous or desperate enough to commit suicide, especially since they had an effective alternative. This was desertion of the plantation, or running-away, as it was called. It started early in the history of the Virgin Islands, and laws applying both to the owners and to the slaves were repeatedly passed in order to curb the practice. The slave-law publicized by Governor Gardelin in September, 1733, for example, reached a high water mark of regulations pertaining to runaways.

From a trickle, running-away assumed greater proportions as plantation agriculture developed and as the treatment of slaves became more severe. The hilly terrain and dense woods of the Virgin Islands provided slaves with hiding places from where they robbed the plantations during the night thereby threatening the owners' prosperity. However, runaways were seldom numerous or bold enough to attack the white colonists and in any event, effective action was taken against them. For example, Governor Lorentz issued a proclamation in 1698 granting freedom to those runaways who returned within a certain period; otherwise they could be shot on sight. More drastic measures were adopted in 1706 when the death penalty was imposed on leaders of runaways, while other participants were to lose a foot.[4]

In an attempt to prevent running-away and marauding, white militias were organized in the various districts and the Free Negro Corps was established, while a major part in tracking down runaways was played by privately organized groups of whites and trusted slaves. As another preventive measure, slaves who were prone to runaway were fitted with spiked-collars to prevent them from ducking under and escaping through the cane-fields.[5]

Runaways never comprised a permanent body in the Virgin Islands such as the maroons in Jamaica, for when the slave-hunt became too successful, the slaves escaped to Puerto Rico. That island had not yet developed a plantation economy and the treatment of slaves there was relatively mild. Besides, runaways were usually employed on works of fortification in the island for one year, after which they were pronounced free and each given a plot of land to cultivate.

Slaves escaping to Puerto Rico became lost to the Virgin Islands slave-owners, a loss which was more strongly felt since only the most robust slaves were prepared to hazard the dangers of the 40-odd miles of ocean separating the Danish islands from the much larger Spanish island. The numbers of runaways were apparently large since for 1745 alone it was estimated that about 300 slaves from St. Thomas and St. Croix had escaped to Puerto Rico. The traffic became highly organized by the runaways themselves, and in St. Croix there was a mountain-hideout called 'Maroons' Hole' just east of Hamm's Bluff, where runaways were safely hidden in a cave whose entrance was protected by poles of a poisonous wood, until they could be transferred to Puerto Rico.[6]

The government of the Virgin Islands made strenuous efforts to prevent slaves from escaping to Puerto Rico, and to this end it tried to block the avenues of escape. For example, slaves who were employed as fishermen became skilled boatsmen, and they were ever alert to steal their masters' boats and sail to freedom. Consequently, numerous regulations cautioned slave-owners to keep their boats chained up threatening them with fines and worse if they failed to do so.

The question of returning fugitive slaves also troubled relations between the governments of the Virgin Islands and Puerto Rico. The argument used by the Spanish authorities in refusing to return runaways was that slaves escaped to Puerto Rico to seek baptism into Roman Catholicism. Not until 1767 did it become possible for Governor-General Baron von Prock to arrange a slave cartel with the Governor of Puerto Rico for the return of runaway slaves. But he had to promise more religious toleration to the Roman Catholics in the Virgin Islands by allowing them to build public places of worship and undertake conversion of slaves.

The problem of runaway slaves appears to have become less troublesome after 1767. Slaves had no desire to escape to the neighboring British colonies where treatment was no better and was possibly even worse than that meted out to slaves in the Virgin Islands. Barring the opportunity to escape to Puerto Rico, runaways would have had to remain in the Virgin Islands to eke out a very precarious existence under continuous threat of capture and severe punishment under the law. When the *Royal Danish American Gazette* began publication in 1770, the description of runaway slaves was advertised in it in yet a further attempt to facilitate their recapture.

It was not until 1838 that the runaway problem revived, occasioned by the abolition of slavery in the British West Indian colonies. Across the Sir Francis Drake Channel from St. John were the British Virgin Islands where the existence of freedom presented a continuous invitation for slaves to escape from the Danish islands. So serious was the problem that at the beginning of 1840, Governor-General von Scholten was forced to station a group of soldiers in Coral Bay and even to institute naval patrols in the area to prevent slaves from escaping.[7]

The St. John Slave Rebellion, 1733 to 1734

When slaves escaped to Puerto Rico, and later to the British colonies, they were seeking freedom outside the slave system of the Virgin Islands, though they also desired freedom right here. Apart from the extremely limited opportunity of purchasing that freedom, the only other means at their disposal was armed uprising. Slave revolts were rare in the Virgin Islands with only two serious ones actually taking place, the first in St. John in 1733 and the second in St. Croix in 1848. In addition, there were two conspiracies in St. Croix in 1746 and 1759, but these did not materialize into revolts.

St. Thomas escaped slave revolts largely because of the relatively short duration of plantation agriculture, and the emphasis on trade. Compared with plantation labor, slave occupations associated with trade were not as exacting and did not involve as much cruel treatment. Also, the white colonists of St. Thomas were organized in area militias and could depend on the support of the Free Negro Corps and on the garrison at Fort Christian in Charlotte Amalie to keep the slaves subdued.

The show of force partly explains why there were no slave rebellions between 1733 and 1848. In St. Croix, for instance, where plantation agriculture flourished through the labor of slaves the forts Christiansvaern and Frederiksvaern had been constructed and garrisoned as much to handle internal disorder as to expel foreign invaders. It is possible too, that some truth resides in the claim that slaves were better treated in the Virgin Islands than elsewhere in the West Indian colonies.[8] The abolition of the slave trade, decreed in 1792 and enforced from 1803, would have shown slave-owners the wisdom of humane treatment since slaves lost through neglect or cruelty could not be replaced by importation. In any case, after 1733 slave-owners had the lessons of the St. John rebellion to refrain from any excessive maltreatment of slaves for fear of the dire consequences involved.

The imbalance of the races in St. John in 1733 was a necessary but not sufficient condition leading slaves to rebel: according to the census of 1733 the island had 208 whites and 1,087 blacks, but in 1728 when there were 123 whites to 677 blacks the imbalance was slightly greater. There were other factors involved in 1733 which caused the rebellion. A major consideration and one which made the situation explosive was the lack of adequate control. At the time order on the island was maintained from Fortsberg in Coral Bay, where the garrison numbered not more than seven men.

St. John was plagued by absentee-landlordism since many of the plantation owners preferred to live in St. Thomas and leave their properties under the control of overseers. The difficulty of finding honest and capable white managers and overseers resulted in the combination of several plantations under one white overseer and even in the use of Negro overseers as managers. Discipline on the plantations was lax and when to this was added the fact that the slaves were mostly African-born and of fairly recent importation, the situation on St. John was well-nigh unmanageable. It is generally believed that St. John had a large number of recently imported El Mina slaves, and the outbreak of the rebellion is usually attributed to them, since they were supposed to be of a violent disposition.

Contributing to the unrest was the serious drought in the spring and summer of 1733, followed in July by a hurricane which caused considerable damage to the struggling crops. An insect plague later on added to the general destruction. The slaves were already threatened with famine when a second hurricane hit the island in early winter and destroyed the few remaining food crops.[9]

Discontent attained the intensity of rebellion from the legal straightjacket in which the slaves found themselves. They had been forbidden in 1726 to sell ground provisions without their masters' permission, and in the following year they were prohibited from observing festivals and from gathering in large groups. Then on September 5, 1733, Governor Gardelin issued his very repressive slave law previously discussed. Faced by death through starvation on the one hand and without an opportunity of being able to improve their condition on the other, the slaves determined to rebel.

The rebellion was originally planned for Christmas 1733, but when Governor Gardelin decided to visit St. John in November, the date of the uprising was brought forward to coincide with his visit. Fortunately for him his tour ended before the trouble began.

The rebellion was carefully planned by the second 'bomba' or slave driver, named Kanta, belonging to the Company, and by the head 'bomba' Class belonging to former Governor Suhm. The outbreak came on Monday morning November 23, 1733 when under the pretence of supplying the fort in Coral Bay with wood, a group of from 12 to 14 slaves, using cutlasses hidden in the bundles, massacred the soldiers in the fort. Only by hiding under his bed was one of the seven soldiers able to escape and to report the incident in St. Thomas. Having killed the soldiers, the slaves raised the flag and fired three cannon shots to signal the island-wide uprising.[10] Among the first victims were Magistrate Johan Reimert Soedtmann and his step-daughter; his wife who was Governor Gardelin's daughter, was in St. Thomas and so escaped slaughter.

Following the initial attack, the rebels divided into two parties, one for the north side and the other for the south side of the island. Armed with flintlocks or pistols and cutlasses, the rebels on the north side killed most but not all the whites they encountered. The surgeon, Cornelius Bodger was saved for his medical skill, and his two young step-sons so they could be made servants. The Company's overseer was saved because some slaves begged clemency for him. In the south side, most of the whites escaped death since they received prior warning from their slaves.

At Caneel Bay plantation, the rebels met with resistance from Johan Jansen and his faithful slaves. Jansen was overcome but the delay here enabled the surviving planters and their families to collect at Pieter Duurloo's plantation. This property on the north-west side of St. John was accessible from St. Thomas and had several cannon to defend it against sea and land invaders. The women and children were transferred to outlying cays for further removal to St. Thomas at the same time that preparations were made to meet the expected attack. Defending the plantation were 40 whites and 25 faithful slaves, most of whom had guns. Future events demonstrated that the slaves' skill at guerilla warfare was not matched by proficiency in siege warfare; the result was that their attack on Duurloo was ineffective.

Meanwhile, reinforcements had arrived from St. Thomas where fear of a similar outbreak suggested assistance to the planters in St. John. The intention was to confine the rebellion to the smaller island, and on November 24, food and ammunition were sent to Duurloo. In addition, a force of 18 soldiers under the command of a sergeant, and several creole slaves armed with guns arrived to assist the beseiged. Later, further reinforcements arrived, including the Free Negro Corps under Mingo Tamarin and other slaves belonging to planters in St. Thomas. The fort in Coral Bay was recaptured with the loss of only two men, and Duurloo relieved. For some time the rebels used the Suhm plantation as their rendezvous, but before Christmas they were driven off and scattered all over the island.

The rebel slaves continued to rob and burn one plantation after another despite the strength of the forces pursuing them. The rough terrain of St. John and the slaves' knowledge of jungle fighting enabled them to evade capture while stratagems to entrap them failed. Willem Vessuup, a white man wanted for murder, tempted them to enter his boat in return for gunpowder which they sorely needed. Vessuup hoped that by capturing the rebels he would win his own reprieve. The rebels, however, refused to be enticed, and in return promised Vessuup ten slaves in exchange for ten barrels of powder. Enough rebels had been killed though to raise the fear of plague in St. John.

Foreign aid first came from the British when in February, 1734 assistance was received from a Captain Tallard of an English man-of-war visiting Tortola. He sent 60 men to St. John to join in the pursuit, but when they were ambushed and four killed, the British force withdrew.

Another British attempt under Captain John Maddox from St. Kitts who landed in St. John with 50 volunteers in March, 1734 suffered a similar fate. When after a vain and wearying search, they were surprised and three men killed and five others wounded, Maddox fled from St. John the very next day.

All attempts by Danes and British to dislodge or to exterminate the rebels had failed so far. After trying in vain to secure further help from the British Governor of St. Kitts, Governor Gardelin turned with success to the French Governor of Martinique. Knowledge of the negotiated sale of St. Croix to the Danes led the French governor to send two ships with 228 soldiers under the command of an experienced officer, Longueville. The French soldiers were trained in jungle warfare and from April 24 to May 27, 1734 they under-took a systematic search of St. John despite heavy rains. They encountered a group of rebels on a reef on April 29, and killed some before the others escaped. The rebels, however, preferred death by suicide – on May 9, 11 dead rebels were found, and while one week later, eight others surrendered. on May 24, 24 were found dead on an isolated headland (Mary's Point).

The French soon after returned to Martinique though the rebellion was not quite over. It was reported in August, 1734 that 14 rebels both men and women, led by one Prince, a slave belonging to Madame Elizabeth Runnels, were still at large on St. John. They were unarmed, and by promising them a free pardon, the Danish officer, Didrik Oettingen was able to capture them. Prince was beheaded, and all the others were punished, most of them by execution. In this inglorious way the rebellion was finally suppressed. For his part, Oettingen received high praise and a lieutenancy in St. Croix.

From an estimate made in February, 1734, it was shown that only 146 slaves, or 14 percent of the slave population, were implicated in the rebellion.[11] Slaves did not readily resort to rebellion, under the worst of conditions. Nor were they easily inveigled into rebellion against the recognized authorities who had military forces at their command, and could depend upon assistance from abroad. The great majority of them remained faithful or acquiescent while a number of them actually took an active part in suppressing the rebellion. The death of six of these slaves entitled their owners to compensation. Of 92 plantations listed during the rebellion, 48 were shown to have suffered damage, and 44 to have escaped it; despite the disorder cultivation had already been resumed on 62 of them by the time the count was taken. While about a quarter of the white population had been killed by the rebels, valuable buildings had been wholly or partly burned, and the total financial loss was estimated at 7,905 rigsdalers.[12]

The rebellion not only resulted in the loss of life, labor and property but it also strained relations between masters and slaves. Apparently it taught the whites both to be more vigilant and to treat their slaves more humanely. St. John developed rapidly after 1734 and by 1739, the population of 1,414 was several hundred more than the pre-rebellion period, and there were 208 whites. However, the white adult male population had declined from 97 in 1733 to 73 in 1739.

Many planters seized the opportunity presented by the acquisition of the fertile island of St. Croix to transfer their resources there. To that extent, St. Croix benefited from the rebellion of 1733. With their slaves and other moveable capital, they contributed to the rapid expansion of this the largest plantation island in the Danish colony. That St. Croix had no violent upheaval before 1848 may be attributed in large measure to the painful lessons learned from the slave revolt in St. John.

The Slave Conspiracies of 1746 and 1759

Slave-owners in the Virgin Islands were hypersensitive to the possibilities of slave uprisings after 1733. Not only must they not be allowed to take place, but if threatened were to be suppressed as quickly and as vigorously as possible. Rebellions were to be nipped in the bud, and to ensure order various preventive measures were introduced after 1733. Slaves were not permitted to gather in groups beyond a certain number and after certain specified hours in the day. Moreover, owners were required to keep white managers constantly on their plantations when they themselves could not be present. Because of vigilance, a threatened rebellion in 1746 by a large number of runaway slaves in St. Croix was prevented from taking place. Mingo Tamarin and his Free Negro Corps hunted down the troublesome runaways and brought them under submission.[13]

In an island where the whites were out-numbered by the slaves by 1,690 to 11,807, as it was around 1759, the situation was pregnant with potential danger. Swift action had prevented an insurrection in 1746, but the slaves remained in a restless condition. When rebellion threatened again in 1759, the authorities were prepared to act promptly as the occasion warranted.[14]

The leading conspirators of the planned revolt seemed to have been William Davis, a free-negro, and his three confederates. One of these was Sam Hector who could read and write, and Michel and Quaco of whom little is known. Plans were carefully laid and the uprising was set for the Christmas holidays of 1759. Each slave was to kill his master or overseer, and take what arms could be found. They were then to split into two bodies, those in the east to assemble under Quaco at Coleman's plantation near Christiansted, and those in the west to assemble under Hector in Frederiksted where they were to seize the fort. All those with weapons were then to proceed to Christiansted to capture the fort there; on the way they were to burn all plantations and kill all the white people they met.

After the successful takeover of the island, William Davis was to be governor-general, Michel was to be second-in-command, while Sam Hector was to be captain of the town. The leaders made sure that the participants were bound by solemn oath, but the enthusiasm of Cudjo, who knew the secret, outstripped his caution. Upon enquiring of a white overseer how much longer it was to Christmas, Cudjo remarked, 'I hope by that time to be a . . . Petit Maitre.' On another occasion he sought and obtained a dozen bullets from a white artisan, and upon being questioned by another white man he voiced the threat, 'You shall be the first that I shall kill.'

These conversations were reported to the authorities, and the governor-general ordered an investigation set for December 11, 1759. What followed was an over-wrought, fearful reaction by the white people, that is, arrest, torture, conviction and execution. Cudjo at first denied his conversations but later admitted to them when his brother Quamina voluntarily testified against him. Cudjo then implicated William Davis who, when promised banishment rather than execution, talked freely and exposed others. Davis later committed suicide by cutting his throat in repentance for his betrayal of his friends. Of those accused of complicity in the plot, thirteen men were executed, including Sam Hecto,̄, two were broken on the wheel, four were burnt alive, four were pinched with hot tongs and hanged − some by the neck, others by the legs − and three were gibbeted. Ten others were transported and sold to the Spaniards, while 59 men and women were acquitted. Revenge touched even the dead William Davis whose body was dragged through the streets of Christiansted, and then suspended and burnt at the stake.

PETER VON SCHOLTEN

Peter von Scholten and his plans for Emancipation

Not until 1848 did the slaves again rise in defiance of the constituted authority as the culmination of a series of events involving the emancipation of slaves. In this respect the career of Peter von Scholten needs to be examined in some detail, since his association with the Virgin Islands and his attitude towards the non-white population largely determined the outcome of emancipation.

Peter von Scholten first came to the Virgin Islands in 1804 as an Ensign and was later promoted to second lieutenant in the Danish West Indian army. His father, Colonel Casimir von Scholten, was Commandant of Fort Christian in St. Thomas, and in 1807 when the British captured the island, both Peter and his father were taken to England as prisoners of war. The following year, they were released and sent to Denmark where Peter became an adjutant to King Frederik VI. He won the affection of his sovereign and was appointed Royal Weigher in Charlotte Amalie in 1814. Promotion came fairly rapidly: in 1822 he became Intendant of Customs, in 1823 Governor of St. Thomas, and in 1827 acting Governor-General of all the Virgin Islands. His acquaintance with the Virgin Islands was already about 23 years and he was to spend exactly 21 years more here.[15]

Ostentatious display was one facet of von Scholten's character; he had only an elementary education and no real culture, but he loved good food, wine, parties, handsome uniforms and beautiful houses. He had a propensity for lavish spending which exceeded his salary, and Government House in Christiansted, and 'Bulowsminde' a beautiful country-house outside Christiansted, bear testimony to his love of splendor and spending. His seemingly reckless use of money particularly his use of public funds for private affairs was widely criticized by the Commerce Collegium. But von Scholten had a very conscientious and warm-hearted personality: he was charming, boisterous, and loved a good joke; and he was beloved by the negro and colored population of the Virgin Islands who referred to him fondly as 'Massa Peter.'[16]

That Peter von Scholten reciprocated the affection of the black and colored people was evident not only by his intimate association with the free-colored woman Anna Elizabeth Heegaard but by his efforts to ameliorate the condition under which slaves, free-blacks and free-coloreds lived.[17] Because of his attention to these lower orders of society von Scholten was disliked and opposed by other white people. As if to compensate for their animosity, he enjoyed the confidence and friendship of King Frederik VI with whom he settled many matters through private correspondence.

The Act of Emancipation passed by the British Parliament in August, 1833, encouraged von Scholten to propose the freeing of slaves in the Virgin Islands. According to his plan of 1834 slaves were to be given one-sixth of their freedom immediately after the plan was accepted, to take the form of one free week-day off when slaves could work for their masters for wages. The money so earned was to be paid into the colonial treasury and used at the end of the year to pay for another portion of the individual slave's freedom according to his or her assessed value. This process would be repeated until slaves had become completely free. In addition, the parents of new-born slaves were to have the right to buy their freedom at a settled price. The plan was unacceptable to both officials and planters and was not implemented;[18] instead, concessions were made by the decree of November 22, 1834, already discussed.

When von Scholten returned to the Virgin Islands in 1840 after a two-year visit to Denmark, he brought a suggestion from the new king Christian VIII for which he was asked to win the planters' approval. Under this scheme slaves were to be given one full day off every week for which they were to be paid if their services were needed. In addition, all slaves over eight years of age were to be paid ten skillings a week during the harvest season. The money so earned could be used by the slaves to buy their freedom.[19]

The plan of 1840 involved a more gradual emancipation than the plan of 1834, and the planters' reaction to it varied. Those on St. John agreed to grant a half-day off on Saturday for the whole year, plus 14 skillings a week for good work. The planters on St. Thomas rejected the plan outright but their decision could not be decisive since they were comparatively few.

The attitude of the St. Croix planters who represented 10,000 slaves was more important; but while the majority agreed to give slaves Saturday off for the whole year, they refused to make any payments by which slaves could buy their freedom. The minority on the other hand, were prepared to give only half-day on Saturday and would make no payment; rather, they wanted a guarantee that they would be able to keep their slaves for the next 15 years without any change. With this unfavorable response von Scholten returned to Denmark in 1842, and was able to secure a Royal ordinance dated February 18, 1843, by which planters were forced to grant their slaves Saturdays off unless they wanted to hire their services at 40 skillings for each Saturday.[20]

The Slave Revolt of 1848 and the Proclamation of Emancipation

Responsible opinion in Denmark undoubtedly favored the emancipation of slaves in the Virgin Islands, though for financial reasons, it was
necessary to compromise with the slave-owners. Planters had already
shown their unwillingness to accept any solution which involved
financial loss to or the payment of money by them. If slaves were freed
outright, it might be necessary for the Danish government to award
them compensation for the loss of their property in slaves. Britain had
already led the way in 1834 by awarding financial compensation to
British colonial slave-owners. But the Virgin Islands had declined so
much economically that it was doubted that they were worth the value
of the compensation that would be involved.

However, by 1847 it appeared that a compromise solution to the
emancipation problem had been found, which seemed satisfactory to all
slave-owners, including the planters. It was embodied in a royal decree
of July 28, 1847 which provided that from that date all children born
to slaves were to be free, but that present slaves should be free only
after an interim period of twelve years, 'so that the interest of all
parties be safeguarded and the necessary preparations for the transition
be made.'[21]

But the Danish Government reckoned without the attitude of the
slaves themselves who had not been considered important.enough to be
consulted. They were dissatisfied with the terms of the decree and
expressed their dissatisfaction by open protest in July, 1848 during a
period of general unrest both in Europe and in the West Indies. There
were revolutionary uprisings in France, Italy and Germany; even
Denmark itself was affected by an outbreak of violence in Copenhagen
and revolution in the dukedoms. News of revolutions in Europe reached
the Virgin Islands by May, 1848 and from Martinique and Guadeloupe
came further news of slave revolts aimed at freedom. Whether the
authorities in the Virgin Islands expected a similar outbreak is uncertain, though the Spanish Governor in Puerto Rico was led to offer von
Scholten military assistance should he require it. Only when the revolt
was imminent were 'strange reports' bruited of slaves' refusal to work
and of their intent to demand freedom. Few if any of the white
population had any suspicion of revolt, and the reports were dismissed
as 'idle rumors and scandals.'[22]

The revolt began in the rural areas in the west end of St. Croix during the late evening of Sunday, July 2, 1848 heralded by the ringing of bells and the blowing of conch shells. At first, the slaves confined themselves to noisy demonstrations, but the white population became considerably alarmed. At about 7 o'clock on the morning of July 3, slaves poured into Frederiksted where they plundered and demolished a few houses including those of the police officer and the judge. The white major who headed the Brand corps which was assisting in keeping the peace, barely escaped with his life when he was attacked by a colored woman wielding an axe. A large number of slaves gathered in front of the fort and demanded their freedom;[23] they were not fired at since it was feared that they might seek revenge by burning down the town and massacring the whites. Indeed, the whole revolt was marked by considerable restraint by both slaves and whites. When their demands went unheard, the slaves worked their fury by plundering and destroying the house of a merchant named Moore, who had recommended that they should be shot down. One of the leaders of the revolting slaves in the west-end was 'General' Buddhoe, a personable black laborer who directed the forces of resistance with considerable daring and skill.[24] Meanwhile, the white inhabitants were in hiding or were escaping on board the ships in the harbor.[25]

Governor-General von Scholten who had only a few hours before returned from an official visit to St. Thomas, received news of the outbreak at about 2 o'clock on the morning of July 3. He decided to remain in Christiansted until he had received definite news from Frederiksted of the state of affairs in the West End. Nevertheless, a detachment of 60 men under the command of Lieutenant Holstein was instructed to take a position on the Centerline Road between Frederiksted and Christiansted. On receiving further reports of worsening conditions in Frederiksted, von Scholten decided at about noon to head for that town.[26] Immediately on his arrival, and on his own authority, he proclaimed the freedom of all slaves in the Virgin Islands. Formal proclamations were printed in Danish and in English that same night and later distributed. The essential portion which embraced all the provisions of the proclamation, was as follows:[27]

1. All unfree in the Danish West-Indian Islands are from today emancipated.
2. The estate Negroes retain for three months from date the use of the houses and provision grounds which they have hitherto possessed.

3. Labor is in future to be paid for by agreements but allowance to cease.
4. The maintenance of the old and infirm, who are not able to work, is until further determination, to be furnished by the late owners.

Von Scholten's declaration of emancipation did not end the revolt in the west, nor did it prevent its spread to the east. Disorder continued in the west where numerous plantations were plundered and destroyed, and military units marched into the rural areas to overawe the slaves. Several turbulent days elapsed before the refugees were inclined to leave the vessels to which they had resorted, and to return to their homes. Slaves who were apparently satisfied with von Scholten's proclamation, including 'General' Buddhoe, were instrumental in catching those who continued pillaging, and carrying them to the fort.[28]

Fighting began in Christiansted even before the news of von Scholten's declaration of freedom was received. Major Falbe had taken steps to defend Christiansted and had blocked the roads leading to it. When about two thousand slaves threatened to march on the town, Lieutenant McCutchin ordered his troops to open fire with grapeshot and several slaves were killed and many others wounded. The crowd dispersed and next morning (July 4) von Scholten had to ride over the island in an effort to stop the plundering of plantations, and to quiet the slaves with the assurance that they were indeed free. The following day, a detachment of troops numbering 60 cavalry and about 140 infantry under Major Falbe, was successful in dispersing two large groups of slaves who were ransacking plantations St. John's and Mon Bijou.[29]

The depredations, however, continued, and a bloody encounter occurred on July 5 between the detachment stationed on the Centerline Road and a group of slaves who surrounded and bombarded them with stones. The soldiers at first fired warning shots, and when these did not help, they shot into the crowd, killing three and wounding many.[30]

On the morning of July 6, when von Scholten rode again from government house in his attempt to calm the slaves, he encountered a group of planters in the harbor-square in Christiansted, who reproached him severely for the rebellion and emancipation. For days von Scholten had driven himself physically, and this attack broke his morale; he returned to government house where he collapsed after muttering his resignation. A provisional government was established in Christiansted, but the officials in Frederiksted refused to acknowledge it and formed their own. This dual control continued until Oberst von Oxholm arrived from St. Thomas on July 8, and was handed over the command by von Scholten. On the same day, 580 Spanish troops arrived from Puerto Rico at the request of von Scholten.[31]

By this time, the revolt was almost at an end; hundreds of prisoners had been brought into the forts and some plantations had resumed operations. The presence of the Spanish troops broke all resistance, and peace was once more restored. The rioters were subsequently tried by court-martial and several were shot. Of the leaders of the revolt who had later assisted the authorities, 'General' Buddhoe of the West End was banished to Trinidad from where he reportedly went to Curacao and then to the United States. Another leader, Martin King of the East End, was imprisoned for two years, and later employed as a rat-catcher on a plantation in St. Croix.[32]

As soon as he was well enough for a sea trip, von Scholten left for Denmark on July 14, 1848. His declaration of emancipation was not reversed, but was confirmed by a royal proclamation issued on September 22, 1848. Von Scholten, however, had many enemies and he was charged for neglecting to take the measures necessary for the adequate protection of the Virgin Islands and to prevent the revolt. He was even accused of instigating the revolt just to have the chance of declaring the emancipation of slaves. Following a court martial, von Scholten was found guilty on February 5, 1851 of dereliction of duty, but he was acquitted by the unanimous decision of the Danish Supreme Court given on April 29 the next year.[33]

Conclusion

The protest of slaves had eventually given them their freedom; but it is doubtful whether they would have achieved even this measure of success had it not been for Peter von Scholten who sacrificed his career on their behalf. The royal decree of July 28, 1847 had required the setting up of a committee composed of members of the colonial government, and other experienced men, under the chairmanship of the Governor-General. It was to plan the administrative and legislative measures which would be necessary to prepare slaves for freedom, and 'when they have obtained their freedom, to provide for their subsistence, for the cultivation of the plantations by means of free labor'.

No action had been taken by July 2, 1848 and the abrupt declaration of freedom made it more than ever necessary for plans to be formulated. What these plans were would, of course, depend upon the structure and growth rate of the economy and, above all, the attitudes, skills, and capacity for labor of the freed people.

[1] Cf. Orlando Patterson, *The Sociology of Slavery*. (Fairleigh Dickinson University Press, 1969) pp. 273-283.
[2] Adam Smith, *The Wealth of Nations*. (London, J. M. Dent & Sons Ltd., 1960 Edition) Vol. 1, p. 345.
[3] C. G. A. Oldendorp, Geschichte der Mission der evangelischen Bruder auf der carabaischen Inseln S. Thomas, S. Croix und S. Jan. (Barby, 1777) Vol. 1, mentioned in Jens Vibaek, *Dansk Vestindien 1755-1848: Vestindiens Storhedstid.* (Fremad, Denmark, 1966) p. 151.
[4] Governors of St. Thomas. Orders issued for Observance by Inhabitants 1672-1726. (The Bancroft Collection at Berkeley).
[5] Steffen Linvald, *Sukker & Rom.* (Kobenhavn, 1967) p. 24.
[6] Vibaek, op. cit., pp. 152-154.
[7] George Truman, John Jackson and Thos. B. Longstreth, *Narrative of a Visit to the West Indies in 1840 and 1841.* (Philadelphia, Merrihew and Thompson, 1844) p. 21.
[8] Emil Valdemar Lose, 'Kort Udsigt over den Danske Lutherske Missions Historie paa St. Croix, St. Thomas, og St. Jan.' (*Nordisk Missions Tidsskrift*, 1, Kjobenhavn, 1890) p. 6; Waldemar Westergaard, *The Danish West Indies Under Company Rule* (1671-1754). (New York, The Macmillan Company, 1917) p. 38; P.P. 1789, Vol. 26, No. 646a, Pt. 3. Report of the Lords' Committee on the Slave Trade, mentioned in Richard B. Sheridan, 'Africa and the Caribbean in the Atlantic Slave Trade.' (*The American Historical Review*, Vol. 77, No. 1, February, 1972) p. 31.
[9] Westergaard, op. cit., p. 166.
[10] C. F. Paludan, 'Blade af de danske-vestindiske Oers Historie.' (*Museum; Tidsskrift for Historie og Geografi, Vol. 3, Copenhagen, 1894)* pp. 341-365.
[11] Westergaard, op. cit., p. 176.
[12] Ibid., p. 177.
[13] Waldemar Westergaard, 'Account of the Negro Rebellion on St. Croix, Danish West Indies, 1759.' (*Journal of Negro History*, Vol. 11, Jan., 1926) pp. 50-51.
[14] Ibid., pp. 51-61.
[15] H. Lawaetz, *Peter v. Scholten. Vestindiske Tidsbilleder fra den sidste Generalguvernors dage.* (Kobenhavn, 1940) pp. 11-34.
[16] Trelawney Wentworth, *The West India Sketch Book.* (London, 1834) pp. 258-259.
[17] H. F. Garde, 'Anna Heegaard og Peter von Scholten.' (*Personalhistorisk Tidsskrift*, Vol. 78, 1958) pp. 25-38; 'Peter von Scholten.' (*Virgin Islands View*, July, 1966).
[18] Vibaek, op. cit., pp. 271-272.
[19] Ibid., pp. 277-278.

[20] Ibid., p. 279; Lawaetz, op. cit., p. 157.
[21] Carlo Christensen, *Peter von Scholten. A Chapter of the History of the Virgin Islands.* (Denmark, Gadgaard Nielsens Bogtrykkeri, 1955) pp. 19-20.
[22] John P. Knox, *A Historical Account of St. Thomas, W.I.* (New York, Charles Scribner, 1852) pp. 112-114.
[23] 'Documents Relating to the Danish West Indies.' (*Journal of Negro History*, Vol. 11, 1926) pp. 302-309.
[24] *Bernhard von Peterson, En historical Beretning om de danske-vestindiske Oer.* (Copenhagen, 1855) pp. 106-109.
[25] Knox, op. cit., p. 113.
[26] Lawaetz, op. cit., pp. 174-191.
[27] Carlo Christensen, op. cit., pp. 25-26.
[28] Knox, op. cit., p. 116.
[29] Charles Edwin Taylor, *Leaflets from the Danish West Indies: descriptive of the Social, Political and Commercial Condition of these Islands.* (London, 1888) pp. 141-142.
[30] Vibaek, op. cit., pp. 293-294.
[31] 'Documents Relating to the Danish West Indies . . .' pp. 313-317; Taylor, op. cit., pp. 143-144; Knox, op. cit., pp. 119-121.
[32] Taylor, op. cit., pp. 144-145.
[33] Carlo Christensen, op. cit., pp. 28-32.

Chapter 11

The Religious Denominations

Ethnic and religious diversity were marked features of the Danish colonial society where the peoples represented included Danes, Dutch, English, French, German, Jew and African. Although the Virgin Islands were Danish, the Danes were by no means a majority of the white population. Consequently, it was of some importance that the views of the other peoples in religion as in other matters should be recognized and respected if harmony were to prevail among them.

The multiplicity of nationalities explains the multiplicity of religious denominations which ministered to the religious needs of the people. Thus the Lutheran Church ministered to the Danes, the Reformed Dutch Church served the Dutch and probably the Germans also, the Moravians were missionaries to the Africans, and the Episcopal or Anglican Church served the British. Catholics of various nationalities in time became numerous enough to support their own Church, while the Jews maintained an exclusive position in religion and worshipped separately in their synagogue.

Except the Jews, congregations commonly consisted of different nationalities, the Catholics being most diverse in this respect. The French Huguenots, though at first served by their own Protestant priest, soon became part of the Reformed Dutch and Lutheran Churches. The multi-nationality of congregations resulted in part from the inadequacy or non-availability of suitable places of worship, but more so from the absence of ministers. Because of the high death-rate among incumbent ministers and the difficulty of securing either initial appointments or replacements, few of the pioneer settlers of St. Thomas were always represented by priests of their own religious leaning. Hence the people of the unserved denominations turned to one of the others whose beliefs and practices approximated most closely to their own.[1]

The Establishment of Organized Religion

Since the European colonies tended to reflect the religious orientation of their mother countries, it is not surprising that the official religion of the Virgin Islands was Lutheranism which was the state religion of Denmark at the time. However, early Danish colonizers wanted to establish their settlement on firm religious foundations, and so were quite tolerant of other religious denominations in their West Indian colony.

When Erik Neilsen Smit undertook the colonization of St. Thomas in 1665, he enlisted the services of a Lutheran theological candidate named Kjeld Jensen Slagelse. According to his contract with Smit, Slagelse agreed to 'serve the congregation which Erik Smit intends, in the name of God and according to royal instructions given him, to move to and congregate in the said island of St. Thomas.' In return Slagelse was to receive a number of clearly defined privileges pertaining to land and buildings which were made inheritable by pastors in succession to him.[2] Thus religion was seen not as a temporary expedient to cater only for the immediate needs of the colonial enterprise, but also as an essential requirement of a permanent undertaking.

Reaffirmation of faith in the value of religion to strengthen the foundation of any new settlement undertaken was explicit in the Charter granted to the Danish West India Company on March 11, 1671. To the concessions accorded in the Virgin Islands to Lutheran ministers, were added others in Denmark. For those who served in the Virgin Islands, special privileges awaited them in the mother-country where they would be given priority in appointments to vacant benefices and paid by the state.[3]

Slagelse had been the personal selection of Erik Smit one of the directors of the Company who organized the colonizing expedition of 1665. The practice of the first Company became a precedent for the second when in 1671 the directors of the Danish West India Company made their selection of a Lutheran minister for their new colony. Though no mention of this power was made in the Charter, the original agreement apparently was allowed to govern the renewed appointment. On this occasion the choice was again Kjeld Jensen Slagelse who unfortunately died at sea on April 25, 1672 on his way to St. Thomas.[4]

Future appointments continued to be made by the directors of the Company and the Slagelse contract of 1665 was apparently modified and applied to his successors. The privileges offered both in the Virgin Islands and in Denmark operated as incentives to attract future ministers, and existing practices were codified in clause 14 of the renewed Charter granted to the Company on September 28, 1697.[5]

In return for privileges granted, it became necessary for the Crown to exercise more control over the appointment of ministers. Accordingly, regulations were issued in 1734 to the effect that pastoral appointments in the Lutheran Church were to be confirmed by the king. Because of the favored position of the Reformed Dutch Church in the Virgin Islands at the time, the provision was also applied to it.[6]

The appointment of Lutheran priests was not allowed to be idle expressions of Danish resolve to promote a stable society based on sound Christian principles. This was evident in the first orders issued by Governor Iversen on August 8, 1672 in which the religious duties of the colonists were clearly indicated:

1. Every person who speaks Danish is bound to attend service every Sunday in Christian's fort when the drum beats, and on failure of doing so is to pay a fine of *twenty-five pounds of tobacco.*
2. Persons of all other nations are bound to attend service every Sunday afternoon at the same place, under the same penalty.
3. Every householder shall encourage his servants to be pious, and have morning and evening prayers; and if he allows them to do work on Sunday which might have been done on Saturday, or if he occupies servants of other people in his employ, he is, for every offense, to pay fifty pounds of tobacco.[7]

The extent to which these orders were observed or enforced is not known. That they could not have been mere pious exhortations is suggested by Iversen's consistent firmness in other matters relating to the government of St. Thomas. Despite the lax administration of Iversen's immediate successors, the Esmits, religious practices continued to be observed. Afterwards, religious observances were placed on a more even keel by the establishment of more stable governments.

The need to foster Christianity in St. Thomas was seen also by the close cooperation between the Lutherans and members of the Reformed Dutch Church. Cooperation was suggested mainly by the desire to secure the fullest support of the Dutch colonists, which was essential for the success of the colonization enterprise.

Cooperation between the two denominations was given practical expression when the Dutch were allowed to use the Lutheran place of worship in Fort Christian to conduct their services until they could construct their own separate building. For the sake of convenience, the Lutheran services were held in the morning while those of the Dutch were held in the afternoon. The cooperation was extended even further; occasionally the Reformed Dutch Church became destitute of a pastor, and on these occasions his functions were performed by the Lutheran clergyman.

The Reformed Dutch Church was given official recognition in 1716 when a delegation of planters to Copenhagen secured permission on behalf of the members of the Reformed Dutch Church for the latter to nominate their own minister for approval by the Danish king.[8]

Concerning the establishment of the other more important religious groups, the Roman Catholics, the Jews, and the Anglicans can be given brief mention. As already indicated, religious toleration was practiced in the Virgin Islands from the beginning of colonization, even though only Lutherans and Dutch Reformists were permitted to hold public worship for many years. It was not until 1754 that Roman Catholics, except Jesuits, were allowed to build churches and introduce clergymen in the Virgin Islands for the purpose of public worship.[9] Following the agreement with Puerto Rico in 1767 for the return of runaway slaves, Roman Catholicism was encouraged especially among the black population, though the Catholic Church was forbidden to draw converts from the other denominations, or to 'make any converts of whites.'[10] Despite the restrictions from which it suffered, Catholicism soon grew to become the largest religious denomination in the Virgin Islands.[11]

Like other segments of the population, Jews became permanent residents of St. Thomas from the earliest years of its settlement. They were so few at first that no formal religious organization was attempted, and it can be surmized that they worshipped privately. However, following the sack of St. Eustatius by the British Admiral Rodney in 1781, substantial numbers of Jews migrated to the Virgin Islands, thereby introducing organized Judaism here.[12]

Because of the more heavy concentration of British settlers in St. Croix, the Anglican Church first took root in this island. In St. Thomas, the Anglicans were for many years never sufficiently numerous to establish a separate congregation; consequently, they joined other denominations, primarily the Reformed congregation, for public worship. Later, their numbers increased through the immigration of English colonists from the other West Indian islands, making it possible for the Anglicans to become better organized. The first minister was Rev. Nicholas McLaughlin who came to St. Thomas from Tortola and conducted services beginning in 1820.[13]

Lutheran Proselytizing Among the Negro Population

The various Christian denominations concentrated on the needs of the white minority rather than on those of the black majority. No direct effort was made to incorporate Negroes into the Christian fold; they were left to do so on their own accord, and in time, free-negroes became members of all the Christian denominations. Judaism was not evangelistic and the Jews comprised an exclusive class of worshippers. As far as the slaves were concerned, they were neglected by all other denominations except the Lutherans. Even so, missionary work among them was not begun until 1757, and then a separate mission was established to devote itself exclusively to the work of Negro conversion.

Though nothing was accomplished for some years, missionary work among the slaves of St. Thomas was discussed by the Royal College of Missions in 1739. Denmark at the time was undergoing a spiritual revival founded on Pietism and this stimulated a concern to convert 'heathens' to Christianity. The colonial administration favored the idea since its desire was to promote stable society. After the slave rebellion in St. John in 1733, the need for the stabilizing influence of Christianity among the slaves must have been strongly desired. Nothing, however, was done during the remaining period of the rule of the Danish West India Company.

New proposals were submitted to the Danish king in January, 1755 for the introduction of a Lutheran mission in the Virgin Islands to work among the slaves. This was approved and eventually ten Lutheran missionaries, comprising six catechists and four under-catechists were dispatched to the Virgin Islands. The catechists were to serve six years and receive 150 rigsdalers a year. Few of them lived or remained in the

Virgin Islands long enough to serve the entire period. Of the ten missionaries sent out in 1757, one died on the voyage, two were assigned to St. Thomas, one to St. John, and the remaining six to St. Croix.[14]

Since the missionaries were not ordained priests, they were required to work in close cooperation with the Lutheran pastors who were to perform the necessary acts of baptism and communion required after the missionaries had achieved the conversion of the slaves. Their record was essentially one of death, desertion or dismissal. Roughly three years after the arrival of the nine catechists only three remained. In 1759 two Lutheran missionaries, and in 1766 six others, were sent out to the Virgin Islands to succeed those who had either died or left. Of these replacements three died within a year of arrival.[15]

The record of death and desertion did not speak well for the effectiveness of Lutheran missionary activity. Indeed, in St. Thomas and St. Croix the results were meager while in St. John where no mission work was done between 1759 and 1766, the situation was even worse.

The Moravian Missionaries and the Slaves

Compared with the Lutherans, the Moravian missionaries were more numerous and successful in winning black converts. The Virgin Islands were unique among West Indian colonies in that the initiative for the education of Negroes was taken by a Negro.

Count Zinzendorf of Germany went to Denmark in 1731 to be present at the coronation of Christian VI, and there his servants became acquainted with the Negro Anthony Ulrich, possibly a slave, from St. Thomas. Anthony told them of the miseries of the slaves in the colony, and of the desire of many of them to be taught the Christian religion. On his return to Germany, Zinzendorf related the incident to the Moravian Brethren whom he had given asylum in Herrnhut, a part of his domains. Later, Anthony himself visited Herrnhut, and to his previous plea, added that the labors of the slaves were so incessant that they would find no leisure for religious instruction; their teacher himself must become a slave, so that he could educate them during their working hours.[16]

As a result of the representations made by Anthony, two brethren, Leonard Dober a potter originally from Wurtenberg, and David

Nitchsmann a carpenter from Zauchtenthal, were selected as missionaries for St. Thomas. They were expected to earn their living by practicing their craft as their compatriots in Herrnhut were doing at the time. The two missionaries arrived at St. Thomas on December 13, 1732, but Dober was soon left alone when Nitchsmann returned to Europe in April, 1733. Dober could not practice his skill as a potter because of the lack of suitable clay, and after serving as steward to Governor Gardelin, he eventually became an overseer on one of the island's plantations. However, in August, 1734 he himself left St. Thomas for Herrnhut where he had been appointed to the post of Elder.[17]

From the beginning in St. Thomas, Moravian missionary activity spread to St. Croix and St. John. Already in June, 1734 fourteen other missionaries, four of whom were accompanied by their wives, arrived to augment the work in St. Thomas and extend it to St. Croix. As in the case of the Lutherans, mortality was high among the Moravians. For instance, during the two years 1734 and 1735, as many as 17 out of a total of 39 missionaries to St. Croix died; because of illness, nine others returned to Herrnhut.[18] The situation was no better in St. Thomas, and it was not until Friederich Martin arrived in March, 1736, that consistent work was begun.

Methods which were first developed in the Virgin Islands formed the basis of later Moravian missionary activities elsewhere in the West Indies. Unlike other denominations, the Moravians were concerned chiefly with the spiritual condition of slaves and did not actively recruit white members. Contrary to the belief of white skeptics, Moravians believed that Negroes were capable of genuine conversion. From the beginning of their mission in St. Thomas, 'They made it clear that Christ had died for blacks as well as whites.'[19] Underlying their activities was the assumption that slaves possessed the capacity to understand and follow the Christian religion.

Their approach was designed not only to convert the Negroes but also to keep them within the Christian fold. The basic lines of approach were suggested by Count Zinzendorf himself: the means of conversion included exemplary personal conduct by the missionaries themselves, and they were required to be cheerful, humble, and diligent in their work. Considerable importance was attached to their personal devotion and good conduct in presenting the Christian doctrine. In their preaching the missionaries were to concentrate on Christ's suffering and death to save mankind.

Above: FRIEDERICH MARTIN
Below: FRIEDENSTHAL IN ST. CROIX

Above: NEW HERRNHUT IN ST. THOMAS
Below: BETHANY IN ST. JOHN

Friederich Martin was the religious innovator in the Virgin Islands and he was responsible for establishing the mission on solid foundations during his long ministry from 1736 to 1750. His achievements led him to be called 'The Apostle to the Negroes', and when he died he was buried on plantation 'La Grande Princesse' in St. Croix. Martin sought to make the mission as self-supporting as possible through the purchase and development of plantations such as New Herrnhut in St. Thomas, Friedensthal in St. Croix and Bethany in St. John. By operating their own plantations with slave labor, the Moravians ensured themselves of a livelihood and also that potential converts were close at hand to make their pastoral work easier. In addition, Martin sought to systematize the internal organization of the mission by imposing a rigid discipline on those converted and to ensure, by means of adequate supervision, that no convert should lapse from his new faith. To provide this supervision a formal church organization was created consisting of a sacramental system, class meetings, and a hierarchy of church assistants. Lastly, Martin adopted the personal interview to meet and invite slaves to attend religious meetings.[20]

Martin believed that children should be taught religious precepts at an early age, but was apparently not in favor of baptizing them. This policy was changed when Johannes von Watteville, a Moravian leader, visited the Virgin Islands in 1749 and recommended that children of believing parents should be baptized as soon after birth as was convenient. Von Watteville was also responsible for relaxing the strict discipline imposed by allowing rejected converts to be received back into the mission after sincere repentance.[21] The first two decades of the mission saw the formulation of the basic principles for teaching Christianity to the Negroes, and Moravian missionaries found little reason to alter them during the remainder of slavery.

The Attitude of Slave-Owners to the Moravians

The Moravian missionaries had little in common with the Protestant clergy whose nationality and culture were generally those of the plantocracy, and being Germans they were regarded as foreigners. Their assimilation into the society was made more difficult by the fact that unlike most of the white men in the Virgin Islands, they engaged in manual work to make their living. Such work was usually left to the Negro population so that the missionaries 'lost caste' by indulging in occupations like planting and building.[22]

In the early years of their service here, the missionaries were faced with suspicion from the planters. This stemmed from fear that the Moravians, by working with the slaves, would spread ideas of social equality which would lead eventually to slave revolts. The work of the missionaries was thus seen as a threat to the existing social order.

Missionary endeavor was thwarted for a time following the St. John rebellion of 1733. Slaves were not only forbidden to hold intercourse with the missionaries, but the latter were also thrown into prison in October, 1737. Apparently they remained there until January, 1739, when Count Zinzendorf visited St. Thomas, and on his representations to the Governor they were freed. Thereafter slaves were allowed to attend religious meetings but only at night after their daily work was ended. Notwithstanding this privilege, acts of violence were still committed against slaves, and even the missionaries themselves were maltreated. For a time, therefore, the precaution was taken of holding services in nearby woods, and of appointing watchmen to guard the congregation against sudden attacks.[23]

Though these outrages against missionary activities were suppressed, the legal freedom of the Moravians to preach was not secured. The campaign for such freedom was led by Count Zinzendorf who used his good offices with the Danish court to present two petitions to the king and queen from the male and female black congregations in the Virgin Islands. As a result of these entreaties, the Moravians were granted toleration and protection to preach to the slaves.[24] The Royal order had the effect of reducing opposition towards the missionaries, even though it could not quite eliminate it.

Of more importance in creating an acceptance of the missionaries was the fact that after a time a noticeable change in the behavior of the slaves was observed. Instead of promoting greater resistance to slavery, religion served to make slaves more industrious workers and more obedient to their masters' orders. Besides, slaves became less inclined to resist their lot by rebelling and running away. This change of attitude served to convince slave-owners that their own interests were served by missionary activities. Consequently, slaves were even encouraged to attend religious meetings although the evangelizing had to be done at evenings after their daily work was over.

The colonial government also acknowledged the beneficial effects of the labor of the missionaries. Following the threatened rebellion of 1759, the authorities became even more favorable to missionary endeavor. Slaves who attended Moravian religious meetings were exempted from the curfew which began at seven o'clock at night provided they could produce a certificate signed by one of the missionaries.[25] Respectability and encouragement were given to Moravian efforts when Thomas de Malleville, the first native Governor General of the Virgin Islands became an adherent of the mission in 1796.

The attitude of the Moravians, also, was one of cooperation with the authorities since their success depended upon the toleration and assistance which they received from the white colonists. It was necessary that they should not alienate but attract the sympathy of slave-owners and other responsible people for the task they were undertaking. They, therefore, sought to avoid conflict with the secular power by disavowing any concern with politics and by accepting slavery as the basis of the social structure of the colony.

Moravian missionaries owned and worked slaves not only to have people on hand to convert, but also to demonstrate their acceptance of slavery.[26] They conciliated the slave-owners by preaching to their slave audiences the duty of obedience and submission. After the cessation of the slave trade from January, 1803 the slave-owners themselves saw the necessity of fuller cooperation with the missionaries. They depended entirely on the colonial labor force since slaves could no longer be replaced by imports from Africa. In order to get the maximum benefit from slaves, they solicited the assistance of their ministers. In so doing they had to give more assistance for the missionaries to perform their duties.

The principal functions of the ministers of the Christian denominations were to preach the gospel, baptize the converts, administer the communion and perform funeral rites. Because of their unique position, the Lutheran clergy might be asked to fill positions in the colonial government. Thus at one time Slagelse was acting-governor, and Stoud became a member of the Council of St. Croix.[27] These were rare instances, however; the involvement of the clergy in political affairs did not occur often since the Virgin Islands did not seem to lack sufficiently qualified men to participate in the political affairs of the colony. In any case, the pastors or missionaries of other denominations were not accorded even limited political privileges; they were left to concentrate their attention on the religious needs of their congregations.

The white population of the Virgin Islands did not seem to have responded well to the efforts of their ministers. Writing from St. Croix in January, 1741 Pastor Stoud referred to the 'unruly and lawless people who care neither for the government nor for religion.' Again, in 1777, Kingo, the Lutheran missionary wrote of the members of the council, the most powerful and influential body of St. Thomians, 'There is none righteous among them, no not one; they are all corrupt in their ways.'[28] That the white males were seldom more than nominal church-goers may be surmized from their dealings with pirates and smugglers and their concubinage with the black and colored population.

Negro Education: Missionary Initiative and Government Assistance

The Negro population was undoubtedly aware of the benefits which they derived from the Christian denominations. Education was recognized as one of the attributes of the 'good' society holding out the promise of a better life beyond the experiences of plantation agriculture for those who would acquire it. This explains the slaves' desire to be taught and the fervor with which they embraced the Christian religion. The denominations were seen as the medium through which they could acquire the attributes essential for advancement. During the first fifty years of Moravian efforts until August, 1782, as many as 8,833 adults and 2,974 children had been baptized. However, for various reasons, during the same period 2,381 adults and 975 children had died.[29]

One of the difficulties experienced by all those who preached to the slaves was that of language, and newly-imported slaves presented the greatest communication problem. Even after they were 'seasoned' to colonial life, they had to use one or the other of the dominant languages – Dutch in St. Thomas, English in St. Croix, and in some cases a mixture of several languages. In St. Thomas a conglomerate language called Negro-Dutch-Creole developed, while in St. Croix English persisted. In St. Thomas the Moravians quickly learned the new dialect, but in St. Croix their ignorance of English retarded their work considerably. Beginning in 1784, it was decided to translate portions of the Bible and other study-aids into the vernacular of the Negroes. Valuable assistance in this respect was obtained from Joackim Melchior Magens, a resident of St. John, who was also responsible for producing a dictionary of Negro-Dutch-Creole.[30]

It was to be expected that those who engaged in evangelical work should emphasize religious education as was evident in the work of both the Moravian and Lutheran missionaries. Secular education was largely neglected though reading and writing skills could be acquired through the teaching offered by the missionaries. It would appear that at his home, the Moravian missionary, Friederich Martin, kept a small boarding school where Negro children were taught to read and write.[31] This endeavor could not have been on a large scale, but Martin's example was followed by his successors.

The lead in establishing schools for Negroes was taken by the Lutheran missionaries beginning in 1773 when Niels Olufsen Salling arrived. The school he established, however, was used primarily for teaching the knowledge needed to pass confirmation examinations. Even so, it was not until 1798 that the Lutheran example was followed by the Moravians when the heirs of the Schimmelmann plantations in St. Croix granted permission for the Moravians to begin a regular school for the Negro children on their plantations. In St. John, a school was also opened at Emmaus, a Moravian church-plantation acquired in 1782, to accommodate the children of that island.

Unlike the British government, the government of Denmark was keenly interested in the education of the Negro population of its slave colony. However, it envisaged its role to be one rather of cooperation with the religious denominations than of independent action and a subsidy was thus given to the Lutheran mission to undertake educational services. However, in 1783 a royal commission recommended that steps should be taken to educate all Negroes in the Virgin Islands. Since the Lutheran mission was small compared with the Moravian mission, it suggested that the subsidy should be transferred from the Lutherans to the Moravians. This move, however, was strenuously opposed by the College of Church Inspection in Denmark since it threatened to bring Lutheran missionary work in the Virgin Islands to an end. As a result of this representation, the plan was abandoned.

Denmark made the first attempt in 1787 to introduce public schools for slaves in the Virgin Islands under the supervision and guidance of the Lutheran missionaries. The teachers or 'school managers' were to be selected from among 'the most well-behaved and capable Free Negroes, who at the same time shall be church clerks and funeral managers for the mission congregations,' and their salary was to be paid from the pew rents collected at mission services.[32] As a result of these provisions, four public schools were established by 1790, three in St. Croix and one in St. Thomas.

With the growth in the number of public schools, the financial provision made in 1787 could not for long support them. Accordingly, from 1819 some of the fines collected in the law courts of the Virgin Islands were used to defray educational expenses. The additional money eased the situation but did not satisfy requirements, and so an annual budget of 6,700 rigsdalers was established in 1832 for education in the Virgin Islands.

Governor-General Peter von Scholten was concerned in the 1830's to improve the condition of the slaves in the Virgin Islands. To achieve this objective he sought to introduce a system of free, compulsory and universal education through an ordinance of June 4, 1839 which provided for the institution of compulsory public education throughout the Virgin Islands for children between the ages of six and thirteen years. The schools were to be operated by the Moravian missionaries, and their direction was in turn to be supervised by the Lutherans through a commission in each island consisting of the Lutheran minister as chairman, the chief of police, a member of the Council, and another member nominated by the Governor-General.[33]

By involving both the Moravians and the Lutherans, von Scholten undoubtedly hoped to secure the cooperation of these major interest groups, and at the same time avoid inter-denominational jealousy and conflict. Also, it was essential to include the Moravians for financial reasons since their active participation in the education scheme would help to minimize costs. Furthermore, since there was at the time an adequate number of Moravian missionaries in the Virgin Islands, it would not be necessary to bring many additional teachers here from Denmark.

The education plan was early acted upon in St. Croix where on May 16, 1841 the first school was opened on plantation 'La Grande Princesse', and by 1842, eight schools were established in the island. In St. John and in St. Thomas lack of funds delayed implementation of the ordinance until 1844 and 1846 respectively. The new schools did not affect those denominational schools already in existence in the three islands. But as in the denominational schools, the role of the Church in the public educational system meant that education generally had a strong religious flavor.[34]

Impact of Christianity on the Slave Society

The crux of Christianity was the improvement of the moral character of the slaves, and because of this objective, religious activity received support from slave-owners. But the denominations were responsible for doing more than making slaves more obedient, industrious and peaceful workers. Their teaching of Christian ethics was aimed at dissociating the slaves from their African practices which were regarded as violating Christian principles. The general belief was that 'The more they are acquainted with the Gospel, the more they lose those ideas, which arose from their former heathenish life.'[35] Two of the African practices which ame under close attention were polygamy and obeahism: polygamy was the practice of one man having more than one wife, while obeahism was a form of witchcraft centering on belief in the occult. Negroes were discouraged from indulging in such practices even to the extend of exclusion from the denominations.

By seeking to break down African 'heathenism' and to inculcate Christian European values among the Negroes, the denominations sought to achieve passive acceptance of slavery and subordination. They succeeded to a considerable extent, for slaves were disinclined to protest against their subordinate position in the society. This was especially so after the slave trade was abolished when there were dwindling numbers of Africans with memories of a freedom recently lost and with hopes of achieving violent emancipation from the oppressions of their white masters.

The primary concern of the missionaries was the conversion of slaves to Christianity, but they did not stop there. Some of the black converts were selected to assist the missionaries in exhorting and supervising converts, and instructing the catechumens. In the performance of these duties, the black assistants tended to work alongside the white assistants. In addition, Negro assistants are known to have conducted services in the absence of white missionaries. These Negroes were able to rise to positions of responsibility, respect and leadership, first within the denominations themselves and later within the community as a whole.

That some of the Negroes were faithful and dedicated servants of the denominations is evidenced by the life and service of men like Nathaniel and Cornelius who were associated with the Moravians.[36] Nathaniel of St. Croix had 'lived in ignorance and the practice of heathen abominations till in his fortieth year.' He was baptized by Friederich Martin in 1744, and until his death in 1802 at the age of 98 years, remained a staunch supporter of the Morvavians. Cornelius was a slave until 1767, employed as a master-mason on the Royal (afterwards,

Schimmelmann) plantations in St. Croix. Because of his competence he was able to buy the freedom first of his wife, then of himself, and later of his six children. Baptized in 1749, he was a devout Christian and faithful Moravian and assisted in the building of six of the Moravian chapels in the Virgin Islands. He was appointed an assistant in the mission in 1754, and until his death in 1801 proved to be a 'generous and sympathizing friend and adviser' to the aged and needy. He was an eloquent speaker and could express himself in Creole, Dutch, Danish, German and English.

The denominations gave the Negroes who comprised the inferior social class an opportunity to associate with a type of social organization which was acceptable to their white superiors. Their presence within the denominations, therefore, gave the Negroes not only the opportunity to secure self-expression but also a degree of social recognition and acceptance by the white community.

The overtures of the Christian denominations to the European community did not receive the widespread support that the missionaries received from the Negro community. The Europeans' lack of enthusiasm for religion was reflected in their disinclination to encourage their slaves to attend religious worship. This tendency was marked in the early nineteenth century when the inhabitants of the agricultural islands of St. Croix and St. John were suffering from economic decline and when those in St. Thomas were concentrating their efforts more and more in trade. Furthermore, the educational reforms introduced by Governor-General von Scholten had the effect of making the Negroes less dependent upon the denominations. The net result was that there was a diminution of religious fervor among the slave population of the Virgin Islands in the nineteenth century. After his visits to St. Croix in the winters of 1835 and 1836, Sylvester Hovey observed that 'not more than a thousand are usually present at public worship on the Sabbath, in all the churches of the different denominations.'[37]

Conclusion

The activities of the religious denominations in the Virgin Islands had been encouraged from the very start of Danish colonization. Beginning in St. Thomas, organized religion was extended to St. John and St. Croix, since it was seen as a stabilizing force in the colonial society. The variety of religious denominations came to reflect the heterogeneity of the society — multi-national in composition and class, and race-divided in structure.

The denominations were divided between those which concentrated their activities among the white population and those which emphasized the conversion of the Negroes to Christianity. Despite their differing areas of emphasis, all the denominations alike suffered from high mortality among their ministers or missionaries, and to some extent from the lack of adequate places of worship. For the slaves the education offered by the denominations presented the opportunity to widen their experiences beyond the bounds of the plantations. For all Negroes, education held out the promise, however distant, of a higher social status.

The social aspirations of the Negroes accounted for their early attraction to Christianity, but those who worked among the slaves had to contend with the resistance, passive or active, of slave-owners. In the absence of positive encouragement from their masters, slaves lapsed in religious devotion when changing circumstances made their connection with the denominations less essential for social mobility.

[1] Frederick Lutheran Church 1666-1966. A Brief History of the Lutheran Congregation on the island of St. Thomas during its first three centuries. (n.d.)
[2] Jens Larsen, *Virgin Islands Story.* (Fortress Press, Philadelphia, 1950) pp. 1-7.
[3] Waldemar Westergaard, *The Danish West Indies Under Company Rule* (1671-1754). (New York, The Macmillan Company, 1917) p. 295.
[4] Kay Larsen, *Dansk Vestindien, 1666-1917.* (Copenhagen, 1927) p. 22.
[5] Westergaard, op. cit., p. 302.
[6] Ibid., p. 24.
[7] John P. Knox, *A Historical Account of St. Thomas, W.I.* (New York, Charles Scribner, 1852) pp. 48-49.
[8] Westergaard, op. cit., p. 190.
[9] Joseph G. Daly, 'Archbishop John Carroll and the Virgin Islands.' (*The Catholic Historical Review*, Vol. LIII, No. 3, October, 1967) pp. 306-307.
[10] Danish West Indies. *Laws, Statutes, etc. Rescript – Royal Ordinance of April, 1777.* (Copenhagen, 1777).
[11] Peter von Scholten, Report on the Regulations on Slavery in the Danish Island of St. Croix 1834-1838. (Von Scholten Collection, Virgin Islands Public Library, MMS).
[12] Hugo Bieber, 'Virgin Islands.' (*The Universal Jewish Encyclopedia*) pp. 425-426; Isidor Paiewonsky, *Jewish Historical Development in the Virgin Islands 1665-1959.* (St. Thomas, 1959); Albert A. Campbell, 'Note on the Jewish Community of St. Thomas, U.S. Virgin Islands.' (*Jewish Social Studies*, Vol. 4, No. 2, April, 1942) pp. 161-162.

[13] Knox, op. cit., pp. 156-158; E. Hutson, *A Short History of the Anglican Church in St. Thomas, Danish West Indies, 1848-1898.* (St. Thomas, 1899).

[14] Hans Ludwig Koch, 'Den Danske Mission i Vestindien.' (*Kirkehistoriske Samlinger.* Series 5, Vol. 3, Kjobenhavn, 1905) pp. 144-181; Emil Valdemar Lose, 'Kort Udsigt over den Danske Lutherske Missions Historie paa St. Croix, St. Thomas, og St. Jan.' (*Nordisk Missions Tidsskrift,* 1, Kjobenhavn, 1890) pp. 1-37.

[15] Kay Larsen, op. cit., p. 119.

[16] John Holmes, *Historical Sketches of the Missions of the United Brethren for Propagating the Gospel among the Heathen from their Commencement to the year 1817.* (London, 1827) pp. 1-3.

[17] C. G. A. Oldendorp, *Geschichte der Mission der evangelischen Bruder auf der carabaischen Inseln S. Thomas, S. Croix und S. Jan.* (Barby, 1777)

[18] H. Lawaetz, *Brodremenighedens Mission: Dansk-Vestindien, 1769-1848.* (Kjobenhavn, 1902) p. 21.

[19] J. E. Hutton, *A History of Moravian Missions.* (London, Moravian Publication Office, 1922) p. 29.

[20] Ibid., pp. 38-41; *Preben Ramlov, Brodrene og Slaverne Et blad af Dansk Vestindiens historie.* (Kristeligt Dagblads Forlag, 1968) pp. 136-148.

[21] Holmes, op. cit., p. 301.

[22] Hutton, op. cit., p. 48.

[23] Holmes, op. cit., pp.297-298.

[24] Ibid., pp. 298-300.

[25] Ibid., p. 307.

[26] Oliver W. Furley, 'Moravian Missionaries and Slaves in the West Indies.' (*Caribbean Studies,* Vol. 5, No. 2, July, 1965) pp. 4 and 15-16.

[27] Jens Larsen, op. cit., pp. 10-11; Westergaard, op. cit., p. 224.

[28] Kay Larsen, op. cit., p. 108; Koch, op. cit., p. 161.

[29] Holmes, op. cit., p. 309.

[30] Jens Larsen, op. cit., pp. 102-128.

[31] Hutton, op. cit., p. 40.

[32] Jens Larsen, op. cit., p. 97.

[33] Kay Larsen, op. cit., pp. 244-246; Lose, op. cit., p. 30.

[34] R. C. Foster, *The Story of Education in St. Croix, 1841-1941.* (Mimeo., 1941)

[35] *Instructions for the Members of the Unitas Fratum who minister in the Gospel among the Heathen.* (London, 1784).

[36] Holmes, op. cit., pp. 317-321.

[37] Sylvester Hovey, *Letters from the West Indies.* (New York, 1838) p. 31. Cf. George Truman, John Jackson and Thos. B. Longstreth, *Narrative of a Visit to the West Indies in 1840 and 1841.* (Philadelphia, Merrihew and Thompson, 1844) pp. 20-21, where these Quakers observed that in St. Thomas, 'the standard of morality was very low among the colored people, and . . . that a small amount of care is bestowed by the religious sects tolerated, towards elevating their condition, and it is probable but little pains will be taken in this respect, while they remain in the condition of slaves.'

Chapter 12

Constitutional Reforms under the Crown

The Danish Crown acquired the assets of the Danish West India Company in 1754 and henceforth became responsible for the government of the Virgin Islands and for the management of colonial affairs. With the dissolution of the Company it was necessary to create a partly new administration in Denmark to assume the responsibilities hitherto borne by it. A reorganized administration in the Virgin Islands was also called for, one which could work in harmony with the central administration, and enable the central administration to work without friction with the colonists. This last condition was essential since it was largely due to opposition from the colonists that the Danish West India Company had been forced into dissolution.

Administrative Reorganization Under the Crown

In keeping with the need for reform, a special office was established in Denmark under the Danish Chamber of Finance on November .28, 1754 to deal with colonial affairs. Known as the 'renteskriverkontor,' it was placed under the management of Peder Mariager, one of the most efficient officials in Copenhagen of the defunct Danish West India Company. Mariager had played a prominent part in the transfer negotiations between the Crown and Company, by preparing for the Crown a study of the Company since its establishment. The 'renteskriverkontor' was in general control over colonial affairs, but particular departments such as the Danish Chancellery, the military college, and the mission college, dealt with specific matters with which they were concerned.[1]

The 'renteskriverkontor' under the Chamber of Finance managed West Indian affairs only until February 15, 1760 when it was replaced by a newly established West Indian and Guinea General Finance and Customs Office. The colonies were to remain under the direction of this office except for a brief period between January 6, 1771 and January 21, 1773. The central administration in Copenhagen had extensive powers in decision-making, but this often created difficulties for the colonies since communication between them and Denmark was slow.

The greatest challenge was to create a new administration in the Virgin Islands. At the transfer, the Company had made no effort to protect the future welfare of its officials, and the general feeling among them was one of bitterness at their abandonment. Under the circumstances, however, their services could not be dispensed with. Thus the lack of people with adequate knowledge of colonial affairs made a complete change of officials impossible in the short run, and continuity of administration was a matter of some necessity because of the distance between Denmark and the West Indies.

Administrative arrangements under the Crown were somewhat more complex than they had been under the Company. There were still two administrative divisions: St. Thomas and St. John together, and St. Croix separately. Each division had its own Council, but in addition to these, there was a General Council or government for the entire group. In order to achieve co-ordination of function there was some overlapping of membership between the local and the general councils as can be seen from their composition.

The General Council consisted of the Governor-General, a chief administrative officer or prefect, and a government secretary. The Council of St. Thomas and St. John consisted of the Governor-General (when he was present), the Commandant, the chief administrative officer (when he was present), a chamberlain or treasurer and a secretary. The Council of St. Croix consisted of the Governor-General, the chief administrative officer, the judge of the Court of Appeal, a chamberlain or treasurer, and a secretary who was the same person as for the General Council.[2]

St. Croix supplanted St. Thomas as the center of administration when in 1755 the Governor-General moved his residence to St. Croix. With him were the two officials, the judge of the Court of Appeal and the administrative officer. The reason for the change was undoubtedly the sugar-producing potential of St. Croix compared with the other islands, and the presence of the Governor-General was considered necessary to give direction to its development. Also, events of the recent past had demonstrated that in the absence of strong central control, the council of St. Croix was politically volatile. Thus it was decided to place the Governor-General where he could exercise effective leadership and firm control.

The Governor-General was to be the highest civil and military official in the islands, and he was not allowed to leave them without royal permission. Though limits of his authority were not made explicit, his dependence on the Danish government was emphasized. This apparent ambiguity often led to disagreements with the Office of Finance, since the Governor-General made decisions on his own initiative. The instructions issued to the Commandant of St. Thomas were similar to those of the Governor-General whose position he assumed when the Governor-General was absent. Moreover, the Commandant presided over meetings of the Council of St. Thomas and St. John.

Under Crown government was established a new chief administrative officer or amtmand, whose main duty was the supervision of the royal plantations which had been inherited from the Company. This was his most regular function all others being subject to continuous change. Accordingly, when H. C. Schimmelmann purchased the plantations in 1763, the office was abolished the following year.

Also deserving of mention were the chamberlains (or kammereren) who acted as foremen or supervisors of the warehouses, as bookkeepers, and as directors of auctions. Revenue collection was taken care of by two treasurers and customs officers. Chamberlains were superior officers as was evident from their membership of the respective local councils. Their duty was to take care of the payments received 'in natura' by the government, and of the proceeds from the sale of goods which arrived from Denmark. Later, they became responsible for the administration of the military stores, but then they were relieved of the duties of bookkeeper.

There was also a number of subordinate officials, some of whom had been Company's employees; others were men who had worked in the East Indies and in Guinea. Two weighing-masters took care of the compulsory public weighing of the raw products of the islands at the time of export, while several surveyors handled the surveying and distribution of Crown lands. Then there were overseers of the royal plantations, warehouse assistants, customs inspectors, surgeons, policemen and finally the pilot and seamen of the government's boats.

Besides the general and local councils, the islands continued to have their burgher councils members of which were appointed from the various Quarters of the islands by a combined process of election and nomination. The burghers of each Quarter elected three property holders one of whom was selected by the Governor-General to represent the Quarter in the burgher council. The chairman of the burgher council bore the title of 'stadshauptmand'.[3] The burgher councils had the power to make proposals to the Governor-General for the better government of the islands, to assist in the assessment of taxation, and to suggest methods for the disbursement of public funds. These liberties gave the burgher councils considerable independence of action and brought them into frequent conflict with the Governor-General.

The Prelude to Reform

After the constitutional and administrative arrangements made by the Crown in the period immediately following the take-over, no major changes took place until 1852. By that time, social transformations in the Virgin Islands and constitutional changes in Denmark, suggested the need for reform.

Following the slave rebellion and the departure of Peter von Scholten for Denmark in July, 1848 the position of Acting Governor-General was given to Peter Hansen. In January, 1849 a little more than a month after he had arrived in the islands, Hansen dismissed the caretaker government that had administered the islands since von Scholten's departure and assumed control himself.

There was much to be done since emancipation had created a new class of free people, and the social system had to be adjusted to cater for them. New problems included the regulation of employer-employee relationships and reforms in the system of taxation, the judicial system, the poor laws and the education system. Hansen was temperamentally unsuited to the task: he was benevolent but slow, firm but quiet. He had worked in the Danish East Indies and was quite unfamiliar with conditions in the Virgin Islands where he found it difficult to understand the divergent interests. The business men in St. Thomas were preoccupied with questions of trade and trade regulation, whereas planters in St. Croix demanded compensation for the loss of their property in slaves. Since the new Governor-General did not have answers to these and other problems, public enthusiasm over his appointment decreased. The colored population had no cause to welcome him since they had cherished the expectation that von Scholten would return. Government employees themselves became very reserved in their attitude: rumors of constitutional reform made them fearful that their own positions might be jeopardized.

Reform of the constitution of the Virgin Islands was the declared intention of the Danish government. Such reform in Denmark itself in 1848-1849 was seen as involving changes in the entire colonial administration as well.[4] Denmark's constitutional change from absolute monarchy to parliamentary democracy necessitated major changes in the position of the Governor-General. Hitherto the chief executive had almost absolute powers as the representative of the absolutist Danish king; now it might be necessary for him to share his power with a representative body.

A major consideration for constitutional reform touched upon the interests of the newly-emancipated slaves who were now qualified for similar social privileges as other free people. If the governmental system was to be more democratic, the question would naturally arise as to their role in it. From the absence of any reference to them in serious discussions, it was probably assumed that they would not be actively involved in the political process. Their exclusion, therefore, raised the question as to how best their interests could be safe-guarded given the continuation of the old ruling class in power. A possible solution was to share political power between the governments of Denmark and the Virgin Islands. In this way the former could act as a check on colonial privileged interests and at the same time influence the adoption of measures for the benefit of the underprivileged.

Constitutional changes in the Virgin Islands stemmed partly from the need to make the colony reflect the division of political power in Denmark itself. It stemmed partly also from changes in communication, since the operation of steam-ships was bringing the Virgin Islands into quicker contact with Denmark. The first changes affecting the position of the Governor-General came in June, 1849: he could no longer issue permanent decrees but only temporary regulations in cases of urgency where delays caused in waiting for confirmation from Denmark would create harm; otherwise, all decisions were to be made in Denmark.[5]

The Virgin Islands became a more integral part of Denmark after the promulgation of the new Danish constitution: colonial affairs were brought under the Ministry of Finance and a minister in Copenhagen became responsible for all decisions affecting the islands. Furthermore, constitutional changes included modifications in titles and designations. In the period from 1849 to 1855 the heads of government in St. Thomas and St. John became known as Presidents rather than Commandants, the appellation Governor-General was shortened to that of Governor, and the designation of the islands was changed from that of 'Danish West Indies' to 'Danish West India Possessions.'[6] It is noteworthy that quasi-military titles were replaced by others that were more civilian in connotation.

Whether to give the islands direct representation in the Danish Rigsdag or permit them to have individual representative assemblies were the major problems facing the constitution-makers. Representation in the Rigsdag foundered partly on the problem of voting rights. The Virgin Islands were not closely linked to Denmark in the sense that both whites and Negroes spoke the language of the mother-country. Besides, not many of them were Danish citizens, and it was considered unwise to give the non-citizens such political rights. At the same time, since Danish citizens formed only a small part of the population of the islands, representation could not be limited to them. Furthermore, colonial planters and merchants took little or no interest in being represented in the Rigsdag, since they believed that their influence would be minimal.

If the Virgin Islands were not to be given representation in the Danish Rigsdag, the question of local representative bodies then arose. The distance between the islands, and their quite different economic structures — commerce in St. Thomas and agriculture in St. Croix — were the chief reasons advanced for proposing two separate Councils for them. It was believed that too much centralization would impair the ability of the islands to develop their own resources. On the other hand, it was shown that other economic interests than the obvious ones, as well as their common cultural elements, indicated a degree of similarity.

The Colonial Law of March 26, 1852 and Associated Changes

Amid the welter of confusing and often conflicting opinions, the Colonial Law of March 26, 1852 was passed. It established a single Colonial Council for the Virgin Islands with the right to 'deliberative cooperation in the exercise of the legislative power.' In each case of law-making the Council would be allowed to make its recommendations after which, acting through his minister, the king would make ordinances for the colony. Existing Danish laws could be extended to the islands, and more specific colonial legislation could be passed dealing with such matters as education, poor relief, the militia, public roads, hedges and enclosures, labor, trade, servitude, vagrancy, sanitation, fire and the police.

The Council could also initiate recommendations concerning the use of Danish laws and ordinances in the islands, and get its recommendations presented in the Rigsdag. The king and the Rigsdag together could make laws concerning all other matters, but the recommendations of the Colonial Council had to be obtained before any law could be approved for the islands. Temporary regulations could in special cases be issued by the Governor, but they were to be discussed at the next meeting of the Council.

The Colonial Council was to consist of sixteen members elected by the people and four members nominated by the king. For purposes of election, the islands were divided into four electoral districts: Christiansted, which was to elect five members, Frederiksted, three, St. Thomas, six, and St. John, two. Both elected and nominated members would serve four-year terms, but every second year, half of them would retire, though re-election and re-nomination were permitted.

Voting rights were given to every man of unblemished character who was at least 25 years of age and at least 5 years resident in the islands. He had to have either a yearly income of $500 Danish West Indian or paid at least $5 Danish West Indian in land or building tax. The voter should have resided for at least one year in the electoral district at the time the election took place. Except for this last provision concerning residence in the electoral district, candidates for election had to be qualified in all other respects as voters. Detailed regulations governed the conduct of elections. In the event of tie votes, the drawing of lots was to decide the issue. The nomination of the king's representatives was to be done either by the king himself or by the Governor on his behalf after the elections had taken place.

Both Danish and English could be used in the deliberations of the Council, and Council minutes were to be kept in both languages also, though written reports had to be only in Danish. The meetings of the Council were not public but an abstract of its proceedings was to be published both in Danish and English. Moreover, the Council could decide its own procedures and could request the Governor to supply information concerning the condition of the colony.

The islands continued to have their burgher councils in addition to the constitutional machinery established by the Colonial Law of 1852. Reform of these burgher councils had been discussed before 1848 such as in 1840 when the burgher council of St. Croix regretted that the members were still elected from eight quarters of the island, rather than from the towns of Christiansted and Frederiksted where there were concentrations of population. It was further regretted that the planters had the sole right of election to the council. Reform was effected on May 4, 1849 when the right to vote or of candidature was extended to every inhabitant who was 25 years old and over, who was a citizen, or who paid at least $8 in land or building tax to the local treasury.[7] When the reform was adopted in St. Thomas on December 8, 1851, the qualification for voters was a commercial tax of $8, and for candidates a store tax of $50, paid annually into the local treasury.[8]

A major reform was effected on May 9, 1855 by which St. Thomas, St. John and St. Croix, were kept as independent and separate municipalities. Each burgher council had the right to make proposals for the general good of the municipality, and to appoint members to commissions to deal with matters relating to schools, hospitals and the public welfare. The life of each burgher council was limited to four years and only men over sixty years of age could refuse to become members if elected. Barred from membership were the Governor, President and relatives of burgher councillors, as well as more than one member of any one commercial establishment. Family or group interests, therefore, could not gain priority over community interests.[9]

The Virgin Islands Under the New Constitution

St. Thomas, St. John and St. Croix elected the first Colonial Council for the Virgin Islands on August 30, 1852, and the number of voters was quite large especially among the more educated burghers. The work of the Council seemed well cut out: the labor act needed revision, new regulations were required for domestic servants and vagrants, judicial reform was overdue, and a well-organized education system was needed in St. Thomas and St. John. Another matter at issue was the extent to which the laws of Denmark should be applied to the Virgin Islands, while of major interest was the colonial budget relating to revenues and expenditures.

The Colonial Council desired greater economy in government and administration, and a majority of the members wished to abolish the executive or administrative head of St. Thomas. To this the Governor agreed but only if the Council provided steamship connections between St. Thomas and St. Croix. Rejecting this proposal were the St. Thomas representatives and the Danish finance minister who thought it more convenient to have the governor, the government secretary and clerical staff residing in St. Thomas, which was at that time the West Indian center for steamships to and from Europe. This transfer was in turn opposed by a majority of the Colonial Council as being too expensive.

Economy was more a slogan than a reality as the meetings of the Colonial Council progressed; instead of retrenchment, expansion of the administration came to be considered essential. Thus Governor Johan F. Schlegel, who had assumed the governorship in 1855, informed the Danish minister of finance in April, 1859 that more and better employees would be needed should the colonial government pass all the measures that were necessary. The Colonial Council itself seemed to have come around to the point where it favored maintaining some of the traditional grandeur of the governor's position. This attitude was reflected in an upsurge of spending on such things as large public buildings and lawns, immaculate barracks for the soldiers, and rich uniforms for the officers of government.

Government expenditures concentrated on St. Croix only widened the rift which early became evident in the relationship between this island and St. Thomas. From the very beginning the representatives from St. Thomas agitated for a special council to take care of the commercial interests of their island. Even greater dissatisfaction came from the designation of St. Croix as the venue for all sessions of the Colonial Council. As such, the representatives from St. Thomas could not be persuaded to undertake the voyage to St. Croix to occupy their seats on the Council, and so it was not possible to convene the Colonial Council between 1856 and 1859.[10] Even when the Colonial Council met in 1859 and 1861, the representatives from the commercial class were conspicuous by their absence. One source of grievance was alleged to be the government's failure to expand the harbor of St. Thomas.

St. Thomians were particularly concerned about the source and destination of colonial revenues. In the six years from 1855 to 1861, the budgets of St. Thomas and St. John showed an average annual surplus of $39,000, while that of St. Croix showed an average annual deficit of $11,000. The combined colonial budget surplus was thus $28,000, which meant that the St. Thomas and St. John surplus was used to erase the St. Croix deficit. It was the general opinion that this should not be so and that each island should be held responsible for its own expenditures.[11]

Agitation by St. Thomians for their own colonial council increased after 1862, and it coincided with a much wider movement for the constitutional reform of the relationship between the Virgin Islands and Denmark. In its legislative capacity, the role of the Colonial Council was primarily advisory with the actual adoption of policies depending on the Danish government. Virgin Islanders were unhappy with the way the Danish government was handling colonial affairs.

The central administration in Copenhagen seemed to have destroyed the initiative of the colonial officials by its suspicions and continuous intervention in minute matters. The governors especially were caught in a dilemma between service to the Danish government and the need to introduce reforms in the islands. Consequently, nothing much was accomplished because of delays and misunderstandings. The filling of even minor colonial posts with people from Denmark when there were qualified people in the islands who had previously done the same jobs was a great source of irritation.

The political impasse was such that its solution called not only for a separate Colonial Council for St. Thomas, but also for a redefinition of the relationship between Denmark and the entire Virgin Islands.[12] Denmark's new constitution of 1855 called for the transfer of colonial affairs from the Ministry of Finance to a newly established Ministry of the Interior. However, this rearrangement was short-lived and three years later colonial affairs were returned to the Ministry of Finance. Provisional changes were also made in the Virgin Islands in September 1863 when two Colonial Councils were created, one for St. Thomas and St. John and another for St. Croix. Membership in each Council consisted of eight elected members and two members nominated by the king. Each administration was allowed to operate its own budget, and municipal responsibilities which had hitherto been borne by the burgher councils were taken over by the two new Colonial Councils.[13] The official designation of the Virgin Islands was changed from 'Danish West Indian Possessions' to 'Danish West Indian Islands' whereby the offensive stigma of being the private property of Denmark was removed. The constitutional arrangements had a short life for they were soon superseded by the Colonial Law of November 27, 1863.

The Colonial Law of November 27, 1863

The Colonial Law of 1863 gave the Virgin Islands a constitution which was more detailed and in some cases more specific than that of 1852. Its provisions sought a compromise solution for the political problems which had troubled St. Thomas and St. Croix in relation with each other and, together, with Denmark.[14]

For purposes of election and representation, the Virgin Islands were divided into two districts of higher authority: St. Croix became one municipality; St. Thomas and St. John, another. Each municipality obtained its own separate Colonial Council which could participate in lawmaking and in the administration of the municipality. The Council of St. Croix was to consist of thirteen elected members and five members nominated by the king, while the ratio in St. Thomas and St. John was eleven to four. The members were elected for four years, but half of them had to retire every second year, the first time by the drawing of lots.

The franchise was held by every man of unblemished character who was at least 25 years of age, held Danish citizenship, and had resided five years in the Virgin Islands. Besides he must possess property in the municipality which produced an income of at least $75 in St. Croix, and St. John, and $150 in St. Thomas, or he must have an income of $500. Eligibility for election required two years residence in the municipality besides being a registered voter. Officials in the colonial government were not eligible for candidature.

Voting was to be by open declaration of choice of candidates, not by secret ballot, and each voter had as many votes as there were members to be elected for the district. Following the practice adopted for election to the burgher council, no one eligible for candidature could refuse election to the Colonial Council except for good reasons. This ruling was intended to curb the continual withdrawals and re-elections which had hampered the work of the Colonial Council under the previous Colonial Law.

The Colonial Councils were to meet every second month, and meetings were to be open to the public. Minutes as well as decisions of each Council were to be written in both Danish and English. Regulations had to be discussed and passed three times by the Councils before they could be enforced, but appropriations needed to be passed twice only. Each Colonial Council could ask for changes in the laws and regulations of the islands, and the Governor as well as members could introduce bills.

Laws for the Virgin Islands could be made by the Colonial Councils but in cooperation with the Danish king and Rigsdag. Laws applicable to the municipalities could be passed in Denmark but the Colonial Councils had first to be consulted. As previously, the Governor was permitted to issue temporary laws and regulations though only under very special circumstances.

Each municipality had its own treasury, and the colonial revenue which had previously gone to the national treasury in Denmark now remained in the municipalities which became responsible for all colonial expenditures except certain pensions. For the first ten years, St. Thomas had to pay $28,000 a year into the Danish treasury, which represented the average yearly surplus of the Virgin Islands budget for the period 1855-1861. Since the surplus had come from St. Thomas receipts, St. Croix was exempted from such payments. The annual budgets had to be approved by the king and then presented to the Rigsdag.

Of some importance was the final section of the Colonial Law of 1863 which contained new provisions relating to the rights and liberties of burghers. These included property rights, inviolability of habitation, freedom of the press and the formation of societies. Also included were freedom of movement, equality before the law, the right to free education and maintenance of the poor. As the state church, the Lutheran Church was to receive financial support from public funds. Assistance to other denominations could only be granted under special circumstances and then by special permission. However, no one could be deprived of his civil and political rights on account of his religion.

The Virgin Islands under the Colonial Law of 1863

Cooperation among the Governor, Colonial Council and Danish Rigsdag and government resulted in the Colonial Law which took effect on April 1, 1865. However, the number of voters was small and there was failing political interest among the more educated classes. Despite the efforts made by the colonial administrations either orally or through the newspapers, hardly half of the people with an income of $500 (who numbered a little more than 400) ever registered to vote, while a small fraction of those registered exercised the franchise.[15] Also, despite constitutional safeguards several of the elected members

H

found valid excuses for vacating their seats in the Colonial Councils.

The lack of political enthusiasm during the last years of the 1860's and even after was due largely to the expectation of the people that the islands would be transferred to the United States. In January, 1868, the voters of St. Thomas and St. John voted over-whelmingly in favor of the transfer, though on this special occasion the franchise was extended to all men over 25 years of age and of unblemished character. It was the continuing ambition of the representatives of St. Thomas to get the seat of government transferred to their island and for the Councils to be given independent power to make laws relating to the internal affairs of the respective municipalities.[16] St. Thomians, too, were concerned with the particular problem of getting the hated annual contribution of $28,000 to the Danish treasury, either removed or reduced. Crucians, for their part, had a special interest, namely, the procurement of a loan from the Danish government to assist the economically depressed planters.

Despite some dissatisfaction, the Colonial Law of 1863 remained in force until 1906 when it was modified. Numerous concessions were granted which served to remove the major causes of discontent in the islands. The first change was introduced in February, 1871 when the Governor's official residence was transferred from Christiansted in St. Croix to Charlotte Amalie in St. Thomas. The residence of the President was subsequently removed from St. Thomas to St. Croix.[17] The change in the Governor's residence was considered necessary not only because of local demands but also because of the need to rescue St. Thomas from the adverse conditions causing its economic decline.

The second change was the Danish law which took effect on April 10, 1874 whereby St. Thomas was released from the obligation to pay $28,000 annually into the Danish treasury. Also, St. Croix obtained the much desired financial assistance in 1876 when it was granted a loan of two million kroner by the Danish government to undertake the construction of a central factory, and a further temporary loan of 600,000 kroner for general purposes.[18]

Virgin Islands government in the period 1865 to 1906 was marked by alternate periods of slothful negligence and energetic performance. Friction between the Councils and the Governor was common, especially when the Governor showed himself opposed to colonial demands. Such was the case when Janus August Garde became Governor in September, 1872. He condemned Denmark's seeming encouragement of the idea of self-government for the islands which had resulted in considerable agitation. In one controversy he went so far as to dissolve the Colonial Council of St. Thomas and St. John.[19]

In order to give the Governor more control, Garde recommended in January, 1879, that the office of President should be abolished, that in future the Governor should divide his time equally between St. Thomas and St. Croix, and 'while living on one, make frequent trips to the other island.' He suggested also that each colonial treasury should pay half of his salary, and that a government secretary be appointed for St. Croix as well as for St. Thomas.[20] This reform which was intended to create a balance in the administration of the two municipalities was not effected before Garde was forced to leave the Virgin Islands in March, 1881 as a result of the many charges which were brought against him following the laborers' revolt of 1878.

The office of President was abolished in April, 1883, and henceforth the Governor became the superior authority in both municipalities. He could, however, entrust his authority to a resident government secretary for the 'daily current business of administration in the district, in which he at any time is not personally present.'[21]

The Colonial Law of April 6, 1906

Constitutional reform after 1863 was closely related to economic reform in the hope that by strengthening the political machinery the colonial economy could be strengthened. During the last quarter of the nineteenth century Virgin Islanders continued to hope for and to believe in an eventual American take-over of the islands, hence their apathy in politics. Similar hopes and beliefs by the Danish government led to neglect of the economic welfare of the islands which continued to decline.

Denmark's rejection of the transfer Treaty of 1902 made it imperative that something should be done to assist the islands. Accordingly a Royal Commission was appointed under the leadership of F. T. M. M. Nordlien to investigate and report on measures that should be taken to improve conditions in the islands including the question of whether the Colonial Law of 1863 should be changed. In its report dated August 26, 1903, the Commission recommended that there be a combined council for all three islands, St. Thomas, St. John and St. Croix, as well as the two municipal councils. It recommended, also that the islands should be represented in the Danish Rigsdag.[22] The constitution which was given in the Colonial Law of April 6, 1906, however, sought reform along other lines which tended to correct some of the abuses of the existing system.[23]

The Colonial Councils rejected the idea of representation in the Danish Rigsdag as well as the proposal of a combined council for all the islands. Except in three instances, the Colonial Law of 1906 resembled in all other important respects the Colonial Law of 1863: firstly, it made clear the position of the Governor; secondly, it included certain important financial provisions; and, thirdly, it provided for changes in the franchise and system of voting.

The Colonial Law of 1906 upheld the law of 1883 regarding the superior authority of the Governor in both of the municipalities. His delegation of authority was further extended with respect to 'the daily current business of administration in the district in which he at any time is not personally present,' in an attempt to strengthen the administration by making it unnecessary to shift the Government Secretary to and fro as the Governor moved between St. Thomas and St. Croix. In his absence authority was to be vested in the Government Secretary in St. Thomas or in a Dispatching Secretary in St. Croix.

The main changes effected by the financial provisions of the Colonial Law of 1906 concerned the remittance of the unpaid balance of the loan given to St. Croix in 1876, and requiring St. Croix to pay 75,000 francs (that is, $15,000 Danish West Indian) a year as a contribution to the general expenses of Denmark. St. Thomas was exempted from such payments for the time being, but the entire matter was subject to review after ten years to determine how much each municipality should pay.

The franchise was extended by lowering the financial qualifications of voters. Henceforth, eligibility to vote went to those who had property yielding a yearly rent of at least 300 francs (or $60 D.W.I.) in St. Croix and St. John, and 700 francs (or $140 D.W.I.) in St. Thomas, or an annual income of at least 1500 francs (or $300 D.W.I.). All other qualifications remained unchanged, but the system of voting was amended by the introduction of the secret ballot.

Conclusion

All three of the Colonial Laws passed in 1852, 1863 and 1906 rested on an extremely limited franchise, even though each succeeding one was an improvement of the one which went before. Emphasis on property and income in the financial provisions of the franchise clauses resulted in the mass of the people of the Virgin Islands being denied the vote even though they might have been qualified in other respects. Thus the laboring population was denied a voice in the management of affairs directly related to them.

The system of government in the Virgin Islands was not crown colony government in the sense that the Crown governed through its representatives in Denmark in the person of a responsible minister of government, or in the Virgin Islands in the person of the Governor. Neither was it full representative government in the sense that elected representatives of the people were solely responsible for legislation. Rather it was a combination of the two systems designed to hold the balance between the various classes in the Virgin Islands. Those who were qualified to vote elected their representatives, but these men did not have full power of initiating and adopting legislation. Their power was limited to the extent that the Crown-nominated members were able to exercise a modifying influence.

Between 1852 and 1863, the role of the Colonial Council was purely advisory, and the participation of the Crown and the Danish Rigsdag in legislation served to ensure that legislation was not confined to the interest of any one particular group to the detriment of any other. Sectional jealousies and conflicts, and the distance separating Denmark from the Virgin Islands, however, enabled the local inhabitants to have more or less of their own way in the regulation of colonial affairs. The governor or his representative proved helpless in the maelstrom of internal conflict which characterized the affairs of the Virgin Islands in those years.

After the introduction of the Colonial Law of 1863, the Councils were given greater legislative power. However, the presence of nominated members together with the participation of the Danish Crown and Rigsdag served to exercise a controlling influence. The separation of political power into two Colonial Councils, one for each municipality, tended to lessen if not to remove sectional conflicts. Each Council could better handle the problems peculiar to its respective municipality, but complete accord was impossible so long as the governor resided in one or other of the municipalities.

Part of the success of the Colonial Law of 1863 was due to the spirit of compromise and conciliation on the part of the imperial government. Its success may also be attributed to its basic compatibility with the

character of the society of the Virgin Islands. With only few changes in 1906, the constitution of 1863 remained intact until the United States acquisition of the islands in 1917. Even so, the political structure then in existence was retained and continued until 1936. Long before then it had become obsolete and was eventually replaced by the first Organic Act of the Virgin Islands passed by the Congress of the United States.

[1] Jens Vibaek, *Dansk Vestindien 1755-1848: Vestindiens Storhedstid.* (Fremad, Denmark, 1966) pp. 11-12.

[2] Ibid., pp. 13-14.

[3] Ibid., pp. 40-41.

[4] *Denmark. An Official Handbook.* (Krak, Copenhagen, 1970) pp. 110-112.

[5] Fridlev Skrubbeltrang, *Dansk Vestindien 1848-1880: Politiske Brydninger og Social Uro.* (Fremad, Denmark, 1967) p. 31.

[6] Ibid., pp. 31-32.

[7] 11te Anordning af 1849 Jeg Peter Hansen, 4 de Mai, 1849. (*St. Croix Avis*, May 10, 1849. No. 560).

[8] Bekjendtgjorelse by Feddersen, 8 Dec., 1851. (*St. Thomae Tidende*, Dec. 27, 1851).

[9] Ordinance concerning the Burgher-Councils in the Danish West India Possessions, 9th May, 1855. (*St. Croix Avis,* October 12, 19, and 26, 1855).

[10] Proceedings of the Colonial Council, 7 Dec., 1859. (*St. Thomae Tidende*, Jan. 7, 1860).

[11] St. Croix. Extract of the Governor's Speech in the Meeting of the Colonial Council on the 26th January, 1863. (*St. Thomae Tidende*, Jan. 31, 1863); Remarks to the Draft of a Colonial Law for the Danish West India Possessions. (*St. Thomae Tidende*, April 11, 1863).

[12] Remarks to the Draft of a Colonial Law for the Danish West India Possessions. (*St. Thomae Tidende*, April 15, 1863).

[13] Committee Report. (*St. Thomae Tidende*, May 20, 1863); Decree of Frederik VII of 26 September, 1863. (*St. Thomae Tidende*, Jan. 20, 1864).

[14] *Collection of the most important Laws, Ordinances, Publications etc., valid in or referring to the Danish West India Islands and issued since the Colonial Law of the 26th of March, 1852.* (Copenhagen, Printed by J. H. Schultz, 1884) pp. 84-102.

[15] Communication to the Editor, 4 November, 1868. (*St. Thomae Tidende*, Nov. 7, 1868), shows that out of a total population in St. Thomas of about 13,000, only 268 persons were registered to vote out of a possible 650, and of those registered only 35 voted in the 1868 elections.

[16] Petition of the Inhabitants of St. Thomas addressed to His Majesty the King of Denmark, 11 July, 1870. (*St. Thomae Tidende*, July 13, 1870; St. Croix Avis, July 19, 1870).

[17] Editorial. (*St. Thomae Tidende*, Jan. 11, 1871); Editorial. (*St. Croix Avis*, Jan. 17, 1871).

[18] The Central Factory Question. (*St. Croix Avis*, April 15, 1876); *Collection of the most important Laws, Ordinances, Publications*, etc:, pp. 230-232.

[19] Skrubbeltrang, op. cit., p. 67.

[20] Ibid., p. 68.

[21] *Collection of the most important Laws, Ordinances, Publications*, etc., p. 260.

[22] The Commission's Report. (*St. Thomae Tidende*, October 10, 1903).

[23] D. C. Canegata, *St. Croix at the 20th Century. A Chapter in its History.* (Carlton Press, Inc., New York, 1968).

Chapter 13

The Aftermath of Slavery

As for Europe, so for the Virgin Islands, the year 1848 can be called the 'annus mirabilis.' As in Europe so in the Virgin Islands, the year 1848 was marked by the clash of rival ideologies. Instead of being nationalism and liberalism versus despotism as in Europe, it was slavery versus freedom in the Virgin Islands, exemplified by the revolt of the slaves in St. Croix against their masters. Following the revolt, slaves were emancipated and a new class of free people emerged. As already seen, social transformation was matched by equally important changes in the political system of the islands; in addition, their economy was considerably affected after 1848.

Economic life was in part influence by the changed relationship between the laboring population and the ruling class, although such changes were more marked in St. Croix than in St. Thomas. The latter island had acquired a considerable reputation as an emporium of trade by 1848, and in the two ensuing decades its importance grew. Thereafter the island suffered a recession. In contrast, the economy of St. Croix traditionally based on agriculture was already in decline by 1848, and this condition was to continue for the rest of the nineteenth century. The state of the economy of the Virgin Islands after 1848 was to determine the social and economic behavior of the people, and the political status of the Virgin Islands as Danish possessions.

The Decline of St. Thomas as a Trade Emporium

The commercial importance of St. Thomas stemmed from its central

THE ST. THOMAS HARBOR SHOWING:
Above: THE FLOATING DOCK
Below: DESTRUCTION CAUSED BY 1867 HURRICANE

position in the West Indies for most American and European shipping lines whose vessels brought freight orders for the different parts of the Caribbean. Since the freight market was concentrated in St. Thomas, ships seeking cargoes had to stop here to get in touch with their owners. St. Thomas had a large, commodious and deep harbor around which Charlotte Amalie the capital was built. It could accommodate many large ships and had the reputation of offering adequate shelter against the ravages of hurricanes. In St. Thomas were established all the facilities of shipping, namely, coaling stations or bunkers for refuelling, wharves for unloading cargoes, tanks for watering, and after 1867, a drydock for cleaning and repairing vessels.

The island, however, suffered several major disasters during the second half of the nineteenth century which affected it adversely. Two cholera epidemics devastated the island belying the notion of its natural healthiness; the first in 1853-1854 killed 1,865 people (1,500 in Charlotte Amalie alone), while the second in 1866-1867 which occurred despite the cutting of a channel in the Frenchtown area to prevent accumulation of debris in the harbor, resulted in the death of from 1,200 to 1,300 people.[1] Epidemics of malaria, such as that in May-June, 1853 which killed 100 persons in St. Thomas, contributed to the same end. Finally, the hurricane of November, 1867 followed by an earthquake and a tidal wave, completed the job of destroying the reputation of St. Thomas as a 'safe' haven.

As a result of the hurricane many ships in the harbor including steamships, sailing ships and lighters were tossed on shore while the lighthouse at the entrance of the harbor was completely destroyed. The result of the earthquake with its tidal wave was equally destructive. The force of the tidal wave threatened to dash two American warships and other vessels in the harbor against the rocks. A beautiful steel bridge over 300 feet long which a Liverpool company had constructed with steel pillars screwed down in the rock foundation of the harbor, collapsed and sank.[2] On August 21 and October 23, 1871 new hurricanes hit St. Thomas destroying 400 houses, greatly damaging the hospital and barracks, and killing several people.[3] The net result of these disasters was a setback in the island's trade; hereafter expansion ceased as shipping companies began to contemplate alternatives to the entrepot in St. Thomas.

Circumstances after 1871 made it easier to consider alternatives. Most noteworthy was the establishment of telegraphic connection between the West Indies and Europe and the United States; no longer must European and American traders resort to the West Indies to acquire current market information. Contributing to the decline was the increasing use of steamships and the establishment of direct and regular connection between the Caribbean, Europe and the United States. The advantages of direct contact were reinforced by active competition by other islands to wrest some of the commercial benefits previously enjoyed by St. Thomas. The most energetic of these was Barbados which, because of its favorable position as the most easterly of the West Indian islands, became the port of call of many steamships. That Barbados was a serious competitor became clearly evident in 1885 when the head-quarters of the Royal Mail Steam Packet Company was transferred from St. Thomas to that island.

The move away from St. Thomas was also caused by the inconveniences which became increasingly evident in the physical environment of the harbor. While sailing ships could easily be accommodated, the harbor was proving too small and too shallow for the steamships of greater length and draught that called here. Difficulty in obtaining sufficient space for turning was evident when several large ships were simultaneously in the harbor. The floating dock which could accommodate ships of a maximum of 2,500 tons soon became too small, and nothing was done to remedy it. The provisioning of ships in the harbor was unsatisfactory, since ships' provisions were dutiable. Besides, one firm had a virtual monopoly of supplying coal and water and reputedly charged exorbitant prices. Ships reportedly avoided these charges by going to St. Lucia to coal, and to San Juan, Puerto Rico, to water.

St. Thomas lost its importance as a distributing center of trade in the Caribbean during the last decades of the nineteenth century. The island lapsed into a stopover for various shipping lines moving between the Caribbean and Europe and North America such as the Hamburg-American line, the West India and Pacific Steam Ship Company, the Harrison Line of Liverpool, the French Compagnie Générale Transatlantique, the Bordeaux line and the Quebec Steam Ship Company. These lines continued to sustain St. Thomas as a coaling station even though much of the business was transferred to other West Indian ports.

Shipping statistics pointed to the rise and decline of St. Thomas after 1848. The number of steamships calling at the island increased from 91 in 1850 to 240 in 1867, and to 353 in 1875. Thereafter the tempo slackened, though the number increased to 415 in 1880. The downward trend continued and by 1902 only 370 steamships called at St. Thomas.[4]

Changes in Agricultural Practices, 1848-1878

Unlike St. Thomas, the economy of St. Croix and of St. John was based generally on agriculture and more specifically on sugar production. Economic decline in these islands which had set in before emancipation became even more severe after 1848. For example, except for the period from 1861 to 1870, production of sugar from St. Croix declined during the years 1850 and 1880. Thus between 1851 and 1855 the yearly average in millions of pounds was 15.1, from 1857 to 1859 it was 13.4, and from 1871 to 1880 it was 12.9.[5] The export of rum and molasses showed similar fluctuations. As far as St. John was concerned, it was reported in 1870 that there was only one estate still in sugarcane cultivation.[6]

Growing competition from beet sugar was one important cause of the continued decline of the sugar industry since it led to a disastrous fall in the price of cane sugar, and since subsidized, or bounty-fed European beet sugar crowded unsubsidized West Indian cane sugar out of European markets.[7] Inefficient methods of production in the Virgin Islands made it impossible for cane sugar producers here to compete on anything like equal terms with beet-sugar producers in Europe.

Even the Danish tax structure discriminated against colonial sugar for the product of the Virgin Islands paid an import duty that was higher than the production tax levied on beet sugar produced in Denmark. In addition to this fact Virgin Islands sugar was subject to a further export duty and was faced with the cost of shipping to Denmark. These expenses added to the cost of cane sugar in the European market.[8]

Virgin Islanders reacted to unfavorable marketing conditions in Denmark by seeking out alternative markets for their produce. The United States market was the chief alternative, but even there the Virgin Islands product faced competition from European beet sugar and from Cuban and Puerto Rican cane sugar.

Declining prices and market discrimination led the planters to cut production costs and diversify the agricultural economy by introducing new crops and new techniques. Emancipation changed the status of the laboring population from that of slaves who had been forced to give their services to their masters without wages, to that of paid employees. Planters sought to reduce costs by employing at low wages as few of these paid laborers as possible. Alternatively, they resorted to labor-saving implements of husbandry, such as ploughs, and more efficient manufacturing devices which had been grossly neglected during slavery. Fields also received heavier applications of manure and other fertilizers.

To meet added expenditures, planters were assisted after 1853 by the financial compensation of $50 which they received for each of their freed slaves regardless of age or sex.[9] The compensation enabled them to convert their factories from windmills and animal-mills to steam-mills which thereby increased from 40 in 1852, to 61 in 1857, and to 67 in 1875. Conversely, the number of windmills declined from 106 in 1855, to 45 in 1865, and to 17 in 1878. Only twelve animal-mills continued to operate in 1855, and by 1878 only one survived.[10] St. Croix's first central factory was established in 1878, aided by a loan of two million kroner from the Danish government. Capacity production required the sugarcane grown on several neighboring plantations.

Steam power increased both the capacity and efficiency of milling, and as much as 65 percent or more of the juice of sugarcanes was extracted, amounting to a 10 to 15 percent increase over old milling techniques. The use of the vacuum pan for the more rapid crystallization of sugar through centrifugation was introduced in the central factory in 1878. Lower unit costs of production, together with the manufacture of 'crystal' instead of muscovado sugar, enabled the central factory to encroach slowly on smaller milling establishments; but it was not until 1916 that the last factory producing muscovado sugar went out of operation.

Precedents were not lacking for economic diversification, since minor staples had been produced by Virgin Islanders prior to the advent of large-scale sugar production. Advantage was taken of the American Civil War (1861-1865) to revive the cultivation of cotton on a large scale to supply the European markets which had been cut off from access to American supplies. The peak was reached in 1865-1866 when 71,000 pounds of cotton were exported,[11] but St. Croix was forced to abandon cotton cultivation after the Civil War when the Southern States resumed production.

Cattle rearing was also expanded by converting plantations into pastures, and as many as 80 plantations had become 'cattle ranches,' by 1870, though results were not very satisfactory. Between 1850 and

1865, for example, the number of cattle increased by 25 percent from 5,249 to 6,528, and little or no success attended the effort to promote animal husbandry later on.[12] Even so, in St. John the rearing of livestock had superseded agriculture to such an extent that the island could be described as a mere 'sheep-path.'[13]

The Labor Problem, 1848-1878

Emancipation came suddenly to the Virgin Islands before adequate preparations could be made for the parties involved. The proclamation of July 3, 1848 was a temporary measure to serve until the relationship between employers and the laboring population could be more fully defined. A working committee of six was appointed on July 10, 1848 from among the planters of St. Croix to formulate rules and regulations to govern the working conditions of the laborers. By an order issued on July 29, 1848 the committee stipulated that the laborers should seek regular employment somewhere, either on the plantation to which they had previously belonged or elsewhere. Laborers had to be on a yearly contract which specified the amount of work and its nature, as well as the wages to be paid. Laborers who refused to work or who demanded higher wages than the average were to be reported to the committee. Because there was little unoccupied land in the Virgin Islands on which the laborers could settle without violating the law of possession, it was confidently believed that they would be compelled to work on the plantations in order to earn their livelihood.[14]

The July, 1848 regulations were replaced six months later, on January 26, 1849 by a more elaborate ordinance issued by the Governor-General Peter Hansen.[15] Contracts were to be effective from October to October, and notice of non-renewal by either side could only be given once a year in the month of August. The working week was to consist of five days as during slavery with Saturday and Sunday free, though workers were subject to compensatory employment on Saturday. Laborers were free to take on, or to refuse extra work, but they had to look after the plantation animals as was customary and to serve as watchmen. In return for his services on the plantation, each laborer was to be provided by the employer with a house for his family as well as a plot of land for cultivation.

Laborers were divided into three classes as during slavery and wages were to be 15, 10 and 5 cents a day according to the class. If laborers were given their customary rations of flour and fish, 25 cents each were to be deducted from their wages each week. Parents were to receive the payments for work done by the children. Artisans, who were also divided into three categories, were in a more favorable position, being allowed 20, 12 or 7 cents a day as the case might be.

For all workers, work on Saturdays could be meted out as punishment for negligence, and the pay was then the regular daily rate. Absence from work by laborers was punished by loss of pay, and parents were fined if they kept their children away from work. No worker could collect wood, grass, vegetables and fruits from the plantation, or to cut cane, or burn charcoal, without permission. Lastly, the maintenance of a sick or aged person rested equally on that person's family and on the employer and was no longer the latter's sole responsibility as before.

For some time after emancipation, laborers remained on the plantations though many of them opposed yearly contracts under the July, 1848 regulations since to them it seemed not very far removed from bondage. Indeed, the regulations issued in January, 1849, were interpreted by the laborers as an attempt to force them back into slavery. The employers themselves contributed to the dissatisfaction. Accustomed as they were to the conditions of slavery, they could not make the adjustments that were necessary under the new state of affairs. They looked forward to operating their plantations with the usual number of laborers at wages they considered reasonable. In addition, they sought to evade the responsibilites for maintenance of old and sick laborers, or of those who were otherwise unable to work.

Even before January, 1849, laborers had begun to leave the plantations for the towns where they sought employment as apprentices in trades. After January, 1849 the process gathered greater momentum,[16] and dissatisfaction crystallized on July 2, 1849 when the laborers on 77 plantations in the center district of St. Croix refused to work. The 'strike' was short-lived for the workers were soon forced back to work by the police and gendarme. Many of them took advantage of their legal right and signified their intention in August, 1849 not to renew or enter into contracts with their employers.[17] Many went into the towns where they took up trades or became servants and seamstresses. Other workers migrated from St. Croix to St. Thomas to seek employment on the docks. However, this practice was curtailed by the adoption of the compulsory passport system; by limiting the number of passports issued, migration from St. Croix to St.

Thomas could be controlled.

Some of the workers who went to live in the towns supplemented their meager earnings by means of wage labor on plantations. These so-called 'porters' were hired on a day-to-day basis instead of being bound by contract, and despite their recruitment, planters complained that workers were too few and unreliable. From an estimated 15,328 workers in 1846, the number had declined by 1853 to 12,865 of whom an estimated 3,000 were unfit for work. It was estimated in 1854 that 25 percent of the effective working force had been lost in the six years since emancipation.

Immigration was one possible means to secure a more adequate and dependable supply of laborers, and in December, 1851 the first immigrants arrived from Madeira destined to work on the plantations. Their numbers were inadequate and as the demand for 'foreigners' became stronger, a committee was appointed to investigate the problem. By 1860 it was necessary to impose additional taxation to pay for the immigration of laborers. An immigration fund was created in St. Croix by floating a loan of $65,000 and in order to meet immigration expenses, planters had to pay 10ᶜ an acre on useful land while those who obtained immigrant laborers for 5 years had to pay $12.[18]

Laborers from the British islands were attracted by the promise of higher wages and of more favorable conditions of employment. Barbadians began to arrive between 1860 and 1861 and, in addition, a small number of freemen from the Dutch West Indies migrated to St. Croix after they were emancipated on July 1, 1863; by 1864 as many as 1,700 immigrants had arrived from Barbados and St. Eustatius.[19] A relatively large number of laborers also came from the British Virgin Islands but most of them sought employment on the coaling wharves of St. Thomas.

About 318 indentured Indians arrived in 1863 at a cost of $112 each, but few of them served beyond their first contract of five years. In fact, as many as 253 Indians returned to their home-land in 1868 carrying almost $12,000. The remainder contracted for a further term until 1873 when nearly all of them left for Trinidad via St. Thomas; the few who stayed remained under the protection of the British consulate.

Generally speaking, the effort to attract agricultural laborers for the plantations did not produce very satisfactory results, as further evidenced by the large group of laborers of French origin who arrived from St. Bartholomew, in the 1870's. Almost without exception, they settled in St. Thomas where they formed two separate and distinct communities: those who settled in 'Frenchtown' in the west part of Charlotte Amalie were engaged chiefly in fishing; the second group lived in the northwestern side of St. Thomas and were farmers and occasional fishermen.[20]

The Agricultural Laborers' Revolt in St. Croix, October 1878

Meanwhile, the migration of a large number of dissatisfied workers to the towns could not but threaten the public peace. Dissatisfaction reached boiling point in October, 1878 when violence again broke out in St. Croix. It is significant that the outbreak occurred on October 1, the day that yearly contracts were brought into operation. Indeed, the disorder was in nature a protest against the provisions of the labor regulations in force and the manner in which they were executed.[21] The annual contract itself was declared to be tantamount to slavery, to the extent that laborers who failed to give timely notice of termination of their contract were compelled to work for the plantation for another year even if they did not wish to do so.

THE LABORERS' REVOLT, 1878

Other conditions of employment created grievances, and contributed to the outbreak of violence. Wages were not only low but they fell below the provisions of the labor ordinance, the maximum of ten cents a day being actually paid instead of fifteen cents. The injustice was more strongly felt when the central factory began paying thirty-five cents a day upon its completion in 1878. To discontent over low wages was added complaints of frequent abuse by managers of the prerogative given them by the labor ordinance to impose monetary fines for certain offences. It was to the financial advantage of managers to impose heavy fines as often as possible since these fines accrued to them as added income.[22] Even when workers were permitted to collect firewood, fruits and grass, to burn coal, to keep poultry and livestock, and to receive rations, these were no more than similar privileges granted during slavery. In some cases they were even less, and many laborers came to believe that there was no difference between slavery and freedom.

Laborers seeking to leave St. Croix encountered barriers erected by the police authorities. Applicants for passports had to reveal how much money they possessed, while a further barrier to emigration was government prohibition of passenger transportation between the islands at a crucial time. Thus denied outlets to other islands, workers without contracts could then be forced by the police to take a job after they had gone three days without work.[23]

October 1, 1878 was a critical date in the life of St. Croix with many laborers congregated in Frederiksted, some seeking new jobs, some planning to emigrate and others to enjoy themselves.[24] The rum-shops did a thriving business and the crowd was boisterously gay. By 4:00 p.m. the mood of the crowd had changed: a large group could be seen gathered at the corner of Dronningens and Kongens Tvaergade, and threats of violence could be heard. The cause was a rumor to the effect that passports were no longer being issued, that several dollars were required in order to obtain a passport, and that several persons had been detained in Frederiksted on their way to Vieques. To deal with the threatening crowd, the police were summoned. They dealt rather heavy-handed with a drunk, Henry Trottman, who fell into a gutter and cut his foot, and was taken to the hospital. The police then tried to arrest one of the crowd named Joseph LaGrange, but he was rescued by the people.[25]

While the police were trying to entice the people to enter the Fort to lock them up there, or to get them to go home, one Felicia James shouted that Henry Trottman had died from the treatment he had received from the police. Apparently this was not so, but the people were aroused. An increasing number gathered before the Fort and started to throw stones to which the police replied with bullets. Consequently, the crowd tore down the outer gate of the Fort and threw it into the sea. However, they were brought up before the inner gate which they tried in vain to storm, and they were stopped by the shooting of the soldiers assisted by a few civilians. The crowd decided to take revenge in the town where shops were ransacked and their contents spilled into the streets and burned. Fires were set to private dwellings in the town as well as to the government Customs House. People seeking shelter from the anger of the crowd escaped on board the ship 'Carib' lying in the harbor, or they sought asylum in the churches.[26]

Meanwhile, a messenger had been dispatched to secure military help from Christiansted, but the dangerous situation caused considerable delay. Not until the morning of October 2, did Lieutenant H. R. L. Ostermann arrive in Frederiksted with an armed force consisting of six cavalrymen, thirteen infantry and two wagons.[27] Much of the destruction committed by the people was attributed later to this delay in the arrival of the troops. Assistance from St. Thomas was also delayed because the telegraph connection between St. Croix and St. Thomas was closed for the night. It was not until 7:30 A.M. of October 2, that Governor J. A. Garde in St. Thomas received news of the trouble. Immediately the Governor with Lieutenant Baron H. F. A. Eggers and 52 officers and privates and a Doctor Pontoppidan left for St. Croix on board the Royal Mail Steam Packet ship 'Arno'. Guided by information that Frederiksted and the whole of the West End had fallen to the people, the Governor landed in Christiansted where military preparations were made to defend the town against possible attack. Martial law was declared, and parties of troops were dispatched into the country parts to maintain law and order.[28]

Meanwhile, in Frederiksted, the arrival of Ostermann and his troops turned the tide of the affray. The Fort was reinforced, and the streets cleared. Assisted by civilian volunteers, Ostermann forced the crowd to evacuate the town.[29] The consequences proved disastrous, for the anger of the people was now turned against the plantations and plantation buildings. People who were not originally involved were forced to join the bands. Uncommitted laborers were asked the simple question, 'Our side?'; if they did not answer, or if they answered in the negative, they were beaten. Consequently, many laborers sought to escape punishment by hiding at the approach of an attacking party. On many plantations managers and drivers were warned before a raiding party arrived, and thus were able to hide. Sticks were the only weapon carried, and fire was the principal means of destruction. Rioters kept a sharp lookout for the approach of troops, and at the cry of 'volunteers' they would seek hasty shelter.[30]

The upheaval lasted several days despite the arrival at Frederiksted of the French warship 'La Bourdonnais' and the British warship 'Tourmaline' on October 4, and of the United States warship 'Plymouth' a little later. These vessels had been summoned by the French, British and American consuls in St. Thomas and the commanders of all three warships offered their assistance to quell the revolt as did the governor of Puerto Rico.

Governor Garde politely refused these offers; he believed that no further assistance was necessary, since the force of the revolt had already been broken and the revolting laborers were sufficiently intimidated. Though he was later severely criticised for not making use of the offers, the Governor believed that his refusal was necessary to avoid further bloodshed and reduction of the labor force. However, some guns were borrowed from the British warship by the St. Croix volunteers.[31]

On October 5, the Governor ordered all laborers to return to their respective plantations on pain of being treated as rebels. They could not leave the plantation without a pass from their employers indicating that they had left on a lawful errand. Despite this proclamation, eighteen persons escaped to Tortola; later attempts to secure their return by extradition failed.[32] At Butler Bay another group of seventeen men was taken, while prisoners were daily taken to the Forts.

Around the middle of October, peace again prevailed on St. Croix and Lieutenant Eggers and twenty-five men returned to St. Thomas. The uprising seemed to have been a spontaneous rather than a planned outbreak, since it did not show any sign of being organized. Indeed, dissension was rife in the ranks of the insurgents, while leadership on an island-wide basis was lacking. Groups operated independently, and individual groups followed the direction of separate leaders such as John Lewis, Thomas Graydon, Francis Leonard, William Jones and William Arnold. Two of the most prominent leaders were James de Silva and Joseph Parris. Women also featured prominently as leaders of the revolt, including Mary Thomas, otherwise known as 'Queen Mary' who called herself Captain, Rebecca Frederik, and Axelline Salomon known as 'the black Amazon'.

Destruction was great with the districts most seriously affected being King, Queen and Prince's Quarters, as well as West End and Northside Quarters. Out of 87 plantations in these districts, only 37 were spared, and the loss suffered by 53 plantations amounted to $603,800, including a loss of $70,000 in crops. Hardest hit were River, Plessens, Mt. Pleasant, Carlton, Whim, Two Williams, Concordia, Good Hope, Camporico, and Wheel of Fortune where most of the mills were destroyed as well as the great houses, and even some of the workers' houses. On 48 plantations the produce, and on 43 the furniture and other miscellaneous items were destroyed. Few animals were lost, even if stables were destroyed. A total of 879 acres were destroyed at a total loss of $83,320 on 24 plantations where individual losses ranged from $300 to $10,500. The destruction in Frederiksted was estimated at $297,000, of which $11,516 was suffered by the colonial government resulting from the loss of public buildings such as the customs-house, the courthouse and schools.[33]

In order to relieve the distress, the Danish government gave permission on January 17, 1879 for the colonial government to borrow $300,000 to help the planters and house-owners. Later, the inhabitants of Frederiksted were granted $55,000 and a loan of $50,000 to be repaid in 10 years, in order to repair their losses.[34]

Black fatalities numbering 60 far exceeded those of the whites only three of whom including two soldiers were killed. Statistics of laborers who died do not include 14 women killed as the result of the explosion of the rum casks at Grove Place, and 12 laborers who were condemned to death by a special court convened by Governor Garde on October 5, 1878.[35] The trial of the 403 laborers who had been arrested continued for about one and a half years; eventually 336 were freed and the others sentenced to imprisonment. The trial revealed active participation of the newly arrived immigrants from the other West Indian islands. Of the so-called leaders, two were from Barbados, and one each from St. Eustatius, Antigua, St. Kitts and Jamaica. Among the other participants imprisoned, eleven were from Barbados, nine from Antigua and four from other islands. However, the only four women imprisoned were native born.

Development Schemes: First Phase, 1878-1902

Two inter-connected developments after 1878 were measures to prevent labor troubles and efforts to expand plantation production. The early reforms were directed more specifically at St. Croix since both St. Thomas and St. John had escaped the outbreak of disorder. The emphasis of St. Thomas on commerce and the employment of laborers on the docks and wharves at higher wages than those obtained by agricultural laborers served to prevent the outbreak of violence. St. John escaped also because its agricultural laborers, despite passport requirements, could move to and secure alternative employment as porters and carriers in St. Thomas. As a consequence, the population of St. John fell from 2,228 in 1850 to 1,574 in 1860, to 1,054 in 1870, to 944 in 1880. During the same period, despite the ravages of epidemics, the population of St. Thomas rose from 13,666 in 1850 to 14,389 in 1880.

The first reform of October 24, 1879, was intended to regulate the employment of labor. The main clauses in this ordinance concerned contracts which had been the source of so much dissatisfaction before 1878. Contracts were no longer to be only on a yearly basis; instead, the term could be varied at will. However, nothing was stated about changes in the length of the working day, the wages to be offered, or how they should be paid.[36]

The 1879 ordinance represented no great improvement over the 1849 ordinance, especially regarding wages and actual conditions of work. This was the reason why many laborers continued to leave the plantations for the towns where generally they lived under very poor conditions. Work could usually be found for a few days of the week, which enabled the people to eke out a bare subsistence. Workers continued to seek part-time employment on the plantations for which they were given five-cents more each day than those under contract. Since they received no food, part-time laborers suffered a disadvantage compared with regular workers. However, they retained the right to dispose of their time, which added freedom was regarded as more than adequate compensation for the loss of material benefits from regular employment.

In addition to those laborers who resorted to the towns where some of them became traders, there were others who engaged in fishing. Others sought a better way of life by emigrating to such places as Vieques, Puerto Rico, Cuba and Panama, where regular work could be found.

In order to achieve the dual goals of community stability and agricultural production, the parcelling-out system was adopted;[37] It involved the subdivision of plantations or parts of plantations and their sale to those laborers who wished to establish themselves as peasant proprietors. The initiative was taken by the colonial government which held several estates either in its own right or by means of tax foreclosure. These plantations were either useless to the government or were resulting in financial loss.

Following the example of the government were certain planters who were willing to dispose of part of their landed property. Declining land values motivated both sellers and buyers, for the former feared even lower prices if opportunities were not grasped, and the latter found the low prices attractive and within their ability to pay.

Land values declined rapidly after 1850, to such an extent that the total plantation wealth of St. Croix, which was estimated at $2.9 million in 1851, had been halved by 1870. After 1870 the value of plantations decreased further as seen in the case of 'Enfield Green' of 375 acres which in 1868 was sold for $70,000, and resold in 1882 for only $41,000. Another example was 'Lower Love' of 300 acres which was sold for $45,000 in 1870, and resold for $25,000 in 1882.[38] Land was roughly one-half the total value of these sugar plantations which remained in operation; cattle ranches and abandoned plantations without works obviously commanded much lower prices. Plots sold to prospective peasants ranged at first from 1 to 10 acres, and later when the trend gathered momentum from 8 to 28 acres in area. The laborers were allegedly given generous terms of purchase.

The initiative in parcelling-out and disposing of plantations to laborers was taken by the colonial government in 1883. The policy seemed to have been applied to all three islands, St. Croix, St. Thomas and St. John, though it acquired greater significance in St. Croix. At first the private plantation owners were hesitant to take similar steps. Indeed, the measure met with some opposition, since it threatened to deprive the planters of some of their most enterprising and industrious workers. More or less off-setting the loss of labor, however, was the opportunity to dispose of the less valuable portions of their plantations which lay in bush or were on steep hills. To work such areas would have involved too much expense and labor which the planters could ill-afford. Moreover, if the 'squatter,' as the peasant was wrongfully called since he had legal right to the property, planted sugarcane this would be disposed of at the factory to the financial advantage of the planter.

Sugarcane production in St. Croix expanded in large measure as a consequence of the parcelling-out system. During the three years, 1891, 1892, and 1893, small-holders on former government plantations produced 1,052,480 lb., 7,148,090 lb. and 4,545,990 lb. of sugarcane respectively. Of a total of 138,064,520 lb. of sugarcane delivered at the co-operative factory in 1901 as much as 36,284,700 lb. or 26 percent came from peasant holdings. The smallholders on former government plantations produced 12,898,460 lb., and in addition, sugarcane grown by 'squatters' was delivered at other private factories. Thus, in 1901, small holders delivered at 'La Grange' 7,081,090 lb. of sugarcane, and 3,777,630 lb. at 'Lower Love'.[39]

The parcelling-out system was beneficial to laborers and to the community apart from the production of sugarcane. To the laborers the possession of land was a sure way of improving their standard of living, and regular employment for their own benefit was assured. Besides sugarcane, the 'squatter' grew food crops such as yams and other culinary plants, both for himself and family, and for sale. Some animals also were reared for food and power. The community as a whole benefited since the system encouraged the growth of a middle-class which was interested in peaceful and stable communal relations.

The parcelling-out system, however, suffered from a number of drawbacks which tended to modify the gains obtained from it. Some tracts were larger than could be conveniently handled by the squatter and his family, with the result that they were subdivided and leased to other laborers. Renters commonly worked the soil to exhaustion without the application of manure since such manure produced from animals reared was generally sold. For this reason, renters held land on short leases, usually for one year at a time, so they could move elsewhere when the returns of a particular plot became uneconomic. Moreover, renters were notoriously unreliable producers with always an eye on the main chance. During periods of drought they were reported to have chopped off the tops of the sugarcane before they matured, and to have sold them as green fodder, with the result that the sugarcane became sour. Many squatters, moreover, did not live upon their plots, but rather in the towns where they increased the problems of urban dwelling.[40]

Stimulus to agricultural improvement in St. Croix motivated the establishment in 1895 of a Botanical Experiment Station located on 11.75 acres of land on plantation 'La Grange'. Its main purpose was to encourage a diversified economy which was considered essential in view of the crisis in the sugar industry. Experiments centered chiefly on tobacco and annatto since they were suited to the soil and climate not only of St. Croix but of the entire Virgin Islands.[41]

The Experiment Station met with disappointing results, due largely to the paucity of funds to carry out the individual experiments, buy necessary machinery and equipment, and employ experts from abroad. Moreover, the Station itself was unsuitably located on comparatively poor soil which did not facilitate experimentation. The water was of poor quality and the supply inadequate. Lastly, the Station was located too far away from the main centers of population so that few peasants and planters came to get planting material and beneficial knowledge.

Development Schemes: Second Phase, 1902-1916

Unsatisfactory economic conditions in the Virgin Islands went far to induce the Danish government to enter into treaty negotiations in 1902 for the transfer of the islands to the United States. The failure of this treaty, however, led the Danish government to adopt measures for the economic development of the Virgin Islands. The first action taken was the appointment of a royal commission on November 18, 1902 to investigate and recommend measures to improve basic conditions of life in the islands. The subsequent work of the commission had the effect of focusing Danish attention on and creating new interest in the Virgin Islands.

The role of the Danish government consisted mainly in encouraging private enterprise, such as the Danish Plantation Company organized in 1903. Under the Company's management cattle, cotton, and sugar production were expanded in St. Croix, and bay-oil, lime, and cattle production were promoted in St. John. Bay-oil from St. John was manufactured into bay-rum in St. Thomas, using alcohol or rum. The Company owned or controlled land in St. Thomas but it was not productively cultivated, and the Company's main activities remained cotton and sugar production in St. Croix. Since it had no factories of its own, most of its cane went to the West India Sugar Factory, commonly known as the Bethlehem Central Factory, organized in 1904. The Factory itself operated twenty-three plantations of its own in St. Croix, twenty of which grew sugarcane and the other three cotton.[42]

A further stimulus came in 1910 when a Department of Agriculture and an Agricultural Experiment Station were established in St. Croix. The site selected for the Station was 'Anna's Hope' a plantation of 225 acres which was fairly level and of good fertility located in the center of the island. The work of the Station centred on the development of types of sugarcane best able to resist pest and diseases and suited to the various parts of St. Croix.

Other development projects sought to improve trade and commerce and were applied more or less to St. Thomas. The limited facilities of the Colonial Bank, the only institution of its kind in the Virgin Islands since 1898 when the St. Thomas Bank ceased operations, impeded the growth of trade. Therefore, the National Bank of the Danish West Indies was established on June 20, 1904 to do business in the islands, and it was given a monopoly over the issue of bank-notes for thirty years.[43]

Reorganization and improvement of the harbor of St. Thomas was intended to encourage shipping. The harbor authority became an independent body in 1904 with a governing board and a treasury of its own. Six years later, the Board was empowered to issue $100,000 worth of four per cent bonds, which were guaranteed by the government, thereby enabling improvements to be made in harbor facilities.

The final stimulus to development was the organization in October, 1912 of the Danish West India Company, an off-spring of the East Asiatic Company (Ltd), founded in 1897. In an attempt to assist the Virgin Islands, the East Asiatic Company had established a successful business here in 1903, and on Hassel Island it operated one of the finest and most modern coaling depots in the West Indies. The Danish West India Company was operated from Copenhagen until October, 1915 when the headquarters were moved to St. Thomas. The Company had ambitious plans to make the island the best equipped port in the Caribbean and its harbor was located on its present site on land reclaimed in Long Bay. Quays and wharves measured 3,200 feet and were provided with modern methods for securing vessels alongside. From 1915 the interests of the East Asiatic Company were handled by the Danish West India Company, which proved to be an important facet to its activities.[44]

Each measure introduced after 1902 was to some extent successful, but their combined effect was inadequate to arrest economic decline. St. Croix had three major sugar factories in 1916, 'Bethlehem', 'La Grange' and the St. Croix Sugar Factory which together produced about seven-eighths of the island's sugar. The remainder was produced by eight other small mills. Already by 1916, several small plantations were using their entire sugarcane crop only for the production of rum. The same year witnessed the passage of the Homestead Act whereby a fund of one million francs ($200,000 D.W.I.) was established to purchase land and encourage small holdings in the Virgin Islands. It came too late to be of any value, for shortly after the islands passed under the control of the United States.

Cotton cultivation was abandoned by 1916 due at first to the appearance of insect pests in the fields and later to the outbreak of the First World War which made it difficult to ship the product to the customary market in Britain. By that time also the Agricultural Experiment Station was not yet fully organized to be of effective assistance to planters.

The war seriously affected the shipping of St. Thomas, which by 1916 had reportedly diminished 'nearly to the vanishing point'.[45] A direct result was that the Colonial Bank ceased to operate in St. Thomas. The war also worsened the difficulties of the National Bank of the Danish West Indies which since its creation in 1904 had never transacted a brisk business. The Danish West India Company suffered from the difficulty in procuring all the funds — estimated at $7,000,000 — necessary to undertake its projects. Along with the rest of the Virgin Islands it was adversely affected by the hurricane of October 9, 1916 which did great damage to its harbor facilities.

The improvements expected from the economic measures did not fully materialize, and even in those areas of achievement the ordinary man did not benefit. First class agricultural laborers in St. Croix (and St. Thomas) earned no more than 20c each day of nine hours work. In St. Thomas, laborers associated with shipping and the wharves were much better off and earned as much as $1.00 a day. However, with the depression in shipping during the war their plight was as great as that of the agricultural laborers. In addition to unemployment, workers suffered from an increase in the price of food caused by the war.

One response of Virgin Islanders to unfavorable living conditions was emigration which by 1916 had become almost customary. Since emancipation population in the Virgin Islands had fallen steadily from 39,614 in 1850, to 33,763 in 1880, to 32,786 in 1890, to 30,527 in 1901, and to 27,086 in 1911. By 1917 when a United States census was taken, the population had decreased to 26,051. Part of this decline can be explained in terms of the epidemic outbreak of diseases during the 1850's and 1860's, and of the high death rate in the islands, but the most persistent cause was the emigration of laborers seeking better employment opportunities elsewhere.

D. HAMILTON JACKSON

WOMEN COAL CARRIERS

Workers who remained sought to improve their lot by means of labor unions through collective bargaining. The first labor union was organized in St. Croix in 1915 by D. Hamilton Jackson, and it called a strike among the sugarcane workers in the island in January, 1916. As a result of the strike and subsequent negotiations between workers and employers' representatives, wages for first class workers were increased to between 30c and 35c a day, and overtime pay was conceded at 4c an hour. Following the example of the St. Croix laborers, coal-carriers in St. Thomas also struck. A labor union was organized by George A. Moorehead representing some 2,700 workers, and as a result of its stand an agreement was secured from the Danish West India Company in December, 1916 to increase the pay to coal-carriers from 1c to 2c a basket.[46] Even before this, Jackson had been sent by his union to Denmark in order to voice their grievances. Meanwhile, labor unrest had induced the Danish government to dispatch the warship 'Valkyrien' to the Virgin Islands to assist in maintaining the peace if necessary. It left only when the islands were handed over to the United States on March 31, 1917.

Conclusion

The post-emancipation era from 1848 to 1917 constituted a difficult period for the peoples of the Virgin Islands as both ex-slaves and ex-slave owners sought to adjust to the new labor situation created by emancipation. Social instability was accompanied by economic dislocation: the economy of the islands based on the twin pillars of commerce in St. Thomas and agriculture in St. Croix experienced almost continuous decline despite the measures adopted to counteract it. A direct consequence was that the islands lost their value as colonial possessions, and the desire was created and sustained to dispose of them.

[1] Fridlev Skrubbeltrang, *Dansk Vestindien 1848-1880: Politiske Brydninger og Social Uro.* (Fremad, Denmark, 1967) pp. 105-106.
[2] *St. Croix Avis,* November 8, 1867; *St. Thomae Tidende,* November 13, 16 and 23, 1867.
[3] *St. Croix Avis,* August 25 and 29, 1871; Skrubbeltrang, op. cit., p. 103.
[4] Considerations regarding the Conditions in the Danish West India Islands. Submitted by the West India Commission decreed by His Majesty's Resolution of

November 18, 1902. (Copenhagen, 1903) Translated from the Original Danish by Harold Larson. Division of Interior Department Archives. The National Archives, Washington D.C. 1939, p. 28.

[5] Statistics regarding landed properties in the island of St. Croix from 1816 to 1857 with a table showing the quantity of sugar shipped from 1835 to 1840 and from 1850-1857. (St. Croix, 1859); Statistics concerning Sugar Production in St. Croix from 1862-1889. (St. Croix, 1892); Statistics concerning Sugar Production in St. Croix from 1890-1902. (St. Croix, 1905).

[6] Translation from the Dagbladet, 9th June. (*St. Thomae Tidende*, September 7, 1870).

[7] R. W. Beachey, *The British West Indies Sugar Industry in the late 19th Century*. (Oxford, Basil Blackwell, 1957) pp. 51-60, 141-146 and 166-169.

[8] Translation from the Dagbladet, 9th June. (*St. Thomae Tidende*, September 7, 1870).

[9] *The St. Croix Agricultural Reporter*, No. 2, July 22, 1864.

[10] Skrubbeltrang, op. cit., p. 112.

[11] Waldemar Westergaard, *The Danish West Indies Under Company Rule* (1671-1754). (New York, The Macmillan Company, 1917) p. 254.

[12] Considerations regarding the Conditions in the Danish West India Islands . . . p.16.

[13] Translation from the 'Supplement to Dagbladet' of 8th September, 1870. No. 211. (*St. Thomae Tidende*, October 12, 1870); Translation from the Dagbladet, Copenhagen, the 2nd of May, 1970. (*St. Thomae Tidende*, June 4, 1970).

[14] Labor Regulations of 29th July, 1848. (*St. Croix Avis*, August 14, 1848).

[15] Provisional Act to regulate the relations between the proprietors of landed estates and the rural population of free labourers. (*St. Croix Avis*, January 29, 1849).

[16] [Ole Svenson, (Ed.)], *Three Towns: Conservation and Renewal of Charlotte Amalia, Christiansted and Frederiksted of the U.S. Virgin Islands*. (Tutein & Koch, Copenhagen, 1964?) pp. 26-27, 55-57 and 78-79.

[17] Skrubbeltrang, op. cit., p. 18.

[18] Proceedings of the Colonial Council. Extraordinary Session, 1862. (*St. Thomae Tidende*, March 5, 12, 26 and 29, and April 5 and 16, 1862).

[19] Skrubbeltrang, op. cit., p. 174.

[20] Earl B. Shaw, 'The Chachas of St. Thomas.' (*The Scientific Monthly*, Feb., 1934) pp. 136-145; Lubin Pickwood, *Social Survey of the French Settlements at Carenage and the Northside*. (Mimeo., 1941?); Rev. Father Guillo, *Report on the Cha Chas*. (Mimeo., 1933).

[21] Charles Edwin Taylor, *Leaflets from the Danish West Indies: Descriptive of the Social, Political and Commercial Condition of these Islands*. (London, 1888) p. 154.

[22] Report of the Royal Commission. (*St. Croix Avis*, November 12, 1879).

[23] Ibid.

[24] Editorial. (*St. Croix Avis*, October 5, 1878).

[25] Report to the Governor of the Danish West India Islands, concerning the events which took place in Frederiksted the 1st October, 1878 and the night following, rendered by acting Policemaster in the Jurisdiction of Frederiksted, R.

Petersen. (*St. Croix Avis*, November 30, 1878).

[26] Ibid.

[27] Ibid.

[28] Publication of October 2nd, 1878 by August Garde. (*St. Croix Avis*, October 5, 1878).

[29] Report to the Governor . . . by R. Petersen. (*St. Croix Avis*, November 30, 1878).

[30] Proceedings of the Colonial Council for St. Croix, 6 November, 1878. (*St. Croix Avis*, November 23, 1878).

[31] Ibid.

[32] Proclamations of 5th October, 1878 by August Garde. (*St. Croix Avis*, October 5, 1878); Arrival of Some of the Escaped Rioters in Tortola. (*St. Croix Avis*, October 16, 1878).

[33] Skrubbeltrang, op. cit., pp. 214-215; Cf. Editorial (*St. Croix Avis*, October 12 and 23, 1878).

[34] *Collection of the most important Laws, Ordinances, Publications etc., valid in or referring to the Danish West India Islands, and issued since the Colonial Law of the 26th of March, 1852* (Copenhagen, 1884) p. 250.

[35] Proclamation of 5th October, 1878 by Janus August Garde. (*St. Croix Avis*, October 5, 1878).

[36] *Collection of the most important Laws, Ordinances, Publications etc.*, pp. 250-255.

[37] Considerations regarding the Conditions in the Danish West India Islands . . . pp. 8-9.

[38] P. P. Sveistrup, *Bidrag til de Tidligere Dansk-Vestindiske oers Okonomiske Historie. Med Saerligh Henblik paa Sukkerproduktion og Sukkerhandel.* (Kobenhavn, Nielsen & Lydiches Bogtrykkeri, 1942) p. 70.

[39] Considerations regarding the Conditions in the Danish West India Islands . . . pp. 9 and 11.

[40] Ibid., p. 11.

[41] Ibid., pp. 11-12.

[42] Luther K. Zabriskie, *The Virgin Islands of the United States of America: Historical and Descriptive, Commercial and Industrial. Facts, Figures and Resources.* (G. P. Putnam's Sons, New York and London, 1918) pp. 166-171 and 178-181.

[43] Ibid., pp. 118-123 and 163-166.

[44] H. G. Brock, Philip S. Smith and W. A. Tucker, *The Danish West Indies: Their Resources and Commercial Importance.* (Washington, Department of Commerce, Special Agents Series. No. 129, 1917).

[45] Ibid., p. 64.

[46] Zabriskie, op. cit., pp. 130-142.

Chapter 14

The Sale and Purchase

After being in the possession of Denmark for varying lengths of time extending for almost two hundred and forty-five years in the case of St. Thomas the Virgin Islands were sold to the United States of America. The transfer was effected on March 31, 1917, culminating a protracted series of negotiations commenced as early as 1865. The willingness of Denmark to sell stemmed basically from the economic relationship which existed between colony and mother-country, whereas the desire of the United States to buy resulted mainly from the demands of national and international politics.

The Reasons for Sale by Denmark

The declining economy of the Virgin Islands made them a colonial liability. Even in the pre-emancipation era, it is doubtful whether the islands were of much financial value to Denmark apart from certain vested interests. They indeed produced some revenue to the Danish exchequer, but there were expenses to be met from the appointment and remuneration of colonial officers. After emancipation, the condition of financial weakness of the Virgin Islands was severely aggravated by the increase of colonial expenditures and an increasing inability to meet those expenditures from local revenues.

The need to cater to the wants of the ex-slave population led to increased colonial expenditures after emancipation. Though some of the burden was shifted to employers, public expenditure on the poor and infirm proved to be an increasing one. Moreover, expenses for the education of the children of the laboring population increased substantially. These were additional to the cost of essential services given through courts, judges, the police, prison, the revenue departments, public health, roads, and fire department. Additional expenses included the salaries as well as pensions of colonial officers.

Compared with other budgetary items, the military establishment proved to be a most costly branch of colonial government. Since the islands benefited from the military protection, they were held responsible for meeting necessary expenditures. In 1851 the troops totalled 540 men divided into three companies requiring over half of the budget of the Virgin Islands to be maintained. From the feeling that all this expenditure was unnecessary both the army and the military expenditures were reduced in the 1860's and 1870's, so that by 1877 the former numbered 187 men while the latter amounted to $60,000. The reduction of the military force was considered one reason for the Laborers' Revolt of 1878, and after the disturbances the army was once more increased so that in the fiscal year 1879-1880 expenses totalled $82,614. This amount remained more or less constant during the remainder of the century imposing a severe burden upon the slim financial resources of the Virgin Islands.[1]

Increasing expenditures were not matched by a corresponding increase in revenues partly because emancipation ended the poll tax which had been levied on slave owners during slavery. The pre-emancipation land-tax was retained but it was levied only on cultivated land, and revenues diminished as more and more land went out of cultivation. The tax on land and another on buildings constituted the main direct taxes levied in the Virgin Islands. But all direct taxes together produced less than one-third of the revenue of the islands. The greater part of colonial revenues came from indirect taxes, of which customs duties brought in the largest amount. The emphasis in St. Thomas on commerce and in St. Croix on agriculture made for different systems of taxation, but in neither case could taxes be raised too high for fear of discouraging trade or production. The result was that duties were either very low or non-existent. Little hope of reforming either the direct or indirect taxes remained by the end of the nineteenth century.[2]

Increasing expenditures and declining revenues could mean only recurring deficits and growing indebtedness. Before 1879, the common budget of St. Thomas and St. John fluctuated between years of surplus and years of deficit. After 1879, however, surpluses disappeared and deficits increased steadily; in some years the latter was as high as $90,000. St. Croix's financial condition was similar, with deficits in certain years amounting to over $80,000. Table 3 shows the state of the budgets of St. Thomas and St. John and of St. Croix for selected years from 1866 to 1900.[3]

TABLE 3

Budgetary Surplus or Deficit of St. Thomas
and St. John and of St. Croix for selected
years from 1866 to 1900
(given in the nearest thousand dollars)

Year	St. Thomas and St. John				St. Croix			
	Reve-nue	Ex-pense	Sur-plus	Deficit	Reve-nue	Ex-pense	Sur-plus	Deficit
1865-1866	211	201	10	–	190	179	11	–
1870-1871	215	189	26	–	206	225	–	19
1875-1876	203	205	–	2	296	340	–	44
1880-1881	177	204	–	27	170	199	–	29
1885-1886	140	186	–	46	150	200	–	50
1890-1891	112	174	–	62	151	202	–	51
1891-1892	106	173	–	67	114	197	–	83
1892-1893	101	174	–	73	143	199	–	56
1893-1894	106	174	–	68	160	199	–	39
1894-1895	93	185	–	92	150	198	–	48
1895-1896	109	171	–	62	142	197	–	55
1896-1897	96	165	–	69	166	198	–	32
1897-1898	91	169	–	78	163	200	–	37
1898-1899	98	180	–	82	145	255	–	110
1899-1900	96	180	–	84	155	253	–	98

Rising indebtedness was the consequence of recurrent budgetary deficits. In 1871 the indebtedness of St. Thomas and St. John to the Danish treasury was $51,153, while that of St. Croix was $71.856. Even though the Danish treasury assumed the expenses of the Governor and President, the debt continued to rise so that by March, 1898, the indebtedness of St. Thomas and St. John was $1,045,418 while that of St. Croix was $984,124. Besides, St. Croix had to repay certain special loans amounting to $238,012 in 1897 on which it had been unable to pay even the interest since 1884.[4] Economic measures which were introduced after 1902 succeeded in reducing the combined deficits of the three islands but only to an annual average of $22,470 during the period 1910-1917.[5]

Denmark could ill-afford the extra expenditures which its colonies required, and its financial position became particularly critical after its war with Prussia in 1864. Besides, both public and private resources were restricted to finance industrialization at home; sale of overseas territory might better enable Denmark to meet its financial require-ments. A precedent for disposal of the West India colony was established in September, 1850, when Denmark sold its possessions in West Africa to Great Britain.

It was the inability of the Virgin Islands to pay their way which eventually led to their sale. So too did the decline of the islands as a market for the produce of Denmark and as a source of raw materials to feed Danish industries. This situation had developed even before emancipation and continued after it as can be seen from trade statistics. Table 4 shows the marked decline in colonial sugar exports to Denmark, the percentage declining from 12.1 in 1897 to 1.0 in 1901;[6] the remainder of the sugar found a market in the United States. In 1911, Denmark received less than two percent of the sugar of the Virgin Islands.

Table 4
Sugar Export from the Virgin Islands, 1897-1901

Year	Total Export	To Denmark
1897	28,714,494 lb.	3,497,341 lb.
1898	24,159,139 lb.	1,490,702 lb.
1899	30,479,469 lb.	343,220 lb.
1900	16,967,455 lb.	300,290 lb.
1901	29,118,522 lb.	300,290 lb.

The market for Danish products in the Virgin Islands was chiefly at St. Thomas; Table 5 shows that, compared with other nations, Danish exports to St. Thomas amounted to only 3.1 percent of the overall import trade of St. Thomas in 1884-89 and 2.1 percent in 1889-94.[7]

Table 5
Imports into St. Thomas 1884-1894
(Annual Averages)

Country	1884-1889	1889-1894
Denmark	$ 48,105	$ 27,902
U.S.A.	346,020	359,683
Britain	487,000	296,000
France	167,000	104,000
Germany	138,000	106,000
Elsewhere	342,289	413,760
	$1,528,414	$1,307,345

Danish trade with St. Croix declined substantially also. Between 1884-89 and 1889-94 Danish average annual exports to St. Croix fell from $24,278 to $19,387 while imports declined from $70,885 to $52,934. These figures illustrate not only a decline but also an adverse balance in Denmark's trade of $46,607 in the first period and of $33,547 in the second period.[8]

Socially, the Virgin Islands were little tied to Denmark. Apart from some administrative officers and the army personnel, only a small minority of the white population of the islands was Danish.[9] The Danish language was hardly spoken, and English was the popular language spoken and taught in the schools. English was even adopted as one of the official languages, and teachers were recruited in the British islands to teach in the schools. The currency in circulation was not the Danish rigsdaler (or krone which replaced the rigsdaler) but rather the Spanish Alfonso and doubloon in gold, and a number of Danish West Indian coins in silver and bronze.[10]

On the whole, the tokens of sentiment which should have linked the colony to the mother-country were sadly absent. Denmark thus approached the sale of the islands with a detached attitude while the majority of the local inhabitants were not sufficiently patriotic to oppose the transfer.

United States Interest in the Virgin Islands

The United States had a long association with the Virgin Islands, especially in the field of commerce which extended as far back as the early eighteenth century. The trading relationship continued and expanded so that by the end of the nineteenth century trade with the United States accounted for approximately one third of the Virgin Islands imports. Growing contact with the United States led many Virgin Islanders to believe that they would gain by a transfer of suzerainty.

Because of the economic decline of the Virgin Islands, their purchase by the United States could not have been considered worthwhile as a mere business venture. But there were more important considerations which aroused the interest of Americans and led to the eventual purchase of the islands.

To the United States the greater value of the Virgin Islands lay in harbors and naval stations; as such they could be important for trade as well as for military purposes. The overwhelming need for a suitable port in the West Indies was demonstrated during the American Civil War (1861-1865) when it was necessary for the Federal navy to find a berth for damaged ships and a holding-place for seized Confederate vessels.[11] A similar need became evident whenever United States economic interests or the national security appeared to be threatened.

The need for military bases at strategic points in the Caribbean was given point by the projected construction of the Panama Canal. The acquisition of the Virgin Islands became important for two reasons: to enable the United States to defend the approaches to the Panama Canal, and to prevent the islands from falling under the control of nations hostile to the United States. For these reasons, not even did the United States annexation of Puerto Rico and influence in Cuba, following the Spanish-American War of 1898, reduce the American desire to acquire the Virgin Islands.

The Panama Canal emphasized the need for a central coaling depot in the mid-Atlantic for ships en route from Europe to Central America. Besides, American vessels bound to and from South America could refuel here which meant business for Americans especially since St. Thomas had long acquired a reputation as a coaling station of considerable importance. The value of a coaling-station in terms of military strategy also could not be overlooked. As it was observed, 'A navy of modern fighting machines without coaling-stations in peace or war will mean maritime paralysis when war comes.'[12] Fleets could move between the United States and the Virgin Islands and seldom be observed since these islands were on the perimeter of the Lesser

Antilles. Alternatively, from the islands the United States could observe the disposition of European ships in the Caribbean.[13]

Considerations of defense and naval accommodation might not have been sufficient inducements to United States acquisition if they had not been coupled with fear that the Virgin Islands might come under the control of an unfriendly or enemy power. There were reasonable causes for alarm such as, for instance, Spain's reported attempt in the early 1860's to buy the Virgin Islands from Denmark, and Britain's seemingly hostile attitude to the Union government during the Civil War. The United States was also fearful of France since it had opposed French intervention in Mexico.[14]

Spain, Britain and France all held territories in the West Indies; it was a debatable point whether under the Monroe Doctrine forbidding European nations to acquire new territory in the western hemisphere, the United States could prevent the transfer of the Virgin Islands from Denmark to any one of these nations. It was otherwise, however, where another nation not already possessing colonies in the West Indies was concerned.

Such a nation was Germany. Rumors that Germany was ambitious to acquire territory in the West Indies, and more specifically the Virgin Islands, aroused American fear of the extension of German power in the region. The interests of national security dictated that the German move be countered. In view of the other advantages which the Virgin Islands possessed, the idea of purchase suggested itself. Seen in retrospect, the fear that Germany desired a foothold in the Caribbean was based on conjecture than on fact, but this did not make the fear any less real.

United States desire to acquire the Virgin Islands coincided with a growing imperialist attitude in the country in the nineteenth century. The need for political and economic reconstruction after the Civil War distracted American attention from the acquisition of overseas territory. However, a change in attitude occurred in the last decade of the century expressed by American intervention in the Cuban struggle for independence and in war with Spain. As defined then, American imperialism was essentially protective and not acquisitive,[15] but there was nothing in the national policy which forbade the acquisition of colonies through purchase.

Above: WILLIAM H. SEWARD
Below: WALDEMAR RUDOLPH RAASLØFF

The Treaty of October 24, 1867

The question of American acquisition of the Virgin Islands was raised and discussed during President Andrew Jackson's first administration when American merchants had pressed their claims against Denmark for the settlement of debts.[16] The question, however, generated little enthusiasm since not much value was attached to the Virgin Islands then.

Until the outbreak of the American Civil War there were occasional fruitless expressions of opinion favoring the purchase and even seizure of all the West Indies including the Virgin Islands. These were sectional attitudes and came generally from the southern states which were interested in more slave territory. They came, too, from the party of 'Young America' motivated by belief in the manifest destiny of the United States to extend order and good government in the western hemisphere.[17]

In Denmark, also, the question of the future possession of the Virgin Islands came up for discussion. First raised in 1846, the question did not attract enough support to warrant debate in the Danish Rigsdag until 1852. Opinion was strongly divided on the issue whether Denmark was able and willing to keep the islands. Opposition leaders eventually won with the argument that the sale would be unwise since the issue was not yet pressing.[18]

The initiative in opening genuine negotiations for the purchase of the Virgin Islands was taken by the United States Secretary of State, William H. Seward, an ardent expansionist, shortly before the close of the American Civil War. Included among the guests at a dinner given by the French chargé d'affaires in Washington on January 7, 1865, were Seward and General Waldemar R. Raasloff the Danish minister in Washington who had long occupied that position and was very popular among American officials. It was at this dinner party that Seward approached Raasloff with a proposition to purchase the islands.[19]

The initiation of discussions, however, was followed by long delay in reaching agreement. On the American side, a carriage accident to Seward temporarily incapacitating him for business, and later the assassination of President Lincoln and the wounding of Seward himself, combined to defer negotiations for some time. Further delay occurred due to Seward's plan to inspect the Virgin Islands themselves and to assess their worth, which was accomplished in January, 1866. Though favorably impressed, he did not pursue the matter vigorously until after

January, 1867 when the United States was offered Samana Bay Harbor in Santo Domingo for purchase or lease.[20]

On the Danish side also there were several reasons for slow progress. The Conservative government in Denmark in 1865 was disinclined to sell the Virgin Islands since Denmark had recently lost the two duchies of Schleswig and Holstein to Prussia and Austria the previous year and felt much humiliated. Even when it was replaced by a Liberal government more favorably inclined towards the transfer delay occurred since Prussia was opposed to the sale and fear of possible aggression by that country against Denmark demanded caution. The likelihood of opposition from France under the Treaty of June, 1733 governing the sale of St. Croix, suggested delay also. Besides, Danes feared that a sales treaty with the United States would not secure the approval of the Senate because of its feud with President Andrew Johnson, Lincoln's successor.[21]

Reassured by the prompt manner in which the United States had concluded the treaty with Russia for the purchase of Alaska, the Danes reacted more favorably to American overtures after May, 1867. Nevertheless, deadlock over the question of price and the consultation of local opinion delayed negotiations until October 24, 1867 when the treaty was finally signed at Copenhagen.[22] The favorable reception of the treaty in Denmark was aided by the work of Senator James R. Doolittle of Wisconsin as a special agent sent to assist Yeaman in Copenhagen, and a friendly visit by Admiral Farragat with his fleet to Copenhagen.[23]

The Treaty of 1867 provided for the American acquisition of St. Thomas and St. John for $7.5 million with the understanding that the inhabitants of these islands would be allowed to express their agreement through a plebiscite. Moreover, it provided for the protection of the liberty, religion and private rights of Virgin Islanders. It also made provision regarding citizenship: those who remained in the islands after the transfer were to choose within two years whether they wished to retain Danish or acquire United States citizenship; those who did not express a desire for change at the end of that time would be considered 'to have elected to become citizens of the United States.'

The question which was likely to cause concern in the Virgin Islands was that of commercial policy so much so that some understanding about the future operation of the level of tariffs in St. Thomas was necessary before a vote could be risked. It was largely on Seward's assurance, and the feeling that the United States could be relied upon for fair dealing, that the plebiscite was allowed.[24] The vote in St. Thomas was taken on January 9, 1868, and in St. John on the following day. In St. Thomas, the vote was 1,039 for and only 22 against the Treaty; in St. John, it was 205 for and none against. The voting was conducted amid much expression of patriotism in favor of the United States.[25]

As far as the islanders were concerned, the transfer was settled; but it was still necessary for the Treaty to be ratified by the Danish Rigsdag and the American Senate. The former presented no difficulty; when the Treaty was brought before it, it was passed and promptly signed by the king on January 31, 1868.[26]

The reception of the Treaty in the United States was far from favorable. At the time the attention of the American Congress and public was diverted by the impeachment of President Johnson. The deadline for the ratification of the Treaty was February 24, 1868, but Seward was forced to seek an extension of the time limit to October 14, 1869, which was granted. American dalliance, however, was embarrassing to the Danish government, and the appearance of Raasloff before the Senate foreign relations committee during the winter of 1868-1869 to press for ratification evoked no favorable response. The congressional session of 1869 did not discuss the Treaty and on March 30, 1869, it was laid on the table which was a gentle method of rejection. The time for ratification was further extended to April 14, 1870 but the death blow came before then on March 22, 1870 when the foreign relations committee recommended that the Senate should not 'advise and consent to the ratification.'[27]

Several factors were responsible for the failure of the Treaty of 1867. Public indifference after the Civil War when there was a reaction against the expansionist policy of Seward featured prominently. Americans were more concerned with social and economic reconstruction and development of the American West than with territorial acquisition overseas. The United States lapsed into a policy of isolation, turning its capital and energy inwards rather than outwards. Imperialism waned and the navy was allowed to dwindle to insignificant proportions so that need to acquire naval stations in the Atlantic no longer became pressing.

The attitude of the United States Senate was crucial since it had the power to ratify or reject treaties. The political differences between President Johnson and Congress, the widespread belief that the Treaty was secretly negotiated by Seward without the prior consent of the

Senate, and the lack of enthusiasm shown by the influential Senator Charles Sumner, chairman of the Senate foreign relations committee, and his failure to make sincere efforts to secure ratification, were all factors which led to the failure of the 1867 Treaty. Both President Lincoln and President Johnson had approved of the purchase, but President Grant disavowed any such action by his predecessors. Some Senators even questioned the constitutionality of the Treaty while others rejected the policy of annexing territory non-contiguous to the United States.[28]

There was fear that acquisition of the Virgin Islands would focus enemy attention upon them in case of war, thereby requiring a great increase of American military and naval force for their defense. There was a general belief, also that the islands were not worth the price. To secure $7.5 million from the House of Representatives was considered well-nigh impossible in view of the recent unpopular purchase of Alaska referred to as 'Seward's folly.' The damage to buildings and ships (including the United States ship 'Monongahela' which was thrown up into the Strand in Frederiksted) and of property generally, by the hurricane, earthquake and tidal wave of 1867, was used with telling effect. 'Immediately everyone began to make fun of the treaty, as one for the annexation of hurricanes and earthquakes, and the subject was fairly "laughed out of the Court" '.[29]

Abortive Negotiations: The Approaches of the 1890's

Though not abandoned, the question of the purchase of the Virgin Islands was not raised for twenty-two years after the Treaty of 1867 was defeated. These years were filled with rumors and counter-rumors of German territorial ambitions in the Caribbean, which caused much anxiety in the United States.[30] Denmark was still desirous of selling the islands to the United States and in November, 1892, the question was again raised at diplomatic level. Clark E. Carr, the United States minister in Copenhagen called on J. B. S. Estrup, the Danish Prime Minister, in connection with some exhibits for the Columbian Exposition at Chicago and reference was made by the Prime Minister to the rejected Treaty of 1867. He intimated that his government would be willing to cede the islands at the price named in that Treaty.

Following the exchange between the two ministers, the matter was referred to Baron Otto Reedtz-Thott, minister of foreign affairs, who after reporting it to the king, informed Carr that the proposition to sell would be favorably considered by the Danish government. Thereupon, Carr informed the United States government, stressing the importance of the islands for naval bases in the Caribbean, and strongly favoring the sale.

To this move initiated by Denmark, the United States Secretary of State, John W. Foster, was entirely sympathetic. The time, however, was inopportune. Presidential elections had already been held and President Harrison had been overwhelmingly defeated by Grover Cleveland. There was not enough time before the end of Harrison's term to draft a treaty and have it ratified, and Cleveland was opposed to the transaction. To begin negotiations, therefore, would have been useless, since they would certainly have been discontinued or repudiated when the new President assumed office in March, 1893.[31] Denmark acknowledged the difficulty and dropped the matter with the expressed willingness to re-open the subject if the proposed Panama Canal materialized, and if it was necessary for the United States to acquire a port in the West Indies.

The question of sale was again taken up three years later when at the beginning of 1896, the United States press took up the subject. It was stated that Denmark had an agent in the United States who was trying to sell the islands, and that if the United States was not inclined to purchase them, Germany would. These rumors came to the notice of John E. Risley, the United States minister in Copenhagen, who soon learned from the Danish government that the report was without foundation. Risley was informed that there were no attempts to sell the Virgin Islands either to the United States or to Germany, but it was hinted that a proposition to reopen the subject would probably be received with favor.

On January 3, 1896, Senator Lodge of Massachusetts introduced a resolution directing the foreign relations committee to inquire and report to the Senate whether or not the Danish West Indies could be bought then, or if not bought by the United States whether it was probable that some other nation would purchase them. Upon this the Senate made no recommendation, nor was it clear what the views of Secretary of State Olney were on the subject. Consequently, nothing came out of this movement and there was another short lapse of time.[32]

Between January, 1897 and April, 1898, quiet semi-official negotiations transpired between Denmark and the United States. The accredited representative of the Danish government in the United States was Niels Gron, a Dane by birth, but a United States citizen by adoption. Gron represented a very conservative sale committee in Denmark and after a long, tedious procedure the affair was almost settled. Unfortunately the Spanish-American War intervened. Not only was the attention of the United States diverted to the more important matter of winning the war, but Denmark dropped the attempt to sell the islands out of courtesy to Spain.[33]

The Treaty of January 24, 1902

Negotiations to purchase the Virgin Islands were deferred pending settlement of questions arising out of the Spanish-American War. During 1900, however, the United States government again began to make overtures to Denmark. Near the end of the following year, negotiations between Secretary of State John Hay and Constantine Brun, the Danish minister in Washington, were practically concluded in another attempt at transfer.

The Treaty concluding the efforts of these diplomats was brought about largely by a Danish adventurer Captain Walter Christmas-Dirckinck-Holmfeld who hoped to gain ten percent of the sales price on the successful completion of the transaction. Due to his influence, the United States sent an agent, Henry White, Secretary of the United States Embassy in Britain, to Denmark 'to negotiate the purchase. Christmas acted as interpreter for White to the representative of the Danish Prime Minister. He also visited the United States, and in many ways assisted the United States government in the preliminaries which led to the conclusion of the Treaty on January 24, 1902.[34]

The Treaty of 1902 differed from the Treaty of 1867 by being drafted in Washington, and placed first before the United States Senate. The sovereignty held by Denmark over the entire Virgin Islands was transferred to the United States without holding the latter responsible for the debts of the islands. The sum agreed upon for all three of the islands was five million dollars, and the time limit for ratification was set for July 24, 1902.

The inhabitants of the Virgin Islands were granted full property, religious and civil rights, and the choice of remaining in or leaving the islands at their pleasure. They were given two years to decide whether they wanted to remain Danish subjects, at the end of which time, if no declaration had been made to the effect, they were to be considered nationals of the United States. It was left to Congress to determine 'the civil rights and the political status of the inhabitants of the islands'.

No vote was taken in the Virgin Islands with regard to the sale of the islands, but majority opinion locally, still smarting from the United States rejection of the previous treaty, was clearly against the sale. In the United States conservative opinion generally favored the purchase of the Virgin Islands because of their value as harbors and coaling depots the need for which had again been plainly seen during the Spanish-American War. But there also some strong sentiment against the purchase. However, when President Roosevelt sent the Treaty to the Senate on January 27, 1902, little opposition was voiced from that body.[35] The Treaty was ratified on February 17, 1902, and signed by the President on March 1, 1902. Charges that high United States officials had been bribed into accepting the Treaty were later proved to be unfounded.

In Denmark, the Treaty did not receive such favorable reception as in the United States.[36] When it was brought up for discussion in the Danish Rigsdag it was passed quite easily by the Folketing, or lower house which consisted of elected representatives of the people. However, in the Landsting, or upper house, composed of the landed aristocracy it met with decided opposition. In the final vote, thirty-two members voted for and thirty-two voted against the ratification. The Treaty, therefore, was vetoed on a tie vote.

During the summer of 1902, the question of the proposed cession was considerably agitated in Denmark and a wave of patriotism had swept the country. The Folketing, however, took a practical view of the situation considering the islands' failing economy and indebtedness and Denmark's own inability to maintain them.

The Landsting was not moved by such considerations. In September, 1902, fresh elections to the upper house had been held with the hope that a majority in favor of the sale would be elected. Christian IX was not favorably disposed to the sale though he had as a constitutional monarch of necessity to agree to the Treaty, and his private attitude undoubtedly influenced the Landsting. Besides, the humiliation felt by the United States' rejection of the Treaty of 1867, contributed greatly to the opposition to the Treaty of 1902 and the situation was worsened by the political differences between the Conservative-dominated Landsting and the Liberal-dominated Folketing.

Business influence might have helped to defeat the Treaty, since

Danish businessmen needed a West Indian harbor to develop trade with Latin America. Some members of the Landsting were closely related to business interests through marriage and Danish capitalists were stockholders in the new East Asia West India Improvement Company which held a 99-year lease on the St. Thomas harbor. The fact that Prince Waldemar, sixth son of Christian IX, was President of the Company, helps to explain why his very popular wife actively lobbied against the Treaty. German influence also might have played a part though it is easy to exaggerate it.[37] Of more importance was sentiment: the thought of losing another colonial possession went against the pride of the aristocratic Landsting.

The Treaty of August 4, 1916 and the Transfer

The Treaty of 1867 had been frustrated by the adverse attitude of the United States, while the Treaty of 1902 met with an unfavorable reception in the Danish Landsting. Whether it was American negligence or Danish recalcitrance, the United States had the upper hand since it could invoke the Monroe Doctrine to prevent the sale of the Virgin Islands to another power. Senator Henry Cabot Lodge made this point clear when he warned that the transfer of the islands to another European power 'would be an infraction of the Monroe Doctrine'.[38] Lodge spoke with the powerful backing of the Senate foreign relations committee; he also undoubtedly expressed the view of the United States government, and of the overwhelming majority of the American public. Firm action was thought necessary to protect national security and vital American economic interests in Central and South America especially as the Panama Canal was assuming reality.

Fear that Germany wanted a foothold in the Caribbean was real but unfounded, and it served to focus attention on the Virgin Islands which were deemed easy prey for Germany's ambitions. Matters came to a head during World War I: in the event of Denmark's being overrun and conquered by Germany, Danish colonies would almost certainly become German possessions. Besides, the possibility of United States involvement in the war could not be overlooked, especially in view of the German submarine campaign and the attendant loss of American lives and property. Not only would an additional base be necessary in the Atlantic, but the United States could not permit Germany to acquire such a base from which to launch attacks. The purchase of the Virgin

Islands became a matter of urgency.[39]

Before the outbreak of the war, the Danish attitude was one of detachment towards what was considered United States 'arrogance and imperialistic tendencies'. The work of the highly popular Dr. Maurice Francis Egan, the United States minister to Copenhagen, since 1907, however, had done much to allay suspicions. Even so, it was not until May, 1915 that the question of the transfer of the Virgin Islands was again raised officially. It had been the hope of the Danish government that the opening of the Panama Canal in 1914 would revive the trade of St. Thomas. However, when it became increasingly evident that this hope would not materialize Denmark was more willing to consider sale.

Instructions were given to Dr. Egan in June, 1915 by Secretary of State Robert Lansing to reopen negotiations though secrecy and discretion were urged. Two months later Egan consulted with the Danish Foreign Minister, Erik de Scavenius who allegedly asked for $30 million for the islands and in October, 1915, Lansing himself discussed the matter with Constantin Brun, the Danish minister in Washington. At first the Danish government hesitated but was later induced to change by the American promise of 'certain commercial privileges in favor of Danish subjects', by the warning that Germany might overrun Denmark in order to acquire the Virgin Islands, and by the threat of outright American annexation of the islands in order to prevent them from becoming German territory. These pressures together with the more favorable attitude of the Danish public to the United States, undoubtedly made the Danish government more responsive to the American approach.[40]

After October, 1915, it was a matter of negotiating what price was to be paid for the Virgin Islands, and by January, 1916, agreement was reached on $25 million as a compromise between the Danish demand for $27 million and the American offer of $20 million. The succeeding months were occupied in negotiating terms acceptable to both sides, especially with regard to free trade and citizenship, and finally on August 4, 1916, the Treaty of cession was signed at the Hotel Biltmore in New York City, by Lansing and Constantin Brun on behalf of their respective governments.[41]

According to the Treaty, the United States government agreed to pay Denmark the sum of $25 million in return for the possession of the entire Danish West Indies. Private property rights were to continue unimpaired, and power was reserved to the United States Congress, subject to the stipulations of the Treaty, to determine 'the civil rights and the political status of the inhabitants' of the Virgin Islands.

A most important provision of the Treaty related to citizenship. Danish citizens residing in the islands were to be allowed to remain or leave at will, retaining all the rights of property in either case. Those choosing to remain were to enjoy all the rights and liberties secured to them by the laws then in force, unless such laws should be altered, in which event they were not to be placed in a less favorable position than before.

Danish citizenship could be preserved by making a declaration to that effect before a court of record within one year from ratification. People not electing to preserve Danish citizenship were to be deemed to have accepted 'citizenship of the United States'. Danish citizens who preserved their citizenship could still renounce it and elect 'citizenship in the United States' and admission to the nationality thereof on the same terms provided for other Virgin Islanders.

President Wilson transmitted the Treaty to Senate on August 8, 1916, and following little opposition, it was approved by that body on September 7. In Denmark, differences over the proposed sale precipitated a political crisis, but the impasse was overcome by submitting the question to a national referendum. The voting on December 15, was 283,694 for and 157,596 against the sale. When the question was brought before the Rigsda, the Folketing voted 90 for and 16 against while the Landsting taking a cue from the national verdict voted 40 to 19 in favor of ratification. On December 22, 1916 the Treaty received the king's signature. On January 16, 1917, it was signed by President Wilson, and ratifications were exchanged on the following day.[42]

Opinion in the Virgin Islands was overwhelmingly in favor of the sale. On August 16, 1916 a cable to Denmark signed by 21 planters expressed support for the sale. Later in the same month resolutions were passed unanimously by the Colonial Councils of St. Croix and St. Thomas and St. John, urgently requesting the Danish government to ratify the Treaty. While the matter was being discussed in the Danish Rigsdag, a delegation of six prominent Virgin Islanders, three from each municipality, including Dr. Viggo Christiansen members of the St. Chomas Council, and A. E. Stakemann member of the St. Croix Council were selected to go to Denmark to support the sale. Local opinion was instrumental in influencing Danish acceptance of the Treaty.[43]

Formal transfer ceremonies were held in St. Thomas and St. Croix beginning at 4:00 p.m. on March 31, 1917. They were preceded on February 18, b7 a farewell service held in the Reformed Dutch Church

THE TRANSFER CEREMONY – ST. THOMAS

in St. Thomas, which the Danish Acting-Governor Commander Henri Konow and his officials attended. On March 31, the ceremonies were preceded by the signing of a transfer agreement in Fort Christian by Commander Konow and U.S. Commander Edwin T. Pollack representing the new American governor of the Virgin Islands. Afterwards, in the presence of guards of honor and to the tune of the national anthems of the respective countries the Danish 'Dannebrog' was lowered and the United States 'Stars and Stripes' was raised. A 21-gun salute was fired from the Fort. In Christiansted and Frederiksted in St. Croix similar ceremonies were held at the Forts by officials representing Denmark and the United States.[44]

The occasion was a solemn one. The ceremonies were witnessed by crowds of people with mixed emotions: sadness by a few on parting from Denmark and hope by the majority for a better life under the United States.

Conclusion

With the transfer of the Virgin Islands from Denmark to the United States one era in their history ended while another began. Latterly, the transfer had been eagerly awaited by the native population in general, and hopes ran high. Association with the United States was somehow regarded as the formula to cure the economic and social ills from which they were suffering.

However, the acquisition of the Virgin Islands was conceived differently by the United States which was motivated by other considerations than the desires and needs of the colonial peoples. The islands had not been bought for their economic potentials; indeed, despite the reputation which St. Thomas had acquired as a trading center, the Virgin Islands were not sought after for their commercial advantages. In any case, telegraph and steamship communication had done much to decentralize commerce between Europe or the United States with Caribbean territories. Rather, the primary value of the Virgin Islands was the advantages which they possessed as a coaling depot and a military base to promote or safeguard vital United States economic interests in the region.

The conception of the islands as a military base rather than as a colony with natural resources to be developed in the interest of the people was to determine United States attitudes and policies in future years.

[1] Charles W. Tooke, 'The Danish Colonial Fiscal System in the West Indies.' (In *Essays in Colonial Finance*. Publications of the American Economic Association. Vol. 1, No. 3, 1900).

[2] United States Congress. 57th Congress, 1st Session. House Document. No. 15. Part 7. *Danish West India Islands, Their Commerce, Production, Population, Area, etc.* (Washington, 1902) pp. 2770-2771.

[3] Tooke, op. cit., pp. 157-158.

[4] Ibid.

[5] Luther Harris Evans, *The Virgin Islands from Naval Base to New Deal.* (Ann Arbor, Michigan, 1945) p. 146.

[6] Considerations regarding the Conditions in the Danish West India Islands: Submitted by the West Indian Commission by His Majesty's Resolution of November 18, 1902. (Copenhagen, 1903) p. 25.

[7] United States Congress . . . House Document No. 15, pp. 2774-2775.

[8] Ibid., pp. 2773 and 2839-2842.

[9] N. Parker Willis, *Health Trip to the Tropics.* (New York, Charles Scribner, 1853) p. 62.

[10] Considerations regarding the Conditions in the Danish West India Islands . . . pp. 18-19.

[11] Halvdan Koht, 'The Origin of Seward's Plan to Purchase the Danish West Indies.' (*The American Historical Review*, Vol. 50, No. 4, Oct., 1944) p. 763.

[12] Harper's Weekly, April 23, 1898, p. 395.

[13] Theodore L. Stoddard, 'The Danish West Indies: Key to the Caribbean.' (*American Review of Reviews*, 1916); Theodore L. Stoddard, 'Strategic Value of the Danish West Indies.' (*Journal of Geography*, Vol. 15, 1916).

[14] Koht, op. cit., p. 763.

[15] Dexter Perkins, *A History of the Monroe Doctrine.* (Boston, Little Brown, 1955).

[16] Niles Register, Vol. 39, November 13, 1830.

[17] Arndt M. Stickles, 'The Danish West Indies and American Ownership.' (*The Journal of American History*, Vol. VII, No. 1, 1913) p. 856.

[18] Jens Vibaek, *Dansk Vestindien 1755-1848: Vestindiens Storhedstid.* (Fremad, Denmark, 1966) pp. 69-71.

[19] Charles Callan Tansill, *The Purchase of the Danish West Indies.* (Baltimore, The Johns Hopkins Press, 1932) pp. 5-11.

[20] Ibid., pp. 12-43.

[21] Ibid., Chapter 1, passim.

[22] *The St. Thomas Treaty. A Series of Letters to the Boston Daily Advertiser.* (New York, 1869) pp. 5-14.

[23] Tansill, op. cit., pp. 50-51 and 67-68.

[24] Olive Risley Seward, 'A Diplomatic Episode.' (*Scribner's Magazine*, October, 1887) pp. 594-596; *The St. Thomas Treaty. A Series of Letters . . .* pp. 11-21.

[25] James Parton, *The Danish Islands: Are We Bound in Honor to Pay for Them?* (Boston, 1869) pp. 38-39.

[26] Ibid., pp. 39-43.

[27] Stickles, op. cit., pp. 860-863.

[28] Tansill, op. cit., pp. 99-151.

[29] Pierce Papers: Quoted in Tansill, op. cit., p. 145.
[30] Tansill, op. cit., pp. 154-192.
[31] Willis Fletcher Johnson, 'The Story of the Danish Islands.' (*The North American Review*, Sept., 1916) pp. 387-388.
[32] Stickles, op. cit., p. 866.
[33] Ibid.
[34] Georg Norregard, *Dansk Vestindien 1880-1917: Reformforsog og Salgsforhandlinger.* (Fremad, Denmark, 1967) pp. 31-55; Tansill, op. cit., pp. 218-285.
[35] United States Congress. 57th Congress, 1st Session. Senate Document. Cession of the Danish Islands in the West Indies. Message from the President of the United States transmitting a Treaty between the United States and Denmark providing for their cession to the United States of certain islands in the West Indies. Document No. 284. (Washington, 1902).
[36] Tansill, op. cit., pp. 345-371; Stickles, op. cit., pp. 870-872.
[37] Johnson, op. cit., p. 389.
[38] United States Congress. Senate Document No. 284, p. 19.
[39] J. B. Scott, 'Purchase of the Danish West Indies by the United States of America.' (*American Journal of International Law*, Vol. 10, 1916).
[40] Maurice Francis Egan, *Ten Years Near the German Frontier.* (New York, 1919) pp. 256-288.
[41] Tansill, op. cit., pp. 467-496.
[42] Norregard, op. cit., pp. 118-128. Note, however, that Norregard gives 286,694 votes for the sale in the referendum.
[43] Darwin D. Creque, *The U.S. Virgins and the Eastern Caribbean.* (Whitmore Publishing Co., Philadelphia, 1968) p. 68.
[44] Frits Lawaetz, The Story of the First Transfer Day. (*The Virgin Islands Times*, March 30, 1967); Joseph Alexander, The Story of Transfer of V.I. (*St. Croix Avis*, March 28, 1970); Luther K. Zabriskie, *The Virgin Islands of the United States of America.* (G. P. Putnam's Sons, New York and London, 1918) pp. 294-317.

Chapter 15

The American Dilemma

The Virgin Islands were handed over to the United States on March 31, 1917, and one week later on April 6, the United States joined the First World War against Germany. The islands had been acquired largely because of their strategic importance for military purposes, but as a naval base they did not play any significant part during the war. After the end of the war in 1918, whatever military importance they had, declined even further.

The military factor apart, the United States had very little reason to acquire the islands. Agriculturally and commercially they were unimportant since long before the acquisition they were in decline. After 1918 they were a doubtful naval asset. Only a persisting fear that the islands could prove dangerous if they were allowed to pass to a nation hostile to the United States led to their retention.

Political Organization in 1917

The conception of the Virgin Islands as a military base rather than as an area valuable for its economic resources determined the political attitude of the United States to its newly acquired territory. In turn, the type of government established was to determine attitudes towards social and economic problems as well as local reactions to the American presence.

Despite the measures introduced by Denmark for the economic regeneration of the Virgin Islands, both a viable economy and an efficient system of social services were lacking. Political power was under the control of an exclusive and privileged class of moneyed people who were jealous of their power and unwilling to share it. The important question which the United States had to resolve was whether it should assume the entire responsibility for the economic and social welfare of its new possession by maintaining the political status quo, or whether it should encourage democratic institutions to enable the people to participate in their own development. In short, the issue was one of continuing autocratic government or introducing those democratic principles of government being practiced in the United States. Because the Virgin Islands were conceived primarily as a naval base, and because the people as a whole were inexperienced in operating a democratic system, the first alternative was implemented.

By an Act of the Congress of the United States passed on March 3, 1917, provision was made for the government of the Virgin Islands. Basically, the system of colonial government introduced by Denmark through the Colonial Law of 1906 was retained. Executive power was vested in the President of the United States but he could delegate his powers to a governor and 'such person or persons' whom he might appoint. These persons could be appointed from among army or navy personnel an authorization which was possible because of the status of the Virgin Islands as an unincorporated territory of the United States. In effect, the functions performed by the governor, the government secretary, the dispatching secretary (equivalent to lieutenant governor) of St. Croix and other senior officials were conferred upon officers of the United States Navy.[1]

No executive order was ever issued covering the relationship of the Navy Department to the government of the Virgin Islands. However, in a letter of October 12, 1922, the President directed the governor to forward his annual reports to him through the Secretary of the Navy. This meager involvement of the Navy Department was used to support the claim of the naval administration that it was civilian in its operation.

The system of government introduced by the Act of March 3, 1917, was intended to be temporary and was to last only until the next session of Congress when permanent legislation would be passed. The entry of the United States into the First World War, however, postponed any immediate action in this direction. Even after the war came to an end in November, 1918, there was no immediate attempt at constitutional reform. The delay in implementing the provision of the Act of March, 1917, relating to the introduction of permanent legislation, and the reaction to it, greatly influenced the nature of political relationship in the Virgin Islands.

Naval Achievements: Social Reforms

In their administration of the Virgin Islands, the naval officers concentrated on the improvement of social services as a result of an early study of the needs of the society.[2] Achievements pertained to the areas of public health, water supply, roads and streets, police, fire protection and public education.[3]

During the first year of its administration the Navy reorganized the hospitals in St. Thomas and St. Croix, and improved their equipment, and a survey was made of the sanitary condition of Charlotte Amalie. During the following years the training of native nurses was pushed, the personnel and equipment of the hospitals were increased, and better provision was also made for the sanitary supervision of food. The entire population of the Virgin Islands was vaccinated against smallpox, infant and maternal welfare was improved, a sanitary code was formulated and mosquito control was made effective.[4] One result of these measures was the fall in the death rate from 35.4 per thousand during the period 1911 to 1917, to 25.0 during the period 1918 to 1922, and to 19.5 in 1926.

Closely connected with the question of health was that of providing a reliable and safe water supply and of sewage disposal. A serious drought in 1924 showed the need for urgent action to conserve water, and a number of concrete reservoirs each fed by a paved catchment was constructed in St. Thomas, while the Creque Dam was built and a number of wells was drilled in St. Croix. These measures were able to reduce to a large extent the suffering usually experienced by the people in times of drought. With regard to sewage disposal, a night-soil removal service was introduced shortly after the United States assumed control followed by a partial institution of a salt water flushing system.

Some attempt was made to improve the roads of the Virgin Islands but not much was accomplished; even the little that was achieved was done slowly. In the main, efforts were confined to road maintenance and to experimentation with small sections of macadam and oil-surfaced roads.

Compared with its road building program, the naval administration achieved more substantial results in organizing the police force and fire protection. A police force composed of natives was organized and ordinances were passed to control its numbers and administration. In order to improve the inadequate fire fighting services inherited from the Danes, the Americans introduced fire departments, installed salt water pumping systems and purchased adequate equipment with which to fight fires.

The greatest achievement of the naval administration was in the field of education. New school buildings were erected, others were repaired or reconstructed, and teaching facilities were improved. More teachers were employed, teacher-training was expanded and salaries were raised to the point where teaching became one of the best paid occupations in the islands. Improved curricula along American lines were introduced with greater emphasis on junior and senior high school education, and schools were secularized except for the Catholic schools attached to the French community. The improvements introduced were reflected in increased appropriations. During the period 1910-1917, the average annual expenditure on education was $21,433; it was increased to $57,967 in 1919, to $66,000 in 1920, to $80,140 in 1921, and to $109,090 in 1922. For the next ten years expenditure averaged about $100,000. From 1918 to 1930, the average monthly salary of teachers increased from $16 to $50 while the annual expenditure for each pupil rose from $10 to $33.[5]

Naval Administration: Economic Bypass

The energy and initiative shown by the Navy in introducing new or improved measures to deal with the social services were not matched by similar vigor to improve the economy of the Virgin Islands. The emphasis in St. Croix on agriculture and in St. Thomas on trade indicated the directions in which development could take place. The administration, however, was either unwilling or unable to act. Even when it was moved to act, its attitude was one of transferred responsibility.[6] In St. Croix the agricultural experiment station was placed under the Department of Agriculture, but appropriations were reduced from an annual average of $3,938 during the period 1910-1917, to $632 during the period 1918-1931. The work of the station was largely experimental, though it assisted to some extent in demonstrating better farming techniques. However, the adminis-tration preferred to work through the schools by having the pupils cultivate small school gardens, a policy which could hardly be expected to produce good or lasting results.

In response to a joint resolution of the colonial councils, the governor created a department of agriculture, commerce and labor in 1924 to investigate and advise on the fundamental economic problems of the Virgin Islands. Few if any benefits resulted chiefly because it was located in St. Thomas and it was headed by the Navy chaplain who was no agricultural expert. The administration assisted some plantation owners by drilling wells to give additional supplies of water and by facilitating the marketing of cattle in Puerto Rico.[7] These efforts, however, were either not very important or showed the administration's willingness to follow rather than to lead.

The administration was obstructive or inactive in other respects. Thus it resisted all demands made by planters for the importation of cheap labor from British West Indian islands but favored the importation of Puerto Ricans who were American citizens, even though their labor was more expensive. With regard to the redistribution of land, the administration favored the formation of homesteads but it took no active steps to implement such a policy. Indeed, the involvement of governors in agriculture was more or less confined to the settlement of labor disputes between employers and laborers.[8] One explanation for their failure to devise and implement schemes for agricultural reform was the frequent change of governors — no less than six between 1917 and 1927 — which further frustrated any hope of achieving continuity of policy.

The government's attitude was reflected in the continuous decrease of cultivation and consequently of production. For example, cultivated areas declined from 12,220 acres in 1916, to 9,662 acres in 1922, to 9,148 acres in 1928, and to 4,686 acres in 1932. The production of sugar showed the same trend: while the average annual production during the period 1910-1917 was 13.5 million pounds, production had fallen to 3.57 million pounds by 1931.[9]

The production of rum declined as a result of lower sugar cane production but more so from the extension to the Virgin Islands in 1921 of the Prohibition Act of the United States passed the previous year which forbade the manufacture and sale of rum here. Virgin Islanders sought to retrieve the situation by turning to the production of bay rum instead, and for several years after 1921 the annual export of that commodity averaged 100,000 gallons approximately. During the last years of the prohibition which ended in 1933 bay rum production was more than double that of the 1916-1917 peak of 47,000 gallons.[10] Like sugar and rum, cotton production also suffered. The war had made the exportation of cotton almost impossible and production was practically abandoned; after the war, cotton cultivation was revived but on an extremely limited scale.[11]

Inefficient administration was not totally responsible for the economic decline of the Virgin Islands. Following the post-war boom which lasted until about 1922, the 1920's were marked by depression. Unfavorable weather conditions climaxed by the hurricanes of 1924 and 1928, and a drop in the price of sugar, were major drawbacks to agriculture in the Virgin Islands. The situation was made worse by the world economic depression in the years 1929 to 1932 during which the Bethlehem and the La Grange plantations went out of operation. Even before then many properties had been abandoned, buildings had deteriorated, and fields had been over-run by bush. Expected financial investment by private Americans did not materialize in order to stimulate development.[12]

In addition to its inability to improve the economy of the Virgin Islands, the naval administration showed itself incapable of adopting and implementing an adequate revenue system or of fully executing the tax system in force. After 1917 the Virgin Islands continued to rely for the most part on the traditional means of raising revenue. The duties on sugar exported were changed from five percent ad valorem to $8 a ton which lasted until 1927 when it was reduced to $6 a ton. But the most notable innovation in the tax system was a local income tax which was introduced in 1918 and which was replaced in 1921 by the federal income tax. The proceeds of this tax, after the cost of collection had been deducted, were paid into the local treasury. However, to some extent the benefits derived from the addition of the income tax was reduced by the removal of duties on goods imported from the United States.[13]

During the period of naval administration, the revenues of the Virgin Islands showed no appreciable increase over those of the last years of the Danish administration. Thus while the average annual revenue for the period 1910-1917 was $260,066, the period 1918-1931 produced $267,778. On the other hand, there was a large increase in government expenditures as a result of the introduction of new or improved social services. Thus while annual expenditures for the entire Virgin Islands averaged $269,412 during the period 1910-1917, they increased to an annual average of $472,234 during the period 1918-1931.[14] The failure of revenues to keep pace with expenditures meant that there were recurring budgetary deficits. Deficits were nothing new, but they were much larger during the American period than they had been during the Danish period. The deficits created after 1917 were met by financial grants passed by the United States Congress a condition which made Virgin Islanders disinclined to adopt new and extended taxation.

The condition of economic regression led to the emigration of Virgin Islanders, many of them to the United States where employment opportunities were better. Others left for Panama, Cuba and Puerto Rico which were United States or United States dominated territories. According to the census of November, 1917, the population of the Virgin Islands totalled 26,051; by 1930 it had declined to 22,012 showing a decrease of 4,039, or 15.5 percent.[15] Actual emigration would be greater than indicated by census returns of total population since after 1917 the population of the Virgin Islands was augmented by the immigration of Puerto Ricans, Americans, and natural increase due to improved health standards.

Civilian Administration and the New Deal

By 1931 the Virgin Islands had degenerated to the point where they could be referred to as the 'effective poorhouse' of the United States, a charge which was made by President Herbert Hoover after a visit to the islands in March, 1931.[16] The naval administration had improved social services but it had proved inept or negligent in stimulating economic development. This failure had resulted in heavy deficit fundings by the Federal Government, which it was considered necessary to reduce. By developing the economy of the islands, it was hoped that they would pay their way without further aid from Washington. Accordingly, President Hoover accepted the recommendations of Herbert D. Brown, Chief of the Efficiency Bureau of the United States, for the economic rehabilitation of the Virgin Islands. Although social services were to continue to receive attention, greater emphasis was to be placed on economic regeneration.[17]

The plan for the economic rehabilitation of the Virgin Islands made for such administrative changes as replacing naval officers by civilian officials. From 1931 the United States Department of the Interior was given the responsibility for administering the affairs of the islands. This Department with experience in other acquired and underdeveloped territories of the United States was seen as 'peculiarly adapted to the task.'[18] Under this arrangement the first civilian governor was appointed with responsibility to implement the rehabilitation program. He was Dr. Paul M. Pearson, a Quaker and former professor of public speaking at Swarthmore College, who had shown executive ability in organizing an extensive Chautauqua circuit in the United States.[19]

The major activity of the new administration centered upon the homesteading program which involved firstly, the acquisition of land through Federal appropriations. The bankruptcy in 1930 of the Bethlehem plantations which occupied 2,211 acres in St. Croix, provided a favorable opportunity to get good land for homesteading. Initially, however, the project was delayed by legal encumbrances and it was not until September, 1934, that the plantations were bought for $90,000. In the meantime a number of other plantations in St. Croix had been purchased, including Whim of 1,415 acres, La Grande Princesse of 712 acres, and the Northside plantations of 1,440 acres, at the cost of $20,000, $23,000 and $13,350 respectively. In St. Thomas, the Lindbergh Bay plantation of 508 acres was purchased for $20,000.[20]

About 850 acres of Whim, 500 acres of La Grande Princesse, and practically all of the Bethlehem and Northside plantations were suitable for peasant cultivation, and they were subdivided into plots averaging 6 acres each. Lindbergh Bay plantation was less suitable for agriculture; nevertheless plots ranging from three to eight acres were laid out. Both in St. Croix and in St. Thomas plots were sold to the laboring population, at moderate prices compared to rental. For instance, although 6-acre plots could be rented for $50 to $72 a year, similar plots could be bought for less than $240 with interest at four percent a year, or at an annual cost to the purchaser of $18.26. Purchasers were given 20 years to pay off the debt.[21]

The homesteading program embraced a home-building project to enable people to live on their plots. With federal assistance a number of two and three room houses were constructed at a cost of about $200 each The cost of the houses had to be repaid on terms similar to those for homesteads.[22]

In order to administer the homestead program and overall economic development, the Virgin Islands Company was chartered on April 9, 1934. Its creation stemmed from the relative lack of experience of the local administration in operating measures of this kind and from the shortage of local expertise. The general plan was for the Company to promote industrial development through the acquisition and cultivation of abandoned land, to provide employment opportunities for the people, and to assist peasant farmers in whatever ways necessary.[23]

Other measures to improve the economy of the Virgin Islands related to the improvement of the port facilities of St. Thomas, and to the promotion of tourism. Ship dues, consisting of tonnage taxes on bunker coal and fuel oil, were suspended in 1934,[24] the effect of which was a ten percent increase in shipping during the first year of its implementation. To promote tourism, hotel facilities were constructed to add to the only two existing hotels, the Grand Hotel and the American Hotel, which were inadequate to accommodate tourists. In 1933 the Bluebeard Castle plantation was purchased and a twenty-room hotel was constructed at a cost of $101,750.[25]

While the rehabilitation program had as its main objective the development of the islands economy, it was not intended that social services should be neglected. For example, the education program was designed as support to the homesteading program, and the major achievement was the establishment of a vocational institute in St. Croix for the promotion of native crafts. Besides, scholarships were secured for Virgin Islands teachers to study at Hampton Institute and Howard University. In other areas of education, the Pearson administration continued and improved upon the methods of the naval governors.[26]

The administration's health program was integrated to some extent with its education program. Thus nursery schools were introduced to teach childcare, and health and welfare work was conducted through the schools. During 1933-1934, malaria was brought under greater control through a program designed to eradicate the anopheles mosquito by filling in certain swamps.[27] Serious research on filariasis was conducted in St. Croix and improvements were made in the regulations governing sanitary and health measures.

Other policies and programs of the Pearson administration were less successful. Like the previous naval administration, it sought to create a feeling of satisfaction and well-being among the public by organizing many concerts and entertainments. The tendency to use trifling achievements to indicate a return to prosperity conflicted harshly with reality and redounded to the discredit of the administration. Economic depression was quite obvious and it was reflected in the decline of revenues, moderate in St. Thomas but heavy in St. Croix, despite some increases in taxation. Comparing the periods 1918-1931 and 1932-1934, there was a fall in revenue from an annual average of $257,479 to $200,557[U.S.]. Table 6 indicates the major areas where decline was experienced in each municipality.[28]

Against the background of decreasing revenue the Pearson administration was faced with the continuing problem of heavier expenditures.
During the period 1932-1935, expenditures amounted to an annual
average of $421,943, leaving a substantial deficit of $197,434 to be met
by federal appropriations.

Table 6
Public Revenue of the Virgin Islands:
1918-1831 and 1932-1934
(Annual Averages)

		St. Thomas St. John	St. Croix	Total
1918-1931				
Direct Taxes		$ 72,124	$ 56,435	$128,559
Indirect Taxes		20,514	69,290	89,804
Sundry Taxes		22,181	16,933	39,114
	Total	$114,819	$142,658	$257,477
Income Tax		28,676	22,343	51,019
Customs Duties		9,047	55,615	64,662
1932-1934				
Direct Taxes		$ 55,596	$ 46,390	$101,986
Indirect Taxes		22,473	39,692	62,165
Sundry Taxes		19,875	16,531	36,406
	Total	$ 97,944	$102,613	$200,557
Income Tax		7,032	3,888	10,920
Customs Duties		5,267	30,145	35,412

Political Aspirations and Political Impasse

Economic depression had the effect of aggravating discontent created
by the social and political grievances from which the people were
suffering. When Virgin Islanders were brought under the sovereignty of
the United States, they believed that they would be accorded all the
rights and privileges of United States citizens. Instead, they were denied

such citizenship and the anticipated political franchise. The extension of citizenship to Virgin Islanders, of course was important from a constitutional standpoint; without it, any Act granting adult suffrage to United States citizens in the Virgin Islands would automatically have denied the vote to the majority of Virgin Islanders.

The treaty of August, 1916 providing for the transfer of the Virgin Islands from Denmark to the United States was not very clear on the question of citizenship. The relevant provision of the treaty was subject to misinterpretation and had been generally interpreted by the islanders to mean automatic citizenship of the United States for all Virgin Islanders. No explanation had been offered by the Danish government, by the United States administration, or by the colonial governments to disabuse them of this notion. The official United States interpretation of the treaty, however, was that the inhabitants of the Virgin Islands had American nationality and were entitled to the protection of the Government, but that they did not have the civil and political status of citizens. In short, they were nationals but not citizens of the United States.[29]

It was not until ten years after the transfer, on February 25, 1927, that a congressional enactment granted United States citizenship to several categories of Virgin Islanders. These included all natives of the islands and residents on and after January 17, 1917, and those who had removed to the United States and Puerto Rico before or after January 17, 1917, who had not become citizens of any foreign country. Children born in the Virgin Islands on or after January 17, 1917, were also granted citizenship.

A further Act of Congress passed on June 28, 1932 filled any gaps that might have been left in the 1927 Act. It provided that all natives of the Virgin Islands who were then living in the United States, in the Virgin Islands, or in any other United States territory who were not citizens of any foreign country, regardless of their place of residence on January 17, 1917, should be granted United States citizenship. Furthermore, natives of the Virgin Islands who were resident in foreign countries were not subject to the United States immigration quota system, or to the head tax, passport and immigration visa requirements for admission to the United States.

The failure to develop the economy and the delay in granting citizenship caused considerable discontent in the Virgin Islands. The causes of dissatisfaction, however, went much further. These were inherent in the political system in which political power was

K

centralized. For the large majority of Virgin Islanders the retention of the property qualifications meant the denial to them of the franchise. The electorate was extremely limited: in St. Thomas and St. John it never exceeded 961 after 1919, and until reform was effected in 1936, averaged about 750; in St. Croix with a much larger population the electorate never exceeded 491 and averaged about 475 during the period after 1917.[30] For the entire Virgin Islands, the electorate was approximately 5.5 percent of the entire population with considerable imbalance in the numerical size of the electoral districts even though they might have equal representation in the Councils. Political power was held by and exercised on behalf of vested interest. Even so, however, under the Act of March 3, 1917, the Colonial Councils were severely limited in control over taxation, and they could not override the governor's legislative veto.

The situation developed where a dissatisfied population sought the franchise and elected representatives sought greater political power. The two objectives were by no means complementary: the unfranchised wanted the power to vote for men who could cater to their interest; the representatives had no intention of sharing their political power if it might lead to the adoption of measures inimical to their interests. The opposition to the political system was stronger in St. Croix where it was tinged with sectional jealousies stemming in part from the small representation and in part from the continued existence of the seat of government in St. Thomas.

The fact that the Virgin Islands were governed by a naval administration also contributed to political unrest. To begin with, there was a stereotype of prejudice in the islands against a military government. The naval officers were themselves jealous of their own powers and were not disposed to share them. The 'military, civil and judicial powers' given to the governors by the Act of March 3, 1917, were interpreted so as to expand their power while withholding support from any move to increase the autonomy of the Virgin Islands. But there was also the need to maintain a certain amount of political calm if anything was to be accomplished. Naval governors recognized that responsible local opinion should be heeded, and to some extent, more in St. Thomas than in St. Croix, they aligned themselves with the vested interests of the islands. This alliance of the naval administration with the traditional political class placed it in the worst possible light, and aroused the suspicions and dislike of those who were seeking political power.

The political strategy of the naval administration was not very effective. It resorted to the use of jail sentences for offenders on a variety of charges, or it reacted to the worst criticism in a conciliatory manner, in either case bringing disrepute upon itself.[31] The naval officers sought to dazzle the public by the splendor of their uniforms rather than to concede popular demands. On occasion the governor adopted a highhanded attitude in dealing with the Colonial Councils and with political leaders. Finally, a political crisis developed in St. Croix in May, 1925 when the governor dissolved the Colonial Council there and more than a year elapsed before the Council would meet again to transact business.[32] The incident stimulated local demand for the replacement of the naval by a civilian administration and for fulfillment of the 1917 promise for a more permanent system.

Congress Takes Action: Political Reforms

While recognizing the need for constitutional reform in the Virgin Islands, the United States Congress was undecided about the wisdom of granting a permanent constitution. Between 1924 and 1927 several proposed bills for constitutional reform were discussed by congressional committees on insular affairs, but none was adopted.[33] Conflicting opinions over the need for reform go far to explain the lack of consensus in Congress.

In the Virgin Islands, the governor, the business community, and the majority of the members of the Councils were opposed to any change in the system of government. On the other hand, the popular press under the control of such men as Rothschild Francis, and the intelligentsia, prominent among whom was D. Hamilton Jackson, favored reform. They were supported by the American Civil Liberties Union composed of Virgin Islanders living in the United States. The powerful voice of Casper Holstein, a Crucian who had migrated to the United States and had become wealthy, was also raised on behalf of Virgin Islanders.[34] The argument was made by the reformists and denied by their opponents that there were 'plenty of Virgin Islanders' capable of filling all positions below those of governor, government secretary and dispatching secretary.

Members of the congressional committees began to see the demand for reform as a selfish desire by some men for political power and for the spoils of office, and to doubt whether the advocates of reform were really expressing the desire of the people. The fact that the greatest opposition came from St. Croix, whereas most responsible opinion in St. Thomas favored the existing political system, gave the suggestion of sectional differences. This in turn posed the problem of drafting a constitution which would be satisfactory to both communities.

After the failure to adopt a constitution in 1927, no further attempt at such reform was made until about five years later when abortive discussions were again held by congressional committees on a draft constitution submitted by Governor Pearson.[35] In the meantime, in order to appease local discontent, compromise was sought through two measures, namely, the grant of citizenship by the Act passed by Congress on February 25, 1927, and the replacement of the naval administration by a civil administration in 1931. As already seen, the latter change was made to facilitate the adoption of a program for economic development of the Virgin Islands. As a further indication of the separation of the Navy from Virgin Islands affairs, responsibility for the administration of the Virgin Islands was transferred to the United States Department of the Interior. Later, in July, 1934, a Division of Territories and Island Possessions was organized within the Department of the Interior to exercise jurisdiction over the Virgin Islands.

The change in administration did not bring to an end the demand for reform which to some extent became more intense. The movement for reform in the Virgin Islands coincided with the entire West Indian demand for a greater democratization of the political process. West Indians generally were apt to attribute the current widespread economic depression to their lack of political power and their demands were more or less the same — the extension of the suffrage, and a greater measure of political autonomy for the representative bodies. With the acquisition of political power, it was argued, the people could then work to implement those measures which would cater to their own interests.[36]

Compared with the naval governors, Governor Pearson showed considerable skill in dealing with political reformists. He outplayed the opposition in publicizing his case and in lobbying the United States Congress and administration. His success only increased the frustration and resistance of his opponents, and intense pressures were applied to get rid of him, even to the extent of favoring the restoration of naval officers to administer the islands.[37]

Virgin Islanders may not have been suffering from economic and social deprivation as much as other West Indians at the time, but their lack of political power was nevertheless just as real. Riots broke out in St. Kitts in 1935, but even before that Virgin Islanders showed the road to constitutional reform by resort to violence. On the evening of October 16, 1934, led by Morris Davis and others, a protest march was staged at the Market Place in Charlotte Amalie, St. Thomas. The march was held without police permission, but when the police attempted to arrest Morris Davis, violence broke out. The outbreak, however, seemed to have been kept under control by the leaders. Beyond the acting police director sustaining a fractured skull and other policemen being beaten, no damage to life or property was reported.[38]

The October, 1934 outbreak resulted in a congressional investigation of the Virgin Islands which culminated in the removal of Pearson from the governorship.[39] He was succeeded in 1935 by Lawrence Cramer, Lieutenant Governor under him, who had resided in St. Croix where he had demonstrated considerable political skill in dealing with his political opponents. His approach was a judicious blend of firmness, frankness and a willingness to compromise. He recognized the need for constitutional reform and his governorship witnessed the adoption of two constitutional measures. Firstly, the franchise was extended to women as a result of a legal decision given in December, 1935 by District Court Judge Levirt of St. Thomas.[40] Secondly, and of far more importance, the first Organic Act was passed by the United States Congress on June 22, 1936.

The constitution introduced by the Organic Act of 1936 was a blend of Danish provisions in force at the time with some expedients based upon American principles and practices. Nevertheless, the Act represented a considerable extension of political power. The division of the Virgin Islands into two municipalities, namely St. Thomas and St. John, and St. Croix, was preserved. Each municipality also retained its Council with a life of two years and with power to initiate and pass legislation for that municipality. The Council of St. Thomas and St. John was to consist of seven elected members and that of St. Croix of nine elected members. Elected representatives would include three members at large — two in St. Thomas-St. John and one in St. Croix — but there would be no nominated members.

In addition to the two Municipal Councils, there was to be a Legislative Assembly of the Virgin Islands consisting of the members of the combined Councils. It was to be convened by the governor, and it was to meet in St. Thomas at least once a year to enact legislation applicable to the Virgin Islands as a whole.

Qualifications for candidates to the Municipal Councils included citizenship of the United States, a minimum age of 25 years, and three years residence in the Virgin Islands prior to the election. The franchise was extended to all residents, including women, who were citizens of the United States, and who were over 21 years of age. All property and income qualifications were abolished, but voters had to be able to read and write the English language.

Executive power in the Virgin Islands was vested in the governor to be appointed by the President of the United States with the advice and consent of the Senate. The governor was empowered to exercise the legislative veto which could be overridden by a two-thirds majority of a Council, but with final decision reserved for the President of the United States. Finally, the governor was placed under the supervision of the United States Secretary of the Interior to whom he had to report annually the transactions of the Virgin Islands government for transmission to Congress.

Conclusion

When the United States acquired the Virgin Islands in 1917, it was faced with the dilemma of having to choose between the introduction of democracy and the retention of autocracy in the islands. In 1917 the choice was autocracy under the administration of naval officers; it was not until 1936 that the dilemma was resolved in favor of democracy after five years of civil administration. The Organic Act of 1936 was passed as the result of considerable pressure exerted by the local population upon the relevant authorities in the United States. That the governors of the Virgin Islands came under attack was due as much to their shortcomings as to the fact that they were the local representatives of the United States administration that was denying Virgin Islanders essential and much desired rights.

Much had been accomplished by the naval administration by way of introducing an improved system of social services, while the civil administration had sought to develop the economy through the establishment of homesteading to promote agricultural production. Throughout the periods of naval and civil administration invaluable financial assistance was given by the Congress of the United States, but munificence was no compensation for the denial of political power. Inspired by the United States ideals of democracy and equality, Virgin

Islanders showed much impatience with their exclusion from the political process.

The Organic Act of 1936, as James Bough stated it, 'was a clear and impressive expansion within the area of self-government for the people of the Virgin Islands brought about by the time honored and well tried principle of widening the franchise to ensure the participation of the masses of the people.'[41] With its adoption, the Act brought the Virgin Islands to the forefront of political and constitutional development in the West Indies. Paternal government had been replaced by responsible government, and it was left to be seen whether responsible government was compatible with good government.

[1] For some of the implications of an unincorporated versus an incorporated territorial status, see Julius W. Pratt, *America's Colonial Experiment. How the United States Gained, Governed, and In Part Gave Away a Colonial Empire.* (Prentice Hall, Inc., New York, 1950) pp. 157-164.
[2] Report of the Governor of the Virgin Islands for 1917, passim.
[3] Annual Reports of the Governors of the Virgin Islands, 1917-1931.
[4] Knud Knud-Hansen, *From Denmark to the Virgin Islands.* (Dorrance & Company, Inc., 1947) pp. 103-109.
[5] Charles F. Reid, *Education in the Territories and Outlying Possessions of the United States.* (Bureau of Publications, Teachers College, Columbia University, New York, 1941) pp. 458-469.
[6] Thomas H. Dickinson, 'Economic Crisis in the Virgin Islands.' (*Current History*, Vol. 27, No. 3, December, 1927) pp. 378-381.
[7] Rosalyn L. Spitzer, Political and Social Development in the Virgin Islands to 1940. (Unpublished Master's Thesis, New York University, June, 1964) p. 37.
[8] Luther Harris Evans, *The Virgin Islands from Naval Base to New Deal.* (J. W. Edwards, Ann Arbor, Michigan, 1945) pp. 274-275.
[9] Longfield Smith, *Sugarcane in St. Croix.* (Washington, Government Printing Office, 1921) pp. 3-6; Annual Report of the Governor of the Virgin Islands, 1932, p. 13,
[10] Donald D. Hoover, 'The Virgin Islands under American Rule.' (*Foreign Affairs, Vol. 4, No. 3, April, 1926)* p. 505; Earl Bennet Shaw, 'The Bay Oil Industry of St. John.' *(Economic Geography*, Vol. 10, No. 2, April, 1934) pp. 143-146.
[11] Longfield Smith, *Sea Island Cotton in St. Croix.* (Washington, Government Printing Office, 1921) pp. 3-4.
[12] Earl B. Shaw, 'St. Croix: A Marginal Sugar Producing Island.' (*The Geographical Review*, Vol. XXIII, No. 3, July, 1933) pp. 414-422; R. G. Woolbert, 'Rehabilitation in the Virgin Islands.' (*Foreign Affairs*, Vol. 17, No. 4, July, 1939) pp. 801-802; Earl Fernando Brady, The Economy of the U.S. Virgin Islands. (Unpublished Master Thesis, University of Puerto Rico, May, 1968) p. 16.

[13] Evans, op. cit., pp. 140-150 and 167-186.

[14] Ibid., pp. 145-146 and 153-162.

[15] *Census of the Virgin Islands of the United States, November, 1917.*
(Washington, 1918) pp. 36-52; Annual Report of the Governor of the Virgin
Islands, 1930, pp. 9-11.

[16] *New York Times*, March 27, 1931; Earl B. Shaw, 'The Poor House of the
United States.' (*Scientific Monthly*, Vol. 41, August, 1935) pp. 131-140.

[17] Pratt. op. cit., pp. 285-287.

[18] Ibid., p. 217.

[19] *New York Times*, March 27, 1931.

[20] Evans, op. cit., pp. 304-306.

[21] Ibid., pp. 304-305.

[22] Lawrence W. Cramer, 'The Virgin Islands Look Up.' (*Opportunity*, Vol. XVI,
May, 1938) pp. 134-137.

[23] Isaac Dookhan, 'The Virgin Islands Company and Corporation: The Plan for
Economic Rehabilitation in the Virgin Islands.' (*The Journal of Caribbean History*,
Vol. 4, May, 1972) pp. 57-58.

[24] Earl Bennet Shaw, 'St. Thomas carries its Coal.' (*Journal of Geography*. Vol.
34, No. 6, September, 1935) pp. 229-236.

[25] Annual Reports of the Governors of the Virgin Islands, 1928 (pp. 72-73),
1933 (p. 5), 1934 (p. 14) and 1935 (pp. 17-18).

[26] Reid, op. cit., pp. 471-482 and 488-490; Katherine M. Cook, *Public
Education in the Virgin Islands.* (Washington, 1934) pp. 15-31.

[27] Knud-Hansen, op. cit., pp. 127-131.

[28] Evans, op. cit., pp. 146-186 and 195-202.

[29] Sixty-Ninth Congress. First Session. Hearings before the Committee on
Territories and Insular Possessions, United States Senate, on S.3228 and S.4005.
(Washington, 1926) pp.47-48.

[30] Cf. Ibid., p. 54, where it is stated that in 1925 'there were only 762 qualified
voters in St. Thomas, which was about one-third of the adult males; and only 417
voters in St. Croix, which is about one-third of the adult males.'

[31] Lucius J. M. Malmin, 'Autocracy in the Virgin Islands.' (*Nation, CXXI,
October 21, 1925)* pp. 470-473.

[32] Sixty-Ninth Congress. First Session. Hearings before the Committee on
Territories and Insular Possessions, United States Senate, on S.3228 and S.4005.
(Washington, 1926) passim; Sixty-Ninth Congress. Second Session. Hearings before
the Committee on Territories and Insular Possessions, United States Senate, on
S.3228, S.4005 and S.4550. (Washington, 1926) passim.

[33] Ibid.; Sixty-Ninth Congress. First Session. Hearings before the Committee on
Insular Affairs, House of Representatives, on H.R.10865. (Washington, 1927);
Sixty-Ninth Congress. Second Session. Hearings before the Committee on
Territorial and Insular Possessions, United States Senate, on S.3228, S.4005 and
S.4550. Part 2. (Washington, 1927).

[34] Casper Holstein, 'The Virgin Islands.' (*Opportunity*, Vol. 3, No. 34, October,
1925) pp. 304-306; Casper Holstein, 'Congress and the Virgin Islands.'
(*Opportunity*, Vol. 4, No. 43, July, 1926) pp. 222; Casper Holstein, 'The Virgin
Islands: Past and Present.' (*Opportunity*, Vol. 4, No. 47, November, 1926) pp.
344-345.

[35] Seventy-Second Congress. Second Session. Joint Hearings before the Committee on Territories and Insular Affairs, United States Senate and Committee on Insular Affairs, House of Representatives, on S.5457 and H R. 14319. Bills to provide a civil government for the Virgin Islands of the United States. (Washington, 1933).
[36] Paul Blanshard, *Democracy and Empire in the Caribbean. A Contemporary Review.* (New York, The Macmillan Company, 1947) pp. 21-28.
[37] Luther Harris Evans, 'Unrest in the Virgin Islands.' (*Foreign Policy Report,* Vol. 11, No. 2, March, 1935) pp. 14-24; Raymond Gram Swing, 'Storm over the Virgin Islands.' (*Nation,* Vol. 141, No. 3655, July, 1935) pp. 95-96.
[38] J. Antonio Jarvis, *A Brief History of the Virgin Islands.* (The Art Shop, St. Thomas, Virgin Islands, 1938) pp. 178-179.
[39] Seventy-Fourth Congress. House. Committee on Territories and Insular Affairs. Report of proceedings held on the Organic Act for the Virgin Islands. Vols. 1 and 2. (Washington, 1936); Seventy-Fourth Congress. Second Session. House Committee on Insular Affairs, on H.R.11751 (Washington, 1936).
[40] Valdemar A. Hill, (Sr.), *A Golden Jubilee. (Virgin Islanders on the Go Under the American Flag.)* (Carlton Press, Inc., New York, 1967) p. 117.
[41] James A. Bough and Roy C. Macridis, (Ed.), *Virgin Islands America's Caribbean Outpost. The Evolution of Self Government.* (The Walter F. Williams Publishing Company, 1970) p. 122.

Chapter 16

Modern Times

By 1936 when the first Organic Act was passed, the main lines for future development in the Virgin Islands had already been indicated. Economically, agriculture based on the traditional money-crop, sugar-cane, was failing and attempts were being made through the homestead program to stimulate it. Furthermore, as was evidenced by the construction of the Bluebeard Castle Hotel, tourism was attracting attention as a desirable alternative, and later on, economic diversification was to be sought by the promotion of industry.

Politically, universal adult suffrage had been granted with the unique qualification that voters should be literate in English. Political development after 1936 would be in the direction of increasing self-government compatible with the political maturity and economic viability of Virgin Islanders. Socially, both the naval and civilian administrations had acknowledged their responsibility to provide essential services in the islands such as in the fields of education, health and housing. This responsibility was to continue under the stimulus of greater local participation in the political process.

The United States had become increasingly conscious of its responsibility for the welfare of the Virgin Islands and this was reflected in the large sums of money granted for rehabilitation and improvement purposes. No longer were the islands to have the reputation of being the forgotten and neglected territory of the United States. Instead of existing in a 'step-child relation to Uncle Sam's family' the Virgin Islands were to become more and more 'a showpiece of democracy' in the western hemisphere.

Economic Transformation

Continued attempts were made to revive the sugar industry after 1936 through vigorous efforts to involve the small producer in the productive process. Sugar production was stimulated by creating more homesteads since experience had shown that agricultural laborers were competent to operate small farms, given the necessary encouragement and assistance. For instance, small farmers in 1937 produced 16,117 tons of sugarcane valued at $53,081, and three more estates were bought by the government, two in St. Croix and one in St. Thomas, for apportionment and distribution to homesteaders.[1] Further purchases increased the acreage under homesteading to 3,552 acres in 1940 when there were 828 small farms compared with 329 in 1930. As suggested by these statistics, the average size of the farms was about 4.28 acres.[2]

Homesteads were smaller in St. Thomas than in St. Croix in keeping with their respective concentration on food crop and sugarcane production. In St. Croix plots averaged 6.37 acres but this acreage proved to be too small to provide adequate family income as well as to enable repayment of loans taken from government under the Homestead Act to acquire the land. The policy was adopted, therefore, of dividing among adjacent homesteaders plots reverting to government in cases of death of the previous owners or of cancellation of contracts. This procedure resulted in increasing the average size of homesteads to 7.75 acres.[3]

The plantation system of sugarcane cultivation had almost disappeared by the late 1930's when only two grinding mills were still in operation to process all sugarcanes grown on the island. This arrangement, however, worked to the disadvantage of the small farmers. For every 100 pounds of sugarcane delivered, the farmers received the value of six pounds of sugar based on current raw sugar prices in the New York Commodity Exchange. No attention was paid to the sucrose content of the sugarcane except when it had dropped so low as to make it advantageous to the manufacturer to offer less than the six pounds value Small farmers had little incentive to continue sugarcane cultivation.[4]

World War II saw further deterioration of the agricultural economy. The Virgin Islands became important as a naval base, and steps were taken to fortify them against the eventuality of enemy intrusion in the Caribbean. The construction of military establishments drew away from agriculture laborers who were attracted by the higher wages offered. After the close of the war in 1945, many laborers were unwilling to return to agriculture which gave them a bare subsistence. In 1946 only about 500 peasant farms with an average size of 5.8 acres were in existence in the Virgin Islands.[5]

Steps were taken to remove the barriers to production in an effort to reverse the drift away from agriculture. Thus in 1942 the municipal council of St. Croix with the approval of the United States administration repealed the export duty of $6 a ton on sugar which was one of the burdens on the industry. But this measure was not sufficient to prevent the closing of the two sugar factories, and in 1944 the Virgin Islands Company was forced to reopen the central factory at Bethlehem in order to process sugarcane produced in the island. Its function was continued by the Virgin Islands Corporation which replaced it in 1949, largely because it employed many laborers.[6]

The activities of the Agricultural Station in St. Croix and of the sub-station in St. Thomas were also continued and focused on experiment, extension services and agricultural education. However, they suffered from a lack of funds and from recurring change or lack of personnel qualified to give direction and stability to their programs. They failed to develop crops for export and settled down to concentrate on truck-farming to provide food for the island-communities.[7] In an effort to stimulate agricultural production, beginning in 1961 the government offered a subsidy of $1 for each ton of cane produced and $50 for each new acre of cane cultivated, but the practice ceased after a few years.[8] The failure of this policy led to the phased withdrawal of sugar production which was brought to an end in 1966 when the Bethlehem factory was closed.[9] However, rum production has continued on a large scale ever since the repeal of the prohibition in 1933.

The swing away from agriculture stemmed largely from the attraction of tourism which began in earnest in the early 1950's. The upsurge followed expanded promotional efforts especially after 1952 with the creation of the Tourist Development Board and the production of an annual carnival. The result was a tenfold increase in tourism during that decade, though the total number of tourists was still relatively small. It was not until after the Cuban Revolution in 1959 and the closing of Cuba to Americans that tourism in the Virgin Islands experienced substantial growth, both absolutely and relatively. The number of tourists increased from 16,000 in 1949, to 164,000 in 1959, and to 1,122,317 in 1969.[10]

Preferential treatment under United States customs regulations and the ability to buy imported luxury goods at virtually free-port prices were the major factors responsible for attracting tourists. Average tourist expenditure rose from $87 in 1950 to a peak of $150 in 1963 and then fell to $100 in 1969.[11] The fall was partly due to larger numbers of lower-income tourists and partly to economic recession in the United States. The actual expenditures involved, however, rose from $16,070,000 in 1958 to $112,268,245 in 1969.[12]

Compared with tourism, growth in industry became important only in the 1960's. Since the 1930's handicrafts had been encouraged through a cooperative but they never attracted many people and in later years handicrafts were imported to meet the demand locally. As early as 1949 legislation was passed providing for designated tax exemption and industrial subsidies for eight years to new industries which qualified with a minimum investment of $10,000.[13] The Act, however, lay idle.

Until 1959 the only attempt to introduce an industry was made in 1951 when an experimental button factory was established in St. Thomas. Then in 1959 watch assembly operations were started in the Virgin Islands, utilizing parts imported from various foreign countries. By the mid-1960's production had jumped to 4.5 million units despite the shortage of skilled labor, and by 1967, sixteen watch companies were located in the Virgin Islands.[14]

Two other major industries were established in St. Croix in 1966 — Hess Oil Virgin Islands Corporation and Harvey Alumina Virgin Islands, Inc., — with a combined investment estimated at about $100 million. The oil refinery processes crude oil purchased from Venezuelan producers, and in return for a ten-year quota to ship 15,000 barrels of petroleum a day to the United States, the Corporation agreed to pay to the Virgin Islands government a royalty of 50 cents a barrel. This was equivalent to $7,500 a day, and the money was earmarked for financing conservation and beautification projects in the islands. Harvey Alumina processes bauxite from Australia and West Africa into alumina which is then shipped to refining plants in the United States and in Norway. Tariff preferences and tax advantages extended under an Industrial Incentive Act as well as relatively low wages paid to workers made it advantageous for these Companies to operate here.[15]

The swing from agriculture to tourism and industry was revolutionary in its consequences and was manifested by the dynamic growth of the Virgin Islands within the past two decades. The agricultural sector as a whole came to provide few employment opportunities, and agriculture became and has remained a marginal economic activity. Some cattle for meat and dairy products and some vegetables continued to be produced, but the bulk of Virgin Islands food needs continued to be imported, thereby contributing to the very high cost of living.

The economic expansion generated by tourism and industry affected all aspects of life and living in the Virgin Islands. Retail trade was the main beneficiary of the boom in tourism aided by a low six percent duty on luxury goods. A great number of businesses, large and small, came into existence in St. Thomas and St. Croix to cater to tourists, as did the construction of hotels and sea-side resorts. The development of St. John from a neglected undeveloped island into a major tourist resort was a result of private initiative and government enterprise through the National Park Service.[16]

Overseas trade has increased: expressed in millions of dollars imports into the Virgin Islands rose from 3.6 in 1936, to 9.5 in 1948, and to 260.2 in 1969; exports rose from $793,651 to $1.7 million, and to $123.4 million during the same period.[17] As a result of the increased shipping involved in tourism and trade, it was necessary to deepen the harbors of the Virgin Islands, and to construct or improve dock facilities.

Government revenues also increased as a result of the economic expansion for apart from federal grants, deficit appropriations and matching funds, revenues came from taxes on real property, profits, customs and excise, incomes and licences. Between 1936 and 1969 revenues for all the Virgin Islands increased from $288,438 to $96,511,513 from all sources.[18]

Increasing revenues allowed government to increase substantially its expenditure on social services, such as health, education, welfare and on public housing. It enabled government to increase the wages of its employees also. The average monthly salary of teachers, for instance, which was $50 in 1930 increased to $293 in 1959 and to $729 in 1969. Following the passage of the 'Hill's Wage and Hour Act' in 1941 and 'Harrigan's Wage and Hour Act' in 1947 providing for minimum hourly wages for various categories of workers, corresponding developments took place in the private sector involved in construction, tourism and industry. In 1966 a wage order established an elaborate code of minimum wages for several categories of workers ranging from 75 cents to $2.50 an hour.[19]

The demand for land was also a direct consequence of the development of tourism, both for the construction of homes and such tourist facilities as hotels. Land over-looking the sea or bordering on beaches was the most desirable. The high demand for this commodity naturally increased its value, and it was calculated that land prices have doubled every four or five years since 1950.[20]

Increasing prosperity resulted in a phenomenal increase in population from 24,889 in 1940, to 26,665 in 1950, to 32,099 in 1960, and to 63,200 in 1970, according to official statistics. Within the last ten years, the population increased by 96.9 percent, compared with a 20.4 percent increase during the previous decade. Some of the newcomers were mainland (United States) citizens or 'continentals' as they were referred to locally, who came to live or were attracted by investment and employment opportunities in the islands. Population increased also as the possibility of more lucrative employment under better conditions reduced the number of prospective Virgin Islander emigrants and encouraged others living abroad to return.

Immigrant West Indians from Puerto Rico and the British, French and Dutch islands accounted for the greater part of the growth in population. These people were originally brought in to perform work for which the local labor force was inadequate. Under United States immigration laws passed, Puerto Ricans being United States citizens, had been given preference over other West Indians in work available on the sugar plantations. During the Second World War, however, labor shortage forced the United States to admit these West Indians or 'aliens' as they were called, to work on the military establishments. After the war 'aliens' were repatriated but were allowed to re-enter along with other Puerto Ricans to engage in farming.[21] With the growth of tourism aliens came to the Virgin Islands in ever-increasing numbers because of the better wages offered here, and moved into other kinds of occupation directly or indirectly associated with tourism and industry. Their services were vital for the maintenance of a viable economy.

The state of the economy, that is, the extent to which the Virgin Islands needed or were dependent on the United States for financial assistance, and conversely, the extent to which they were able independently to maintain all the functions of government, was the underlying factor of constitutional reform and political changes in the Virgin Islands.

The Revised Organic Act of 1954

The Organic Act of 1936 was in operation for 18 years in the Virgin Islands before it was revised by the United States Congress. Reform stemmed from certain basic weaknesses in the original Act and culminated certain other developments in the direction of greater self-government by the people of the Virgin Islands. It was intended by the revised Act to promote further the growing political consciousness of Virgin Islanders and to achieve greater economy and efficiency of government.[22]

The Organic Act of 1936 had created two municipalities in the Virgin Islands each with its own legislative body and administrative departments. The consequent overlapping and duplication of activities did not only increase administrative expenses that were wholly out of keeping with the size, population and revenues of the islands, but they hindered concerted action and bred particularism within the two municipalities. The common Legislative Assembly was unable to redress the balance between the two separate councils. Nevertheless, it was able to achieve some important successes such as, for instance, in the field of social welfare, and these successes indicated the desirability of having a single legislative body only which would represent both municipalities and bring them together.

After 1936 there was a growing trend towards greater participation by Virgin Islanders in local affairs and important administrative positions in the islands were given to qualified Virgin Islanders. A major step in the direction was taken when a resident Virgin Islander, Morris de Castro, was appointed as governor in 1950. His appointment could be construed as a significant step in recognizing the ability of the people of the Virgin Islands to govern themselves and manage their own affairs.

Besides, Virgin Islanders had achieved a high level of political maturity and awareness by 1952 due primarily to the greater activity of political parties in presenting political issues to the electors in order to win their support. Weekly broadcasts introduced by Morris de Castro bringing to the people 'a resumé of governmental operations and stating the opinions of the administration in all public issues,' made them more fully aware of the need for change.[23] Congressional observers were impressed by the level of public enthusiasm for reform.

The need to revise the Organic Act was further suggested by the possibilities which such revision would have for further political development of Virgin Islanders. This was in the direction of the two-party system, the development of which was clearly desirable if the interests of the entire Virgin Islands were to be served instead of sectional interests as hitherto.[24]

The essential provisions of the Revised Organic Act expressed the need for improvement of, economy in, and unification and simplification of the structure of government.[25] The two municipal councils were abolished and replaced by a single legislative body termed the 'Legislature of the Virgin Islands,' to be located in St. Thomas, the seat of government. The islands of St. Thomas, St. Croix and St. John were made three separate voting districts and were to return two, two and one members respectively to the legislature. In addition to these five members, an additional six members-at-large were to be elected from the Virgin Islands as a whole. Particular representation of individual islands was thus combined with general representation to ensure that matters would be dealt with on a territorial basis. Each voter had as many votes as there were representatives for his district, as well as two extra votes for two only of the members-at-large.

The legislative responsibility of all members, or 'senators' as they were called, was still limited to the extent that they could not pass laws in conflict with congressional legislation applicable to the Virgin Islands. However, Congress no longer had reserved power to annul any legislation passed in the Virgin Islands. Locally, greater cognizance was to be given to the legislature's authority by requiring the governor to report back to the legislature any vetoed legislation within ten days after it had been presented to him instead of within thirty days as previously. If the bill was not returned within ten days it was to become law.

After 1954 members of the legislature were to be paid salaries to be fixed by the members themselves. This was a move away from dependence upon the moneyed class and was intended to appeal to talent so that the legislative business would be better served.

Another provision designed to improve the government and extend the scope of self-government was that which abolished the language qualification for voters. Under the Organic Act of 1936, the vote was limited to men and women, otherwise qualified by age and citizenship, who could read and write the English language. As a result thousands of Spanish-speaking people of Puerto Rican origin living in the Virgin Islands were denied the franchise. These people were now given the vote.

L

In order to improve administrative efficiency, the governor was empowered to reorganize and consolidate all existing executive departments, bureaus, boards, commissions and other agencies of government into not more than nine departments. He was given one year after the passing of the Act to effect this change after which no other department or agency of government could be created without the prior approval of the Secretary of the Interior. However, adjustments could be made within each department to promote efficiency.

The economic or fiscal provisions of the Revised Organic Act strengthened the economic base of government. Permanent United States residents living in the Virgin Islands could satisfy federal income tax obligations by paying their taxes on income obtained from all sources, whether inside or outside the Virgin Islands, into the Treasury of the Virgin Islands. In addition, the proceeds of customs duties, all quarantine, passport, immigration and naturalization fees collected in the Virgin Islands were to be deposited into the local Treasury, after the cost of collecting them had been deducted.

Of more importance was the granting of a concession for which Virgin Islanders had long asked, namely, a financial contribution by the United States to the revenues of the Virgin Islands on the basis of matching-funds. The United States agreed to give to the Virgin Islands an amount of money equal to the revenues collected in the islands from all sources. The federal contribution would come from the internal revenues collected from imports into the United States of goods produced in the Virgin Islands. Besides, a further sum of $1,000,000 or the balance of such internal revenues whichever was greater, was to be made available to the Virgin Islands for 'emergency purposes and essential public projects.' Such surplus appropriations, however, were not to exceed $5,000,000.

To ensure that both the matching-funds and the surplus-balance were properly spent, the approval of the President or his designated representative had to be obtained before any expenditure was made. Furthermore, the legislature was authorized to issue bonds limited to $10 million to finance public improvement or specific public undertaking. Lastly, the Office of Government Comptroller for the Virgin Islands was created independent of local control to audit the government's accounts and report to the pertinent authorities all failures to collect revenues as well as extravagant, excessive, unnecessary, or irregular expenditures.

The Revised Organic Act of 1954 provided the legal base for the political and administrative re-organization of the Virgin Islands. The first elections to the new legislature under the Act were held in November, 1954, and under executive orders issued by the governor, departmental reorganization was effected the following year. After the reorganization the following departments were created to serve the entire Virgin Islands, namely, agriculture and labor, education, finance, health, property and procurement, public safety, public works, social welfare and tourism and trade. The codification of the islands' laws followed as a necessary consequence from the creation of a single legislative body and from the unification of administrative departments. Codification of three separate bodies of laws was a mammoth undertaking and it was not until 1957 that it was completed.[26]

The Elective Governor Act, 1968 and Subsequent Political Reform

The Elective Governor Act of 1968 stemmed from the favorable working of the Revised Organic Act of 1954, since by the mid-1960's Virgin Islanders had demonstrated that they had benefited from the political education and were prepared to assume greater responsibility. By that time, also, the economy of the islands had improved sufficiently to enable the people to undertake more and more of the financial responsibility for their own government which was being borne by the Federal Government.

Virgin Islanders were also affected by the international winds of change in the direction of a greater measure of internal self-government and independence from external control. The document which issued from these aspirations was the Report of the Constitutional Convention of the Virgin Islands of 1964-1965. Its recommendations included an elective governor and lieutenant governor for four-year terms, the continuation of existing representation but without any limitation on voting for members-at-large, a Resident Commissioner or delegate to the United States House of Representatives, and the right of Virgin Islanders to vote in national elections for the President and Vice-President of the United States. In addition, the Convention recommended the lowering of the voting age to 18 years, the abolition of the Presidential veto on laws passed locally, and the appointment of the Comptroller by the governor with the consent of the legislature.[27]

The long Democratic administration from 1961 under the energetic governorship of Ralph Paiewonsky, scion of a wealthy Jewish family of St. Thomas, undoubtedly contributed greatly to constitutional reform. It was more than mere coincidence that the Paiewonsky administration coincided with the period of unprecedented prosperity in the 1960's. Himself a successful businessman, Paiewonsky tackled the job of government in the spirit of the entrepreneur. Schemes for the economic and social improvement of the Virgin Islands were studied and implemented: an end was brought to the decadent sugar industry; tourism and industry were boosted; and large-scale investors, such as Hess and Harvey, were encouraged.[28] The resulting boom held promise for greater economic viability of the Virgin Islands in the future. Paiewonsky's encouragement of investors from abroad was not without local opposition, but despite it, he was able to achieve peaceful and progressive government. The creation of a viable economy combined with able administration greatly increased the confidence of congressional leaders in the political maturity of Virgin Islanders.

The first changes in the Revised Organic Act of the Virgin Islands were made in 1966 when in keeping with United States Court decisions the voting power of electors was changed. The 'two-out-of-six' principle hitherto in existence was replaced by that of 'one-man, one-vote' in the election of members-at-large to the legislature since it was believed that democracy in the Virgin Islands would thereby be strengthened. The same consideration governed the second reform increasing the membership of the legislature from 11 to 15 members. Of these representatives, five were to be elected from St. Thomas, five from St. Croix, one from St. John and four at-large.[29] Also motivating this reform was the growth of population and the need to consider more and more sophisticated and complex legislative proposals. The increased representation would enable the legislature to function more efficiently by making more and larger committees possible.

Political aspirations went beyond reforms of the franchise and the legislature to include the popular election of governors. Ever since 1917 the governors of the Virgin Islands had been appointed by the President of the United States with the advice and consent of the Senate. In 1966 and 1967 the committees and subcommittees on insular affairs of the Senate and House of Representatives held hearings on and approved the proposal for an elective governor for the Virgin Islands and the appropriate legislation was passed in August, 1968. It was recognized that the time was 'ripe for taking the progressive step toward a territorial government' which was 'fully responsible and responsive to local needs and to the local electorate.'[30]

A number of drawbacks were inherent in the principle of having appointed governors. A Presidential appointee was beyond the scope of recall by the people, and to this denial of privilege was added the fact that even though occasionally Virgin Islanders had been appointed governors there was no legal stipulation that all governors were to be Virgin Islanders. As such, there was no guarantee that local leadership would be trained at the highest level as was the intent of the policy of having appointed governors. Another important consideration was that an appointed governor, no matter how wisely or carefully selected, need not be the popular choice. Besides, both the selection of non-Virgin Islanders as governors and their appointment by an authority other than Virgin Islanders constituted a denial of the democratic desire for self-government of Virgin Islanders.

The Virgin Islands Elective Governor Act of August, 1968 was one essentially to increase the political power of the people and their elected representatives in the legislature. Beginning from November 3, 1970 and continuing every four years qualified Virgin Islanders could elect by majority vote their own governor and, jointly with him, a lieutenant governor. The power of the electorate extended beyond the election of their chief executives; provision was also made for the recall of the governor through a referendum by those who had voted at his election.

The powers of the members of the legislature also were significantly increased, of greatest importance being the expansion of their legislative power. Under the Act, the Presidential veto over local legislation was removed; the governor could no longer over-ride a legislative veto over his veto by referring the legislation to the President. If two-thirds of the members of the legislature over-rode the governor's veto of a bill it became law.

Some other measures passed by the Federal Congress or by the local legislature, depending on their respective competence, were also expressive of the political maturity of Virgin Islanders. The most important of these was a congressional enactment authorizing the election of a non-voting Virgin Islands delegate to the federal House of Representatives despite the fact that the islands pay no federal income tax and have a relatively small population. When brought into operation in 1973 this measure gave the delegate a voice in Congress both on national and Virgin Islands issues, and has served to ensure that the welfare of the Virgin Islands is not overlooked in federal legislation especially those allocating funds.[31] Other measures passed locally reflected the demographic changes (and in part the increasing prosperity of St. John). Reapportionment legislation in 1968 gave St. Thomas-St. John seven seats in the legislature, St. Croix six, and two at-large members of whom one was to be a resident of St. John. Four years later, further reapportionment gave seven seats each to St. Thomas-St. John and St. Croix, and one at-large member who was to be a resident of St. John.[32] Lastly, the base of representation was significantly widened by the adoption locally of two further measures: firstly, the franchise was given to Virgin Islanders between 18 and 21 years of age; and, secondly, the absentee ballot was extended to Virgin Islands members of the armed forces and students who would be outside the territory at the time of election.[33]

The Emergence of Political Parties

The rise of political parties was a major development of the period since 1936. Constitutional changes served to stimulate party organization, and political parties, in turn, worked for changes in the local political system.

Before 1936 individuals with common political objectives or policies formed loosely knit and temporary associations, but candidates for elections operated on a personal basis instead of in parties. Occasionally groups of candidates came together and presented themselves to the voters but such groupings were temporary and did not survive the elections. Persons elected under the aegis of any such group did not consider themselves bound to maintain the position they canvassed.[34]

By the Organic Act of 1936, all the members of the two municipal Councils were to be elected on the basis of universal suffrage and there were no longer any nominated members. The organization of political parties on the basis of popular support and the adoption of policies which could appeal to the newly-enfranchised people, were now possible. As a result a new group of political leaders emerged who sought political power with popular support. In order to give strength to their movement against previously entrenched political leaders, their organization into political parties became necessary.

The 'Progressive Guide' founded in St. Thomas in 1937 was the first cohesive and dynamic political party in the Virgin Islands. The principal organizers of the party were Omar Brown, Carlos Downing, Roy P. Gordon, Oswald Harris, Valdemar Hill, Sr., Aubrey C. Ottley and Henry V. Richards, Jr.[35] The activities of the party were more or less restricted to St. Thomas; an attempt by the Progressive Guide to extend itself to St. Croix in 1942 did not achieve any appreciable success. This was partly due to insular jealousies and partly to the hold which the traditional ruling class continued to have on St. Croix politics. The fact that the two islands were parts of separate municipalities each with its own council underlined the difficulties of organizing a political party on a territorial basis.

The education of the local public and the winning of elections were only part of the work of the Progressive Guide; it also had to keep in close touch with public opinion and the political parties in the United States. This was tacit acknowledgement of the importance of Congress and the United States administration in the politics of the islands. In the 1930's there existed in the Virgin Islands a Republican Club and a Democratic Club which were affiliated with the national parties. Both of these clubs sent delegates to national conventions, but their members did not all take an active interest in local politics and whenever they did so they operated more or less as independents. In order to maintain continuous contact with the national parties, the Progressive Guide organized both Republican and Democratic committees within itself, each working in close relation with its national counterpart.

The Progressive Guide owed much of its popularity to the measures introduced and passed in the Council and conveyed to the public in its slogan banner, 'Square Deal.' It won all of the elected seats in 1940 and thereafter dominated the Council. In its selection of candidates for election, however, it tended to give preference to older members. Consequently in 1946 a group of young liberal dissenters broke away, and under the leadership of Earle B. Ottley, a journalist, launched the Liberal Party. Some time elapsed before the new party became firmly established, and in the 1948 elections it won only one seat.[36] The Progressive Guide continued to attract heavy support because of its use of the 'spoils system' to award jobs to its supporters.

The adoption in 1948 of the Merit System by which jobs were to be given to qualified persons saw the beginning of the end of the Progressive Guide. By 1952 it was defunct, and the Liberal Party was reorganized the same year as the Unity Party of the Virgin Islands. Also in 1952, a Democratic Party was organized in St. Thomas by Ralph Paiewonsky, Francisco Corneiro and James Bough, among others, with affiliations with the national Democratic Party.[37] Its existence was to create a problem of national party affiliation for the Unity Party, a condition which it was to correct in later years.

St. Croix lagged behind St. Thomas in political party organization, and for some time after 1936 Crucian politics continued to be controlled by those who had been accustomed to wield political power. Laboring interests were served by the St. Croix Labor Union which had been formed in 1915 by D. Hamilton Jackson, but the Union was not active in politics except as a vehicle of protest. A change came after World War II when disbanded soldiers returned home from the United States and from among these ex-servicemen a new class of political leaders emerged. They decided to operate through the Labor Union, since this was a working-man's organization. Headed by Ludwig Harrigan, president of the Labor Union, they gained control of the municipal council of St. Croix in the general election of 1946.

Organized in St. Croix in 1947 by Stanley Farrelly, Roy P. Gordon, Charles Clarke and Louis Brown among others, the Republican Party demonstrated the growing awareness of the people of the value of the two-party system. It was a reaction of Crucians to the existence of political parties in St. Thomas and could claim affiliation with the national Republican Party.

A landmark in the history of political parties in the Virgin Islands was the Revised Organic Act of 1954. The essential provisions of this Act which affected political parties were the single legislature and the election to it of six members-at-large. By the second provision the six members had to be elected by all of the people of the Virgin Islands. As such, therefore, it became necessary for the political parties to extend their activities over the entire territory — the Unity Party and Democratic Party to St. Croix, and the Republican Party to St. Thomas.

After 1954 three major political parties existed in the Virgin Islands — the Unity Party, the Democratic Party and the Republican Party. Control of the legislature swung between the Unity Party on the one hand and a coalition of Democrats and Republicans on the other. The Republican Party was not very powerful, however, and by and large control of the legislature passed between the Unity Party and the Democratic Party. The 1962 election was significant for later developments since the Unity Party secured six and the Democratic Party five of the eleven legislative seats.

Despite its legislative successes the Unity Party was handicapped by the fact that it lacked affiliation with one of the national parties. The only way by which it could secure this was to take over one of the local parties, and the Democratic Party was the obvious choice. The local Republican Party was affiliated with the national Republican Party, but in terms of members it could not be of much value to the Unity Party. Affiliation with the Democratic Party on the other hand would not only give the necessary national contact but at the same time convert a powerful adversary into an ally.

Using its majority in the legislature, the Unity Party passed a Revised Election Code in February, 1963 which permitted an individual to register membership with a political party of his choice without the approval of that party. Previously, parties decided who should be their members, and the implications of the new regulation were quickly recognized and challenged in the law courts. The United States District Court in the Virgin Islands ruled against the measure, but its decision was reversed by the Third Circuit Court of Appeals.[38]

Shortly after the Unity Party was formally dissolved and its members registered with the Democratic Party. Henceforth the Democratic Party consisted of two undefined sections distinguished by their election symbols: the Unity or 'Mortar and Pestle' Democrats and the old or 'Donkey' Democrats. Both factions claimed to be the true Democratic Party and during elections tended to operate as separate parties. Their combined political strength, however, was considerable. Thus in the 1964 elections when the 'Mortar and Pestle' Democrats won six seats and the 'Donkey' Democrats won five, they controlled the entire legislature. The Republican Party failed to secure five percent of the votes cast. Its poor showing and its small membership of about 500 in 1966 compared with the Democratic Party's overwhelming support raised the question as to whether a two-party system did in fact exist in the Virgin Islands.[39]

Both its overwhelming strength and its polarization in two groups worked to the disadvantage of the Democratic Party. In the first instance, it was easier to bring charges of corruption and of favoritism against it. In the second instance, it was easier for dissension to develop within and divide the party. This was especially so since it had the support of the local Democratic administration which had been in power since 1961. Charges of political patronage and of corruption were levied against it when it supported the administrations's policies of bringing back Virgin Islanders from abroad and securing jobs for them, and of developing tourism and industry by encouraging private capital and labor from the United States.

It would appear that the Democratic Party appealed to the intellectual and propertied classes of the Virgin Islands. Even though it probably did so with the best of intentions and in the belief that all the people of the Virgin Islands would benefit from increased prosperity initiated by a relatively few, it alienated a fairly considerable body of Virgin Islanders. Under these conditions it was easier for rival political parties to emerge.

The general elections of 1968 were contested by an independent body of dissatisfied Democrats. Though they won no seats, they obtained more than the five percent of the votes required for the registration of a new political party. Accordingly, the Independent Citizens' Movement was organized appealing primarily to the working class. Its titular leader was Cyril E. King who had been Government Secretary since 1961 and had for some time in 1969 acted as governor. The Independent Citizens' Movement was well aware of national party affiliations, and one of the sponsors of Cyril King for the elected governorship in November, 1970 was no other than Hubert Humphrey, leader of the national Democratic Party. At the elections, King lost his bid to become governor: failing to obtain an outright majority in the general elections, he was finally defeated by Dr. Melvin Evans, governor since July, 1969, at the run-off elections. Nevertheless, his party won six of the legislative seats while the Democratic Party won six and the Republican Party won three.

In order to exercise effective control over the legislature, and in order to counter effectively the influence of the Independent Citizens' Movement, the Democratic and Republican parties came together in a loose coalition after the elections. This was practical politics. However, the ease with which the Independent Citizens' Movement attracted popular support and the extent to which it did so, show that party politics in the Virgin Islands are still in a fluid state and that the search for stable political forms to reflect popular attitudes and desires goes on.

Social Changes After 1936

After 1936 and more especially after the Second World War increasing attention was given to the adoption and implementation of schemes for the improvement of social services and for raising the standard of living in the Virgin Islands. The adoption of measures to effect social changes was largely the outcome of the operation of the economic and political systems. However, the basic factor demanding change was the desire of the people for a better way of life.

After 1936 Virgin Islanders like other peoples in dependent territories elsewhere were influenced more and more by the 'revolution of rising expectations.' Generally, they aspired to American standards with which they had come into contact through living in the United States or through experience with American tourists coming to the Virgin Islands. Newspapers, radio and television also served to draw attention to American standards locally. Moreover, the swing from the laissez-faire philosophy to that of the welfare state in the political economy of the Virgin Islands since the 1930's was conducive to social reform, while the increasing participation of Virgin Islanders in government and administration facilitated the formulation and execution of measures to improve social conditions.

The adoption of schemes of social improvement could not have been possible without the economic prosperity experienced by the Virgin Islands after 1936. As has already been shown, local resources were backed by substantial federal funds, especially after 1954 with the implementation of the policy of matching-funds. The availability of resources for social services has to be seen not only in terms of increased government revenues but also in terms of increased wages of the people. If increased revenues enabled the government to introduce necessary improvements, higher wages enabled the people to avail themselves of them in those cases where payment was required.

After 1936 some notable successes were achieved by way of improved social services. The major problems related to health, social welfare, water, education, housing and transportation. A major step was taken to improve health services when in 1953 the Knud-Hansen Memorial Hospital in St. Thomas, a modern 116-bed institution, and the Charles Harwood Memorial Hospital in Christiansted, St. Croix, a modern 60-bed hospital, were opened. In addition, the Frederiksted Public Health Facility and the Morris F. de Castro Clinic at Cruz Bay, St. John, were also brought into operation.[40] A vigorous recruitment policy among foreign doctors desirous of entering the United States eased the shortage of doctors while the policy of post-graduate training for medical doctors and of in-service training for nurses helped to improve their efficiency. To overcome the problem of sewage disposal especially the use of night-soil cans, facilities for salt-water flushing were extended in the towns and central sewer mains were installed. In the country, the move was away from pit latrines and towards the adoption of the flush system and septic tanks, which by the late 1950's was generally accepted by the people. With regard to garbage disposal, the adoption of the trucking service and the construction of dumps at central points served to ensure more sanitary surroundings.[41]

Before 1954 the only department in the Virgin Islands to have been organized on a territorial basis was that dealing with social welfare. The legislative base for social welfare activities in the Virgin Islands was laid in 1943 when the Legislative Assembly passed the Social Welfare Act. However, the Act did not begin to take effect until 1947 when Title V of the Federal Social Security Act was extended to the Virgin Islands providing for a federally supported and municipally sponsored program of child welfare, maternal and child health and crippled children's services. The public assistance and the old age and survivors insurance provisions of the Federal Social Security Act were extended to the Virgin Islands in 1950 and 1951 respectively.[42] The adoption of the federal legislation made possible the development of uniform standards of assistance and services throughout the Virgin Islands as well as centralized supervision and policy development necessary for federal participation in the program. The executive arm was the Social Welfare Department.

In addition to the operation of the Social Welfare Department and acting in conjunction with it were the Community Chests of St. Thomas and St. Croix organized in August, 1938 and December, 1954 respectively. These were two separate and distinct voluntary and charitable organizations providing help in those areas of need where federal and local government programs could not effectively operate because of lack of funds and the restrictions placed on government operations.[43]

Closely connected with the question of health were problems relating to the provision of an adequate supply of potable water ·and of adequate housing. Because of the low rainfall and recurrent droughts, water shortage was a continuous problem and after 1936 the situation was aggravated by the heavy growth of tourism and population and by the introduction of industries. The problem was particularly acute in St. Thomas where wells could not be drilled. In order to maintain adequate supplies of water, therefore, more reservoirs were constructed and barging of water from Puerto Rico was continued on a larger scale.[44] The desalination of sea-water was undertaken from 1962, while in St.

Croix wells were drilled by government to meet the increasing demand for water.[45] In St. John a number of shallow wells was the main source of water supply. In all the islands where the public water supply could not reach, reliance was on basement cisterns, and water was purchased from private suppliers in times of shortage.

The Virgin Islands' government played a prominent role in housing although much of the funds for development came from federal sources. Government activity began in 1950 when a law was passed creating the Virgin Islands Housing Authority, and the Department of Housing and Community Renewal was established in 1962 in order to coordinate and give central direction to government's housing activities. The record of performance of the two bodies was impressive. Between 1952 and 1970 four housing projects with a total of 752 units were completed and rented under the management of the Housing Authority in St. Thomas. In St. Croix during the same period there were six projects with 764 units. Two other projects of 300 units in St. Thomas, and one of 256 units in St. Croix were partly completed and occupied.[46]

The intention of government was to provide low-rent housing, but some of the housing catered to people in the middle-income group in order to facilitate government's recruitment of teachers, nurses and other professional workers. In view of the exorbitant rentals for housing charged in the Virgin Islands the provision of low and middle-income housing was necessary. Under the government housing programs some 595 units of moderate income housing were constructed on government-owned land and sold to qualified persons of moderate income. Moreover, certain community renewal and emergency housing totalling 534 units were built, and land was purchased in anticipation of further construction.

Government involvement in housing, however, did not end with construction. In addition, it operated a homestead and home loan fund in order to encourage and assist people to buy their own sites and build their own homes. Furthermore, private enterprise was encouraged to supplement the efforts of government.

Government performance in the provision of transportation facilities was not as outstanding as its other achievements. Roadbuilding was confined largely to maintaining old roads and to opening new roads to certain tourist resorts and new housing projects. Throughout the period there were large stretches of unpaved or dirt roads. Statistics for St. Croix for 1934, 1944 and 1954 show that while there were 0, 36 and

39 miles respectively of hard-surfaced roads, there were as many as 140, 104 and 111 miles respectively of dirt and gravel roads.[47] A parallel situation existed in St. Thomas and St. John. By 1970 there was but little improvement on all three islands.

The road system was very unsatisfactory: paved surfaces, invariably bituminous macadam, were very unstable and were liable to erosion during rains. Potholes resulted but in many instances complete sections of road surfaces were destroyed as was the case also with dirt roads. The bright spot was the waterfront project in Charlotte Amalie which was completed in 1954 in order ᵗo facilitate shipping and commerce and to enable government better to deal with traffic problems created by the growing number of motor vehicles brought into operation.[48]

For external travel government maintained two airports – Bourne Field (later renamed the Harry S. Truman Airport) in St. Thomas, and the Benedict Field (renamed the Alexander Hamilton Airport) in St. Croix. These were acquired when the United States Navy ceased operations in the Virgin Islands on December 31, 1947, though the Navy retained the right to require the immediate return of the facilities in St. Thomas in the event of a national emergency.[49] In order to cater to larger airplanes the runways of both airports were later lengthened, though geographical considerations imposed restrictions on the extent to which the Harry S. Truman Airport could be developed. A new Alexander Hamilton Airport on St. Croix was completed in 1962, and plans were later made for a new airport for St. Thomas. Airway services were handled by private enterprise.

Tremendous progress in education has been made since 1936 with the assistance of American consultants, and educational programs were developed and maintained at the nursery, elementary and junior and senior high school levels. Schools were operated both by the government and by charitable organizations mainly the religious denominations. The period was marked by the construction of new schools, introduction of improved curricula, and more up-to-date teaching equipment and facilities. Education programs generally were strengthened by policies of in-service teacher training, scholarship loans to permit deserving candidates to improve their professional competence by going abroad for higher education and training, and by evening schools for adults. In both the private and public schools the provision of school lunches and medical care at federal and the local government expense had the effect of making students better able to avail themselves of the education offered. Similarly, the bussing of children to school at the public expense not only enabled them to attend schools of their choice, but brought available education within their easy reach. Adult education was improved when in 1950 the United States Congress extended to the Virgin Islands the benefits of the Vocational Education Act of 1946.[50]

The most outstanding achievement in education in the Virgin Islands was the establishment of the College of the Virgin Islands as a result of the growing need for better trained and more highly qualified personnel in the teaching, nursing and other services in the islands. It sought to avoid the expenses and inconveniences borne by students having to go to the United States for higher education. At the same time, it served to ensure the retention of talent in the Virgin Islands which might otherwise be lost had the students been exposed to the attractions of overseas employment opportunities by being educated abroad.[51]

Beginning in July, 1963 as a two-year liberal arts institution offering programs leading to an associate in arts degree, the College expanded in 1968 into a four-year institution offering courses leading to the baccalaureate degree. As the only institution of higher education, and of research (through the Caribbean Research Institute), in the Virgin Islands, the College represents the place where ideas and programs are developed for the economic, political and social advancement of the territory.[52]

Considerable improvement was achieved in the provision of social services in the Virgin Islands since 1936, but a number of factors limited progress. Unpredictable population growth made it impossible to plan adequately to meet short-term needs. Despite talented Virgin Islanders who returned to or remained in the Virgin Islands, services suffered from a shortage of trained personnel; expatriate labor proved too transitory to allow for the formulation of plans based on their services. For too long did the Virgin Islands operate a dual system of administration, and even when departments were unified in 1955, the geographical separateness of the islands hampered their effective functioning.

Areas of differences

Social tensions among the various peoples of the Virgin Islands have been accentuated by prosperous economic conditions. One area of tension relates to the 'alien' population, and the second to 'native'

Virgin Islanders themselves. As non-citizens of the United States, 'aliens' suffered from the political consequences of their status. Irrespective of the length of their stay, aliens, including permanent residents, were denied participation in the political process either as voters or candidates for election. A large body of people, therefore, lacked the opportunity to direct their affairs.

The economic disadvantages of aliens were equally serious. Aliens were subject to the minimum wage laws of the Virgin Islands but were sometimes denied equal compensation to Virgin Islanders given the same service. This was particularly the case when they were employed by private enterprise. In the high cost economy of the Virgin Islands, the vast majority of aliens worked for substandard wages which made them unable to live on a comparable level with native Virgin Islanders.[53]

Because of their lower economic position, aliens maintained a lower standard of living in terms of housing, food and clothing by comparison with other workers. Indeed, one authority has said that 'the housing situation for the alien population [was] nothing short of a crisis.'[54] It was not until 1969 that public housing was made available to alien residents and it required a legal decision in 1970 to make public education available to all categories of alien children.

Except for action through the courts or by sympathetic appeals to government through the initiative of the Alien Interest Movement created in 1969, aliens lacked effective means to improve their condition. Under United States immigration laws the prospects are remote that many of them will ever become United States citizens. Improvement in their condition depended on the extent to which both federal and local governments were prepared to acknowledge a responsibility for their welfare.

By virtue of their control of the legislature, 'native' Virgin Islanders could overcome many of the problems experienced by aliens, and their status as United States citizens gave them privileges to which aliens could aspire but could not have. On the other hand, their power was limited by the operation of the federal laws in the Virgin Islands and from the consequences of accelerated economic growth based largely on tourism. Economic prosperity necessitated and stemmed from the introduction of outside workers – 'continental' Americans, Puerto Ricans and 'alien' West Indians, made possible through the operation of United States immigration laws. In their own way, whether as United States citizens or non-citizens, these people competed with Virgin

Islanders for jobs available in government service or private enterprise.

Concentrated land ownership and control was a problem which affected aliens and citizens alike. A survey in 1950 revealed that approximately .5 percent of the population owned 80 percent of the land. Much of this land was sold to wealthy outsiders who could afford to pay the high prices demanded. Lands sold included not only home-sites but areas suitable for investment purposes such as those bordering beaches. The great majority of native Virgin Islanders saw little hope of coming into independent possession of land which they could later bequeath to their children. The most that many of them could look forward to was the occupation of land leased from government.

A grievance closely connected with the ownership of land was that of the use of beaches. Theoretically beaches are partly public property (up to high water mark) but in practice whole beaches touching private land were controlled as the property of the land owners. Since they controlled access to beaches landowners effectively controlled beach property. In cases where the public was denied access, their use of beaches depended on their membership of clubs connected with these beaches or upon payment of high entrance fees. The fact that resort areas were controlled by non-Virgin Islanders only served to make the grievance more acute.

Some of the unrest can be attributed to the widespread feeling among Virgin Islanders that they have lost control of their economy. It is true that more and more Virgin Islanders have participated in economic undertakings, partly owing to the work of the Small Business Development Agency since 1969. But the ownership and control of the major industries and big businesses by non-Virgin Islanders with greater competitive power has led the natives to question their role in the future economic development of the islands. This factor, together with being outnumbered population-wise on the one hand, and being faced with difficulties in the acquisition of property on the other, has made Virgin Islanders increasingly fearful of becoming foreigners in their own land.

Beginning with the Organic Act of 1936 and ending with the Elective Governor Act of 1968, Virgin Islanders were given a considerable measure of self-government. Their political status, nevertheless, showed many of the characteristics of a dependent territory. For example the governor still has to report annually to the Secretary of the Interior whose Department continues to supervise Virgin Isalnds affairs. In addition, Presidential consent is still required for capital expenditures of Virgin Islands Treasury funds as established by the Revised Organic Act of 1954. Indeed, effective supervision over the collection and disbursement of money by the local government is exercised by the federally appointed and paid Comptroller who owes no direct responsibility to the local government and cannot be controlled by it.

Constitutional changes in the Virgin Islands are still dependent upon congressional action; the local legislature has no power to initiate reform but can only request it. Federal laws continue to be applicable to the Virgin Islands, and laws passed by the local legislature cannot violate or conflict with federal laws. The Virgin Islands have no control over foreign affairs and cannot initiate relations with a foreign country.

Political advancement in United States territories is not in the decentralized tradition of independence as in the case of British colonies. Rather, in keeping with the concept of federation inherent in the United States constitution it is in the direction of centralization and statehood with the United States. For the Virgin Islands the major inhibiting factor has been the economic dependence of the government on the United States.

Conclusion

The fundamental change which took place in the Virgin Islands after 1936 was the abandonment of agriculture based largely on peasant farming and the development of tourism and industry. The turning point came with the Second World War. Prosperity based on tourism and industry was reflected in part in increased revenues, greater imports and exports, higher wages, and a rapid population growth.

The state of the economy determined to a large extent the nature of political reforms after 1936. First came the consolidation and unification of political institutions in 1954 in response to a need for greater economy and efficiency. This was followed by a greater measure of self-government in 1968 as the islands became more self-sufficient. Greater political representation in 1966 stemmed partly from increased population, but it was also due to government's desire to introduce more improved and modern systems of social services in keeping with popular needs and demands. Greater revenues made this possible.

The emergence of political parties after 1936 gave the people the appropriate means through which to express their wants. By 1970 the

Virgin Islands had not yet attained complete economic self-sufficiency, political fulfillment in statehood, or a fully satisfactory system of social services, but the stage was set for a further thrust forward.

[1] Annual Report of the Governor of the Virgin Islands, 1937, p. 8.
[2] Annual Report of the Governor of the Virgin Islands, 1940, p. 12.
[3] Ibid., pp. 13-14.
[4] Ibid., pp. 5-11.
[5] Annual Report of the Governor of the Virgin Islands, 1946, p. 3.
[6] Isaac Dookhan, 'The Virgin Islands Company and Corporation: The Plan for Economic Rehabilitation in the Virgin Islands.' (*The Journal of Caribbean History*, Vol. 4, May, 1972) pp. 68-69; Report of Proceedings. Hearings held before Subcommittee of the Committee on Interior and Insular Affairs. United States Senate. H.R.2989. Virgin Islands Company Recharter Bill. (Mimeo., 1949).
[7] J. C. Rosenberg, *Cultural and Social Aspects of Agriculture in St. Croix.* (Caribbean Research Institute, 1966); Wendell E. Clement, Wylie D. Goodsell and Solberg, *General Observations on the Agriculture in the Virgin Islands.* (Caribbean Research Institute, January 6, 1966).
[8] Annual Reports of the Governor of the Virgin Islands, 1962 (p. 19) and 1963 (p. 62).
[9] Dookhan, op. cit., pp. 74-76.
[10] Annual Reports of the Governors of the Virgin Islands, 1959 (p. 54) and 1969 (p. 56)
[11] 'The U.S. Virgin Islands. Special Report.' (*World Business*, No.11, April, 1968) p. 8; Annual Report of the Governor of the Virgin Islands, 1969, p. 60.
[12] Annual Reports of the Governors of the Virgin Islands, 1958 (p. 58) and 1969 (p. 60).
[13] Annual Report of the Governor of the Virgin Islands, 1949, p. 2.
[14] Annual Report of the Governor of the Virgin Islands, 1967, p. 36.
[15] The U.S. Virgin Islands. Special Report, pp. 9-11.
[16] Martin Garson Orlins, The Impact of Tourism on the Virgin Islands of the United States. (Unpublished Ph.D. Thesis, Columbia University, 1969).
[17] Annual Reports of the Governors of the Virgin Islands, 1940 (p. 61), 1949 (pp. 22-23) and 1969 (p. 58).
[18] Annual Reports of the Governors of the Virgin Islands, 1937 (p. 5) and 1969 (p. 119).
[19] Valdemar A. Hill, (Sr.), *A Golden Jubilee.* (*Virgin Islanders on the Go Under the American Flag.*) (Carlton Press, Inc., New York, 1967) pp. 132-139; Valdemar A. Hill, (Jr.), Minimum wages in the U.S. Virgin Islands, 1938-1968. (Unpublished Master's Thesis, Puerto Rico, Inter-American University, 1968).
[20] The U.S. Virgin Islands. Special Report, p. 9.
[21] Annual Report of the Governor of the Virgin Islands, 1944, p. 2; U.S. Congress. House. Committee on Insular Affairs. To assist in relieving economic distress in the Virgin Islands. (Washington, 1943-44). Part 111, passim; Report on

the Audit of the Virgin Islands Corporation, 1952. (United States, Government Printing Office, 1953) p. 7; United States Department of Agriculture: Economic Appraisal of the Operations of the Virgin Islands Corporation. (Washington, 1953) p. 1.

[22] Eighty-Second Congress. Second Session. Hearings before the Subcommittee on Territories and Insular Possessions, House of Representatives, on H.R.2644. A Bill to revise the Organic Act of the Virgin Islands of the United States. (Washington, 1952); Eighty-Second Congress. Second Session. Revision of the Organic Act of the Virgin Islands. A Report and Recommendations of the Sub-committee on Territories and Insular Possessions based on Hearings held in the Virgin Islands in January, 1952. (Washington, 1952).

[23] Annual Report of the Governor of the Virgin Islands, 1953, p. 36.

[24] Eighty-Third Congress. Second Session. Virgin Islands Report ... with reference to proposed revision of the Organic Act and the Governmental, Economic and Fiscal Structure in the Islands, with recommendations on the Federally owned Virgin Islands Corporation. (Washington, 1954).

[25] Raymond Lewis Cravens, The Constitutional and Political Status of the Non-Contiguous Areas of the United States. (Unpublished Ph.D. Thesis, University of Kentucky, 1958) pp. 157-166.

[26] Darwin D. Creque, The U.S. Virgins and the Eastern Caribbean. (Whitmore Publishing Co., Philadelphia, 1968) p. 161.

[27] Proceedings of the Constitutional Convention of the Virgin Islands, 1964-1965. (Mimeo., 1965).

[28] Creque, op. cit., pp. 174-184.

[29] Eighty-Ninth Congress. Second Session. Hearings before the Subcommittee on Territorial and Insular Affairs ... March 8, 9; April 19 and 27, 1966. (Washington, 1966).

[30] Ibid., p. 92.

[31] The Daily News, November 3, 1971, and January 19 and March 29, 1972.

[32] The Daily News, May 8 and 9, 1972.

[33] The Daily News, June 17 and August 16, 1972.

[34] Luther Harris Evans, The Virgin Islands from Naval Base to New Deal. (J. W. Edwards, Ann Arbor, Michigan, 1945) p. 83.

[35] Hill, (Sr.), op. cit., p. 128.

[36] Creque, op. cit., pp. 114-115.

[37] Hill, (Sr.), op. cit., p. 143.

[38] The District Court of the Virgin Islands Division of St. Thomas and St. John. Civil No. 260 − 1963. Memorandum of Opinion; United States Court of Appeals for the Third Circuit. No. 15,000 and No. 15,001. Opinion of the Court.

[39] Eighty-Ninth Congress. Second Session. Hearings before the Subcommittee on Territorial and Insular Affairs ... (Washington, 1966) pp. 53 and 57.

[40] Annual Report of the Governor of the Virgin Islands, 1953, p. 13.

[41] Annual Reports of the Governors of the Virgin Islands, 1950-1970, passim.

[42] Annual Reports of the Governors of the Virgin Islands, 1947 (p. 8), 1950 (pp. 15-16) and 1951 (pp. 30-31).

[43] Annual Report of the Governor of the Virgin Islands, 1958, p.47.

[44] Eighty-Fifth Congress. First Session. Activities of the Virgin Islands Govern-

ment and the Virgin Islands Corporation. Hearings before a Sub-committee of the Committee on Government Operations. House of Representatives. (Washington, 1957) pp. 37-38; Economic Report on Industries in the Virgin Islands, United States Department of Labor. (October, 1959) p. 10.

[45] Annual Report of the Governor of the Virgin Islands, 1962, p. 2.

[46] Annual Report for Fiscal Year 1969. Department of Housing and Community Renewal; Annual Report of the Governor of the Virgin Islands, 1970, pp. 104-112.

[47] Annual Report of the Governor of the Virgin Islands, 1954, p. 38.

[48] Ibid., p. 16.

[49] Annual Report of the Governor of the Virgin Islands, 1947, p. 2.

[50] Annual Report of the Governor of the Virgin Islands, 1950, p. 11.

[51] The Governor's Conference on Higher Education in the Virgin Islands, Bluebeard's Castle Hotel, July 27-31, 1961. Conference Workbook. (Mimeo., 1961).

[52] Self-Study Report of the College of the Virgin Islands. Submitted to the Commission on Institutions of Higher Education of the Middle States Association of Colleges and Secondary Schools. (St. Thomas, U.S. Virgin Islands, December 15, 1970).

[53] *Aliens in the United States Virgin Islands: Temporary Workers in a Permanent Economy.* (Prepared by Social, Educational Research and Development, Inc., January, 1968).

[54] *A Profile and Plans for the Temporary Alien Worker Problem in the U.S. Virgin Islands.* (Submitted by Social, Educational Research and Development, Inc., August 5, 1969) p. 4.

Index

CPSIA information can be obtained at www.ICGtesting.com
Printed in the USA
BVOW010038150113

310556BV00002B/3/P